W9-CMP-904

# PRIVATE SPHERE TO WORLD STAGE FROM AUSTEN TO ELIOT

PR468.W6 S24 2008
0134111776784
Sabiston, Elizabeth
 Jean, 1937-
Private sphere to world
 stage from Austen to
     c2008.

2009 07 13

*For Hédi*
*who brought poetry into my life*

250601(00)
$111.60

# Private Sphere to World Stage
# from Austen to Eliot

ELIZABETH SABISTON
*York University, Toronto, Canada*

Library Commons
Georgian College
One Georgian Drive
Barrie, ON
L4M 3X9

DISCARD

ASHGATE

© Elizabeth Sabiston 2008

All rights reserved. No part of this publication may be reproduced, stored in a retrieval system or transmitted in any form or by any means, electronic, mechanical, photocopying, recording or otherwise without the prior permission of the publisher.

Elizabeth Sabiston has asserted her moral right under the Copyright, Designs and Patents Act, 1988, to be identified as the author of this work.

Published by
Ashgate Publishing Limited
Gower House
Croft Road
Aldershot
Hampshire GU11 3HR
England

Ashgate Publishing Company
Suite 420
101 Cherry Street
Burlington, VT 05401-4405
USA

Ashgate website: http://www.ashgate.com

**British Library Cataloguing in Publication Data**
Sabiston, Elizabeth Jean, 1937–
    Private sphere to world stage from Austen to Eliot 1. Austen, Jane, 1775–1817 – Criticism and interpretation 2. English fiction – Women authors – History and criticism 3. English fiction – 19th century – History and criticism 4. Women and literature – Great Britain – History – 19th century 5. Sex role in literature
    I. Title
    823.8'099287

**Library of Congress Cataloging-in-Publication Data**
Sabiston, Elizabeth Jean, 1937–
    Private sphere to world stage from Austen to Eliot / Elizabeth Sabiston.
        p. cm.
    Includes bibliographical references.
    ISBN 978-0-7546-6174-0 (alk. paper)
    1. English literature—Women authors—History and criticism. 2. Women and literature—England—History—19th century. 3. Women—Books and reading—England—History—19th century. 4. Sex role in literature. I. Title.

PR468.W6S24 2007
810.9'928—dc22
                                                          2007025305

ISBN 978-0-7546-6174-0

Printed and bound in Great Britain by MPG Books Ltd, Bodmin, Cornwall.

# Contents

| | | |
|---|---|---|
| *Figure* | | *vii* |
| *Acknowledgments* | | *ix* |
| 1 | Introduction—"Letters to the World": From Private Sphere to World Stage | 1 |
| 2 | Jane Austen's Art of Fiction: The Hidden Manifesto in *Northanger Abbey* and *Persuasion* | 5 |
| 3 | Not Carved in Stone: Women's Hearts and Women's Texts in Charlotte Brontë's *Jane Eyre* | 55 |
| 4 | Cathy's Book: The Ghost-text in Emily Bronte's *Wuthering Heights* | 95 |
| 5 | "The Iron of Slavery in Her Heart": The Literary Relationship of Elizabeth Gaskell and Harriet Beecher Stowe | 131 |
| 6 | George Eliot's *Daniel Deronda*: "A Daniel Come to Judgment" | 151 |
| 7 | Conclusion—and a New Beginning | 189 |
| *Bibliography* | | *193* |
| *Index* | | *205* |

# Figure

6.1    Dante Gabriel Rossetti, "La Pia de Tolomei" (1868–80),    181
       reproduction courtesy of the Spencer Museum of Art,
       The University of Kansas. Lawrence, Kansas. Museum
       purchase: State funds.

# Acknowledgments

A previous version of Chapter 5 was published as "Anglo-American Connections: Elizabeth Gaskell, Harriet Beecher Stowe and 'The Iron of Slavery'" in *The Discourse of Slavery*, ed. Carl Plasa and Betty J. Ring (London and New York: Routledge, 1994). "This is my letter to the world," "I'm Nobody! Who are you?" and "'Twas like a maelstrom" are reprinted by permission of the publishers and the Trustees of Amherst College from *The Poems of Emily Dickinson*, Thomas H. Johnson, ed., Cambridge, Massachusetts: The Belknap Press of Harvard University Press, Copyright © 1951, 1955, 1979, 1983 by the President and Fellows of Harvard College. Every effort has been made to trace or contact all copyright holders. The author would be pleased to rectify any omissions brought to her notice at the earliest opportunity.

I would like to acknowledge the help and support of York University in the form of three sabbatical fellowships which enabled me to travel to the United Kingdom and visit the various regions, sites, and museums associated with my nineteenth-century women novelists. I deeply appreciate the help of my York students, both graduate and undergraduate, in my various courses on Women in Literature and Nineteenth-Century British Women Novelists. Their questions and insights sharpened my own, and several of them are singled out by name in my text. I am grateful for the technical assistance and moral support of Ann Gagné and Peter Paolucci. I would like to thank Ann Donahue, my editor at Ashgate, for her useful, tactful advice, quick responses to my queries, and readiness to expedite matters.

Special thanks are due to my English cousin, Ian Sabiston, for his thoughtful, congenial companionship on our literary excursions in the United Kingdom, and for his "painterly" eye. My dear mother and father, Lowland Scot and Orkney Islander, live on in my memory during this journey back in time. From the beginning, they piqued my curiosity about the nineteenth century, when their own parents were born into an era of great social changes which I wanted to understand. My mother participated in the beginning of this particular literary journey; I only wish she could see the conclusion. Finally, I owe more than I can say to my toughest critic and most ruthless editor, Hédi Bouraoui, for his unwavering encouragement, guidance, and patience.

Elizabeth Sabiston
Toronto
January 2008

# Chapter 1

# Introduction—"Letters to the World": From Private Sphere to World Stage

This is my letter to the World
That never wrote to Me –
The simple News that Nature told –
With tender Majesty

Her Message is committed
To Hands I cannot see –
For love of Her – Sweet – countrymen –
Judge tenderly – of Me
                    Emily Dickinson, c. 1862

 I'm Nobody! Who are you?
Are you – Nobody – too?
Then there's a pair of us?
Don't tell! they'd advertise – you know!

How dreary – to be – Somebody!
How public – like a Frog –
To tell one's name – the livelong June –
To an admiring Bog!
                    Emily Dickinson, c. 1861

In *A Room of One's Own*, Virginia Woolf identifies childlessness as the unifying trait in the women she selects as the four greatest British women novelists of the nineteenth century: Jane Austen, Charlotte Brontë, Emily Brontë, George Eliot.[1] This theory of the biological tradeoff—babies for art—probably influences her decision to relegate a fifth woman novelist, Elizabeth Gaskell, to minor status. It would also probably have led her to neglect a sixth, the American Harriet Beecher Stowe. I have opted, however, to include both the married women with children, Mrs. Gaskell and Mrs. Stowe, in an analysis of a peculiarly feminine contribution to the art of fiction in the nineteenth century, which prepared the way for a Virginia Woolf, a Doris Lessing, a Willa Cather, a Toni Morrison, a Margaret Laurence, an Alice Munro, a Bharati Mukherjee in the twentieth.

The Brontës' contemporary, the American Transcendental poet Emily Dickinson, seems to have signaled several other unifying traits among our six women novelists

---

1    "Save for the possibly relevant fact that not one of them had a child, four more incongruous characters could not have met together in a room" (64).

at least as important as that highlighted by Woolf. Moreover, these traits also link them with a number of their female predecessors in the seventeenth and eighteenth centuries, among them Madame de Lafayette, Charlotte Ramsay Lennox, Fanny Burney (d'Arblay), and Maria Edgeworth. Dickinson writes, "This is my letter to the World / That never wrote to me"; as Virginia Woolf comments, she always imagined that "Anon." was a woman (48).

One major stream of the earliest French and British fiction was the epistolary novel, as practiced, for instance, in Madame de Lafayette's *La Princesse de Clèves* and Samuel Richardson's *Pamela* (1740) and *Clarissa* (1749). Richardson's work influences, among others, Fanny Burney and Jane Austen. Richardson's use of the female as the dominant voice was a reflection of the reality: women as the dominant letter-writers in the private, domestic sphere. In fact, the seed for Richardson's *Pamela* was a book of model letters for maidservants. One can imagine Jane Austen, reading *Pamela*, *Clarissa*, and *Sir Charles Grandison*, saying to herself, "If I can write letters, I can do this too." But for Austen, as for the Brontës, Mrs. Gaskell, and George Eliot, the world never writes to them, never seeks them out, since the pen is perceived by society to be in men's hands: hence the anonymity, or the adoption of male pen names. Like Dickinson, their strength lies in communicating "the simple News that Nature [also personified as a woman] told"—the private, the emotional, woman's physical and spiritual landscape.

Yet writing (even if only for *eventual* publication, posthumously as in Dickinson's case) is by definition a *public* act, and all six of our women novelists were confronted with the dilemma of effecting an elision of public and private spheres, of articulating ranges of experience often considered so personal as to be incommunicable.

Dickinson's more playful poem "I'm Nobody!" could express both their frustration and their quiet triumph at remaining faithful to their female subject and angle of vision, in contrast to the "man's world" of "advertising"—indeed, Dickinson seems to prophesy Madison Avenue. Certainly in Dickinson's day most of the froglike writers telling their name "– the livelong June – / To an admiring Bog!" belonged to the masculine tradition of publication. The Brontës' difficulties in dealing with publishers, not to mention Mrs. Stowe's in cheating herself out of vast wealth in royalties for the first "best-seller," are suggestive of women's malaise and naivety in the domain of literary production and distribution. Charlotte Brontë sold her copyright for 1500 pounds (Woolf 67); Emily Brontë was cheated by her publisher. Harriet Beecher Stowe got only 10 percent royalties on one of the world's first bestsellers because she was too fearful to take the chance of investing in her own talent. No wonder that Virginia Woolf became her own publisher, had Hogarth, "a press of her own," in "that purely patriarchal society" (71).

What the six women novelists treated here have in common is a consciousness of their craft as keen as Virginia Woolf's. As Woolf notes, these women writers emerge not long after the birth of the novel in English: "The novel alone was young enough to be soft in [their] hands" (75). And the novel does not require public performance. Women's consciousness recognized the implications for them of the marriage market theme, particularly in the epistolary form as practiced by Samuel Richardson. Letters in the female voice become an instrument of seduction in Richardson, whose Pamela in some ways effects a more powerful and effective seduction on Mr. B. than his attempted rapes do on her. To carry that concept one step further, Richardson ultimately uses those female letters to effect the seduction of the reader. Thus the text itself becomes identified with the female body and the female consciousness, and passes by way of Charlotte Ramsay Lennox, whose "Female Quixote" is seduced by unrealistic French seventeenth-century romances, Fanny Burney, and Maria Edgeworth, to Jane Austen. As Brigid Brophy has remarked, Jane Austen then takes the novel as she sees it, pulverizes it, and creates a new form that brings the novel to full maturity.

My study focuses on six women novelists—Austen, Charlotte and Emily Brontë, Elizabeth Gaskell, Harriet Beecher Stowe, and George Eliot—in an attempt to demonstrate the relationship between the self-reflexive novel and the emerging female text and voice. That these authors are regarded as "canonical" today only serves to underline their movement from near-anonymity, in the private sphere, to equality with their male contemporaries.

Chapter 2, "Jane Austen's 'Art of Fiction': The Hidden Manifesto," is a rebuttal of Henry James's patronizing treatment of Austen as an unconscious artist composing in the drawing-room in the intervals of dropped stitches. It argues that Austen was at least as conscious of her art as James himself. If she never wrote a manifesto entitled "The Art of Fiction," unlike James, there is a buried manifesto in her comments on the novel in her "The Plan of a Novel" parody of the romance, in *Northanger Abbey* and in *Persuasion*. I have written extensively elsewhere on *Emma*,[2] but will refer briefly to its relationship to "The Plan of a Novel," and to *Northanger* which she seems to have been revising for publication around the same time she was composing *Emma*. I will also glance at instances of intertextuality in *Sense and Sensibility* and *Mansfield Park*, illustrating her awareness of her predecessors and contemporaries.

Chapter 3, "Not Carved in Stone: Women's Hearts and Women's Texts in Charlotte Brontë's *Jane Eyre*," will focus on *Jane Eyre* but also refer briefly to the attempts of other Brontë heroines—such as Shirley Keeldar and Lucy Snowe—to create visual or verbal art works and mythologies that refute the discourses of patriarchy. Lest we think that Brontë's vision excludes male readers as some male texts are popularly supposed to exclude female readers, I will touch on Charlotte Brontë's curious influence on two of those supposedly quintessentially male novelists, the American Herman Melville and the Russian Leo Tolstoy.

Chapter 4, "Cathy's Book: The Ghost-Text in Emily Brontë's *Wuthering Heights*," argues that there are more than two ghosts in *Wuthering Heights*, that the book in which 12-year-old Cathy Earnshaw has inscribed her passionate revolt without let, restraint, or inhibition, is the true story of Wuthering Heights on which Lockwood's and Nelly Dean's narratives merely constitute a gloss. Director William Wyler had the right intuition in having Merle Oberon, as Cathy, made up to resemble a portrait of Emily Bronte in the 1939 film version of *Wuthering Heights*.

---

2    In *The Prison of Womanhood: Four Provincial Heroines in Nineteenth-Century Fiction*, I discussed Austen's Emma and Eliot's Dorothea Brooke as female would-be artists whose attempts at creativity are "silenced"or thwarted by their environment and their own shortcomings.

"'The Iron of Slavery in Her Soul,'" Chapter 5, on "The Literary Relationship of Elizabeth Gaskell and Harriet Beecher Stowe," examines two women writers who use their texts as instruments of social activism, who, like their contemporary Charlotte Brontë, carve their works on the female heart, not in stone.[3] Finally, Chapter 6, "George Eliot's *Daniel Deronda*: 'A Daniel Come to Judgment,'" focuses on the complex relationship between Deronda and Gwendolen Harleth. If the putative heroine is "silenced," Deronda seems to be an androgynous hero whose first name may link him to Shakespeare's Portia in *The Merchant of Venice*, disguised as a male lawyer, and greeted by Shylock as a "wise young judge. A Daniel come to judgment." The Conclusion examines the ramifications and impact of these novelists and their heroines on the twentieth and twenty-first centuries.

But, before Jane Austen, there was Samuel Richardson. And between Richardson and Austen there were the eighteenth-century "mothers of the novel," among whom one of the most important for Austen was Richardson's colleague, Charlotte Ramsay Lennox.

---

3    Stowe is the only American woman novelist I have chosen to include for this particular study. The choice was based largely on her "internationalism," her bestseller status in Great Britain, and on her literary relationships with Elizabeth Gaskell in particular, but also with Charlotte Brontë.

Chapter 2

# Jane Austen's Art of Fiction: The Hidden Manifesto in *Northanger Abbey* and *Persuasion*

### Introduction: The "Nay-Sayers" and the "Janeites"

In addition to anonymity and (at least according to Woolf) childlessness, another quality our nineteenth-century women novelists have in common is their ability to provoke controversy, both in their day and ours. Of the six, probably Jane Austen and Charlotte Brontë have sustained both the most virulent attacks and the most passionate defenses.[1] Critical attacks on Austen have tended to be condescending, on Charlotte Brontë angry, but both occur along gender lines. Henry James's picture of "dear Jane, gentle Jane, everyone's Jane," composing in the drawing-room in the intervals of dropped stitches, is typical of critics who patronize Austen. Actually, Austen was at least as conscious as James of her craft, but buried *her* manifesto in her creative work, rather than writing an essay on "The Art of Fiction."[2] Lionel Trilling, one of the more noteworthy Austen defenders, asked in an unfinished 1975 essay, "Why Read Jane Austen Today?" (He died before completing it, and probably before answering his own question.)

The attackers see her as dated, a snob, an apologist for a hierarchical society, and an advocate of economically determined marriages for upwardly mobile young women. The admirers see her as clear-eyed, candid, lucid, capable of both detached observation and ironic criticism of social institutions, including marriage, which she tends to see as the *only* possible outlet for most young women, perhaps less fortunate than herself in that she has her art and the encouragement of a loving, supportive family. Her Emma Woodhouse claims that marriage is not necessary to her; she is an heiress, financially independent, and she has her own imagination and

---

1    With perhaps the exception of Mrs. Stowe, but for more "programmatic" reasons— her alleged sentimentality and her racial stereotyping.

2    Despite her family's great support of her writing, the inscription on her tombstone in Winchester Cathedral, for which her brother Henry was probably responsible, never mentions her art, but only her Christian virtues. The memorial brass for which the family was also responsible emphasizes that "She openeth her mouth with wisdom and in her tongue is the law of kindness" (Proverbs). One wonders if they were nervous about her portrayals of inept or venal clergymen like Mr. Collins or Mr. Elton. At any rate, the memorial window put up by public subscription in 1900 more than makes up for it, depicting, among other Biblical and theological writers and poets, St. Augustine, often called St. Austen, David and his harp, St. John—"In the beginning was the Word."

supposed art of matchmaking to fall back on. But Emma, a true Female Quixote, lacks the discipline, technique, and detachment of a Jane Austen. Above all, Emma is a snob who never attaches her feminism to a critique of the patriarchy in general—although Mr. Knightley does and will do much to "democratize" her before and after marriage—whereas Austen's sharp, astute observations subtend a critique of the system, a critique which would lead, not perhaps to revolution à la Mary Wollstonecraft, but to evolution in the manner of Nathaniel Hawthorne.

Her work is remarkably congruent with Edward Saïd's position in "The World, the Text, and the Critic" in that Austen would never deny the work's referentiality to the world "out there." Indeed, her treatment, in *Mansfield Park*, of the Antigua material and of William Price's advancement in the navy, and, in *Persuasion*, of Frederick Wentworth's fortunes made in the navy during wartime, shows an author keenly aware of the dawning of the British Empire at the beginning of the nineteenth century, but also aware of its abuses.

Even in her own day, and throughout the ninenteenth century, Austen had both impassioned devotees and acerbic detractors. Among Austen's detractors, regrettably perhaps, was Charlotte Brontë, who accused Austen of lacking passion in her work. But Charlotte was probably at least in part motivated by resistance to that curious figure, George Henry Lewes, and his oft-stated admiration for Austen's control and discipline. A foremost critic in his age, and the model for George Eliot's portrait of the artistic Will Ladislaw in *Middlemarch*, Lewes seems to have been a male feminist, a strong supporter of women's writing. A devotee of Austen, he respected Charlotte Brontë and tried to give her constructive criticism (not all of it sympathetic, notably in the case of *Shirley*). And he was, of course, the common-law husband of George Eliot, who took the first part of her pen name from him.

The funniest detractor is the iconoclastic American Mark Twain who says that "Jane Austen's books ... are absent from this library. Just that one omission alone would make a fairly good library out of a library that hadn't a book in it." He also comments that when he tries to read Austen's novels, he feels "like a barkeeper entering the Kingdom of Heaven," and refers to her characters as "Presbyterians" (quoted by Watt, *JA* 7).[3]

Austen's admirers, past and present, include Lewes and her great Regency contemporary Sir Walter Scott—a false dichotomy, largely unfair to Scott, has been set up between what he himself calls his "Big Bow-Wow strain" and her "exquisite touch, which renders ordinary commonplace things and characters interesting"

---

3    Twain's animus against Calvinism is widely documented. He blamed it in part for the American Civil War. His mother was a Calvinist, and his father an atheist who denounced Christianity in the streets. He thus associates Calvinism with women, in *The Adventures of Huckleberry Finn* and elsewhere, and he focuses in his works on the escape from the world of women. Leslie Fiedler sees, in Fenimore Cooper, Twain, and other practitioners of the American picaresque novel à la *Don Quixote*, the central character as a "man on the run" (26). Somewhat surprisingly, though, Fenimore Cooper, best known as the author of the Leatherstocking Series about Natty Bumppo, the frontier scout, began his writing career in imitation of Jane Austen. If the apparently dominant form in nineteenth-century American fiction was the picaresque or mythic, the novel of manners continued to exist and flourish in the more popular women's writing.

(quoted by Watt 8). Lewes and Tennyson both compared her to Shakespeare. James's great admirer and, in some ways, emulator, E.M. Forster, is also much more attracted to Austen (though the compliment is double-edged): "She is my favorite author! I read and re-read, the mouth open and the mind closed" (19).

By the 1940s, psychoanalytic / Freudian critics began turning their attention to Austen, including D.W. Harding, whose famous essay, "Regulated Hatred in Jane Austen," appeared in *Scrutiny* in 1940. Tony Tanner's more recent insightful introductions to the Penguin texts and his book on Austen represent a continuation of that critical perspective. David Daiches saw Jane Austen as "in a sense a Marxist before Marx" (quoted by Watt 11). The poet W.H. Auden's 1937 "Letter to Lord Byron, Part I" (quoted by Ian Watt and by Park Honan) alludes to her knowledge of economic realities, but is equally applicable to her knowledge of human nature in general:

> You could not shock her more than she shocks me;
> Beside her Joyce seems innocent as grass. (11)

Mark Schorer analyzed the cash nexus embodied in Austen's figurative language in "Fiction and the Matrix of Analogy" (1949). Marvin Mudrick's curmudgeonly work on her ironic narrative point of view and its literary sources, in *Jane Austen: Irony as Defense and Discovery* (1952), prepared the way for numerous critiques of narratology in Austen, pioneered by Wayne C. Booth's *The Rhetoric of Fiction* (1960).

How, then, do we answer Trilling's question, "Why Read Jane Austen Today?" A partial answer seems to be that she has spoken timelessly to succeeding generations of readers and critics in different ways; that the evils she presents still exist today; that her Hawthornesque "meliorism" offers hope for the future; that no one has better delineated the male–female dynamic *as it exists in society*, not in isolation; that, above all, she is completely conscious of what she is doing and of her craft.

But before dealing with her impact on, and reputation among, her contemporaries and successors, male and female, I would like to explore her relationship to a predecessor, one of the so-called "mothers of the novel," Charlotte Ramsay Lennox, author of *The Female Quixote* (1752). Lennox, before Austen, was trying to come to terms with the special relation of women writers to fiction and to reality.

### *The Female Quixote* Revisited

Virginia Woolf asserts that all women writers should lay flowers on the Westminster Abbey grave of Mrs. Aphra Behn, the first known professional woman writer, as "Jane Austen should have laid a wreath upon the grave of Fanny Burney" (rather difficult to do, since Jane Austen predeceased Fanny Burney). Someone in Winchester has taken Virginia Woolf's hint and leaves fresh flowers every day at Jane Austen's memorial and grave in Winchester Cathedral.[4] Austen had other literary "mothers" in addition

---

4    The so-called "Jane Austen revival" is really no surprise for those who were in the know all along. There is a kind of reverence about her grave. I was not surprised to learn that

to Fanny Burney, and one of the most significant of these was Mrs. Lennox. She is particularly influential on Austen's creation of her imaginative, would-be-artist heroines such as Marianne Dashwood in *Sense and Sensibility*, Emma Woodhouse, Catherine Morland in *Northanger Abbey*, and, in a somewhat different sense, Anne Elliot in *Persuasion*.

I have already described Lennox's impact on Austen's *Emma* (1816) in my earlier book *The Prison of Womanhood: Four Provincial Heroines in Nineteenth-Century Fiction*. Today, however, I am rereading *The Female Quixote* as a much more defiant affirmation of women's writing than I had originally thought, and not just as a "put-down" of the female romantic imagination. It anticipates Jane Austen's defense of the art of women's fiction in *Northanger Abbey, Persuasion*, and the burlesque "Plan of a Novel." I remarked earlier that, "As a novel it has little to recommend it, the adventures being stretched beyond the patience of more normal human beings than its heroine's friends and family." On further consideration, I realize that the prolixity may not be altogether Lennox's own fault but a partial result of pecuniary pressures similar to those later confronting Sir Walter Scott. Moreover, several critics have hinted that she was badly advised by two male mentors, the two Samuels, Johnson and Richardson. Richardson was actually the novel's printer, and for some reason the publication was delayed. Duncan Isles guesses that the rather cursory conclusion, the "cure" effected by the divine, Dr. ____, owes its existence more to Richardson's making up for the delay than to Lennox: "My guess ... is that the cure was to have been gradual, and based on a continuation of the Countess's attempt to cure Arabella, which begins so promisingly and yet is abandoned so abruptly and oddly" (*FQ* Appendix 426). Many feminist critics (myself included) would also prefer the cure to be effected by the Countess, herself an admirer of the French romances, but who is able to separate fact from fiction.[5]

To be sure, many critics overstate the case for Arabella as a female "artist." While she must be empowered to critique reality, she *does* desperately require a corrective from it, like her successors, Austen's Marianne Dashwood, Catherine Morland, and Emma Woodhouse. For that reason, Arabella's most effective cure occurs on a non-verbal, visceral level when, in emulation of the Roman Clelia depicted in Mademoiselle de Scudéry's romance, she leaps into the river in order to save her virtue (as she thinks), and almost drowns: it seems that Clelia did not wear quite so many petticoats while swimming across the Tiber! Arabella needs a physical shock to lead her back to reality, as Tom Jones needed the physical shock of believing he had slept with his own mother in order to reform. Arabella is then turned over to the ministrations of the divine Doctor ____, whose function is analogous to that of Fielding's Squire Allworthy.

What is probably most significant about *The Female Quixote* is its intertextuality, the fact that it is a self-reflexive novel *by a woman*. We know that Jane Austen read

---

when someone tried to take a picture of me beside the memorial plaque, I disappeared from it: Jane didn't want to share the space!

5     More depressingly, others, notably Catherine Craft, see the Countess as "silently virtuous and unknown" (834), and, she continues, "The countess personifies that doom to which Arabella must succumb" (837).

it more than once, as Lennox obviously read Mademoiselle de Scudéry's romances more than once. Its self-reflexiveness doubtless stirred Austen's imagination, as well as its link to some of her own spiritual mentors, Dr. Johnson, Richardson, and Fielding. Appearing twelve years after *Pamela*, but only four after *Clarissa* and three after *Tom Jones*, it melds the romance tradition of Richardson with the satirical / parodic tradition of Fielding, a blend which was to prove tremendously fruitful for Austen herself.

If Arabella fails to capture our attention today, unlike the witty Emma Woodhouse or even the comparatively lightweight Catherine Morland, it is largely because the romances with which her imagination is imbued are those of the Scudéry school, voluminous seventeenth-century tomes rarely read in our time. But Lennox did seize on the fact that many were written by women, notably Madeleine de Scudéry and a much greater forerunner of the modern psychological novel, Madame de Lafayette (*La Princesse de Clèves*, 1678).[6]

Lennox's version of the Court of Love / seventeenth-century French romance leads straight to Jane Austen's "Plan of a Novel, According to Hints from Various Quarters," her tongue-in-cheek response to the Reverend James Stanier Clarke, Librarian to the Prince Regent, who had asked her to write a novel either about the House of Saxe-Coburg, or about a clergyman. It is an "anti-*Emma*" whose heroine is all sentiment, no wit. The heroine is orphaned, travels constantly, is pursued by a villain of melodrama, is infinitely talented and absolutely lacking in a sense of humor. As Austen concludes, shedding light on both *Emma* and *Northanger Abbey*: "The name of the work *not* to be *Emma*—but of the same sort as S and S and P and P" (*Discussions*, 6). But the plot outline is that of *The Female Quixote*.

Like the "*Emma*-heroine," Arabella has an imagination nourished by isolation. "Wholly secluded from the world," she had no diversion "but ranging like a nymph through gardens," and no companionship "but that of a grave and melancholy father" (7). She is orphaned early in the novel, like the anti-heroine of "The Plan of a Novel." Like Emma Woodhouse, she is "handsome, clever, and rich." Her father is a courtier disgraced before she was born, who had retired to the country; her mother, like Emma's, long dead.

She dreams of kidnapped maidens, of "ravishment," as it occurs in the romances. Edward, her father's gardener, is to her a prince in disguise, in love with her. In fact, the only thing he covets illicitly is the carp in her father's pond. She mistakes highwaymen for aristocratic "ravishers" and frightens them away. She involves her patient suitor, Mr. Glanville, in duels to protect her honor which is never really in question. She asks other young ladies, including her cousin Miss Glanville, about their "adventures," not realizing that their understanding of this term is not that of the heroines of romance.

When Mr. Glanville falls sick, she thinks that all she needs to do to cure him is to assure him that she does not "hate" him. When her uncle Glanville intervenes on his son's behalf, Arabella thinks that he is pleading his own incestuous wishes!

---

6   This romance tradition itself grew out of the medieval Court of Love developed by women like Eleanor of Aquitaine, Marie de France, and Christine de Pisan.

Mrs. Lennox's judgment of Arabella is ambivalent. Her absurdity is caused by "a country education, and a perfect ignorance of the world" (180). On the other hand, Lennox stresses that the ideal of conduct she finds in the romances is at least superior to Miss Glanville's worldliness.

In order to effect her cure, Mr. Glanville tries to initiate her into Bath society, like Austen's Catherine Morland, and ultimately into London society. Unfortunately, these are the most boring sections of the novel, and the most boring of all is the learned Doctor's diatribe against romances which, as Craft notes, he has apparently "never read" (837). The Countess, who *has* read, loved, and memorized them, while retaining the ability to distinguish them from reality, is unaccountably shuffled off stage. Did Lennox's male mentors insist on a male mentor for her confused heroine?

The text throughout stresses Arabella's art and sense of language. She is impressively learned and charming, except on the subject of the French romance. When Glanville, her cousin-suitor, steers her away from this subject, she is a very sensible young woman; but he never succeeds in steering her for long. He tries to become the male mentor that Henry Tilney is to Catherine Morland, or Mr. Knightley to Emma, but she has her own agenda and endeavors to do some female mentoring herself by introducing him to the world of the romance. Glanville is not a very apt pupil when she orders her servants to bring *Cleopatra*, *Cassandra*, *Clelia*, and *The Grand Cyrus*, two written by a woman (Madeleine de Scudéry), the other two for a largely female readership: "Glanville sat rapt in Admiration at the Sight of so many huge Folio's, written, as he conceived, upon the most trifling Subjects imaginable" (49). Pleasant and witty as he is, he categorizes women's writing and reading, and women's concerns—life, death, love, honor, childbirth—as "trifling," nor does he alter that assessment in the course of the novel. Indeed, at the very end, "as much in Love as he was," he tells his father that he cannot marry Arabella unless she is "cured" (339–40). So it is only Arabella who is to change, not Glanville.

Arabella fails to make the distinction between history and romance on which Henry Tilney insists in *Northanger Abbey*. In fact, she accepts the romance's revisionist view of history. Clelia, for instance, does not swim across the Tiber to save herself and other hostages from political tyranny, but rather "to preserve her Honour from Violation" (62), as Arabella thinks she is doing herself later in the novel.[7] Like Emma Bovary, she reads "herstory," not "history"; Emma Bovary is far more interested in the king's mistresses than in the kings themselves—though she certainly has a point!.

Richard Church and others have noted that what appeals to Arabella in the romances is that they ennoble some rather disreputable historical women, or defend a somewhat tarnished reputation, such as that of Cleopatra: "Cleopatra was really

---

7    The editor, Margaret Dalziel, notes a curious error here on the part of either Arabella or Lennox, or both: Arabella attributes *Clelia* to a male author, Scudéry's brother. If the eror is intentional on Lennox's part, she could be suggesting that Arabella will never be even a would-be artist, or *artiste manquée*, like Emma Woodhouse or Emma Bovary, because she sees writing, authorship, as a male prerogative, and identifies only with fictional heroines, not their creators.

married to *Julius Caesar*" (62)—and so on. Glanville is to repeat her theory to the Young Gentleman who appears later, and who calls Cleopatra "a Whore" (105–6). Needless to say, this is Glanville only trying to placate the imperious, willful Arabella.

Arabella does, in fact, refuse the role of female artist, in an exchange with her cousin Miss Glanville:

> Your History, said Miss *Glanville*! Why, will you write your own History then?
> I shall not write it, said *Arabella*; tho', questionless it will be written after my Death. (110)

In this she is more like Flaubert's Emma than Austen's: Emma Bovary wants to be the chief performer in her drama, whereas Emma Woodhouse wants to be the artist behind the scenes, or offstage, with her little protégée Harriet Smith as the protagonist. Emma Woodhouse is modest, however, about her own appearance, whereas Arabella lives up to the shortened form of her name, "Bella" for beauty, as in "Belle et la Bête," "Beauty and the Beast." Arabella does, however, share the trait of snobbery with Miss Woodhouse. When Miss Glanville asks why it was such a crime for her brother to confess his love to Arabella, Arabella stresses that "Doubtless, ... I am the first Woman of my Quality, that ever was told so by any Man, till after an infinite Number of Services, and secret Sufferings ..." (111).

Arabella engages in a spirited defense of the romance form similar to Jane Austen's defense of novels by women in *Northanger Abbey*. When the rake Sir George Bellmour puts his foot in it by referring to romance subjects as "trifling," Arabella exclaims, "And pray ... What Subjects afford Matter for a more pleasing Variety of Conversation, than those of Beauty and Love?" (149). Sir George is Mr. Glanville's rival as a potential male mentor for Arabella, a much more sinister one. He takes advantage of Arabella's obsession by presenting himself as a *male* composer of romances. His name suggests "Bell" as in "Bella," and "mour," as in "amour," a would-be lover of Bella / Arabella.[8]

Sir George's "artistry" resides in setting himself up as Mr. Glanville's rival. Sir Charles even chides him, "It is pity you are not poor enough to be an Author; you would occupy a Garret in *Grub-street*, with great fame to yourself, and Diversion to the Public."[9] At this Sir George exclaims (sounding like a male Emma), "Oh! Sir, ... I have Stock enough by me, to set up for an Author Tomorrow, if I please: I have no

---

8    His name, moreover, may be an echo of that of the Duc de Nemours in Madame de Lafayette's *La Princesse de Clèves*, which bridged the gap between romance and realistic novel. This work is a classic example of René Girard's "triangular desire" in the French novel, in which the married Princesse de Clèves returns the love of the Duc de Nemours, but loves honor too much to cheapen her marriage by an affair. Nonetheless, the Prince learns of her love for the Duc and dies of a broken heart. But she remains true to him even after his death, finishing her days in a convent. This is, in fact, the kind of novel Arabella *should* be reading, in that it injects the stuff of realism into romance, instead of glossing over kidnappings, ravishments, and soiled reputations.

9    Mrs. Lennox was herself, like Aphra Behn, a professional woman writer with not much money.

less than Five Tragedies, some quite, others almost; Three or Four Essays on Virtue, Happiness, etc. ...." (252).

Sir George's "tale within a tale," in Book VI, analogous to the tale of "The Man on the Hill" in Fielding's *Tom Jones*, takes up almost fifty dull pages, but it leads to an embarrassing self-revelation. Sir George borrows the language of romance (like John Willoughby in *Sense and Sensibility*), without grasping the essentials of honor, duty, *gloire*, chastity. He thus presides over his own unmasking, for his tale reveals promiscuity, inconstancy, imprudence, and lightmindedness. Arabella arrives instantly at a right judgment of Sir George: "In my opinion ... Mr. Glanville spoke too favourably of you, when he called you only inconstant; and if he had added the Epithet of Ungrateful and Unjust, he would have marked your Character better" (250). Jane Austen's cunning rake John Willoughby may have been inspired by Sir George, but so is her thoroughly inept would-be rake John Thorpe in *Northanger Abbey*, who boasts of never having read romances *or* novels except for Lewis's *The Monk* (male Gothic) and Fielding's *Tom Jones*, both of which Austen would have considered to be in somewhat poor taste in that they describe the sexual peccadilloes of their heroes.

Arabella's female romances, on the other hand, like Madame de Lafayette's, extol honor, virtue, and duty (*devoir*). As Craft notes, Arabella not only transforms Cleopatra into a virtuous woman, but also, turning her attention to real women in her life, she even ennobles the fallen woman, Miss Groves, and the prostitute, who becomes in her imagination the Princesse de Gaule. In much the same manner, Emma Woodhouse sees Harriet Smith as the illegitimate offspring of nobility. Nor is Arabella far off the mark: if ever there was a victim of the male libido and of the double standard promoted by the patriarchy, it is Miss Groves. And prostitution is itself a product of a patriarchal system. Her support of other women shines in comparison to an underlying theme of a "modern" age in which women betray other women. Again, witness Miss Glanville, whom some recent critics try to defend, but who seems unmistakably vain, trivial, superficial, jealous, and duplicitous—the product of her contemporary society.

Much of *The Female Quixote* is a satire on language, as is much of *Northanger Abbey*. Arabella is seen by Tinsel, one of the two "Beaux" towards the end, as "a most accomplish'd, incomprehensible Lady" (303). A page later, to everyone's astonishment, she makes a "sensible Speech," which makes Mr. Glanville forget momentarily "all her Absurdities" (304). Even Sir Charles recognizes that at times "his Niece was not only perfectly well in her Understanding, but even better than most others of her Sex" (309). But she is always ordering "Paper and Pens to be brought her," a scribbler, like Pamela. Her father at one point considers burning all her books (54), but dies before he can fulfill his threat.

The past of the romances in some ways compares favorably with the present. At the very end, Arabella still avers to the divine Dr. ____ "that the Difference is not in Favour of the present World," and that her romances, "if they do not describe real Life, give us an Idea of a better Race of Beings than now inhabit the World" (380). The Countess's warning is a two-edged sword: "Custom, said the Countess smiling, changes the very Nature of Things, and what was honourable a thousand Years ago, may probably be look'd upon as infamous now. A Lady in the heroic Age you speak of, would not be thought to possess any great Share of Merit, if she had not been many times carried away by one or other of her insolent Lovers. Whereas a Beauty in this could not pass thro' the Hands of several different Ravishers, without bringing an imputation on her Chastity" (328). But this statement also implies a critique of the present age where honor and duty—and chastity—count for nothing, but only the appearance of them.

Lennox contrasts the double marriages of Sir George and Charlotte Glanville, worldly and contemporary, and Arabella and Mr. Glanville, more idealistic and spiritual: "... the first mentioned Pair were indeed only married in the common Acceptation of the Word; that is, they were privileged to join Fortunes, Equipages, Titles, and Expence; while Mr. *Glanville* and *Arabella* were united, as well in these, as in every Virtue and laudable Affection of the Mind" (383).

Thus Lennox's work foreshadows Jane Austen's in many ways. Not only does Arabella's situation with her father closely resemble Emma Woodhouse's (or that of the anti-heroine of "The Plan of a Novel"), but Arabella's "sensibility" (15) is akin to Marianne Dashwood's in *Sense and Sensibility*. Her father, the Marquis, plans "to use *Persuasions* to effect what he desired" (emphasis mine). Miss Groves's fate *could* be that of Marianne Dashwood, and *is* that of the two Elizas. Miss Groves in her youth, like Catherine Morland, is "a great Romp" (71). Like Marianne Dashwood, Arabella "strained her Ankle" in fear "of being pursued by her apprehended Ravisher." Charlotte Glanville is the false confidante figure that in Austen is to become Lucy Steele—steely Lucy—in *Sense and Sensibility*, Mary Crawford in *Mansfield Park*, and especially Isabella Thorpe in *Northanger Abbey*. Arabella's diatribe against idle ladies (279) is echoed in Mrs. Croft's distinction between "fine ladies" and "rational creatures" in *Persuasion* (94). John Willoughby's opportunistic marriage to Miss Grey echoes that of Charlotte Glanville and Sir George Bellmour.

But Lennox's Arabella—not Lennox herself—has a problem with female artistry that Austen's Emma Woodhouse, Catherine Morland, and Anne Elliot do not. Perhaps the profession of writing is not for "a lady," unless a lady is—like Lennox—down on her luck. Arabella assigns the task of writing her adventures to her maid Lucy, an earthy female Sancho Panza. Lucy is told to take notes of all Arabella's conversations, over her own protests: "I know it is not such simple Girls as I can tell Histories: It is only fit for Clerks, and such sort of People, that are very learned" (121).

Arabella is the first clear example in prose narrative of the imaginative provincial heroine who learns that she cannot impose her own art on life. Lennox launches an imaginative heroine into reality, preparing the way for Jane Austen's more convincing portraits of Emma Woodhouse, Catherine Morland, and Anne Elliot.

## "Haunting the Abbey": The Female Imagination in *Northanger Abbey*

*A Problematical Text*

*Northanger Abbey* (published 1818) is one of the two most problematical of Jane Austen's texts, the other being *Mansfield Park* (1814) : *Mansfield Park* largely because its heroine seems dislikably priggish to many; and *Northanger Abbey* because, as Mudrick puts it, its heroine is altogether too "lightweight." These are not, however, preeminently novels of character, though Jane Austen is constitutionally incapable of writing novels that lack penetrating psychological analysis. In both instances, moreover, we are dealing with novels whose titles are place names, not "Johnsonian" attributes like *Sense and Sensibility* or *Pride and Prejudice*.[10]

In its *ur* form, *Northanger Abbey* may have been a parody of the Gothic tradition in the 1790s, when Gothic romances were at the height of their popularity, but it ended up as something quite different.[11] *Northanger Abbey*, however, is very difficult to date, since no one is certain which parts belonged to the original, from the 1790s, and which from the later, revised edition of 1803. Moreover, we cannot know, apart from the internal evidence of the text, whether or not Austen may have revised it again at Chawton Cottage, possibly just after *Mansfield Park* and around the time she was working on her greatest novel of character, *Emma*, and, later, *Persuasion*, with which it was published posthumously in 1818. If *Mansfield Park* is an *implied* panoramic novel ("implied" because we are never actually transported to London, much less Antigua), which embodies a powerful critique of the abuses of patriarchy and imperialism, then *Northanger Abbey* is an implied, or hidden, manifesto in which Jane Austen embarks on a passionate defense of her craft, and particularly her craft as practiced by women writers. As I have argued earlier, *Emma* is a kind of critical self-portrait of the Artist as a Young Women, but never makes explicit the artistic models and influences on her (apart from Madame de Genlis's *Adelaide and Theodore*, whose plot somewhat parallels Emma's "nunlike" situation with a demanding, hypochondriacal—if not tyrannical—father). In *Northanger Abbey* literary predecessors and contemporaries are discussed explicitly, which makes the novel a treasure trove for those who would like to argue that, contrary to Henry James's opinion, Jane Austen was an artist who knew exactly what she was doing.

## Too "Lightweight" a Heroine?

The novel includes a number of powerful defenses of the form, as well as dialogues on the subject between and among Catherine Morland and Henry and Eleanor Tilney.[12] But that is not where the novel begins. *Northanger Abbey* foregrounds Catherine Morland herself, and presents her as a new kind of anti-romantic anti-heroine, at least up until the age of 17 (also Marianne Dashwood's age). Jane Austen knits together skillfully the development of Catherine's character from innocence to experience, and her own coming to literary maturity.

---

10   As Ann Banfield notes, place equals consciousness in Jane Austen: Austen integrates the novel of consciousness with that of place (Gothic) to create a "novel of consciousness of class and society" (30).

11   Marilyn Butler remarks that Austen's movement from Bath to Northanger may have resulted more from the fact that she was writing for "volume format," not serialization, than from any shifting intentions about the Gothic: "In her three shorter novels—*Northanger Abbey*, *Sense and Sensibility* and *Persuasion*—she uses one of the most emphatic methods of distinguishing between her two parts, a complete change of location" (55).

12   Tony Tanner refers to it as "a self-justifying artefact" (44).

Catherine's imagination can be compared to that of Lennox's Arabella. The modest, unassuming Catherine does not presume to be the author of her own plots; indeed, she does not even read Gothic novels until Isabella Thorpe introduces her to them in Bath. Arabella also aspires to act in someone else's plots, those of the seventeenth-century French romances. Unlike Arabella, however, Catherine does not even aspire to be the principal actress; she accepts for a long time Isabella Thorpe's attempts to (as Mudrick puts it) "parade" as the heroine.

*The Female Quixote* is an important model for *Northanger Abbey*, as well as for *Emma*.[13] Both *The Female Quixote* and *Northanger Abbey* turn on an heiress-plot; in Catherine's case, she is mistaken for an heiress by John Thorpe, who passes the word to General Tilney. Both novels also incorporate mistaken identities (comparable to Emma's mistaking Harriet Smith for a nobleman's by-blow), seduction, and supposed kidnappings (in Catherine's case, a kidnapping in reverse). But Catherine possesses a fount of common sense which soon disabuses her, whereas Arabella's persistent obsessions become irritating. Catherine, as the eldest daughter in a large family of ten, has never had the opportunity to develop the self-referentiality of Arabella.[14]

*A Tale of Two Catherines: The Heiress-Theme*

Austen is careful to introduce her immediately, like Emma, and she is presented as an anti-heroine in the opening paragraphs through a series of negatives. Her father, like Jane Austen's, is a respectable clergyman, "not in the least addicted to locking up his daughters" (1063). Presumably, hints Austen, not all fathers in a patriarchal system practice paternal tyranny. Despite the size of the family, equal only to Fanny Price's Portsmouth connections in *Mansfield Park*, this is an orderly, mutually supportive group of siblings, and, as has been remarked, one of the few in Austen with two very responsible parents. Any parental neglect results from the mother's many lyings-in, but she is "a woman of useful plain sense, with a good temper, and, what is more remarkable, with a good constitution"—considering all those children! (1063). So we have a heroine who is not, even by age 17, overwhelmingly attractive, but, rather, has "strong features." By 15 she is "almost pretty," and "To look *almost* pretty is an acquisition of higher delight to a girl who has been looking plain the first fifteen years of her life than a beauty from her cradle can ever receive" (1064).

What else is Catherine *not*? She is not delicate and fainting, but "fond of all boys' play," as she is raised among brothers (1063). She is, indeed, rather "a romp," as Lennox's poor Miss Groves was in her youth, but fortunately is not to suffer Miss Groves' fate. Nor is Catherine screwed into the usual assortment of "women's accomplishments." Catherine starts music lessons at eight, and ends them at nine, for "she could not bear it." Mrs. Morland allows her to quit, for she "did not insist

---

13   Julie Shaffer also sees *The Female Quixote* as a starting point, where true perception really "means relinquishing delusions of female power" (24).

14   Maria Jerinic notes an essential difference between Arabella and Catherine: unlike Arabella, "Catherine is not looking for the Romantic Suitor or the Gothic Abductor. She assesses each situation and each individual separately rather than working them into an overarching scheme of romance" (140).

on her daughters being accomplished in spite of incapacity or distaste" (1063). We are reminded of Emma, who does play and draw, but never finishes anything she starts. Catherine's "taste for drawing was not superior" (1064). Her father teaches her "writing and accounts," her mother French, but "Her proficiency in either was not remarkable, and she shirked her lessons in both whenever she could" (1064).

As for her literary education, she "had nothing heroic about her" and prefers "tomboy" activities—"cricket, baseball, riding on horseback, and running about the country, at the age of fourteen, to books, or at least books of information ..." She *does* make an exception for books that "were all story and no reflection."

But, as Austen remarks with tongue planted firmly in cheek, "from fifteen to seventeen she was in training for a heroine" (1064). Her readings are suggestive of some of Jane Austen's own favorites: Pope,[15] Gray's Elegy, Thomson, Shakespeare ("Othello," a strange choice dealing with sexual jealousy and power relations). But Catherine, unlike Emma, does not dream of being an originator of form: "though she could not write sonnets, she brought herself to read them" (1065). Is she bright enough to be a heroine? Austen implicitly compares her to Marianne Dashwood, calling "her mind about as ignorant and uninformed as the female mind at seventeen usually is" (1066).

Her greatest deficiency is drawing, but this will not matter until she finds a lover to portray. But why has the heroine no aspiring lover as yet? As Austen explains, incidentally foreshadowing the Gothic mysteries of Northanger Abbey, "But strange things may be generally accounted for if their cause be searched out" (1065). In this case, there are, Austen implies, not only no lords or baronets in the neighborhood, but probably no eligible young men. There is not even any family "who had reared and supported a boy accidentally found at their door" (1065).[16] But, Austen assures us, "when a young lady is to be a heroine, the perverseness of forty surrounding families cannot prevent her. Something must and will happen to throw a hero in her way" (1065).

Enter Mr. and Mrs. Allen, who will expedite her quest for a husband by taking her on a Smollett-esque excursion to Bath, prime husband-hunting territory, where a master of ceremonies is even employed to effect introductions. Catherine is launched into the great world with equal anti-romanticism. Her mother does not worry about seduction or kidnapping, and instead advises her to wrap up "very warm."[17] Her confidante, her sister Sally (Sarah), does not, unlike Lydia Melford's confidante in Smollett's *Adventures of Humphrey Clinker*, insist "on Catherine's writing by

---

15　Though not exactly a favorite, Austen alludes to him significantly in *Sense and Sensibility*. Marianne, who "admires Pope no more than is proper," might have detected Willoughby's duplicity earlier had she read "The Rape of the Lock," a satirical poem echoed in the situation in which young Margaret, Marianne's sister, witnesses Willoughby cutting a lock of her sister's hair as a keepsake—completely improper behavior unless there is a formal engagement.

16　The reference, of course, is to Fielding's *Tom Jones: A Foundling*, and this will not be the only reference to the satirical Fielding in the novel.

17　In Stephen Crane's Civil War novella, *The Red Badge of Courage* (1896), Henry Fleming's mother tells the fledgling soldier *not* to return with his shield or on it, but to wrap up warm and not forget to wash his socks—completely unheroic advice.

every post" (1066)—nor will Catherine do so; Austen raps lightly the tradition of the epistolary novel from which she learned so much and from which she departed so radically. Nor do any mishaps prevent Catherine's successful arrival at Bath. The Allens encounter neither robbers nor tempests, "... nor one lucky overturn to introduce them to the hero" (1067). Catherine "was come to be happy, and she felt happy already" (1067).

Not only does Catherine follow in the footsteps of earlier heroines who, like Arabella, as Rachel Brownstein writes in *On Becoming a Heroine*, find their role models in books, not life, but she also inspires the creation of a later heroine who is *really* an heiress, Catherine Sloper in Henry James's *Washington Square* (1880). Again, the use of a place name as a title suggests that we are looking at a rather larger social vision than the fate of one young woman.

Although James patronized Jane Austen, in *Washington Square* he borrowed from her satirical inversion of the courtship / marriage / presumed heiress theme. James was, in fact, fascinated with the notion of the "Heiress of All the Ages." *Washington Square* was later dramatized, as *The Heiress*, and ultimately filmed (twice), and Catherine was later to be followed by Isabel Archer in *The Portrait of a Lady* (1881), Milly Theale in *The Wings of the Dove* (1902), and Maggie Verver in *The Golden Bowl* (1904).

James's *Washington Square* is a reworking of *Northanger Abbey*, whose plot turns on a misunderstanding about the heroine's wealth, which makes her the potential prey of the stupid would-be rake John Thorpe. More seriously, she could become the victim of the vain, tyrannical General Tilney, who wishes to marry his son Henry to a wealthy young woman. James's Catherine Sloper is, much more sinisterly, the prey of a fortune hunter. She is torn between a tyrannical father, Dr. Sloper, and Morris Townsend, a Europeanized American fortune hunter. James's work could be read, in fact, as a denunciation of the patriarchy, as Austen's could too if we substitute General Tilney for the benevolent father, the Reverend Morland. Inherited wealth would seem to grant young nineteenth-century women financial freedom and independence, but instead leaves them at the mercy of unscrupulous social climbers.

Austen's Catherine Morland[18] is unintentionally misrepresented to General Tilney as the Allens' heiress by John Thorpe. The General has met her when he goes to Bath to take the waters. He invites her to his estate, Northanger Abbey, to push her tentative, beginning relationship with Henry towards courtship and marriage. When the General discovers his mistake, instead of kidnapping the desirable young woman—the fate of Richardson's Pamela and Clarissa and the one Lennox's Arabella envisions—he throws her out and sends her back to her parents in "a hack post-chaise," which disqualifies her as a "Heroine."

A glance at James's opening description of his Catherine confirms his debt to Austen. Catherine Sloper, like Catherine Morland, is an anti-heroine, unromantically conceived and described in negatives. She is *not* beautiful, and has been "a good deal

---

18 Her last name is a tag name—Mor / land—suggesting wishful thinking on the part of both John Thorpe and General Tilney, as her first name is the patron saint of spinsters, a fact more exploited by James than by Austen, since her Catherine does marry.

of a romp." She was "decidedly *not* clever; she was *not* quick with her book," but like Catherine Morland "mustered learning enough to acquit herself respectably in conversation with her contemporaries" (34). Again like Catherine Morland, she is "extremely modest" and unassuming. She is more observer than center of attention on "social occasions," like Catherine Morland at Bath. She is strong and healthy, *not* languid (37). She is also a tomboy, who plays with male cousins as Catherine Morland plays with her brothers.

Catherine Morland is not an heiress to start with; Dr. Sloper threatens to disinherit Catherine Sloper if she persists in her plans to marry Morris Townsend, who walks out on her when Dr. Sloper informs him of the threat. Both Catherines are manipulated by fathers, or father-figures, because of their anticipated inheritances. Austen's ironic ending could equally well be James's, though the latter strikes a more tragic note: "I leave it to be settled by whomsoever it most concerns, whether the tendency of this work be altogether to recommend parental tyranny or reward filial disobedience" (1207).

The internal evidence of *Northanger Abbey* points to the fact that Jane Austen was, if anything, *more* conscious of her craft than Henry James. "Romance" as a subgenre of fiction is defined as "a fictitious tale of wonderful and extraordinary events, characterized by much imagination and idealization." Throughout, the novel explores the distinction between "history" and "romance." Most critics have felt that Henry Tilney, as male mentor, corrects Catherine's imagination, based on romance fiction, with his historical sense. But, like Lennox's Mr. Glanville, Henry is not always and altogether in the right, and Austen recognizes that Catherine's romances are not always and altogether in the wrong. Indeed, romance and history often collide dangerously in this dangerous age. The Gothic tradition reflected the recent traumas of the American Revolution of 1776, the French Revolution of 1789, and the Industrial Revolution. Its imagined terrors constituted a psychological escape from the omnipresent fears of revolution, of class conflicts, of rapid social and technological change.[19] It grew out of not the ordered, classical world of Pope and Johnson, but that of early romanticism; Jane Austen was very much a child of this period of transition.

As we watch Catherine's developing consciousness, we witness, as in Emma Woodhouse, a mixture of right and wrong perceptions, depending on whether they grow out of her social experience, or out of a romance novel plot which becomes a kind of Procrustean bed on which to fit life and real acquaintances. But her "right" perceptions are not always those of the "historian" who, as Austen is well aware, imposes his *own* order, regularizing that which is not always reducible to "sense."[20] Which is the more "fictitious"? Catherine's "imagination of disaster" (one critic

---

19   During the Vietnam War, the violence of, for instance, Sam Peckinpah's films constituted a similar kind of psychological release for young men waiting to be drafted.

20   More than a century later, Norman Mailer was to subtitle his *Armies of the Night*, about the 1967 Peace March on Washington, "The Novel as History, History as the Novel." He takes to task the media's supposedly accurate, "historical" view—for instance, their statistics on the numbers of the war protestors—as "a forest of inaccuracies," and contrasts it to his own limited, subjective, "novelistic" view as participant / recorder.

compares it to James's) derived from Gothic fiction, while overblown, does serve as a corrective to her own sunny 17-year-old disposition, and to Henry's reductions of his own family history to pattern and order.

### Bath: Isabella's False Tutelage

Isabella, who introduces the Gothic to Catherine, is a kind of false mentor, a false confidante like Lucy Steele or Mary Crawford. Her teachings must be transcended by Catherine, the more-than-apt pupil. But Isabella and the Gothic are necessary steps in Catherine's adjustment to adult experience.

The first part of *Northanger Abbey*, the Bath section, is, as has long been noted, a satire on travel literature à la Smollett and Fanny Burney. But through Isabella's "mentoring" and Isabella's and John's machinations, it sets the stage for the second, Gothic section set at Northanger Abbey. Bath provides a presetting, a frame, a social context. In addition, for Austen, as for her later heroine, Anne Elliot, in *Persuasion*, Bath was not necessarily a positive experience, though probably not particularly "Gothic." When her mother announced suddenly, in 1800, that the Reverend George Austen, her father, had decided that he wanted to retire to Bath from Steventon— "Well, girls, it is all settled; we have decided to leave Steventon in such a week, and go to Bath"—it is reported that Jane fainted away. For the inexperienced Catherine, however, who has never been away from home, it is virtually paradise on earth.[21] She just wants to pass uncensured through the crowd. Austen uses her

---

21   Park Honan, Maggie Lane, and others have dealt in some detail with Austen's ambivalence towards Bath. Anna Lefroy was evidently the source for the story of Austen's fainting at her father's news (Honan 155). Honan speculates, from an autobiographical manuscript of Frank Austen's, that their father was "too incapacitated from age and increasing infirmities to discharge his parochial Duties in a manner satisfactory to himself" (quoted by Honan 156). As Honan remarks, Cassandra was absent at this time, and "the tears of a younger daughter were insignificant" (156). Lane says that Austen's attitude towards Bath "was sometimes hostile, frequently ambivalent," but never "dismal," probably because "her own temperament was sunny" (11–12). She also insists that Bath would have been difficult for a writer like Austen to ignore, for better or worse. Her parents married in Bath, in April, 1764 (5), and her father is buried there in Walcot Church (35). Moreover, one of her ancestors, James Brydges, the Duke of Chandos, participated in the creation of Georgian Bath by John Wood, Ralph Allen, and Beau Nash. His second wife, Cassandra Willoughby, gave her first name to Austen's mother and sister, and, Lane adds, "her surname to one of Jane's most charming villains" (5). Anne-Marie Edwards also notes that Bath was "second only to London" (75). She also remarks that "Jane cleverly chooses locations in Bath to suit her charactrers" (79). Like a number of critics Edwards implies an identification between Austen and the two heroines of her "Bath" novels, *Northanger Abbey* and *Persuasion*, remarking that Catherine Morland is "all eager delight" as she approaches Bath for the first time, and quotes her effusion to Henry Tilney, "Oh, who can ever be tired of Bath?" (75). Edwards assumes that *Persuasion* was written 13 years after *Northanger Abbey*, and that her later heroine Anne Elliot's more jaundiced view of the city reflects actual social changes during that period, in which Brighton became more fashionable, and Bath became "more a place to retire to than elope from" (88). Thus, Anne Elliot, "a much more sedate character than Catherine Morland"—she is after all ten years older—"finds 'the white glare' of Bath exhausting and persists 'in a very

late impressionistic style—that of *Persuasion*—to describe Catherine's perceptions. For example, she does not see the dancers, but only the high feathers of the ladies. Soon, however, she begins to yawn because, unlike the heroines of romance, she is not noticed by anyone—yet she is "exceedingly handsome" compared to three years before (1070).

Nor does Mrs. Allen turn out to be the treacherous chaperone of romance—or of Richardson's novels—who would function "by intercepting her letters, ruining her character, or turning her out of doors" (1067). But General Tilney really *does* turn her out of doors in the second section, and realism and romance intersect, or collide. Mrs. Allen is simply incompetent, a flat character with one *idée fixe*—dress, and the shops of Salisbury. She also provides the link to the Thorpes, since she and Mrs. Thorpe were old schoolfellows. They indulge in a *dialogue de sourds* about dress and children which, comments Austen, is what passes for conversation between them. She telescopes Mrs. Thorpe's ramblings in a much less subtle way than she does those of the babbling Miss Bates in *Emma*: "This brief account of the family is intended to supersede the necessity of a long and minute detail from Mrs. Thorpe herself, of her past adventures and sufferings, which might otherwise be expected to occupy the three or four following chapters" (1076).

Catherine's initial experience of Bath is a mixture of pleasure and disappointment. She is introduced to Henry Tilney by the master of ceremonies, Mr. King (a real person in Bath history), early on, but he soon disappears, and Catherine, in a fit of narcissism, sees only people "*nobody* cares about" (really herself)—a statement as sweeping as Mrs. Bennet's reported consciousness that "It is a truth universally acknowledged, that a single man in possession of a good fortune must be in want of a wife" (1). Austen has more than a little fun with Richardson's dictum that a young woman must be devoid of sexual feelings towards her admirer until the marital knot is tied. Austen applies this "legislation" even to dreams and fantasies: "... if it be true, as a celebrated writer has maintained, that no young lady can be justified in falling in love before the gentleman's love is declared,[22] it must be very improper that a young lady should dream of a gentleman before the gentleman is first known to have dreamt of her" (1073).[23]

---

determined, though very silent, disinclination' for the city" (89). Again, however, should we assume that *Northanger Abbey* was not re-edited before final publication? More importantly, can we identify Austen with her two heroines, one so "lightweight," the other, as Austen put it, "almost too good for me"? Her alleged fainting occurred nearest the acknowledged reworking of the earlier novel in 1803, and on May 5, 1801, she wrote, on coming into Bath with the sun in her eyes, "The first view of Bath in fine weather does not answer my expectations; I think I see more distinctly through rain. The sun was got behind everything, and the appearance of the place from the top of Kingsdown was all vapour, shadow, smoke and confusion" (*Map* 6).

22   The reference is to Richardson's letter, No. 97, vol. 1, "Rambler."

23   Jocelyn Harris remarks of Austen's intertextuality that "Male authors as well as female provide origins for her work when she makes a deliberate, powerful, and I believe most conscious choice to revisit and remake those earlier authors, out of respect, companionship, and even love" (88)—and, we might add, irony.

When Henry fails to appear in the Pump Room, the Thorpes appear instead.[24] Catherine's common sense makes of John Thorpe anything but an object of desire. She holds her tongue merely because she is "fearful of hazarding an opinion of [her] own in opposition to that of a self-assured man" (1085). Indeed, she judges him rightly despite his compliments and her own naivety, and tolerates him merely because he was "her brother's friend and her friend's brother" (1084). John gives himself away by revealing his recklessness in buying and selling horses, by his diction—he asks his mother respectfully, "Where did you get that quiz of a hat, it makes you look like an old witch?"—and above all, by his literary taste, or lack of it. When the girls speak to him about Mrs. Radcliffe's *Mysteries of Udolpho*—on which the shadow plot of the Northanger section will be imposed—he says, "I never read novels. I have something else to do" (1081). But a minute later, he adds, proving he *has* read novels, "Novels are all so full of nonsense and stuff. There has not been a tolerably decent one come out since *Tom Jones*, except *The Monk*" (1085). Austen was a sometime admirer of Fielding. But she undoubtedly felt that some of Fielding's more explicit sexual episodes in *Tom Jones* were in poor taste, and in Matthew Lewis's *The Monk*, a lurid tale of murder, incest, violence, she undoubtedly saw one of the most nefarious examples of "male Gothic" which she contrasts to Mrs. Radcliffe's "female Gothic." John is more nuisance than temptation: he prevents her from dancing with Henry, and she receives her first social lesson, "that to go previously engaged to a ball [to John] does not necessarily increase either the dignity or enjoyment of a young lady" (1089). When she sees Henry with an attractive young woman, she does not experience jealousy; in fact, she recognizes that the young woman is Henry's sister Eleanor. When she is frustrated in her desire to dance with Henry, she feels "a violent desire to go home." When there, she does not pine away, but "immediately fell into sound sleep, which lasted nine hours, and from which she awoke perfectly revived, in excellent spirits, with fresh hopes and fresh schemes" (1092). John Thorpe poses no threat to either Catherine's sense or sensibility, except by frustrating her efforts to cultivate the Tilneys.

When she hopes to see more of Eleanor (and Henry) at the Pump Room, John Thorpe once again intervenes to take her on a supposedly pre-engaged ride to Claverton Down, which he accurately describes as "a tumble," and frightens her with his reckless horsemanship. Mrs. Allen, as usual, when appealed to for permission, says, "'Do just as you please, my dear,' ... with the most placid indifference" (1093). Asked to elaborate on the joys of the ride, Catherine cannot lie even "to please Isabella" (1097).

John intervenes once again when Henry has asked her for a third time to dance, claiming he expected to dance with her. She begins to show signs of her old tomboy spirit when she replies, "I wonder you should think so, for you never asked me" (1102). John is a riding, fox-hunting "Barbarian" in the manner of Squire Western in *Tom Jones* or John Willoughby. At last Catherine gets her wish to dance with Henry, who is becoming impatient with John Thorpe and introduces the notion of the promised dance as "a contract of mutual agreeableness" (1103). He then proceeds

---

24 This is the same substitution device Austen uses in *Sense and Sensibility* where one suitor appears when another one is expected.

to declare, "I consider a country-dance as an emblem of marriage," a metaphor that pervades Henry's mentoring. Invited to go for a country walk with Eleanor, "her spirits danced within her, as she danced in her chair all the way home" (1105), which again sounds like the mature Austen style of *Persuasion*, as Anne Elliot also dances in her carriage all the way home.

John Thorpe intrudes once more to prevent the country walk. He lies that he has seen Henry and Eleanor Tilney in Lansdown Road, planning to go as far as Wick Rocks (1108). Since it is raining hard, not the beautiful weather of Udolpho, of Tuscany, or the South of France (1106–7), Catherine finds it plausible that they may have postponed the walk till drier weather, and John persuades her to go to Blaize Castle, which she hopes will be "an edifice like Udolpho" (1109)—anticipating her eagerness to visit Northanger Abbey in the second part. "Are there towers and long galleries?" she asks (1108).[25] Again, Mrs. Allen is not the most authoritarian of guardians when appealed to by John to persuade Catherine to go: "Well, my dear, ... suppose you go" (1108). Even the courteous Henry comments of Catherine's only social outlet at home, visits to Mrs. Allen: "What a picture of intellectual poverty!" (1104).

Predictably, the excursion never reaches Blaize Castle because they set out too late and thoughtlessly, so Catherine has not even that consolation. Moreover, she is a virtual prisoner in John's carriage (like Emma with Mr. Elton), when they pass the Tilneys still in town, proving John's falsehood. Catherine is not shy, finally, at reproaching him: "How could you deceive me so, Mr. Thorpe? ... I had rather, ten thousand times rather, get out now, and walk back to them" (1109). This is as close as Catherine comes to being kidnapped: it is impossible to escape with the reckless John driving the carriage. Mr. Allen, with more sense than his wife, later characterizes it as "a strange wild scheme" (1110). Moreover, while she is out, she has missed Eleanor who had every intention of fulfilling her engagement. Austen describes this news as "heart-rending" from Catherine's point of view, and concludes Chapter 11 melodramatically: "And now I may dismiss my heroine to the sleepless couch which is the true heroine's portion; to a pillow strewed with thorns and wet with tears. And lucky may she think herself, if she get another good night's rest in the course of the next three months" (1111). Of course, next morning, at the beginning of Chapter 12, Catherine awakens "cheerful" and we see her "tripping lightly through the churchyard" as she goes to apologize to Eleanor (1111). However, told Eleanor is out, she subsequently sees her exiting with, apparently, her father, and Catherine is truly disturbed at the apparent "incivility" (1112). What appears to be incivility is no such thing—but it foreshadows the ending when Eleanor is forced to be the bearer of the bad tidings that her father is compelling Catherine's expulsion from Northanger.

---

25  As Lane notes, "Anybody less naïve than Catherine would have known that Blaise Castle was in fact scarcely 30 years old, an 18th century garden folly built by a wealthy sugar merchant, Thomas Farr, to adorn the grounds of his estate just outside Bristol. The joke, between Jane Austen and her contemporary readers, is on Catherine, but the censure is reserved for John Thorpe" (76).

When Catherine sees Henry and his father at the theater, she does not hesitate to apologize impulsively for missing the country walk: "... if Mr. Thorpe would only have stopped, I would have jumped out and run after you" (1113). When Catherine calls for Mrs. Allen's corroboration of her story, the latter, as usual, helpfully replies, "My dear, you tumble my gown!" (1113). Austen notes the beginning of Henry's attraction to this open, frank girl, who is not trapped, unlike Anne Elliot, by public opinion, which Anne's father reveres: "Is there a Henry in the world who could be insensible to such a declaration?" (1113).

When the Thorpes once again try to manipulate her out of the rescheduled country walk with the Tilneys, by substituting another excursion to Clifton, she finally finds the courage to call John a liar—or practically: "If I could not be persuaded into doing what I thought wrong, I never will be tricked into it" (1118). Although she is imposed on longer by the more subtle Isabella than by John, she has already begun to suspect her of "being wanting in tenderness" (1111), or, more bluntly, of lacking interest in Catherine except as a companion / confidante / go-between.[26] When the Thorpes try to spoil the country walk for the second time, and Isabella protests, "These Tilneys seem to swallow up everything else," Catherine starts to see her friends as "ungenerous and selfish" (1116). Catherine defends herself: "If I am wrong, I am doing what I believe to be right." Isabella's reply is sullen and sarcastic: "I suspect ... there is no great struggle" (1117). They even enlist her brother against her when she insists on going to the Tilneys' lodging to apologize. Finally, unlike the heroine of a romance, "my heroine was most unnaturally able to fulfill her engagement, though it was made with the hero himself" (1121). That engagement is the excursion to Beechen Cliff, during which Henry elaborates on what has been subtended all along, the distinction between romance and history.

---

26  Isabella's instrument of deception, like John Willoughby's and Lucy Steele's, is conventional romantic language. As James Thompson writes, "Another excellent index of Austen's self-consciousness about ineffability can be found in the many times she uses such expressions with unmistakeable irony, always in connection with her shallowest characters, thus indicating her awareness of the potential for cliché" (95). Tony Tanner discusses Jane Austen's own resistance to metaphor: "Metaphor may blur and confuse by its overabundance and excess of possible references and other 'worlds'; Jane Austen, it seems, aims at a total transparency ..." (64). This resistance was very much shared by the later George Eliot who time and again, particularly in *The Mill on the Floss* and *Middlemarch*, warns us that images are "the brood of desire" and reflect "the shallow absoluteness of men's judgments." Barbara Horowitz asserts that Catherine learns "that books, as well as people, lie," but she seems to feel that Austen shared the belief of her age "that novels were harmful to the young, particularly to young women" (82). I would argue, rather, that Catherine learns not to distrust books, but to distrust misreadings, including Isabella's, which influence her own. Patricia Meyer Spacks refers to what I have called the "false confidante": every Austen novel "contains at least one unworthy female contemporary of the heroine, frivolous, insensitive or foolish" (160). Honan thinks that Austen's cousin and later sister-in-law, Eliza de Feuillide, may have been the model for Isabella (134)—not very likely, in view of Austen's obvious attachment to the exotic Eliza. Honan does admit that "*Northanger Abbey* does make serious points about social education and language ..." (139).

*Gothic Delusion and Northanger Abbey*

John Thorpe's ridiculous mock-proposal marks the turning-point of the novel, away from Bath and towards Northanger Abbey.[27] It also sounds a warning-note, which Catherine does not understand at the time, that John is vastly overestimating her father's fortune, and hopes to follow his sister's example in marrying the Morlands' wealth. In case she misses the point, he continues, "Did you ever hear the old song, 'Going to one wedding brings on another'?" (1131). Catherine has developed sufficient wit by this point to retort, "But I never sing," in much the same tone Fanny Price uses when she says, "I cannot act." If General Tilney "quantifies" in describing his rooms, his estate, so does John Thorpe: "But you have more good-nature, and all that, than anybody living ... you have so much—so much of everything" (1132). Catherine has her suspicions and says, in general, "If there is a good fortune on one side, there can be no occasion for any on the other. No matter which has it, so that there is enough. I hate the idea of one great fortune looking out for another; and to marry for money I think the wickedest thing in existence. Good day" (1132).[28]

There is a remarkable symmetry in the two parts of the novel, whose actions are structured by a brother–sister team, the Thorpes at Bath, the Tilneys at Northanger. Henry Tilney is the glue that holds the two sections together. John Thorpe is a rather obvious anti-hero, even to Catherine, and one of the enigmas of the novel is how the common-sense Catherine of Fullerton, who acquires social discernment and intelligence, spirit and wit, in her dealings with the Thorpes at Bath, can be so fanciful and deluded at Northanger.[29] Isabella is much more dangerous than her brother, in that some of what she professes appeals to the very young Catherine, as indeed it once did to Austen herself. Isabella—or her readings, rather—appeal to Catherine's imagination as John Thorpe, who is earthy and anti-imagination, can never do. Isabella, in fact, embodies the central theme of the novel—how to separate fact from fiction. She does not create fictions, but merely borrows plots in order to fabricate lies. Like Lucy Steele, she pretends to be sensitive, caring, and romantic, but underneath she is "steely," hardbitten, has her eye on the main chance, and is determined to marry for money.

Isabella is untrustworthy because, like John Willoughby, she professes one set of principles and practices another. Four years older than Catherine, and possessing "great personal beauty" (1075–6), she is ideally situated to dominate the younger woman and capture her imagination. Disappointed in Henry Tilney's

---

27  Dianne Hoeveler asserts that "both worlds are essentially the same, Bath being only what we might recognise as the tamer, 'cooked' daytime version of the 'raw' Northanger, while the Abbey at night, as constructed by Catherine's Gothic imaginings, is the nightmare version of Bath." Both are "equally unreal, rejected by and rejecting the heroine" (121).

28  And there speaks Jane Austen, before much of Henry's mentoring takes effect on Catherine. Austen has more than one spokesperson in the novel.

29  Alan D. McKillop underlines the tension between two roles Catherine is to play: "... Jane Austen's difficulties come from trying to develop both possibilities at the same time. In a sharp opposition between fiction and ordinary life, common sense should have the upper hand, and Catherine by virtue of being commonplace is on the side of common sense. But in the quixotic mode Catherine is to illustrate, not merely to negate, romantic folly" (57).

absence, Catherine finds that "Friendship is certainly the finest balm for the pangs of disappointed love" (1075). Unfortunately, as so often in Austen, such are the conditions of the marriage market that female friendships are often unstable, except among sisters—and sometimes even then (Lydia Bennet, Elizabeth Elliot). Their conversational subjects are vacuous, the youthful parallel to Mrs. Allen's and Mrs. Thorpe's chats: "dress, balls, flirtations and quizzes" (1075). One feels sure that it is Isabella—"Bella" the beauty[30]—who introduces these fascinating subjects to the uninitiated Catherine. Most importantly, since the English weather is often wet, especially in Bath, she introduces Catherine to the world of Gothic fiction: they "shut themselves up to read novels together" (1077). Isabella's unwillingness to separate fact from fiction is a negative but necessary lesson for Catherine in this *Bildungsroman*. It is to be corrected, its gaps filled in, by the male mentor, Henry Tilney, in the second half of the novel.[31]

Isabella seeks to make Catherine the confidante of her secret romance with James Morland, but Catherine is too obtuse to take the hint. She describes James as her ideal man, which Catherine fails to take in. Later, she puts words in Catherine's mouth: "You would have told us that we seemed born for each other, ... my cheeks would have been as red as your roses; I would not have had you by for the world" (1099). Catherine retorts that "I would not have made so improper a remark upon any account ..." (1099). She has good taste by nature. Moreover, she knows her brother is not handsome, as Isabella asserts, and Isabella's assurance that she will prefer his family to hers seems "a pitch of friendship beyond Catherine." It should also be noted that Isabella's ideal mate, like Marianne Dashwood's, must agree with her in everything.

Isabella is favorably disposed only towards men who show interest in her and her friends: the others are condemned in a feminist diatribe worthy of Mary Wollstonecraft—or of Emma Woodhouse, who paraphrases Wollstonecraft to Mr. Knightley in her attack on male judgment. As Isabella generalizes, "They give themselves such airs. They are the most conceited creatures in the world, and think themselves of so much importance!" (1080). She then spots "two odious young men who have been staring at me [not Catherine] this half-hour." Catherine thinks she is relieving Isabella's mind by reporting that the two male offenders have left the Pump Room. Isabella promptly suggests they return to her lodgings in Edgar's Buildings to see her new hat. Catherine warns her they may overtake the young men, and Isabella's classic reply as to *not* avoiding them is, "I have no notion of treating men with such respect. *That* is the way to spoil them" (1081). Austen's ironic scalpel dissects them, setting off "immediately, as fast as they could walk, in pursuit of the two young men" (1081).

Isabella placards her "frankness," which only highlights Catherine's real innocence and sincerity. "You have no disguise," says Mrs. Thorpe to her eldest daughter, whereas Isabella is nothing but disguise (1138). Isabella claims she never loves by halves (1079), and asserts she is "disinterested" materially, while she is

---

30   Her name could be an echo of "Arabella."

31   We do learn that Isabella's literary taste is limited, one-sided; she has not read Richardson's *Sir Charles Grandison*, one of Catherine's—and Austen's—favorite novels (1081).

mentally enumerating her perquisites as James's bride at Fullerton, "with a carriage at her command, a new name on her tickets, and a brilliant exhibition of hoop-rings on her fingers" (1131). "Inconstancy is my aversion," she says, but she is simultaneously tempted by Charles Hodges, and later by Frederick Tilney. When she learns that James is to receive only Mr. Morland's living, of about 400 pounds annually, Isabella expresses her negatives in terms of her own supposed altruism: the income will not supply "the common necessaries of life," says Isabella, and "For myself, it is nothing; I never think of myself" (1137). She also expresses the harsh reality which contradicts her avowed allegiance to the romances: "... after all that romancers may say, there is no doing without money" (1143). Unlike that later Isabella, Isabella Linton in *Wuthering Heights*, she is not the victim of romances, but merely shapes their plots to fit her own purposes. She hints there may be more than one way of Catherine's and her becoming sisters; that is, if Catherine marries Henry Tilney and she marries Captain Frederick Tilney (who is a hollow womanizer).[32]

Isabella is literally absent from the Northanger Abbey section, though she has helped to prepare it. We hear from her one last time, in epistolary form, a letter which is preceded by James's to Catherine. Her revelations, and her rhetoric, are appalling, as she tries to put the blame on James for silence.[33] She also calls on her supposed feminist leanings to defend herself: "Many girls might have been taken in, for never were such attentions; but I knew the fickle sex [meaning Frederick, in whom she has met her match] too well" (1186). Catherine is once again enlisted as go-between, but by now she is judging rightly: "She was ashamed of Isabella, and ashamed of having ever loved her" (1186). She concludes, "She must think me an idiot ..." (1187). The mentoring of Henry in the Northanger Abbey section has freed Catherine of more than one delusion.

### Eleanor Tilney: Gothic Heroine at Northanger Abbey?

Eleanor Tilney is the "sisterly" foil to Isabella, and takes over from her in the second section. When Catherine first meets her at Bath, she realizes she has "more real elegance" than Isabella. Moreover, she seems capable "of being young, attractive, and at a ball, without wanting to fix the attention of every man near her ..." (1090). Eleanor speaks, not profoundly, but "with simplicity and truth, and without personal conceit," in marked contrast to Isabella, who simply ignores Catherine's existence except to confirm her own opinions. Eleanor clears up not only the first mystery of Henry's presence, then absence, at Bath, but also the mystery of the old chest in Catherine's room at Northanger: it is there simply to be out of the way (1155). Eleanor's tale is not told, except parenthetically in the final pages, but *her* love story, not Isabella's, fits the demands of romance fiction: the cruel, tyrannical father who

---

32  Moreover, she disowns all responsibility for flirting with Frederick: "One's eyes must be somewhere," describing herself, with ironic truth, as "absent" (1141). Here, the Lacanian "gaze" seems to distance and objectify not the perceived object, but the perceiver.

33  Only Mary Crawford's final letter in *Mansfield Park*, in which she seems to wish for Tom Bertram's death so that Edmund will inherit the estate, is comparable in its blind self-absorption and narcissism.

splits the lovers up because of the suitor's lack of fortune, a lover who turns out to be noble, and whose "unexpected accession to title and fortune" permits not only her own marriage, but also Catherine and Henry's. Of her lover, whom we never meet, Austen says mock-formulaically, "the most charming young man in the world is instantly before the imagination of us all" (1206). Eleanor is the subdued, pained heroine who appears elsewhere as Elinor Dashwood, Fanny Price, and Anne Elliot. It is characteristic of Austen that embedded in her novel are other potential novels not to be told here, but elsewhere. Life is a limitless storehouse of narratives. Austen also uses this young man to tie up the loose thread of the mysterious missive Catherine finds in the chest: yes, it is a banal laundry list, but it is also romantic, in the way that romance occurs in real life, for it turns out to be Eleanor's lover's laundry list from his visit to Northanger.[34] Austen is playing with the Gothic tradition of offering natural explanations for apparently supernatural phenomena. She also justifies herself for introducing an apparently new character in the final pages: he turns out to have been lurking in the background all along: "... I have only to add (aware that the rules of composition forbid the introduction of a character not connected with my fable) that this was the very gentleman whose negligent servant left behind him that collection of washing-bills, resulting from a long visit at Northanger, by which my heroine was involved in one of her most alarming adventures" (1206–7).

## Henry's Mentoring

Henry's initial mentoring of Catherine in Part One leads directly to the furthering of her education at Northanger Abbey. Katrin Burlin has written probably the most perceptive essay on Henry's mentoring, contrasted to the Thorpes' manipulations. She speaks of the fictive process as "the necessity for the professional novelist in a world thoroughly permeated by delusive fictions." She emphasizes that "Jane Austen's motive is to fight for her craft." Following Joseph Wiesenfarth's *The Errand of Form*, she marks the stages of Henry's education of Catherine. First, when he meets her at Bath, he expresses astonishment that she does not keep a

---

34  Hoeveler, I believe, misreads this laundry list and the presence of linen in the mystery chest: "The linen and the laundry list are the visible residue of women's lost and unpaid labour for the family. The domesticities, rather than reassuring Catherine, should have horrified her" (131). In an age in which the gentry, and even lesser lights, had servants, the only exploitation of women would have been of the servant class—not, I suspect, a topic which would have occurred to Austen then. Eleanor would not have been responsible for the family laundry. Tanner is more astute in comparing Austen's use of chests and wardrobes to that described in Gaston Bachelard's *The Poetics of Space*, particularly the chapter on "Drawers, Chests and Wardrobes." In a parenthetic, but important, paragraph in his chapter "Anger in the Abbey: *Northanger Abbey*," Tanner quotes Bachelard, who offers an "examination of the images of intimacy that are in harmony with drawers and chests, as also with all the other hiding-places in which human beings, great dreamers of locks, keep or hide their secrets" (49). Tanner also rightly emphasizes the word "intimacy," with its implications of sexuality, and sees in the description of the cabinet with, "in the centre, a small door, closed also with a lock and key (which) secured in all probability a cavity of importance,"'"a thinly veiled image of virginity," signifying Catherine's sexual "awakening" (49).

journal—which she presumably promptly begins to do—referring somewhat sardonically to women's "easy style of writing" (1071). Second, he introduces the country dance as a metaphor for marriage: "You will allow that in both man has the advantage of choice, woman only the power of refusal ... You will allow this?" (1103). He then distinguishes between them, and Austen underlines the irony of the courtship where the man tries harder, and marriage where the woman does (1103).

Third, on the walk to Beechen Cliff[35] with Henry and Eleanor, Henry assumes the role of language teacher, on the words "nice" and "amazing." As Eleanor says, he will be citing "Johnson and Blair all the rest of the way" (1122). Henry emphasizes the age gap (like Mr. Knightley) between himself and Catherine: "I had entered upon my studies at Oxford, while you were a good little girl working your sampler at home" (1122). He also enters on the distinction between fiction and history, while Catherine complains about "the men all so good for nothing, and hardly any women at all" (1123). Like Arabella and, later, Emma Bovary, Catherine is interested in "herstory," and presumably here too Jane Austen is subtly correcting Henry's teachings.[36] Craik and others have felt that Henry is too much the authorial voice, and Walton Litz says that Austen has trouble keeping herself out, and embodies her ideas in Henry. But Catherine is not all wrong, nor is Henry all right.

Eleanor misunderstands Catherine when she says, "I have heard that something very shocking indeed will soon come out in London" (1125), meaning a Gothic fiction, but Eleanor thinks of a "dreadful riot." Henry says condescendingly, "My dear Eleanor, the riot is only in your own brain" (1125). But in fact critics, including Litz, have noted that the reference could be to the very real Gordon Riots of the 1780s. So, again, the female perception is not all wrong. D.W. Harding has noted that England at this period was indeed dangerous, and housed "voluntary spies."[37] Surely Jane Austen is speaking with tongue in cheek when she says, "imbecility

---

35  Edwards notes that Beechen Cliff was known as one of the beauty spots around Bath. It seems to me that, as a setting for real-life romance, it anticipates the even more romantic setting of the Undercliff at Lyme, which Austen describes so eloquently in *Persuasion*.

36  Antoinette Burton suggests that Jane Austen's own teenage *History of England*, illustrated by Cassandra, reveals her essential agreement with Catherine: "What make Austen's *History* subversive, and finally, feminist in the most expansive sense of the term is that it dares to suggest that traditional representations of English history [Burton argues that Austen's *History* is a parody of Oliver Goldsmith's *History of England from the Earliest Times to the Death of George II* (1771)] were 'and are', so vulnerable to reinterpretations and the imaginative powers of women readers so great, that the mischievous work of two teenage girls scribbling in the family parlour would easily render 'the History of England' a not so innocuous parody of itself" (47). Honan also sees in Catherine's dialogue with Henry a recapitulation of Austen's own debates with her brothers over the relative virtues of history and romance (142).

37  Gary Kelly elaborates that Austen's linkage of the domestic and feminine with the national reading "is a metaphor and metonymy for success or failure at the national and imperial level in an age of national and international crises ..." (31). Hoeveler argues that "in valorising Henry's smug enlightenment attitude, it would appear that Austen shares or at least would like to share Henry's outlook and privileges, it would appear that Austen wants to be one of the boys" (133). It seems clear, however, that Austen calls Henry's attitude into question, and that she is angry about her age, even if the anger is contained.

in females is a great enhancement of their personal charms" (1124). Catherine has the last word when she says, "I cannot speak well enough to be unintelligible," a wonderful remark as relevant to much of today's critical theory as to Austen's time, and Henry agrees, "Bravo! an excellent satire on modern language" (1135).

The fourth mentoring marks the transition to Northanger. Catherine thinks, "These were thrilling words" at the very name of the Abbey (1139). She dreams of "its long, damp passages, its narrow cells and ruined chapel ... and she could not entirely subdue the hope of some traditional legends, some awful memorials of an injured and ill-fated nun" (114).[38] In Chapter 20 she is off to Northanger Abbey, which constitutes approximately the last third of the book. Henry, as Burlin has remarked, is more eager than she. In the curricle on the way to the Abbey, he whets her appetite for the Gothic, describing real furniture, including a "ponderous chest" (1151), and a housekeeper named Dorothy. "The night was stormy" (1156), but the lodges are "of modern appearance" (1152), and the panes of glass "so large, so clear, so light!" (1153). He prizes her teachableness, yet he seems to love pulling her leg.

The Gothic episodes are played for laughs.[39] One cannot help thinking of Emma Woodhouse's conceit of Miss Bates "haunting the Abbey" (Donwell) were Mr. Knightley to marry Miss Bates's niece Jane Fairfax. Catherine locks the cabinet inadvertently; it was already unlocked—a fitting metaphor for the creation of Gothic mystery. But, as we have already seen, the laundry list she discovers in the mysterious cabinet *does*, in a realistic way, embody romance. Above all, her misgivings about General Tilney *are* validated in a realistic, if not a Gothic, way.[40] Henry and Frederick, both away much of the time, did not have the opportunity of witnessing the domestic tyranny Mrs. Tilney and Eleanor did. If not a Montoni of melodrama, he is the kind of "villain" we do find in real life.[41] And Catherine is not

---

38   This is a motif that does not fail to attract Charlotte Brontë's attention in *Villette*.

39   As Birthe Tandrup writes, *Northanger Abbey* is more a satire on the misreading of Gothic than of the Gothic tradition itself: "It is a truth universally acknowledged by critics that Jane Austen's take-off of the Gothic in *Northanger Abbey* is less an attack on the genre itself than an attack on readers of it who, like Catherine Morland, cannot distinguish between life and fiction" (83). To that end, to correct the character's point of view, "the brief appearance of another viewpoint, that of the narrator as objective truth-teller or norm, sheds an ironic light on what the character just said or thought" (84). Jerinic argues that *The Mysteries of Udolpho* is less a target for satire than a model for *Northanger Abbey*: "Rather than existing as a parody of *Udolpho*, *Northanger Abbey* instead critiques the eighteenth century positioning of the female reader" (147), and particularly a positioning "in which women are educated relying on a reading list constructed by men" (143). Hoeveler sees Mary Wollstonecraft as the mother of Gothic feminism (certainly, her daughter Mary Shelley was a major contributor to it). She asserts that *Northanger Abbey* is a fictional version of Wollstonecraft's *A Vindication of the Rights of Woman*—an overstatement of Austen's more subtle politics and poetics, I think.

40   As Tanner notes, Catherine's very invitation to the Abbey "[emanates] from the patriarchal centre of power" (43).

41   As Paul Morrison stresses, Henry's corrections of Catherine's vision are themselves Gothic: "Henry can release Catherine from her gothic illusions ... only by invoking the ideological standards that are themselves the staple of the gothic, which suggests that the distance between texts will not hold" (5).

just the "simpleton" Henry loves to teach; she will also teach him.⁴² It is tempting to imagine his being embraced by Catherine's outgoing, active, energetic family as he has not been, apart from Eleanor, by his own. Catherine's imaginings of a live Mrs. Tilney imprisoned in her room are probably to lead to Charlotte Brontë's wholly serious version of the "Madwoman in the Attic," Bertha Mason Rochester in *Jane Eyre*.⁴³ And Henry James's *The Turn of the Screw*, in which the governess / narrator may, in fact, be herself mad, undoubtedly owes a substantial debt to both *Northanger Abbey* and *Jane Eyre*.

Finally, the novel seems to lead to an impassioned defense of its own form. Around the time of "The Plan of a Novel" and *Emma*, it seems as if Jane Austen had to work something through about her craft, and particularly her role as a female writer. First, there is the heartfelt apologia for female solidarity at the end of Chapter 5, beginning, "If the heroine of one novel be not patronized by the heroine of another, from whom can she expect protection and regard?" (1077):

> Let us not desert one another; we are an injured body. Although our productions have afforded more extensive and unaffected pleasure than those of any other literary corporation in the world, no species of composition has been so much decried ... and while the abilities of the nine-hundredth abridger of the History of England, or of the man who collects and publishes in a volume some dozen lines of Milton, Pope, and Prior, with a paper from the *Spectator*, and a chapter from Sterne, are eulogised by a thousand pens, there seems almost a general wish of decrying the capacity and undervaluing the labour of the novelist, and of slighting the performances which have only genius, wit and taste to recommend them ... "And what are you reading, Miss ____?" "Oh! it is only a novel!" replies the young lady; while she lays down her book with affected indifference, or momentary shame. "It is only *Cecilia*, or *Camilla*, or *Belinda*"; or, in short, only some work in which the greatest powers of the mind are displayed, in which the most thorough knowledge of human nature, the happiest delineation of its varieties, the liveliest effusions of wit and humour, are conveyed to the world in the best chosen language. (1078)

Lest we miss the point that this is all in praise of female novelists—Fanny Burney, Charlotte Smith, *et al.*—Austen proceeds to compare what would happen if the young lady were reading the *Spectator*, "how proudly would she have produced the book, and told its name!" But Austen adds, "the chances must be against her being occupied by any part of that voluminous publication, of which either the

---

42  As Barbara Horowitz emphasizes, Austen "was the only writer on education who believed that women could teach men as well as learn from them" (126). Comparing Austen's work to that of the authors of conduct books and essays on women's education, such as Hannah More, Jane West, and Mary Hay, Horowitz goes so far as to argue that Catherine considers it her "duty" to uncover the truth of Mrs. Tilney's death (5). Tony Tanner suggests, in a nice phrase, that Catherine is often "wrongly right" (45).

43  Morrison adds, moreover, that Henry's actions sometimes illustrate the male domination of the Gothic: "The staircase down which she [Catherine] suspects Mrs. Tilney has been conveyed ... is the staircase up which Henry ascends: the search for a woman withdrawn from visibility by a man only serves to reveal Catherine's secret suspicions to a man. The principle of gothic incarceration is reversed, but its essential function is reinscribed. Visibility, or, better, legibility is a gender specific trap" (14).

matter or manner would not disgust a young person of taste; the substance of its papers so often consisting in the statement of improbable circumstances, unnatural characters, and topics of conversation, which no longer concern any one living; and their language, too, frequently so coarse as to give no very favourable idea of the age that could endure it." So much for Addison and Steele![44] "Genius, wit, and taste" are her criteria. She makes a claim for high seriousness through language, wit, and knowledge of human nature.[45] This defense of the novel as practiced by women is offered by a kind of floating narrative voice which strikes a personal note.[46] The discussion is followed by Chapter 6, with Isabella's and Catherine's dialogue on literary taste and the Gothic, where Catherine has difficulty separating fact from fiction.

In the final *éclaircissement* at Northanger, when Henry finds Catherine in his mother's room, she has a kind of rude awakening, like Emma: "The visions of romance were over" (1175). But again there is a sting in the tail: Catherine has realized lurid events do not occur, "at least in the midland counties of England," but she is less sure about "the Alps and Pyrenees," France and Italy, and even "the northern and western extremities" of Britain—territory staked out by Austen's "unknown" admirer, Sir Walter Scott, who would doubtless have been amused, and later by those other transplanted Celts in wildest Yorkshire, the Brontë sisters. The narrative moves from Henry's object lesson to Catherine's somewhat muddled application of it:

Charming as were all Mrs. Radcliffe's works, and charming even as were the works of all her imitators, it was not in them perhaps that human nature, at least in the midland counties of England was to be looked for. Of the Alps and Pyrenees, with their pine forests and their vices, they might give a faithful delineation; and Italy, Switzerland, and the South of France, might be as fruitful in horrors as they were there represented. Catherine dared not doubt beyond her own country, and even of that, if hard pressed, would have

---

44   As Honan writes, "There has never been a stronger statement of belief in the novel form" (143–4)—*if* we add, the novel form as practiced by women.

45   Clifford Sisken sees in Austen's defense of the novel and attack on the *Spectator* an indication of her movement towards popular culture: they "point to ... Austen's participation in the historical transformation of the two-tier market into a hierarchical system of what we now know as high versus low culture—a hierarchization that in narrowing the range of proper writing ushered in the disciplinary advent of the new category of Literature" (56). He also ties this newly acclaimed popular culture to women readers and writers, revealing "how other new divisions of knowledge were informed by divisions of gender ..." (63). By the same token, Austen is a deconstructionist *avant la lettre*, interrogating the canonical male tradition. Jocelyn Harris remarks on Austen's self-confidence: "... far from being anxious about the propriety of female invention, Jane Austen actually boasts of it in *Northanger Abbey* when she praises the largely female genre of her novels as being superior in genius, wit ..." (98–9). In another vein, Hoeveler generalizes about the Gothic (not distinguishing between male and female Gothic): "Gothic fiction is not about being equal to men, it is about being morally superior to men. It is about being a victim" (119)—if one needs to equate victimization with moral superiority.

46   Honan calls the narrator "a lithe and slippery eel of great energy which is less than fully controlled" (41).

yielded the northern and western extremities. But in the central part of England there was surely some security even for the existence of a wife not beloved, in the laws of the land, and the manners of the age. Murder was not tolerated, servants were not slaves, and neither poison nor sleeping potions to be procured, like rhubarb, from every druggist. Among the Alps and Pyrenees, perhaps, there were no mixed characters. There, such as were not as spotless as an angel, might have the dispositions of a fiend. But in England it was not so; among the English, she believed, in their hearts and habits, there was a general though unequal mixture of good and bad. (1176)[47]

The ending is of a piece with the realistic-romantic tone of the work. If Henry's love for Catherine is built initially upon gratitude for *her* infatuation, their marriage will be based at least as much upon education—if not more—as it will upon passion. Tanner, reiterating his theme of "Anger in the Abbey," claims that "Happy endings are only the dream of narrative" (55). But this is perhaps to offer too dismal a conclusion to a charming, amusing tale. I am reminded much more strongly of the romantic-realistic comic ending of *Emma*, in which Emma's marriage to Mr. Knightley is facilitated by Mr. Woodhouse's fear of a thief in his poultry-house! As Austen writes, of Emma's concealment from Mr. Knightley of the whole truth about her responsibility for Harriet—in a rare editorial intervention, like her defense of the novel in *Northanger Abbey*:

> Seldom, very seldom, does complete truth belong to any human disclosure; seldom can it happen that something is not a little disguised or a little mistaken; but where, as in this case, though the conduct is mistaken, the feelings are not, it may not be very material. (339)

In *Persuasion*, Anne Elliot does marry into danger, not the Gothic danger of which Catherine Morland dreams, but the very real danger of the Napoleonic Wars and the War of 1812 which gave impetus to the Gothic tradition at the turn of the century.

### *Persuasion*: Silenced Storyteller or New Scheherazade?

It would be tempting to see Anne Elliot as a mature version of Catherine Morland, inasmuch as *Northanger Abbey* and *Persuasion*—"the two 'Bath' novels," as Maggie Lane calls them (11)—were published together posthumously in December, 1817 (1818 on the title page), have the same setting, and have heroines who are victims of "parental tyranny" (though in Catherine's case the "patriarch" is not her own father). But Anne at 19 was already far more mature than Catherine at 17, and, if Catherine must lose her romantic illusions, Anne must learn romance as she grows

---

47   The leaves of rhubarb, it is worth noting, are poisonous. And in the same year in which *Northanger Abbey* was published, Mary Shelley was depicting the "construction" of a bride for the Frankenstein monster in the remote Orkney Islands. Catherine naively underlines what Tanner calls contradictions in Henry's world: "Henry tries to evoke a phantasm of peaceful life from which the possibility of horror and violence has been eradicated" (71), but "If England has become a land of 'voluntary spies,' it is not the secure and calm place Henry Tilney seems to be trying to evoke" (70).

older. Above all, both novels lend themselves to readings as self-reflexive works on the art of the novel.[48]

While *Emma* (1816), which bears strong affinities to *Northanger Abbey*, is almost universally acknowledged as Jane Austen's masterpiece, many readers (including myself) have always had a special fondness for her poignant last-completed novel, *Persuasion*.[49] Barbara Hardy has argued that Anne Elliot is *not* a creative figure (unlike Emma Woodhouse), and that the movement of the novel is towards life, not art, that it is "concerned with living." I would like to stress, however, that Anne, like her predecessor Elinor Dashwood in *Sense and Sensibility*, *does* express aspects of Jane Austen's own creativity: discipline, detachment, shrewd observation of others, an objectivity that Marianne Dashwood, Catherine Morland, and Emma Woodhouse all too woefully lack, although all three possess Austen's spirit, idealism, energy, and, in Emma's case, a wit sometimes pushed to the point of cruelty. Anne is not "an interfering little bitch," as my mother, too unsympathetically I think, called Emma, but a passive observer for whom the *donnée*, given, of the novel is her inability to interfere effectively, to intervene and prevent her father's and sister Elizabeth's vain extravagance, Louisa Musgrove's folly at Lyme, Captain Benwick's grief over his lost love Fanny Harville. Most importantly, she is powerless to let Captain Wentworth know she still loves, has always loved, him. The whole novel points towards the recast final chapters 22 and 23 which contain Anne Elliot's passionate defense of woman's constancy, and her attack on male pens which have perpetuated a literary stereotype of female infidelity or inconstancy. This is a set-piece to be juxtaposed to Jane Austen's own vehement editorial intervention in *Northanger Abbey* on behalf of female writers. Hardy notes that Austen uses the authorial "I" in *Persuasion* for the first time since *Mansfield Park* (unless we count the problematically dated *Northanger Abbey*), but, I believe, the heroine becomes that authorial "I"—observing "eye"—throughout the novel, culminating in Anne's / Austen's defense of her craft. In *Persuasion*, in fact, Austen has written the answer to misogynistic male writers: she has created a heroine who remains constant and faithful to her memory of Captain Frederick Wentworth even when all hope is gone.[50]

## The Heroine as Female Mentor

Jane Austen wrote to her niece Fanny Knight about Anne, "You may perhaps like the Heroine, as she is almost too good for me" (quoted in Butler, 284). We can

---

48  Claudia Johnson suspects, as I do, that the *Northanger Abbey* we have may not be the 1803 version, and that the two novels published in 1817 are implicitly linked: "... they seem unlikely companions, but in Austen's mind their partnership was deeper than the accident of their copublication. *Persuasion* itself speaks to problems that to all appearances pressed on Austen while she was reviewing, perhaps even revising, Northanger Abbey [sic] for publication" (288).

49  It invites the reader's subjectivity: Honan also calls it "her most emotionally powerful work and perhaps the most difficult to judge" (385).

50  Jan Fergus claims that the plot turns on Anne's "recovery of her own sexuality" (75)—but she never lost it! I would say, rather, that what she recovers is her voice, and thereby her activity.

compare this remark to what she has said about some of her other heroines: Elizabeth Bennet—"I must confess that I think her as delightful a creature as ever appeared in print, and how I shall be able to tolerate those who do not like *her* at least I do not know" (*Letters* II: 297 [29 January 1813]; quoted by Mudrick, 93); Fanny Price— "Oh, what has become of all the shyness in the world?"; Emma Woodhouse—"I fear I have created a heroine whom no one but myself will much like" (*Memoir*, 157; quoted in Lascelles, 69).

Austen's spirited, misguided heroines appear in *Bildungsromans*, Elizabeth, Emma, and even Marianne Dashwood in half a *Bildungsroman*. Anne Elliot, however, has nothing to learn, except Wentworth's surviving feelings for her.[51] Indeed, if anyone is "educated" in the course of the novel, it is Wentworth himself, and by a female mentor. Craik points out that Anne is "faultless" from the start; not coincidentally, she is also Austen's most mature heroine, at that crucial age of 27 when, throughout the nineteenth century, a woman had either to find a husband, or be branded a spinster forever.[52]

Anne touches us in a way that few of Austen's other heroines do, for she suffers in silence like Elinor Dashwood, but, unlike Elinor, does not speak (when she does speak) in balanced Johnsonian epigrams! John Bailey has said there are few heroines we love so much (quoted in Wright, 145). And one of the reasons is that, comparable to the Marianne-part of *Sense and Sensibility*, the novel could easily veer towards tragedy. Andrew Wright says that we are never in doubt of the outcome (147), but I—along with Anne—am.

Persuasion *and "Persuasions"*

The title *Persuasion*, while chosen by Henry Austen after his sister's untimely death, seems most appropriate as it suggests an author preoccupied with her art to the very end.[53] The word "persuasion" appears often in the text. Anne as a 19-year-old suffers from "over-persuasion" about Wentworth on the part of Lady Russell (86).[54] Louisa Musgrove is "not so easily persuaded": "When I have made up my mind, I have

---

51  Cheryl Weissman, instead of repeating the *Bildungsroman* comparison, says simply that "Here the focus has veered from character to the perception of character ..." (91). Ann Astell disagrees that this is not a *Bildungsroman*, and stresses that Anne continues to "learn romance" throughout the novel: "... it is so obviously Anne's story" (275). It seems to me, however, that she has already learned romance before the novel begins, but must find her own function and voice. Tanner remarks that "to learn romance [is] a deliberate oxymoron surely," since romance is by definition intuitive rather than cognitive (212).

52  Charlotte Lucas, in *Pride and Prejudice*, is a good case in point of the traditional desperation of the 27-year-old spinster. Tanner sees Anne as a lonely girl, an "in-between girl," caught between father and lover (209).

53  The Jane Austen Society of North America (JASNA) implicitly supports this view in naming its journal *Persuasions*.

54  On that level, as Tanner remarks, the novel is at least as much "about dissuasion" (210).

made it" (109).[55] Her obstinacy—as the reader, or Anne, might see it—calls forth Wentworth's curious parable of the nut; to Louisa he says:

> "Your sister is an amiable creature; but *yours* is the character of decision and firmness, I see ..." "Here is a nut," said he, catching one down from an upper bough. "To exemplify,—a beautiful glossy nut, which, blessed with original strength, has outlived all the storms of autumn. Not a puncture, not a weak spot any where.— "This nut," he continued, with playful solemnity, "—while so many of its brethren have fallen and been trodden under foot, is still in possession of all the happiness that a hazel-nut can be supposed capable of." (110)[56]

Then he points the moral: "My first wish for all, whom I am interested in, is that they should be firm. If Louisa Musgrove would be beautiful and happy in her November of life, she will cherish all her present powers of mind" (110). Of course, ironically, it is the quiet, undemonstrative Anne who has been firm all along, and who is entering the autumn of her life; the headstrong Louisa will precipitate herself off the Cobb at Lyme onto her "nut"!

Lady Russell again attempts to "persuade" Anne to marry William Walter Elliot and secure her birthright, Kellynch, entailed away, like the Bennets' home, to a male heir (216). Kellynch has been called "hollow," and indeed Anne perceives it, and its present proprietor, as such. Nor does it take her long to realize that William Walter Elliot is as "hollow" as Sir Walter, the current owner, when her friend Mrs. Smith reveals the truth about him (after first also trying to "persuade" Anne to marry him in order to intervene with him on her own behalf).

Austen describes ironically Elizabeth Elliot's "internal persuasions" on rank. Elizabeth decides not to entertain by holding a dinner in Bath, which would reveal "the reduction of servants" (224), and instead just asks the Musgroves "for an evening" (225). Wentworth suffers from an "unfortunate persuasion," a false persuasion, about Anne's possible interest in Mr. Elliot. And his jealousy ultimately brings them together again. At that point Anne defends herself spiritedly when he fears she has been listening once more to Lady Russell's "persuasion": "You should not have suspected me now; the case so different, and my age so different. If I was wrong in yielding to persuasion once, remember that it was to persuasion exerted on the side of safety, not of risk. When I yielded, I thought it was to duty; but no duty could be called in aid here. In marrying a man indifferent to me, all risk would have been incurred, and all duty violated" (246). In other words, she here defines "persuasion" only in negative terms, of choosing *not* to do something; it could never lead her towards vice. However, taken in other contexts it can be positive. The term "persuasion" occurs often in Austen's other novels as well. Having her last

---

55   The topic is a projected visit to her sister Henrietta's suitor Charles Hayter at Winthrop, and the comparison is to Henrietta's lack of resolve.

56   Tanner comments sardonically, "a 'nutty' happiness indeed" (233), adding that "Anne is not a 'nut'—that visual image for the ideal wife was curiously infelicitous" (235)— deliberately so, I should think. Johnson also notes that "The most salient feature of the glossy hazel-nut ... is not that it holds impressions well, but that it is not susceptible to them at all" (298).

completed novel called *Persuasion*, whether the title was chosen by her brother or herself, permits the term to take on artistic connotations. Of what is Austen trying to "persuade" her readership? That a woman can write "against" a male tradition in which women are constructed as either profligate seductresses, or passive victims. She creates instead a heroine who, against all odds—an indifferent family, the twin prisons of rank and gender—strives for autonomy and is constant, above all, not only to Wentworth, but especially to herself.

*The Ending(s): Anne as Artist-Critic*

Structurally, it makes sense to start with the concluding chapters, compare that ending to the cancelled chapter, and then work backwards towards the source, Anne's consciousness, and her perceptions of her family and friends.[57] Austen's decision to cancel the first version of the penultimate chapter is vivid testimony to her continuing command of her creative powers to the end of her days. Like Louisa Musgrove, the cancelled chapter is more precipitate than Austen recommends. As soon as Mrs. Smith denounced Mr. Elliot:

> Anne left Westgate Buildings, her mind deeply busy in revolving what she had heard, feeling, thinking, recalling, and foreseeing everything, shocked at Mr. Elliot, sighing over future Kellynch, and pained for Lady Russell, whose confidence in him had been entire. The embarrassment which must be felt from this hour in his presence! How to behave to him? How to get rid of him? What to do by any of the party at home? Where to be blind? Where to be active? It was altogether a confusion of images and doubts ... (255)

Anne runs into Admiral Croft in Gay Street, Bath, "within a few steps of his own door" (255). He has assumed that she and Mr. Elliot are to be married, and invites her in to see his wife, saying, "... there is nobody but Frederick here." Anne thinks to herself, "Such a person to be passed over as a nobody to her!" (256).[58] Events begin to escalate out of control:

> After being allowed to feel quite secure, indifferent, at her ease, to have it burst on her that she was to be the next moment in the same room with him! No time for recollection! for planning behaviour, or regulating manners! There was time only to turn pale before she had passed through the door, and met the astonished eyes of Captain Wentworth, who was sitting by the fire, pretending to read, and prepared for no greater surprise than the Admiral's hasty return. (256)

When Admiral Croft returns from the Post Office, he asks Captain Wentworth to act as go-between for him with Anne, offering to surrender the lease to Kellynch on the misunderstanding that she is to marry Mr. Elliot. Frederick cannot help exclaiming,

---

57  Without granting Anne creativity, Hardy nonetheless says that the "storyteller" in *Persuasion* is Anne's memory. Horowitz notes Anne's many accomplishments, but relates them to women's education rather than to women's artistry: Anne shows "elegance of mind," is an accomplished pianist, a connoisseur of the arts, understands Italian, and is authoritative on both poetry and prose; nor does she conceal that knowledge (67).

58  Her father and sister have thought of her previously as "nobody," "only Anne" (37).

"That I should be the person commissioned on this subject is extraordinary! and believe me, Madam, it is no less painful" (259). The *éclaircissement* is more direct and less subtle than is Jane Austen's wont. Anne disabuses Wentworth instantly: "You are misin—the Admiral is misinformed" (259). Wentworth's "colour was varying." The scene becomes as close to overtly sexual as Austen gets: Wentworth "looked with an expression which had something more than *penetration* in it—something softer ... It was a silent but a very powerful dialogue; on his side supplication, on hers acceptance" (259; emphasis mine). If this had been the final version, it would have been the first successful proposal dramatically staged, rather than performed offstage, in Austen's novels. Wentworth bursts out, "Anne, my own dear Anne!" (260). He now realizes Anne's steadiness and constancy: "(so far from being altered for the worse), she had gained inexpressibly in personal loveliness; and that as to character, hers was now fixed on his mind as *perfection* itself, maintaining the just medium of fortitude and gentleness" (260). The final use of "persuasion" refers to the Admiral's wife who is delighted to have Anne as a prospective sister-in-law: her "particularly friendly manner in parting with her gave Anne the gratifying *persuasion* of her seeing and approving" (263; emphasis mine).

The revised Chapters 22 and 23 delay all the action. Having heard Mrs. Smith's denunciation of Mr. Elliot, "Anne went home to think over all that she had heard" (218). There is a full day's delay, "and Mr. Elliot's character, like the Sultaness Scheherazade's head, must live another day" (233). Again, Austen contextualizes the scene with a simile referring to the archetypal woman artist, Scheherazade, who will die unless she can entertain her husband the Sultan with 1001 Tales, one tale each night. In other words, she would die if she could not speak, so Austen is addressing the "anxiety of authorship" (as Gilbert and Gubar call it) in very female terms. Moreover, Scheherazade is also the female artist who is forced to confront risk. Austen constantly highlights the relationship between domesticity, risk, and art. As is often remarked, in the end Anne marries into risk: "She gloried in being a sailor's wife, but she must pay the tax of quick alarm for belonging to that profession which is, if possible, more distinguished in its domestic virtues than in its national importance" (254).[59] If Anne married into risk, and to a man whose profession is celebrated for its "domestic virtues," Austen too, by breaking silence and writing professionally about the interrelations of private (domestic) and public virtues, was taking risks. Her heroine comes close to Austen in perception and gifts, if not in professionalism. The final chapters of the book slow down the action mainly through the device of letter-writing, as private an art as one can get away with in a drawing room.[60]

---

59   It is Anne who first uses the term "risk," but in connection with Mr. Elliot. If she marries into risk with Frederick, it is because of the danger of his profession. But Anne makes clear that the "risk" she would incur in marrying Mr. Elliot is that of an unsuitable husband, married without love.

60   One thinks of Darcy trying to write to his sister Georgiana despite the interference of Miss Bingley in full pursuit, or of the creaking dining room door at Chawton which alerted Jane to hide her work.

Anne may not become a professional writer, but she has strong ideas on literature and often borrows aphorisms from favorite poets and prose writers. She does not advise the sentimental, bereaved Captain Benwick to give up poetry, but merely to balance Scott and Byron with prose, letters, biographies. Anne does realize with wry amusement, however, that "she had been eloquent on a point in which her own conduct would ill bear examination" (122). Anne considers, moreover, that "it was the misfortune of poetry to be seldom safely enjoyed by those who enjoyed it completely; and that the strong feelings which alone could estimate it truly, were the very feelings which ought to taste it sparingly" (122).[61] While Anne makes no mention of the novel, but only letters and memoirs, letters did graduate to the epistolary novel, and memoirs to the epistolary or autobiographical novel. Although it is not so explicit as in *Northanger Abbey*, and needs to be teased out, Austen seems again to be presenting a defense of the novel, as mediating the lyric (romance) and the biography / essay / history (realism). This is a conjunction Virginia Woolf was later to seize on in her lyric novels, in practice if not in theory. In fact, she valorized poetry as the highest form women writers should strive for, with the novel being an intermediate step because younger, therefore more accessible.[62] Anne recognizes realistically that Benwick will not struggle long with his feelings for the dead Fanny Harville. When Benwick takes up with Louisa Musgrove, injured on the Cobb at Lyme, Anne decides that these two apparently mismatched people were thrown together by "the situation" (177). In fact, Anne dismisses his motives almost as Emma does Harriet Smith's: "He must love somebody" (178).

Austen indulges a romantic love of landscape more in this novel than in any other, and undoubtedly the wave-swept Cobb and Undercliff constitute a thoroughly romantic scene. In the longest description of landscape in an Austen novel, she expatiates on the beauties of Lyme:

> ... the remarkable situation of the town, the principal street almost hurrying into the water, the walk to the Cobb, skirting round the pleasant little bay, which in the season is animated with bathing machines and company, the Cobb itself, its old wonders and new improvements, with the very beautiful line of cliffs stretching out to the east of the town, are what the stranger's eye will seek; and a very strange stranger it must be, who does not see charms in the immediate environs of Lyme, to make him wish to know it better. The scenes in its neighbourhood, Charmouth, with its high grounds and extensive sweeps of country, and still more its sweet retired bay, backed by dark cliffs, where fragments of low rock among the sands make it the happiest spot for watching the flow of the tide, for sitting in unwearied contemplation;—the woody varieties of the cheerful village of Up Lyme, and, above all, Pinny, with its green chasms between *romantic* rocks, where the scattered forest trees and orchards of luxuriant growth declare that many a generation must have passed away since the first partial falling of the cliff prepared the ground for such a state, where a scene so wonderful and so lovely is exhibited, as may more than equal any of the

---

61   The word "safely" again suggests a parallel between the dangers of naval battle and those of authorship.

62   Like Woolf, Austen the prose writer has a passion for poetry.

resembling scenes of the far-famed Isle of Wight: these places must be visited, and visited again, to make the worth of Lyme understood. (117; emphasis mine)[63]

It is almost as though Louisa, and indeed Anne herself, are swallowed up by this landscape and the sea air, powerless to resist. There Anne encounters William Walter Elliot, whose attentions and admiration reawaken her womanhood, but not her love (he does not know at this point that she is his cousin). Her eyes sparkle, her cheeks blush, she speaks more, and Wentworth begins to take more notice of her. Anne's earlier praise of autumn (perhaps her own season, or so she thinks) sounds almost Keatsian or Shelleyan—she did, of course, share with Keats an association with Winchester, with its beautiful walk through the Water Meadows, and she was known to adore long walks in the area around Chawton. By the same token, Anne's "pleasure in this walk [to Winthrop, Charles Hayter's home, as it turns out] must arise from the exercise and the day, from the view of the last smiles of the year upon the tawny leaves and withered hedge, and from repeating to herself some few of the thousand poetical descriptions extant of autumn, that season of peculiar and inexhaustible influence on the mind of taste and tenderness" (107).[64] Anne's musings suggest that Austen is indeed blending the new romanticism with the old classicism, even as she tries to blend poetry and prose, and in this she is very much a child of her age.[65]

---

63   Lest we miss her "intention" (*pace* Wimsatt), Austen actually uses the word "romantic" in the passage. One might compare Catherine Morland's romantic illusions on Beechen Cliff—"That noble hill whose beautiful verdure and hanging coppice render it so striking an object from almost every opening in Bath" (*Map* 2)—when Henry tries to mentor her into realism. Walton Litz refers to "the new importance she gives to natural landscapes" (217), and concludes that, "More than has been generally realized or acknowledged, she was influenced by the Romantic poetry of the early nineteenth century ... In their quiet and restrained fashion, Jane Austen's last works are part of the new movement in English literature" (219). The Harvilles' small house in Lyme embodies "love in a cottage." Tanner remarks that it is "rather like a ship on shore." Certainly, in its situation on the Marine Parade / Esplanade, it seems to embrace nature in both storm and calm. Several critics move from the novel's romantic style to its political stance. Marilyn Butler castigates it as muddled, caught between two worlds, because it does not fit into her "conservative," eighteenth-century box. She says it is "an eighteenth-century novel in search of a centre" (227). Robert Hopkins, however, sees it as "essentially liberal" (273), and Claudia Johnson is of the opinion that Austen *uses* conservatism only in order to be read: "Conservative fiction was Austen's medium because it very quickly became the only fiction there was, other voices being quelled, and Austen persistently subjected its most cherished mythologies to interrogations from which it could not recover" (307).

64   Keats's "Ode to Autumn," celebrating that "season of mists and mellow fruitfulness," is dated later than Austen's novel, and after her death (September 19, 1819, and in Winchester).

65   Several critics note Austen's emphasis on the new individualism associated with romanticism. Hopkins notes the tension between luck and rational or moral judgment, and concludes that, "Given a choice between prudential morality and the truth of love, *Persuasion* argues for love" (272). He goes so far as to see Austen in this novel opting for "existential choice" (174). Mary Poovey, however, feels that Austen rejects individualism, and the changes that can be effected by romantic love: "In her realistic portrayal of the inevitable connections between the public and the private spheres and in her allusions to that complex

In her literary exchange with Captain Harville in the last two chapters, Anne seems to be reconstructing, or reinventing, herself by rejecting the mistaken intentions and manipulations of others.[66] Indeed, as much as in *Northanger Abbey*, Austen makes use of a whole array of false artists who use language to manipulate and misinform Anne: Mrs. Clay and Mrs. Smith, Mr. Elliot, even Elizabeth and Mary, certainly Lady Russell. Lies are generated, and false gossip, leaving Anne very much in Austen's (and the reader's) position in playing the detective role throughout.[67]

It has been noted that Anne's confidants at the end are all male, even in the cancelled chapter: Admiral Croft, Captain Harville, Charles Musgrove, and finally Wentworth himself. A new Scheherazade, she liberates herself by frank discourse with men. Like Isabella Thorpe with Catherine Morland, the women use Anne as *their* confidante without ever letting her tell her own story.[68] Anne liberates herself by accessing the male world, which is also the male literary world. The male world she accesses directly (the literary obliquely) is not that of the old patriarchy, but of the new naval officers / entrepreneurs, as Austen uses the popular form of the novel to access a new public, both male and female.[69] Anne's defense of woman's constancy, much attacked by male writers, represents her counter-thrust. The go-between device employed with Elinor in *Sense and Sensibility*, who is approached by Colonel Brandon to offer Edward Ferrars the living at Delafield so that he may marry Lucy Steele, is used again in a sense, but not so overtly and repetitively as

---

society, beyond the personal interests of her characters, Jane Austen exposes the fallacy of the claim for personal autonomy" (173). It seems to me that, although Austen is rightly suspicious of romantic love as conceived by middle-class borrowings from the medieval Court of Love tradition, Anne's passion for Wentworth is disabused of illusions, but nonetheless it is passion as realistically conceived. Austen does not cease to be a realist for all her interest in romanticism, but I prefer to use the word "realism" to describe a technique which she uses, not an ideology, bourgeois or otherwise. Thus, not only are the Cobb, Lyme, and Bath described with meticulous accuracy, but we can still see the originals of Captain Benwick's and Captain Harville's small pastel houses facing the sea on the Marine Parade.

66   Honan says, "Feminist critics illuminate this scene, and nothing they have said in the twentieth century perhaps would have offended the author" (383). Indeed, Sandra Gilbert quotes a brief sentence from it in a 1986 *New York Times Book Review* article, "From Our Mothers' Libraries: Women Who Created the Novel" (30).

67   Stephanie Barron's series uses Jane Austen herself as the detective, and P.D. James has imagined that if Austen were living today, she would be, among other things, a writer of detective fiction. I have wondered how much Agatha Christie's Miss Jane Marple, who uncovers secrets in country villages, owes to Miss Jane Austen (who, alas, did not live to Miss Marple's ripe old age).

68   Henry James's Maggie Verver is similarly trapped in a prison of silence in his last completed novel, *The Golden Bowl* (1904). One cannot help thinking that the last from both authors was also silence (almost).

69   Honan asserts that "Here Jane Austen is not Tory but Radical [referring to Wentworth's critique of a naval command that cynically sends sailors out in unseaworthy vessels], and her grasp of a war profession gives her story an edge as she treats the Navy, at the present time (the summer of 1814)" (381). He adds that, "Time and change, false feeling and modernity confront her. Like Jane Austen, she [Anne] is an acute, estranged observer" (381). But her overall treatment of the navy (as of modernity) is fair and balanced.

in the cancelled chapter where Admiral Croft asks Wentworth to broach to Anne the subject of surrendering the lease to Kellynch to expedite her supposedly projected marriage to Mr. Elliot. In the revised version, it is Harville, not one of the principals, who is commissioned by Benwick to have set a picture of the latter originally intended for his fiancée, the late Fanny, but now destined for Louisa. This errand leads to a discussion of constancy between Harville and Anne: "Poor Fanny! she would not have forgotten him so soon!" (236). Anne makes an even stronger statement, applying fidelity to all women: "It would not be the nature of any woman who truly loved." In a statement similar to Byron's "Man's love is of man's life a thing apart, 'tis woman's whole existence," Anne asserts:

> "We certainly do not forget you, so soon as you forget us. It is, perhaps, our fate rather than our merit. We cannot help ourselves. We live at home, quiet, confined, and our feelings prey upon us. You are forced to exertion. You have always a profession, pursuits, business of some sort or other, to take you back into the world immediately, and continual occupation and change soon weaken impressions." (236)

She is, of course, thinking of Wentworth and not Benwick, who, as Harville reminds her, "has not been forced upon any exertion" (237). Anne then moves to the argument from nature, that "It must be nature; man's nature, which has done the business for Captain Benwick" (236). In an exchange that sounds very modern, Harville turns the tables with *another* argument from nature:

> "I will not allow it to be more man's nature than woman's to be inconstant and forget those they do love, or have loved. I believe the reverse. I believe in a true analogy between our bodily frames and our mental; and that as our bodies are the strongest, so are our feelings ..." (236)[70]

Anne has an answer for this too—might does not make right:

> "Your feelings may be the strongest," replied Anne, "but the same spirit of analogy will authorize me to assert that ours are the most tender. Man is more robust than woman, but he is not longer-lived; which exactly explains my view of the nature of their attachments." (237)

She adds that men have so many worldly cares, they can scarcely be expected to add women's feelings to all this.

Finally they agree to disagree. Just at this point a clatter is heard: Captain Wentworth's "pen had fallen down;" he has obviously overheard the discussion. Anne suspects as much (has intended as much?). He was supposedly writing a letter in aid of Benwick's painting commission.

Ironically, the "argument" then takes a literary turn, and Wentworth is drawn in. Harville now argues, "all histories are against you, all stories, prose and verse ... I do not think I ever opened a book in my life which had not something to say about woman's inconstancy." He continues, "Songs and proverbs, all talk of women's

---

70 This debate is still with us. The newly discovered size of Einstein's brain (probed by a woman doctor) was immediately applied to the debate over male versus female intelligence: "Bigger is better."

fickleness. But perhaps you will say, these were all written by men" (237). Then comes the most famous, most significant passage from Anne:

> "Perhaps I shall.—Yes, yes, if you please, no reference to examples in books. Men have had every advantage of us in telling their own story. Education has been theirs in so much higher a degree; the pen has been in their hands. I will not allow books to prove anything." (237)

... with the possible exception of Jane Austen's own novels (and those by other women writers). The pen, of course, is not now in Wentworth's hands;[71] he has stopped writing and started listening, and to a female mentor. If this is a novel of education, it is the hero who has to learn.[72]

Anne acknowledges that Harville is right to stress a naval man's suffering in parting from his wife and children.[73] But Anne demurs, saying that while all this is true, men need an object, women only memory: "All the privilege I claim for my own sex (it is not a very amiable one, you need not covet it) is that of loving longest, when existence or when hope is gone" (238).

Captain Wentworth at this point is folding his letter and leaves, but returns immediately with a letter addressed to Anne, not Captain Benwick. Anne reads the most passionate proposal in a Jane Austen novel, and, typically, it must be presented in writing, not delivered orally:

> I can listen no longer in silence. I must speak to you by such means as are within my reach. You pierce my soul. I am half agony, half hope. Tell me not that I am too late, that such precious feelings are gone for ever. I offer myself to you again with a heart even more your own, than when you almost broke it eight years and a half ago. Dare not say that man forgets sooner than woman, that his love has an earlier death. I have loved none but you. Unjust I may have been, weak and resentful I have been, but never inconstant. You alone have brought me to Bath. For you alone I think and plan.—Have you not seen this? Can you fail to have understood my wishes?—I had not waited even these ten days, could I have read your feelings, as I think you must have penetrated mine. I can hardly write. I am every instant hearing something which overpowers me. You sink your voice, but I can distinguish the tones of that voice, when they would be lost on others.—Too good, too excellent creature! You do us justice indeed. You do believe that there is true attachment and constancy among men. Believe it to be most fervent, most undeviating in
>
> F.W. (240)

The language is erotic, sexual: "You pierce my soul ... you must have penetrated mine" (240). Again, Anne is as imprisoned as Elinor Dashwood behind her screens. She looks ill because of lack of privacy, and decides to go home.

---

71   Some feminist critics like to draw the analogy between "pen" and "penis," which seems appropriate here, regardless of the different etymologies.

72   As Toni Morrison said of her reason for using a male central consciousness in *Song of Solomon*, "It's the men who have to learn."

73   Austen refers implicitly back to this exchange at the end of the novel when she celebrates the navy for its domestic virtues.

Charles Musgrove insists on accompanying her, but when they meet Wentworth conveniently in Union Street, Charles, characteristically, is able to go off in search of a gun. Wentworth's and Anne's exchange of vows is summarized in free indirect discourse, without dialogue, so it is again the written word [Austen's] that best conveys passion. At Lyme his eyes were finally opened to Anne's superiority by Louisa's accident: "... he had learnt to distinguish between the steadiness of principle and the obstinacy of self-will, between the darings of heedlessness and the resolution of a collected mind" (240). He now learns that had he returned earlier, having made one capture, Anne would have married him immediately. Wentworth now resolves to be "happier than I deserve" (249). Even Lady Russell is reconciled: "She loved Anne better than she loved her own abilities ..." (251).

In the recent film version we see Anne apparently about to set sail on Wentworth's ship, he who had most observed the sailors' superstition about women being unlucky on board. We know Mrs. Croft accompanies her husband, but the Crofts are, and will remain, childless.[74] Presumably Anne, who is 27, and Wentworth, who is in his early 30s, will have children. But there could be another form of happy ending: a constant exchange of letters from sea to shore and the converse, and perhaps the beginnings of an epistolary novel.

*Anne as Observing "I" / "Eye"*

If we now take a backward look at Anne as observing "eye" / "I," and note her taste, curiosity, wit, and learning, she becomes a heroine very like Jane Austen herself, a truly liberated woman. In Austen's day, at the very beginning of the nineteenth century, there was a remarkable fermentation and social and class change, which also involved redefining the role of women.

*Anne's Family*

Throughout the novel Anne appears as both a social and a literary critic. The text begins with Austen's own attack upon an idle, gentrified patriarchy in the person of Anne's father, Sir Walter Elliot. The first sentence introduces not only Sir Walter, but also his relation to books, a major theme of the text: "Sir Walter Elliot, of Kellynch-hall, in Somersetshire, was a man who, for his own amusement, never took up any book but the Baronetage ..." (35). This description immediately sets up a contrast between him and Anne (or Jane Austen herself).[75] Sir Walter's is a Book of the Dead; it is not fiction, but a moribund reality. His most valued relatives, the

---

74 The film version makes much of Admiral Croft's fondness for the Musgroves' boys, with whom he enjoys playing. Johnson may be pushing her thesis beyond the evidence given when she suggests that the Crofts' childlessness is a conscious choice: "Admiral and Mrs. Croft are not gentry. Far from presiding over a neighborhood, they live most contentedly at sea, unconcerned with the production of heirs or the reproduction of ideologically correct values through the cultivation of local attachments" (289).

75 In the film, Amanda Root is made up to resemble the one picture we have of Jane Austen, by her sister Cassandra.

Dalrymples, represent only the empty status of inheritance, based on death: "... they were nothing."[76]

Sir Walter has chosen regal names for his daughters, like his ancestors since "the first year of Charles II, with all the Marys and Elizabeths they had married" (35). Elizabeth Elliot is a Virgin Queen indeed, at 29 presiding over form and nothing else.[77] Is Mary "Bloody Mary," the other Tudor queen? If so, Anne's name echoes Queen Anne, who presided over an age Jane Austen never ceased to cherish—that of Johnson, Richardson, Pope—even as she moved, like her heroine, towards romanticism.

Sir Walter dislikes the navy, doubtless because of the threat it poses to the old idle patriarchy. He complains that it is "the means of bringing persons of obscure birth into undue distinction"—in other words, an aristocracy of talent—and it destroys a man's looks: "a sailor grows old sooner than any other man" (49). The weatherbeaten, functional Admiral Croft makes the appropriate comment on Kellynch and its owner: "I should think he must be rather a dressy man for his time of life.—Such a number of looking-glasses!" (43).[78] Sir Walter leaves the Crofts contemptuously "to find their own level" at Bath (177), not realizing they would have no interest in the snobbish, inert Dalrymples.[79] When Sir Walter notes Anne's improvement, it is only in terms of her looks: "... he thought her 'less thin in her person, in her cheeks;

---

76  The film depicts them with chalk-like complexions like death-masks. Harding, in his Introduction to the Penguin edition of *Persuasion*, refers back to his 1940 essay on "Regulated Hatred" in Austen, and reminds us of her "much stronger dislike of the society in which she seemed comfortably embedded" (7). He says that in *Persuasion* "the story is embedded in a study of snobbery, snobbery displayed amidst the sharply realized detail, social and physical, of life in country houses and Bath at the end of the Napoleonic Wars" (18). Tanner remarks on "the absence of any real centre or principle of authority" in this world (210). Johnson notes that if "the landed classes have not lost their power, they have lost their prestige and their moral authority for the heroine" (287). Horowitz also says that "the novel's dislike for social position is explicit" (85). Austen's apparent openness to change and her continuing, growing interest in romanticism are implicitly linked.

77  She is the very reverse of "that actress with the lived-in face" (Jeanne Moreau) the critic A Alvarez once described. Elizabeth is rather a Gina Lollobrigida, who reportedly refused to smile broadly, laugh, or, presumably, cry, in order to avoid wrinkles.

78  Tanner associates mirrors with the one book Sir Walter reads, the Baronetage: Sir Walter is "someone fixed in the ultimate solipsism gazing with inexhaustible pleasure into the textual mirror which simply gives him back his name" (209). This is "parenthood as narcissism," Tanner adds. Mr. William Walter Elliot, of almost the same name, is an instance of character as mirror, who also turns out to be narcissistic ("it's all done with mirrors"). Given this father, Horowitz remarks, showing male vanity rather than female, Anne is probably saved by parental neglect.

79  Tanner reads *Persuasion* as a novel of transplantation (to Bath): "... and 'transplanting' is itself both a symptom and a part of a more far-reaching social fragmentation and mobility" (218). Lane notes that, for all the charms of Bath, Austen's characters are often attracted to it "for the wrong reasons" to the point that it sometimes appears "as an evil influence" (95). Not only in the two "Bath" novels, but in the others, transplantation to Bath often augurs ill. Lane mentions such characters as Willoughby, Wickham, Admiral Crawford and his nephew Henry, Mr. and Mrs. Elton, all of whom either sow wild oats in Bath, or go there to hunt a fortune

her skin, her complexion, greatly improved—clearer, fresher. Had she been using anything in particular!' 'No, nothing.' 'Merely Gowland,' he supposed" (158). For him, happiness and commitment have nothing to do with it.

### Of Female Friendships, and Female Betrayals

Lady Russell is a totally ineffectual adversary for Sir Walter, for she admires him in spite of everything, and has evidently entertained hopes of being the second Lady Elliot, not just Anne's surrogate mother. But, alas, from Sir Walter's point of view, she is blemished, and has a "crow's foot about [her] temples" which "had long been a distress to him" (38). Austen defines well her strengths and limitations: "She had a cultivated mind, and was, generally speaking, rational and consistent—but she had prejudices on the side of ancestry; she had a value for rank and consequence, which blinded her a little to the faults of those who possessed them" (42). She exhibits both "pride and prejudice."

Her objections to Wentworth as Anne's suitor were based not only on his lack of fortune, but on his possession of a sense of humor: "Lady Russell had little taste for wit" (56). Douglas Bush notes that her weakness is that she is too social. She is, moreover, inconsistent. While she still does not wish Anne to be married to Wentworth, she resents his apparent attraction to Louisa Musgrove. Her "taste in noises" is also contradictory. While she objects to the rowdy family and children at Uppercross, the sounds of Bath—"the clash of other carriages, the heavy rumble of carts and drays, the bawling of newsmen, muffin-men and milkmen, and the ceaseless clink of pattens"—soothe her (unlike Anne): "No, these were noises which belonged to the winter pleasures; her spirits rose under their influence ..." (149).

She is at her worst when she attempts to "persuade" Anne to marry Mr. Elliot in order to replace her mother eventually at Kellynch, when Mr. Elliot inherits. The imagery she uses suggests her genealogical snobbery: "If he really sought to reconcile himself like a dutiful branch, he must be forgiven for having dismembered himself from the paternal tree" (150). She is, in fact, avowedly (unlike Emma for all her faults), "no match-maker," but a match-breaker (171), as well as a supporter of patriarchy. Anne's judgment is far better. Lady Russell sees her "as the future mistress of Kellynch, the future Lady Elliot" (171), but Austen takes only a paragraph to record Anne's decision: "For a few moments her imagination and her heart were bewitched ... The charm of Kellynch and of 'Lady Elliot' all faded away. She never could accept him. And it was not only that her feelings were still adverse to any man save one; her judgment, on a serious consideration of the possibilities of such a case, was against Mr. Elliot" (172).

Lady Russell is one of three widows ("single women") in the text whose fates could foreshadow an unmarried Anne's in a few years: the other two are the Machiavellian Mrs. Clay and the victimized but gossipy Mrs. Smith.

Mrs. Clay's first name is "Penelope," derived from Ulysses' faithful wife, and probably a satirical touch of Austen's, a parodic gloss on Anne's affirmation of the

---

(95–6). On June 30, 1808, Austen herself wrote, "It is two years tomorrow since we left Bath for Clifton—with what happy feelings of escape!" (97).

"woman's constancy" theme. Like Lady Russell, she has physical defects; Jane Austen, through Lady Russell, makes an otherwise mean-spirited comment about *her* complexion: "That tooth of her's! and those freckles!" (63).[80] But the point is that her flattery of Sir Walter easily erases those defects, in his eyes, for she becomes to him only another mirror for his narcissism. Mrs. Clay supplants Anne, first, with her father and sister Elizabeth, then at Bath. Anne thinks rather harshly at one point of "all the plague of Mrs. Clay" which "her satisfaction in Mr. Elliot outweighed" (159)—ironically, since Mrs. Clay has already set her sights on Mr. Elliot. She lies outright about meeting Mr. Elliot accidentally, instead of by appointment, in Bath-street when he was supposedly "Sunday-visiting" (232).[81] In her, as in himself, Sir Walter sees only the surface of manners, of propriety. Mrs. Clay and Mr. Elliot deserve each other, but it would be a marriage made in hell. *His* motive is to prevent her marrying Sir Walter, and possibly producing a male heir who would threaten his own claim to the estate; *her* motive is to become Lady Elliot by whatever means necessary (a fate Lady Russell would have reserved for Anne).[82] Elizabeth, moreover, whom he has jilted in the past, would be more than willing a second time around.

Mr. Elliot's old letter describing his rupture with Sir Walter and Elizabeth, revealed by Mrs. Smith, is entered as negative evidence, as Wentworth's letter of reconciliation is positive and heartfelt.[83]

Soon enough, however, he proves to be a branch of the same tree as Sir Walter, and recovers his snobbery. His exchange with Anne on "good company" defines the major issues. Anne serves as Austen's spokesperson, as much as, or more than, Henry Tilney in *Northanger Abbey*: "My idea of good company, Mr. Elliot, is the company of clever, well-informed people, who have a great deal of conversation; that is what

---

80   To be fair, Anne (and implicitly Austen) seem to agree. As Anne thinks, "Mrs. Clay had freckles, and a projecting tooth, and a clumsy wrist ..." (62).

81   Mary's description is exact—they are "'standing under the colonnade' which partially encloses the Abbey Churchyard from the street" (Lane, 62).

82   Tanner is perhaps carrying the idea of the hellishness of a match between Mr. Elliot and Mrs. Clay a bit far when he suggests, on the basis of a letter to the *Times Literary Supplement*, that Mrs. Clay may be suffering from syphilis: according to Nora Crook in an October 7, 1983 letter, the "Gowland's Lotion," which Sir Walter mentions to Anne on the basis of its benefits to Mrs. Clay's skin, "contained 'corrosive sublimate of mercy,' which 'had a particular connection with the old fashioned treatment of syphilis.'" Tanner concludes from this evidence that "a hint of syphilis must be intended ... it also suggests the presence of the most ruinous sexual disease among the upper classes" (237). The problem with this is, did Jane Austen know about this particular property of Gowland's? And how upper-class is Mrs. Clay anyway?

83   Mr. Elliot has written:

Give me joy: I have got rid of Sir Walter and Miss ... The baronet, nevertheless, is not unlikely to marry again; he is quite fool enough. If he does, however, they will leave me in peace, which may be a decent equivalent for the reversion. He is worse than last year.

I wish I had any name but Elliot. I am sick of it. The name of Walter I can drop, thank God! ... (210)

I call good company" (162). Mr. Elliot, on the other hand, reveals himself *not* to be a Jane Austen hero:[84]

> "You are mistaken," said he gently, "that is not good company, that is the best. Good company requires only birth, education and manners, and with regard to education is not very nice. Birth and good manners are essential; but a little learning is by no means a dangerous thing in good company, on the contrary, it will do very well. My cousin, Anne, shakes her head. She is not satisfied. She is fastidious." (162)

He further reveals his changed outlook when he asserts that "rank is rank" (163). He is one of Jane Austen's "rakes"—like Willoughby and Wickham—who has no vocation.[85] Ultimately, Anne sees him as worse than Mrs. Clay.

Mrs. Smith is represented as much more ambiguous than the other two widows.[86] Ostensibly, she is Anne's friend and confidante, but she has her own agenda. She too is a talespinner. Anne leaves it to her father "to recollect, that Mrs. Smith was not the only widow in Bath between thirty and forty, with little to live on, and no surname of dignity" (170). She is crippled,[87] but she possesses "the choicest gift of heaven," "that elasticity of mind, that disposition to be comforted, that power of turning readily from evil to good, and of finding employment which carried her out of herself ..." (167). In other words, Anne sees much of herself—perhaps too much—in her old schoolfriend.[88] Mrs. Smith says of Nurse Rooke, as she might say of herself or Anne—or we might say of Jane Austen—"Hers is a line for seeing human nature" (168). But *Mrs. Smith's* "line" is somewhat tainted by ulterior motives: she uses a curious metaphor, for which Anne rebukes her, to describe the gathering of gossip: "The stream is as good as at first; the little rubbish it collects in the turnings, is easily moved away" (211). Bush thinks that Austen would have removed Mrs. Smith if she had had time to revise the novel, but she does function importantly as a foil to Anne and the other women, as well as a confidante. Her husband is another of the "Charlies" in the novel: Musgrove, Musgrove Jr., Hayter, and Smith—again perhaps

---

84    At least one critic, however, Roger Gard, seems to disagree: "The point about Mr. Elliot is that he poses a powerful, as it were reactionary, alternative to the naval alternative, a re-embodiment of what we have previously learnt from Jane Austen to admire in a man" (198). Whatever this is, I do not see a trace of it (though Henry Crawford in *Mansfield Park* does have significant attractions, including his interest in Shakespeare and his ability to act on stage, though his acting in real life is harmful).

85    As Butler says, "... there is very little that is significant for William Walter Elliot to represent" (228). Wright, similarly, sees him as "a red herring" (151). He may have been more fully developed had Austen lived long enough to polish the text, and may have turned into a variation on the sophisticated, clever Henry Crawford, but this is speculative.

86    As Tanner remarks, "Smith" is "the archetypal anonymous English name, a name which is in effect no 'name' at all" (218).

87    Disease and physical fragility represent a thematic infrastructure in the novel: Mary's hypochondria, little Charlie Musgrove's fall, Anne's fragility, Louisa's self-inflicted concussion.

88    Honan says that Anne sees in her "a dark mirror-image of herself' (382)—perhaps of what she could have become if she had married Frederick at 19, and he had been subsequently lost at sea?

a sign of Austen's lack of time to edit, though not to complete.[89] Anne judges Mrs. Smith (and her late husband) after her about-face, when she first encourages Anne to marry Mr. Elliot, then reveals his less-than-pristine character: "... there had been a great deal of general and joint extravagance" (214). Nonetheless, with all her faults, she helps Anne to determine her "line of conduct" (214).

### *"She Learned Romance ...": Anne's Powers of Persuasion*

Anne's consciousness is fully developed at the time the novel begins: "She had been forced into prudence in her youth, she learned romance as she grew older" (58). Like Eliza Bennet, she has learned the importance of intuition and feeling to balance reason. Her confidantes and false confidantes—Lady Russell, Mrs. Clay, Mrs. Smith—have consciousnesses inferior to her own, and merely provide information, clues, differing points of view to sharpen her own. Anne goes from being "nobody," "only Anne" (37), to being "everything" in the novel as she follows Jane Austen's own path from "private" to "public"—whether the latter will include novel-writing, as well as letter-writing, we can only speculate. From being a spirit contained (like James's Maggie Verver), she becomes the persuader, rather than the persuadee. Anne is at first a mystery for the reader to unravel.[90] She is the only sister to resemble her mother: "... her father had found little to admire in her, (so totally different were her delicate features and mild dark eyes from his own)" (37). More importantly, her mother, like Anne, was the family reader, intellectual, and arbiter of order: "While Lady Elliot lived, there has been method, moderation, and economy, which had just kept him [Sir Walter] within his income" (40).

Anne prefers Mary to Elizabeth only because the hypochondriacal Mary needs her: "To be claimed as a good, though in an improper style, is at least better than being rejected as no good at all" (61). When Mary petulantly complains of her husband's going to the Musgroves' party while she remains home with an injured child (little Charlie), she exclaims (rightly), "... I am sure, I am more unfit than any body else to be about the child" (82). Indeed, it is Anne, the born mother, who is induced to remain with her nephew. Mary's husband, Charles Musgrove, has first proposed to Anne, and it is implied that he *could* have been improved with a sensible wife: "As it was, he did nothing with much zeal, but sport; and his time was otherwise trifled away, without benefit from books, or any thing else" (70). Wentworth begins to realize Anne's constancy towards himself when he learns she has rejected Charles Musgrove. Mary's letter, after Louisa's near-fatal fall at Lyme, characteristically

---

89 The film changes Charles Hayter's first name to Philip to avoid confusion. Some critics, however, see the repetitions as deliberate. Johnson writes, "... the redundancy of Hayter's Christian name, doubling with that of Charles Musgrove, calls attention to what is undistinctive about eldest sons in general" (299). It would surely be overdoing it, though, to add Charles Musgrove, Jr., and Charles Smith to the list. Weissman sees "doubleness and refrain" in Persuasion as that of reinvented fairy tales, including the female names in the Baronetage, the Charleses, and the two falls, of little Charlie and, later, of his Aunt Louisa on the Cobb (309).

90 Reginald Farrer wrote, "... Anne Elliot is a puzzling figure in our literature" (Southam 271).

provides the most important nugget of information as an after-thought, after a series of complaints: "... we were rather surprised not to find Captain Benwick of the party, for he had been invited as well as the Harvilles; and what do you think was the reason? Neither more nor less than his being in love with Louisa ..." (176).

Anne's soft spot for the navy is revealed early in the novel, when she rebukes her father: "Sailors work hard enough for their comforts, we must all allow" (49). Her cheeks "flush" when she learns that Mrs. Croft's brother is a Wentworth, though the latter is speaking of the elder brother, the clergyman, not Frederick the sailor who "had come into Somersetshire in the summer of 1806 ..." (55). Anne is never in real doubt of Wentworth's constancy—but of his judgment. Anne's initial rejection / postponement of his suit was a result not only of the "persuasions" of others, but of her own solitude, Mrs. Croft being at "a foreign station" with her husband, and Mary at school (59). Some have seen Anne as too passive, but reading between the lines, we see her as the most active member of her family, who feels her power grow. At first she avoids Kellynch, but becomes increasingly involved with the Crofts. She alerts Elizabeth to Mrs. Clay (common clay?), and hopes that the seed will sprout (63). It is Anne who catalogues her "father's books and pictures" (65), and who bids farewell to her father's tenants. She is everyone's confidante, when she should be chief actor: at Uppercross, "One of the least agreeable circumstances of her residence there, was her being treated with too much confidence by all parties, and being too much in the secret of the complaints of each house" (71).

Anne is an accomplished musician, but has no voice and does not dance—unlike Emma, who plays to an audience (73). She is an "enabler" who plays country dances for the Musgroves, without participating. She has not, however, outlived the age of feeling, though she hopes she has "outlived the age of blushing" (75).[91] At the beginning, Anne is in "a sort of desolate tranquillity" (63)—at peace with herself, but sad. She dreads her first reunion with Wentworth at Uppercross, and can only think afterwards, "It is over! it is over! ... The worst is over!" (85). Mary rubs salt in the wound, reporting his remark, "You were so altered he should not have known you again" (85). Did he say this out of pity? Does she misunderstand his motives? There is a curious passage immediately following in which we start with Anne's reconstruction of Wentworth's consciousness, and end up with his consciousness itself, as given in direct address to his sister:

"So altered that he should not have known her again!" These were words which could not but dwell with her. Yet she soon began to rejoice that she had heard them. They were of sobering tendency ...

... He had thought her wretchedly altered, and, in the first moment of appeal, had spoken as he felt. He had not forgiven Anne Elliot. She had used him ill; deserted and disappointed him ... She had given him up to oblige others. It had been the effect of *over-persuasion*. It had been weakness and timidity.

---

91    Jane Austen also blushed easily, though biographers now think that redness of complexion may have been a symptom of her disease.

He had been most warmly attached to her, and had never seen a woman since whom he thought her equal, but, except from some natural sensation of curiosity, he had no desire of meeting her again. Her power with him was gone for ever.

It was now his object to marry. He was rich, ... ready to fall in love with all the speed which a clear head and quick taste could allow. He had a heart for either of the Miss Musgroves, if they could catch it; a heart, in short, for any pleasing young woman who came in his way, excepting Anne Elliot. This was his only secret exception, when he said to his sister, in answer to her suppositions,

"Yes, here I am, Sophia, quite ready to make a foolish match ..." (86)

Does the transition occur with "He had been most warmly attached to her"? Or with "It was now his object to marry"? The shift is virtually seamless. Do the two merging consciousnesses suggest how alike these lovers are, even in their disappointment?[92] She sets Wentworth's standard when he describes his ideal woman: "A strong mind, with sweetness of manner" (87).

At their second reunion she wants to pass unobserved, fingering mechananically the piano (95–6). His "ceremonious grace" is the worst evil (96), and she makes the excuse of a headache to avoid seeing him at a Musgrove dinner (100). The first time they are alone together (Mary and the Musgrove sisters are upstairs), Captain Wentworth looks out the window (102). When her nephew Walter gets on her back, however, Wentworth releases him: "... some one was taking him from her, though he had bent down her head so much, that his little sturdy hands were unfastened from around her neck, and he was resolutely borne away, before she knew that Captain Wentworth had done it" (103).[93]

Despite her powers of observation, Anne forgoes the "opportunity of watching the loves and jealousies of the four" (103). Like a French classical heroine (or Madame de Lafayette's Princesse de Clèves), her own passions do not blind her. She knows that Captain Wentworth is not in love with either Louisa or Henrietta, and that they are only infatuated with him: "It was a little fever of admiration" (105). She knows that he was wrong only in accepting both of the Musgroves' attentions.

Wentworth's second "rescue" of Anne in Book I occurs when she is fatigued on a Musgrove walking-party; Captain Wentworth helps her into his sister's carriage: "... she owed it to his perception of her fatigue, and his resolution to give her rest" (113).

Anne begins her recovery at Uppercross. The Musgroves belong to the comic part of the novel, which Anne keenly appreciates. They are "large" people (66), and their house is pleasantly untidy: "The portraits themselves seemed to be staring in astonishment" (67). The Musgroves' lack of interest in the Elliots is a great comfort, teaching a lesson, "the art of knowing our own nothingness beyond our own circle" (69).

Anne's wit, like her creator's, is sometimes exercised at the Musgroves' expense. But unlike Emma at Box Hill, she does not utter her witticisms aloud. We are not sure at times whether we are hearing Austen's voice or Anne's. Mrs. Musgrove is

---

92   The film uses the two voices merging to read Wentworth's letter of proposal to Anne.

93   Hardy comments that Anne's relatives are on her back, and David Lodge finds the scene orgasmic.

mourning an apparently worthless son Dick, who had died at sea, having been sent there "because he was stupid and unmanageable on shore ..." (76). Although this sounds like Austen's authorial "I," it later appears that Anne shares Austen's views of Mrs. Musgrove's "large fat sighings over the destiny of a son, whom alive nobody had cared for" (92).[94]

On a whole, however, Anne approves of the senior Musgroves, whose spontaneity contrasts sharply with her own father's pretensions (223). While she does not overvalue the gifts of Henrietta and Louisa, with "the usual stock of accomplishments," she *does* envy their sisterly feeling, "that good-humoured mutual affection, of which she had known so little herself with either of her sisters" (68).[95] Even the family "togetherness" can be a blessing to Anne: as Elinor Dashwood "screens" herself, Anne paradoxically seeks "the solitude and silence which only numbers could give" (111). As in the case of Emma's Highbury, however, the environment also constitutes a prison where they must all meet, whatever happens, including Anne and Captain Wentworth: they "... would have to frequent the same church, and there must be intercourse between the two families" (115).

At Lyme, Anne moves from "passive activity"—"she had to struggle against a great tendency to lowness" (119)—to "public activity" by helping first Captain Benwick, then Henrietta, thus both sexes (121–4).

Volume II represents "a second spring of youth and beauty" for Anne when she is delegated to take charge at Uppercross, while some of the party remain at Lyme with the injured Louisa. She is happiest at Uppercross, knowing she is useful. She immediately forgets Bath: "She had lately lost sight even of her father and sister and Bath. Their concerns had been sunk under those of Uppercross ..." (139). Her pain is alleviated there: "Scenes had passed in Uppercross, which made it precious." (139). Mrs. Croft treats her as "a favorite"—"a couple of steady, sensible women," who are "rational creatures" rather than "fine ladies" (Mrs. Croft's distinction, 94)—and reveals that Captain Wentworth is still concerned for her (141). Unlike Lady Russell, Anne prefers either extreme of noise—"the bustle of Uppercross and the seclusion of Kellynch"—to Bath (149).

In Bath, Anne begins to judge her father's values, and is astounded that he "should find so much to be vain of in the littlenesses of a town" (152). She also begins to judge his language and Elizabeth's, as they convey "under embellishment" the supposed reconciliation with Mr. Elliot.[96] She increasingly mistrusts Mr. Elliot and his "very rapid recovery" from mourning his dead wife (a "commoner" whom he had married for her fortune) (160). In resisting Lady Russell's "persuasions" that

---

94  Austen could be describing her own satirical bent: "Personal size and mental sorrow have certainly no necessary proportions ... But, fair or not fair, there are unbecoming conjunctions, which reason will patronize in vain,—which taste cannot tolerate,— which ridicule will seize" (92).

95  We are far from Lydia Bennet's marital competition with her oldest sister Jane, or the Bertram sisters "wasting gold paper" and fighting for the same man.

96  As Tanner says, "Anne comes to embody what we might call the conscience of language. She, and she alone, always speaks truly, and truly speaks" (220). He also writes elsewhere that all Jane Austen's heroines are "guardians of the language—as their own author so supremely was" (Monaghan, 193).

she marry him, she becomes uneasy about his morals, in the past, if not the present. Anne sees him as "rational, discreet, polished,—but he was not open" (173). Like Mr. Knightley, "She prized the frank, the open-hearted, the eager character beyond all others. Warmth and enthusiasm did captivate her still" (173). She is, in fact, describing Wentworth, whom she still loves, as he continues to see her as his ideal.

Anne's satirical bent is close to Austen's as she considers the unlikely match of Benwick and Louisa: "... of course they had fallen in love over poetry. The idea of Louisa Musgrove turned into a person of literary taste, and sentimental reflection, was amusing, but she had no doubt of its being so" (178). The main concern for her, of course, is the thought of "Captain Wentworth unshackled and free" (178). Anne, for once in her life, thinks in exclamations: "They were too much like joy, senseless joy!" (178).

The pace steps up as Anne's "public" appearances and activities accelerate. Even Mudrick acknowledges that she grows "out of the author's tight, ironic feminine world." Using Benwick as an example, Anne tries to make a point about the compatibility "of spirit and gentleness" (182). Mrs. Croft compares Benwick (a man of action and a reader) with Frederick: "There is something about Frederick more to our taste" (182). But Anne must conceal her full agreement. The Admiral proposes getting Frederick to Bath, and he arrives the next day as the plot speeds up: "Before Mrs. Croft had written, he was arrived; and the very next time Anne walked out, she saw him" (184). It is raining in Bath, which may suggest fertility and new hope, in keeping with Austen's own stated preference for seeing Bath under a rainy sky. He is agitated at meeting Anne, and even moreso when his offer of an umbrella is refused in favor of Mr. Elliot who, to Anne's annoyance, keeps turning up at the wrong time. Anne knows she is not yet "wise and reasonable," and would like to shuffle her cousin off (188).

At the concert a couple of days later Anne finds courage to greet Frederick when she is in the right, while "Elizabeth had turned from him, Lady Russell overlooked him ..." (189). As a woman of principle, she "felt equal to everything which she believed right to be done" (191). Frederick takes care to disabuse her about his feelings for Louisa: "I regard Louisa Musgrove as a very amiable, sweet-tempered girl, and not deficient in understanding; but Benwick is something more. He is a clever man, a reading man" (192). He is astonished at Benwick's apparent ease in forgetting his dead fiancée, Fanny Harville: "A man like him, in his situation! With a heart pierced, wounded, almost broken! Fanny Harville was a very superior creature. ... A man does not recover from such a devotion of the heart to such a woman!—He ought not—he does not" (192). Anne now affirms that "I should very much like to see Lyme again" (193). Anne's emotions are "delightful ... He must love her" (195).

Anne is human (and still girlish) enough to appreciate Frederick's jealousy: "Jealousy of Mr. Elliot! It was the only intelligible motive ... For a moment the gratification was exquisite. But alas! there were very different thoughts to succeed. How was such jealousy to be quieted? ... It was misery to think of Mr. Elliot's attentions" (199). Any pity she has for Mr. Elliot is all at an end, and he begins to seem like an enemy. Her first object at the concert is to avoid him.[97]

Anne becomes a surrogate member (elder sister?) of the Musgrove family: "It [the family atmosphere] was a heartiness, and a warmth, and a sincerity which Anne delighted in the more, from the sad want of such blessings at home" (225). Most importantly, she regains confidence in her own and Wentworth's maturity, and ability to overcome jealousy: "We are not boy and girl, to be captiously irritable, misled by every moment's inadvertence, and wantonly playing with our own happiness" (226).[98] Anne's amazement at Mary's discovery of Mr. Elliot in conversation with Mr. Clay can be read two ways: "'No,' cried Anne quickly, 'it cannot be Mr. Elliot, I assure you. He was to leave Bath at nine this morning, and does not come back till to-morrow'" (226–7). Anne is surprised that he has misled her, and that there is a conjunction of interests between him and Mrs. Clay, whereas Wentworth thinks her reaction argues a degree of intimacy between them. Because Anne is the one who initially refused their engagement, it is she who must move from private suffering to public boldness, and even aggressivity. She exclaims spontaneously, "I am not yet so much changed," but stops, "fearing she hardly knew what misconstruction" (229). She emphasizes her constancy, despite changing appearances, and becomes an active heroine, but one who pays a price of exhaustion (231).

In this seemingly "autumnal" novel, Austen's style becomes livelier, more metaphorical, more vivid, even as the *literal* action of the plot diminishes. Anne is "electrified" by Mrs. Croft's reference to her acquaintance with her brother (75). She "sports with musings of high-wrought love and eternal constancy" as she passes through the streets of Bath (200). Like Catherine Morland, she virtually dances in her carriage. She imagines the little Durands at the concert "with their mouth open to catch the music; like unfledged sparrows ready to be fed" (201). In four words, Austen defines the Dalrymples by the Dowager Viscountess's "three lines of scrawl" (162), and their socializing as "a period of nothing-saying amongst the party" (197).

Anne is finally able to confront and resolve the themes of patriarchy, risk, and artistry. What remains unresolved is her future function as wife of a highly-placed naval officer. We are very aware of her physical frailty: she is no robust Eliza Bennet or Emma Woodhouse. Will she be strong enough for childbirth? Will she be strong enough to join Wentworth on board ship (as the film sanguinely depicts her)?[99]

---

97   Babb says that he "exhibits" her. Bush thinks that Anne sounds somewhat severe on Mr. Elliot's "Sunday travels," more like Fanny Price. But her severity is perhaps a result of her general uneasiness about him, which is borne out when he lies about his Sunday and is discovered meeting Mrs. Clay by assignation.

98   Elizabeth Gaskell's Margaret Hale and John Thornton arrive at a similar conclusion in *North and South* (1853) when they reject traditional definitions of "lady" and "gentleman" for "woman" and "man."

99   Although autobiographical readings are always suspect, Austen herself was inordinately fond of the sea. Two of her brothers were naval officers, and Francis (Frank) nearly became Admiral of the Fleet, but declined the post because he was 89 at the time. Some speculate that Captain Harville may be modelled on Frank Austen. Austen's family lived near the Cobb in Lyme (Edwards, 112–13), and the precarious steps down which Louisa tumbles

What is certain is that if Emma Woodhouse is, as I have called her, the "Self-Portrait of a Lady" as would-be artist—representing herself in her portrait of Harriet, as Austen represents a younger, more bumptious and thoughtless self in Emma—then Anne Elliot is a "Self-Portrait of a Lady as Artist"—a mature woman who is sharply critical, witty, an astute observer who remains in the background, who is a well-informed judge of literature and wise counsellor. In the course of the novel, she has moved from silenced storyteller to passionate advocate of not only women's constancy, but women's writing. We do not see Anne literally becoming an artist, any more than we see Emma, but Austen has created a heroine endowed with all of her own gifts, and none of Emma's defects, a heroine whose ultimate fate is left open, but which could well include writing during Frederick's lengthy absences (she would never be on board ship during battles, and Napoleon is regrouping his forces). If Anne marries into risk, Austen similarly sets sail to risk with her writing career.[100] Austen has, in fact, redefined bravery in female terms and created a courageous, imaginative Scheherazade for the nineteenth century who prepares the way for, among others, Charlotte Brontë's Jane Eyre.

---

were known as "Granny's Teeth" (114–15). Edwards reports that Austen liked sea-bathings so much that she stayed in too long at Lyme and announced herself "unreasonably tired" (112). She notes too that "The little seaside town [Lyme] delighted her," and Austen wrote that "The prospect of spending future summers by the sea ... is very delightful" (111). Like Anne, she loved to spend her day in "unwearied contemplation" of the sea. Historically, Lyme witnessed the battle of Sir Francis Drake against the Spanish Armada (1588), and, still memorialized in Lyme, the Duke of Monmouth's landing in 1685. Although I think his reading over-radicalizes Austen, Tanner claims that she, like Conrad (and I might add Mark Twain), rejects landed society.

100 Edward Saïd uses a ship metaphor to describe Austen's novel: Austen presents "a series of historical changes that her novel rides like a vessel sitting on a mighty sea" (162). Lynda Boren sees Jane Austen's own "creative defiance" in her exchange with Captain Harville: they are "the words of a woman artist struggling to make herself felt both as artist and as woman" (11), and Harris speaks of the transformation of the Romantic to the domestic sphere.

Chapter 3

# Not Carved in Stone: Women's Hearts and Women's Texts in Charlotte Brontë's *Jane Eyre*

## Introduction: A New Kind of Heroine

Charlotte Brontë's Jane Eyre, like Jane Austen's Emma Woodhouse and, in a different sense, Anne Elliot, is a single woman who, for one reason or other, thinks herself exempt from the marriage market. Austen's Emma thinks herself exempt because she is economically independent, and considers (mistakenly) that she does not need marriage to fulfill herself. Jane Eyre, on the other hand, considers herself exempt because she has no financial resources except her own labor as a governess—we may remember that Austen's Jane Fairfax, in a similar situation, refers to the governess-trade as the "slave-trade," implying white slavery or prostitution. Because Jane Eyre has no family, no economic independence, no striking good looks, she sees herself (again mistakenly) as having no attractions in the marriage market. Both heroines attract considerably older, powerful men who reject the idea of the marital marketplace.[1]

Emma paints a portrait of Harriet, her little protégée, because she sees blonde, blue-eyed, somewhat dim Harriet as the conventional heroine of the romances she is reading. Her deepest self—her "serious spirit," as Mr. Knightley calls it—which seems buried in her unconscious, knows that the real model for Harriet's portrait, and the real heroine of Emma's creation, is Emma herself. It is Mr. Knightley's difficult but joyous task to bring this "deepest self" to the surface. By the end, he finds her "faultless in spite of all her faults"—I would add, faultless *because* of all her faults (348)—she challenges him, and one is tempted to speculate beyond the ending that he will continue to have a hard time with her, and that this will be a most stimulating marriage. At the end, she is already matchmaking for little Ann Weston, still a tiny baby in her cradle.

Emma echoes Mary Wollstonecraft in a dialogue with Mr. Knightley about Harriet's attractions. She says, "… till it appears that men are much more philosophic on the subject of beauty than they are generally supposed; till they do fall in love with well-informed minds instead of handsome faces, a girl, with such loveliness as Harriet, has a certainty of being admired and sought after …" (47). This is a very

---

1    For a fuller discussion of Austen's *Emma*, see my book *The Prison of Womanhood: Four Provincial Heroines in Nineteenth-Century Fiction* ( London: Macmillan and New York: St. Martin's, 1987).

close paraphrase of Wollstonecraft: "When do men *fall-in-love* with sense? When do they, with their superiour powers and advantages, turn from the person to the mind? … Men look for beauty and the simper of good-humoured docility …" (*Vind.* 118). Jane Austen had certainly read Wollstonecraft carefully.[2] Mr. Knightley's answer is the most important statement in the novel about female–male relations: "Men of sense, whatever you may chuse to say, do not want silly wives" (48). Austen would doubtless like to agree with him, and perhaps does in this novel, but still there are the Palmers in *Sense and Sensibility*, the Bennets in *Pride and Prejudice*, and even here John and Isabella Knightley—perhaps the source of Emma's fears that even Mr. Knightley could be interested in Harriet. In fact, Harriet is almost a Frankenstein monster Emma has created.

Jane Eyre, by the same token, sketches Blanche Ingram and then herself as a reminder of how little she has to offer Mr. Rochester, putting Blanche in the conventional romantic role in the marriage that Harriet could occupy in *Emma*. Her art becomes a means of controlling her feelings. At the same time Charlotte Brontë is reminding us that the real heroine of her creation is Jane herself. Thus both Austen and Brontë present us with heroines who break the mould, who do not conform to the "Pamela"-standard of beauty and passive goodness—Emma because she is a tall, healthy brunette, autonomous and active; Anne Elliot because she has reached the crucial Austen age of 27, with a delicate prettiness that hardship and loneliness have caused to fade; and Jane because she is "plain" (or thinks she is), prickly, defensive, without any of the obvious attractions. Both authors present us with *Bildungsromans*, which also move towards *Kunstlerromans*—Portraits of the Artist as a Young Woman—or at least a would-be artist. In the slightly different pattern of *Persuasion*, the movement is rather towards life for Anne than towards art. But Austen uses Anne's situation as a means of saying something important about her own art, through Anne's lips as she denounces male literary treatments of the themes of love and woman's constancy and their corollary, the silencing of women. By the end, Anne has moved from private sphere to public and becomes an eloquent defender (to an all-male audience) of the female point of view in literature. The shadow Portrait of the Artist as a Woman, in fact, in both *Emma* and *Persuasion*, is that of Jane Austen herself, and it is a self-portrait.

## Charlotte Brontë's Limitations

In *A Room of One's Own* Virginia Woolf ranks Charlotte Brontë somewhat below Jane Austen as a novelist, although she claims that she had "more genius in her than Jane Austen" (66). The problem Woolf has with Charlotte Brontë is that she feels her gift was marred by anger, citing as proof the passage from *Jane Eyre* when Jane ascends to the leads of Thornfield Hall and contemplates what sounds remarkably like a feminist rebellion, at least on the spiritual level:

---

2   Jane Austen, unlike Wollstonecraft, was not revolutionary, but evolutionary. Emma's feminism is too extreme, from Austen's point of view, but nonetheless Emma does express a certain uneasiness on Austen's part about the nature of female–male relations.

It is in vain to say human beings ought to be satisfied with tranquillity: they must have action; and they will make it if they cannot find it. … Nobody knows how many rebellions besides political rebellions ferment in the masses of life which people earth. Women are supposed to be very calm generally: but women feel just as men feel; they need exercise for their faculties and a field for their efforts as much as their brothers do; they suffer from too rigid a restraint, too absolute a stagnation, precisely as men would suffer; and it is narrow-minded in their more privileged fellow-creatures to say that they ought to confine themselves to making puddings and knitting stockings, to playing on the piano and embroidering bags. It is thoughtless to condemn them, or laugh at them, if they seek to do more or learn more than custom has pronounced necessary for their sex. (96)

Clearly, Woolf sees Jane Eyre as a self-portrait of the artist, but regards the portrait—and the artist—as flawed.

Woolf's criticism was anticipated many years earlier by George Henry Lewes, Charlotte's contemporary (and George Eliot's common-law husband). While he admired *Jane Eyre* for its landscape of the female soul, he faults the novel for being at times *too* inward-looking, which results in "much melodrama and improbability, which smack of the circulating-library …" (Norton Critical Edition 448).

Lord David Cecil, in the late 1930s, was also to pick up on both Lewes's and Woolf's misgivings about Charlotte Brontë and write some really phallic criticism (Mary Ellmann's term) about her: he sees Charlotte Brontë's work as "untutored, unequal," but "inspired" (101), and names her as "our first subjective novelist" (102). Like Lewes, he calls *Jane Eyre* "a roaring melodrama" (107), and points out how nonsensical the plot is. As Cecil puts it, Charlotte Brontë "stretches the long arm of coincidence till it becomes positively dislocated" (108). He also attributes what he sees as her failings in male portraiture to her womanhood: "Serious male characters are always a problem for a woman novelist" (114), while he never once presents the converse problem: that of a male novelist trying to create believable female characters.[3]

*Jane Eyre as Confessional: Title and Name*

*Jane Eyre* is presented, to be sure, in the form of a confessional. It is a *Bildungsroman*, a novel of an education, of an initiation, and thereby also a quest novel, told by a first-person narrator, from a by-definition subjective female point of view. The convention, therefore, is that this manuscript was written by Jane Eyre herself, its subject but also (in this respect like Anne Elliot) the perceiving eye of the novel. That is not to say that Jane Eyre is necessarily Charlotte Brontë. It is a retrospective, which, if we accept the convention, must color and shape Jane's memories of her younger self: ten years have passed since Jane's marriage to Edward Fairfax Rochester. As she concludes, "I have now been married ten years. I know what it is to live entirely for and with what I love best on earth. I hold myself supremely blest—*blest beyond what language*

---

3    There has indeed been speculation that Dickens was endeavoring to go Charlotte Brontë's Jane Eyre one better (not too successfully) in his later use of a female narrative voice, Esther Summerson in *Bleak House* (1853).

*can express*;[4] because I am my husband's life as fully as he is mine" (396; emphasis mine). Some critics have emphasized Jane's gifts as a pictorial, visual artist and have suggested that it is not until Lucy Snowe in *Villette* (1853) that we have a Charlotte Brontë heroine who is a verbal artist. Such a view, however, is only tenable if we forget the written retrospective convention of *Jane Eyre*, whose heroine follows the same path as Charlotte Brontë herself, who ruined her eyesight while young making sketches, and turned increasingly from drawing to writing.

Postmodernist criticism often focuses on writing the body, and the body as text; Jane Eyre, in a sense, both *is* her text and *writes* it.[5] We might, in fact, compare the title of *Jane Eyre* to that of *Pamela*, whose heroine's isolation and vulnerability seem signalled by the absence of her last name—her fate is to be completed by marriage. Or again, we can compare *Emma*, whose heroine's last name is unnecessary, so dominant is her personality.[6] As W.A. Craik has said, Jane Eyre is the novel and the novel is Jane Eyre (107).

Why, then, *Jane Eyre*, not simply *Jane* or *Jane Rochester*? The answer is to be found in the theme of Jane's quest for independence. Although she leaves Rochester on their planned wedding day because Richard Mason reveals Rochester's deception—that he is already married—on another level she needs to leave in any case, to establish her own independence. She returns not as the vulnerable orphan, cast off by her only known relations, the Reeds, but as Jane *Eyre*, furnished with financial independence and a loving family, the good cousins, the *R*ivers, contrasted to the bad cousins, the *R*eeds.[7] Critics like Lewes and Cecil, in fact, fail to recognize what more recent critics have: that the more "melodramatic" elements, in which Brontë *seems* to twist the long arm of coincidence, *are* what the novel is about, for they confer a mythic dimension to the heroine's quest.

Jane's last name, "Eyre," points to this mythopoeic dimension. In terms of what we call onomastics, it embodies a number of linguistic puns, homonyms—clues, in a word, as to how we are to regard its owner. The most obvious association is "Eyre"—"heir," for Jane is finally to come into her patrimony through the faraway death of her uncle, Mr. Eyre, who has been seeking her. "Eyre" also "sounds like" the French "errer"—to wander—and Jane sees herself as "a wanderer on the face of the earth" (197)—from one to another of the several settings where she seeks a home. To "err" in English is also to wander from the truth, to be mistaken. Rochester errs, and Jane almost does. Charlotte Brontë was, of course, fond of showing off her skills in French, acquired in Brussels, the experience she describes in *The Professor* and *Villette* when it seems she, as a pupil-teacher, fell in love with her married employer, M. Héger.

---

4    Charlotte Brontë, however, is able to suggest the multlayered nature of truth through symbolism and dense patterns of imagery.

5    Richardson already presented the body as text in Pamela, who conceals writing about her body, and writes about her body.

6    We might also compare the heroine of Flaubert's *Madame Bovary* (1857), whose identity is completely defined by marital status, whose maiden name (Rouault) most readers forget.

7    The fairy tale aspect of these symmetrical families was as important to Charlotte Brontë as to Charles Dickens in his imagery.

The other French "sound-alike" for Eyre is "aire," a word that appears in the text when little Adèle, who is Francophone, thinks that is the name Jane gives her (89). As the footnote to the Norton Critical Edition mentions, "aire" can mean "area or space," particularly, I believe, a theatrical space, and there are charades and theatricals at Thornfield, in addition to the "unofficial" theatrics of Mr. Rochester. The English derivative of "aire," in fact, is "eyre," and means literally a legal circuit, which could relate it to Jane's inheritance, but also to Rochester's legal tie to Bertha. "Aire" can also mean "nest for a bird of prey," and it has long been noted how frequently Brontë uses bird imagery, usually to describe her characters.[8] Is Rochester the bird of prey at Thornfield? He is described as a falcon at one point (167), an eagle at another. Jane is frequently described as a robin (25), a bird in a cage (122). In keeping with the bird imagery, it should also be noted that an "eyrie" in English is "an eagle's nest." Of course, the English word "air" is also implied, particularly when we see Jane looking *down* on her world from the leads at Thornfield, or when she yearns to take flight. An alternate pronunciation of "Eyre" would be "ire," which brings us back again to Woolf's detection of Charlotte Brontë's (or Jane's) anger—though Adèle's pronunciation settles the issue, the pun is still there. Jane's anger is a problem with Woolf because, like Lewis and Cecil, she sees Jane as a literal projection of her creator, and not just as a fictional construct from whom her creator may be distanced artistically to a greater or lesser degree.[9]

*Charlotte Brontë's Craftsmanship: Structure*

What I am increasingly struck with is how consciously crafted and controlled a novel *Jane Eyre* is. It makes a forceful plea for women's right to feel, to be passionate, to act, but it frames that plea within a tightly wrought structure. In her later novel *Shirley* (1849), Charlotte Brontë inverts the Medusa-Gorgon myth of a female monster who turns men who dare to look her in the face to stone, to a compassionate treatment of the "Old Maids" (the aptly named Misses Mann and Ainly ["only," in Yorkshire dialect]) who are turned to stone by the men who never look on them as sentient beings, and who could foreshadow the fate of one of her heroines, Caroline Helstone, being raised by her rigid, unfeeling clergyman-uncle, the Reverend Helstone (Hailstone—hellfire and brimstone), who, as her potential suitor Robert Moore recognizes, is leaving his fortune to the Church, not Caroline, thereby in all likelihood dooming her to the fate of lifelong spinsterhood—she is just barely saved from it. The mythic frame, nonetheless, controls and shapes the anger.

Earlier, in *Jane Eyre*, and even in the juvenilia, Charlotte Brontë is making not just a feminist plea empowering women to feel, but a woman writer's plea that women be allowed to dip *their* pens into their hearts—not to carve their texts in stone, but to inscribe them on their hearts so those hearts do *not* turn to stone. For this reason Charlotte Brontë appeals so strongly to theorists who see the body as the text, and the text as the body. In Austen's *Persuasion*, Anne Elliot's impassioned critique of

---

8     The "Aire" is also the name of a Yorkshire river near the Brontës' home.

9     Gilbert and Gubar write of Jane, she is "invisible as *air*, the *heir* to nothing, secretly choking with *ire*" (342).

male writers' portrayals of women as flighty and inconstant is comparable. Both pleas are all the more effective because they are rational and carefully constructed.

Charlotte Brontë makes use of a triadic structure to trace her heroine's development. Kathleen Tillotson, in *Novelists of the Eighteen-Forties*, remarks that *Jane Eyre* was one of the first "three-decker novels," not produced loosely in serial form, which permitted authors such as Thackeray and Dickens to respond as they went on, to their audience's reactions to characters or plot, and to compose the remainder to suit their demands and wishes. The quest for independence aligned with feeling is repeated three times until finally it is fulfilled with Jane's return to a chastened Rochester and a Christian marriage of the sort Richardson valorizes in *Pamela*, a way-station on the path to eternity, a model for union with God.

Starting with Ellen Moers in *Literary Women* (1978), critics have focused on the image of the "Red Room" as it appears, with variations, in all three parts of the novel, which correspond to:

A. Gates / head (the Reed family)—Jane's entry into experience.
and
Lo / wood (Mr. Brocklehurst, Miss Temple, Helen Burns)—we might compare the name to Lo / wick in George Eliot's *Middlemarch*, where the wick burns low indeed—Casaubon, also a clergyman, though venial compared to Brocklehurst, is moribund.
B. Thorn / field—where, however, Jane says on arrival, "My couch had no thorns in it that night" (85).
C. Marsh End (Moor House) (the Rivers family)—John Reed is the "bad" cousin, St. John Rivers the "good"—but both bully Jane; one is physically abusive, the other spiritually.
and
Fern / dean (Rochester)—the novel comes full circle, and Jane comes home. But how healthy is Ferndean? Rochester never kept Bertha there, because the climate was unhealthy and damp, and he would not kill her.

In Book I, Jane is imprisoned in the red room at Gateshead as punishment for flying "out of herself" at the bullying John Reed, her first experience of sexual oppression: "The red-room was a spare-chamber, very seldom slept in," with red drapes, carpet, tablecloth, walls (10). There is a "secret" to the red-room, as there is to the third-story room at Thornfield: "Mr. Reed had been dead nine years: it was in this chamber he breathed his last" (11). The terrified ten-year-old Jane imagines that Mr. Reed's ghost appears to her, and faints. As Moers and others have noted, however, red is both a terrifying and a triumphant color to a woman: it can symbolize blood and death, as it does to a man, but to a woman it also symbolizes menstruation and childbirth, which, in the nineteenth century, could be a source of fear, with the high rate of mortality of both infants and women (often as a result of puerperal fever, one of the great killers of the period—it killed Mary Wollstonecraft), but also a source of fulfillment. So if Mr. Reed does appear to Jane in the red room, it would be in a spirit of benevolence, since he is the only one who, in her memory, has ever cared for her. The terror of the ten-year-old may be transformed, in the adult Jane, into a recognition that some "positive" in her life occurred then, namely her separation from Gates / head, where no fulfillment is possible.[10]

At Thornfield, of course, there is another red room—Mr. Rochester's, when the mad Bertha sets fire to it: "Tongues of flame darted round the bed: the curtains were on fire. In the midst of blaze and vapour, Mr. Rochester lay stretched motionless, in deep sleep" (131).[11] This time it is Jane herself who comes to the rescue, in an inversion of the "white knight on a charger" rescuing the damsel in distress, and Mr. Rochester accuses her of plotting to drown him, as he lies in a pool of water.

The "red-room" of Part III is not witnessed by Jane, but described after the fact to her by the former butler (Rochester's father's) at Thornfield. Bertha has finally succeeded in setting fire to Thornfield, and in the attempt to rescue her, Rochester is maimed and blinded.

Another recurrent motif is that of starvation: first at Gateshead, where Jane, as punishment, is not fed in the red room. She considers suicide by starving herself to death. Later, both at Lowood and when she flees Thornfield, she almost does starve. At Lowood the girls are offered "a nauseous mess" of "burnt porridge" for breakfast; Jane comments ironically, "Thanks [were] returned for what we have not got" (39). The stew is "rusty" (44), the portions tiny, and bread and cheese at Miss Temple's, their beloved headmistress, is "nectar and ambrosia" (63).

When she leaves Thornfield after she learns of Rochester's perfidy, she is "destitute" once more (283). Hunger is a "vulture" (288), and she edits much of her suffering (as Huck Finn does in Twain's novel): "Let me condense now. I am sick of the subject" (289). She is practically reduced to begging—for bread from a farmer (289), and, in an echo of the burnt porridge at Lowood, for "a mess of cold porridge" destined for the pigs, from a little girl (290). But Jane always chooses to survive: "Because I know, or believe, Mr. Rochester is still living; and then, to die of want and cold, is a fate to which nature cannot submit passively" (290)—unlike Charlotte's sister Emily's hero / anti-hero Heathcliff (and possibly Cathy) in *Wuthering Heights*.

*Jane's Childhood Conditioning*

When we first meet Jane at Gateshead, she is ten years old, and the narrative effectively ends when she is 20, apart from the retrospective summary written at age 30, when she writes the manuscript and summarizes the history of her marriage to Rochester, concluding with that curious paean to St. John Rivers, whose "glorious sun hastens to its setting" (398).

---

10   One of my students, Caterina Giordano, noted the passage in which Jane returns to consciousness after her ordeal in the red room; the first thing she sees is the fire / blood imagery reduced to the friendly reality of the nursery fire: "In five minutes more the cloud of bewilderment dissolved: I knew quite well that I was in my own bed, and that the red glare was the nursery fire" (15).

11   Does the phrase "tongues of flame" refer to the Pentecostal tongues in the Bible which descended on the disciples after Christ's death, who began speaking in no known language but were understood by all?

There are very few female initiation novels that start with childhood; more typically, an inexperienced 20- or 21-year-old, like Austen's Emma Woodhouse or George Eliot's Dorothea Brooke in *Middlemarch*, is the protagonist. There is at least one example earlier than *Jane Eyre* of a female initiation novel that begins with childhood conditioning, and that is Jane Austen's *Mansfield Park* (1814), in which Fanny Price, a little girl of ten taken from her large impecunious family in Portsmouth to live with wealthy relatives, is treated as an unpaid servant, in a somewhat similar situation to Jane's at Gateshead. Charlotte Brontë surely had Fanny Price in mind; for all her complaints about Jane Austen's lack of passion, she clearly treated some of her works as a model / paradigm on which she could improve. In fact, the "madwoman in the attic" was undoubtedly suggested by Catherine Morland's wild fantasy that General Tilney is keeping his wife a prisoner upstairs at Northanger Abbey. What *cannot* happen in a Jane Austen novel *can* in a Charlotte Brontë, but here, as in Jane Eyre herself, Brontë undoubtedly had an Austen model in mind.

When we first meet little Jane (and this is true of Fanny Price as well), she immediately strikes the note of her "physical inferiority to Eliza, John, and Georgiana Reed" (5), her cousins, the children of the family that takes her in. Abbot, the maid, reinforces Jane's negative sense of her self, calling her "a little toad" compared to the pretty, but spoiled, Georgiana (21). We find Jane, characteristically, "shrined in double retirement" in the *red*-curtained window-seat, escaping, on a "drear November day," into her beloved reading—she is yet another "female Quixote," like Pamela, Charlotte Ramsay Lennox's Arabella in *The Female Quixote* (1751), and Emma Woodhouse before her. We can only guess what Emma Woodhouse read as a child and young woman,[12] but we are told Jane's readings, which help shape her dreams and her life: Bewick's 'History of British Birds' (6)—a source of bird imagery in the novel; Goldsmith's 'History of Rome'—she compares the bully John Reed to the "Roman Emperors" (4); fairy tales—her own situation, like Fanny Price's, has often been compared to Cinderella's; Swift's 'Gulliver's Travels' (17)—Jane with the Reeds is comparable to Gulliver in the land of the giants, and she is soon to set out on her journey; tales of the Arabian Nights (32)—Scheherazade was the archetypal female artist, who would die if she could not tell her tales, 1,001 of them, to keep her husband entertained so he will not have her killed.[13] We can also assume Bunyan's *Pilgrim's Progress* (1678), which frames the closing paragraphs of the novel. Last, but far from least, she is careful to mention among her later readings Richardson's *Pamela*, whose heroine's fate she in some ways emulates by eventually marrying "the Master," her employer, who not coincidentally is a somewhat watered-down Victorian version of the reformed rake.

---

12   We do know that she has read Madame de Genlis' *Adelaide et Théodore*, also critiqued by Wollstonecraft in the *Vindication of the Rights of Woman*. In this moralizing novel the heroine is forced into a convent by a tyrannical father when she refuses to marry the man he has chosen for her, a situation in some ways comparable to Emma's subjection to her father's gentle tyranny, which would make marriage to any young man almost impossible.

13   Jane Austen mentions Scheherazade in *Persuasion*, as we have remarked, significantly at the beginning of the chapter where Anne Elliot implicitly speaks out in favor of women writers by criticizing male writers' perceptions of the female.

Significantly, her first act of rebellion in this household where she seems an alien presence, "a discord in Gateshead Hall," occurs when John Reed seizes her book, denies her access to the library,[14] and flings the book at her, injuring her (8). At this point she flies "*out* of myself, as the French would say" (9). This act of rebellion will ultimately move her, like her creator, from the private, domestic sphere, to the public, first at Lowood, then at Thornfield—to an outside world which, in fact, she has hitherto perceived only in books set in exotic locales, or in travel literature. From this first "book-ish" rebellion will ultimately be written her *own* book—again, an echo of the heroine's progression in Richardson's novel.

Not only do we accept the convention of her writing her own tale, the novel also begins with a book as the instrument of her destiny. John Reed threatens her: "You have no money; your father left you none; you ought to beg" (8). After her flight from Thornfield, and before she reaches Moor House, she is indeed forced to beg. The "master–servant" ploy occurs first with John Reed, foreshadowing her later relationship with Mr. Rochester. Like Dickens's equally lonely Esther Summerson in *Bleak House*, she has only her doll to love, for "human beings must love something" (924).

The first of many reflecting-mirrors[15] (perhaps a metaphor for Jane's and Charlotte's subjective artistic creations?) appears in the red room, where "a great looking-glass … repeated the vacant majesty of the bed and room" (11). This mirror-universe, to the terrified child, seems to project a world beyond the grave. Another "mirror" at Gateshead is the kind but submissive nurse Bessie Lee, who advises Jane to be "bolder" in self-defense (33), who, according to Jane—and we trust her—is naturally good, but has "indifferent ideas of principle or justice" (24). Jane herself combines natural goodness with a strong moral backbone, as she demonstrates in her subsequent relationship with Rochester. It is Bessie who reappears later, bringing Jane news of Gateshead and the Reeds, first in Chapter X (79), later in Chapter XXI (194), informing Jane of John Reed's death and his mother's impending death (194–5). She offers a more flattering—and realistic—mirror to Jane than the maid Abbot. She tells the 18-year-old Jane: "… you are genteel enough; you look like a lady, and it is as much as ever I expected of you: you were no beauty as a child" (80). Bessie moreorless authenticates Jane's narrative. She could be described not only as a mirror but also as a Jamesian *ficelle* or confidante, in a rather limited sense. At Thornfield the limited confidante role will be assumed by Mrs. Fairfax. In no sense is Jane ever as isolated as the powerless Pamela.

Her journey to freedom begins at the symbolically named Gateshead, "an entrance into a new life" (21). Her model is Gulliver, that "most desolate wanderer in most dread and dangerous regions" (17). Despite Bessie Lee's song concluding, "God is a friend to the poor orphan child" (18), Jane prefers to help herself towards independence—"poverty for me was synonymous with degradation"—and she answers the kind pharmacist Mr. Lloyd, "No, I should not like to belong to poor people" (20). Jane is out to make her own opportunities and earn her way, including winning a little love to herself.

---

14  We might compare Virginia Woolf in 1928 at Cambridge.
15  Cynthia A. Linder and others have addressed this subject from different perspectives.

The first way-station on her road to independence is Lowood, where she is indeed among poor people, but does not belong to them. After John Reed, the next male tyrant in her life is the Reverend Mr. Brocklehurst, who has been compared to a Dickensian tyrannical schoolmaster.[16] Kathleen Tillotson, I believe, was the first to point out that the description of him as a tall black column—"a black pillar, such, at least, appeared to me, at first sight, the straight, narrow, sable-clad shape standing *erect* on the rug: the grim face at the top was like a carved mask, placed above the shaft by way of capital" (26; emphasis mine)—is echoed in the description of that other very different man of the cloth, St. John Rivers: "I saw he was of the material from which nature hews her heroes—Christian and Pagan—her lawgivers, her statesmen, her conquerors; a steadfast bulwark for great interests to rest upon; but at the fireside, too often a cold cumbrous column, gloomy and out of place" (346).[17] The image is phallic, representing two forms of male (patriarchal) power, however differently motivated. While Brocklehurst is clearly a bad, hypocritical clergyman, to be contrasted to the "good" clergyman, Rivers, we shall see later that Jane equally resists and fears Rivers' rigidity and Calvinistic obsessiveness. Brocklehurst rationalizes the suffering and oppression of children as being good for their souls, when he preaches to Miss Temple: "Oh madam, when you put bread and cheese, instead of burnt porridge, into these children's mouths, you may indeed feed their vile bodies, but you little think how you starve their immortal souls!" (55). His black clothing associates him with the death of oppressed children like Helen Burns. Jane's morality—"I must keep in good health and not die"—is the common-sense response to such tyranny (27). Charlotte Brontë especially underlines Brocklehurst's hypocrisy when he says to Mrs. Reed, "Consistency, madam, is the first of Christian duties"—a consistency which is consistently not applied to his own prosperous family, his children wearing velvet, silk, and furs provided, presumably, by the funding Brocklehurst diverts from Lowood's coffers into his own pockets (56). When Brocklehurst denounces Jane as a liar, Jane, like Dickens's Jo the crossing-sweeper in *Bleak House*, this "native of a Christian land," is compared by Brocklehurst to "a little heathen who says its prayers to Brahma and kneels before Juggernaut" (58). One cannot help but compare Brocklehurst's attitude to Rivers' missionary zeal in going forth to convert so-called "heathens" in exotic climes—Indian Hindus and Brahmins, who have their own perfectly good religion. This is what is surprising about Jane's positive evocation of Rivers at the end, when all along we have been invited to see foregrounded the misery of the "native" poor of Great Britain, whom Brocklehurst exploits and Rivers ignores (virtually).

A more attractive Christianity is evinced by the other-worldly Helen Burns, who exemplifies patient endurance and the movement through suffering to perfection. As Helen puts it, "… it is weak and silly to say you *cannot bear* what it is your fate to be required to bear" (48). As Jane has rejected poverty, she rejects, though with loving compassion, Helen as a role model. Jane is, in fact, more like Thackeray's Becky

---

16  It has long been accepted that he is based on the real-life William Carus Wilson, head of Cowan Bridge school where two of Charlotte's sisters died.

17  Helene Moglen argues that Rivers completes Helen Burns's other-worldly project (487), but at no time is Helen associated with images of moral rigidity and intransigence.

Sharp in refusing to be passive and submissive: "When we are struck at without a reason, we should strike back again very hard" (50). Jane's own suffering, and that of those around her (even the Reed family, but especially Rochester) causes her ultimately to soften this position, but never to the point of passively accepting total other-worldliness as an immediate goal or end, just as she rejects suicide on the moors, or self-sacrifice with Rivers. Helen, on the other hand, like Rivers in the conclusion, is "looking to the end" (51). Jane needs and prefers the love of human beings: "I cannot bear to be solitary and hated, Helen" (60).

### *"I can always advertise": The Independence Theme*

After Helen dies in Jane's arms, we are told, she rests in an unmarked grave until her old friend returns to it 15 years after her death and raises a grey marble tombstone with Charlotte's less embarrassing tribute to Thackeray,[18] an inscription, "Resurgam," "I shall rise again," derived from Thackeray's Chapter 14 of *Vanity Fair*.[19] This inscription also sets the pattern of *spiritual* death and rebirth for Jane herself which marks the end of each of her sojourns, and the beginning of each new stage of her quest. Helen's death at the end of Chapter IX is, in a sense, shared vicariously by Jane, for, at the beginning of Chapter X, she telescopes or truncates the next eight years of her life into an expository summary: "… to the first ten years of my life, I have given almost as many chapters. But this is not to be a regular autobiography: therefore I now pass a space of eight years almost in silence" (72).[20] The adult Jane is, in a sense, formed by Helen's death, yet another in the series of loved ones who have been lost to her. Her education she summarizes: she has risen to be "the first girl of the first class"; then she begins to teach. She has described her own mind as "analytic" and "questioning." It is Helen, she writes, who "had a turn for narrative," for "informing" (68). But Helen's "turn for narrative" becomes her legacy to Jane, her "heir." Moreover, is it not possible to be both "analytic" and "questioning," and a mistress of "narrative"? Does this formulation not define the psychological novelist?[21] Jane has, in brief, fulfilled Miss Temple's prophecy: "We shall think you what you prove yourself to be" (61), and with Miss Temple's marriage Jane is fully armed to move into the world outside the formerly pestilential Lowood.

Jane declares that only human ties matter: "I had had no communication by letter or message with the outer world … And now I felt that it was not enough … I desired liberty; for liberty I gasped; for liberty I uttered a prayer." But she concludes, "'Then,' I cried, half desperate, 'grant me at least a new servitude!'" (74). Are these sentiments mutually contradictory, or merely an acceptance of the parameters, the

---

18   Her dedication to Thackeray, who *had* a mad wife in an asylum, if not the attic, was to prove a source of great embarrassment and vexation for her.

19   Actually, we cannot be sure whether she borrowed it from him, or the converse, because of the periodical nature of his publication.

20   We might compare her silence over ten years of marriage to Rochester.

21   I am indebted to my friend and colleague, Dr. Phyllis Rozendal, for pointing out yet another link between Helen and Jane: Jane is associated with fire, and Helen "burns" with religious zeal.

circumscription of women's lives as they were lived in the nineteenth century? Is there "liberty" to be found, paradoxically, within the "servitude"? Perhaps a vocation? Paid servitude in place of living on charity?

Jane advertises, and yearns "to go where there was life and movement." Millcote, the nearest town to Thornfield Hall, as Robert B. Heilman has noted, is scarcely a Gothic setting. It is located in the heart of the industrial North of England: "Millcote was a large manufacturing town on the banks of the A___" (77). Indeed, notes Heilman, the more Gothic setting is the dank, unhealthy Ferndean where, in Charlotte Bronte's "New Gothic," Jane spends her marriage with Rochester—a happiness earned and tempered by suffering (459). It is clear she is beginning life again, as at Gateshead: "A phase of my life was closing to-night, a new one opening to-morrow" (78): "Resurgam."

*Rochester and Rivers: "The Dark Is Light Enough"*

The two men who represent a love interest in Jane Eyre's life are polar opposites. A diagram suggesting their completely antithetical natures may clarify Charlotte Brontë's use of male foils.

| Edward Fairfax Rochester | Jane | St. John Rivers |
| --- | --- | --- |
| Dark | green eyes | Blond |
| Vulcan | chestnut hair | Apollo |
| Volcano | | River |
| Fire | | Ice |
| Moon | | Sun |
| False Idol | | Orthodox Religion |
| World | | Other World |
| Eros | | Agape |

What Charlotte Brontë has done is manipulate and re-shape the old blonde–brunette antithesis, usually relevant to heroines, applying it instead to her male characters. That blonde–brunette contrast probably received its most popular expression in the nineteenth century in the novels of Sir Walter Scott, particularly *Ivanhoe* (1820), in which the blonde Anglo-Saxon maiden, Rowena, wins the hero's love, but the brunette Rebecca, who is Jewish, and has knowledge of the healing arts and of the occult, usually appeals more to the reader.[22] As Scott was well aware, this tradition

---

22  Hollywood made a film version in the 1950s with a middle-aging Joan Fontaine as Rowena, and a very young Elizabeth Taylor, in the full bloom of her beauty, as Rebecca—audiences came away doubting Ivanhoe's intelligence and taste for choosing the blonde! Edgar Allan Poe paid homage to the same tradition in his "Ligeia" (1838–39), in which the dead dark heroine takes over the soul of the Anglo-Saxon Lady Rowena.

goes back to the medieval Court of Love, in which the ideal lady, the lady on a pedestal, was always blonde and grey- or blue-eyed.[23]

Both Charlotte Brontë and her sister Emily, author of *Wuthering Heights*, refuse to apply this stereotyping to their heroines. Cathy Earnshaw, in *Wuthering Heights*, is a dangerous, impetuous, self-willed brunette, and Jane Eyre, we learn, has green or hazel eyes and chestnut hair (red highlights). Her coloring, in fact, mediates that of the two men, the extremely dark Rochester and the fair St. John Rivers. In *Wuthering Heights* the contrast is between the very dark Heathcliff, of unknown origin, found as a child on a Liverpool dock, described by some of the characters as an "imp of Satan," and the very fair, civilized, even-tempered Edgar Linton whom Cathy marries, even while her soul remains wedded to Heathcliff's.

Rochester's and Rivers' natures are polarized in ways that their physical differences only begin to suggest. Rochester is associated, in mythology, with the dark god Vulcan at his forge. But Vulcan is also the cuckolded husband. Rivers is connected with Apollo, god of the sun and of poetry (388–9). Rochester himself makes these associations when Jane returns to him. Rochester is linked to the moon, rather than the sun. Again and again moonrise illuminates his dialogues with Jane, notably in the Midsummer Eve scene where he first taunts Jane, who believes that his bride is to be Blanche Ingram, not herself. The moon is presided over by a goddess, indeed the triple goddess, not a god. If Rochester is associated with volcanoes and fire, Rivers is with water (the river of his name), and frozen water, or ice. Rivers is other-worldly and religious to the point of self-abnegation or self-destruction. Rochester, on the other hand, almost becomes a false idol for Jane before their expected marriage. He himself has admitted to her his worldliness in the form of his past excesses, especially sexual. In Denis de Rougemont's terms, from *Love in the Western World*, Rochester would represent Eros, or romantic, passionate love, whereas Rivers would represent Agape, or Christian love in marriage, a marriage based on partnership and spiritual sharing (though it is difficult to imagine Rivers sharing anything), not on passion.[24] But the point remains valid that Jane runs the risk of being swallowed up by Rochester, of losing her selfhood—Robert B. Martin has remarked on the unVictorian way in which they wander in and out of each other's bedrooms (478)—and that the movement of the book has to be towards an independence she must earn before she can choose to share a life with him.

Some modern readers (and some not-so-modern, like George Eliot) want to argue that Jane should have stayed with Rochester in the first instance, since he really does love and care for her, and can have no further relations, marital or otherwise, with Bertha Mason Rochester. Eliot, who had her own reasons for detesting the British

---

23    The tradition is, of course, Eurocentric, and writers like James Baldwin, in "The Dark Is Light Enough" (*Notes of a Native Son*), complain that this stereotype of Anglo-Saxon beauty carries over into, for instance, films made with black actors whose careers, at least throughout the 1950s, flourished most if, like the tragic Dorothy Dandridge (or Halle Berry today, who has played Dandridge), they conformed to so-called *white* standards.

24    Actually, later in life De Rougemont retracted his dichotomizing of Eros and Agape, and admitted that romantic and Christian love can be compatible (see *Pamela*).

laws on divorce,[25] criticized this aspect of the novel: "All self-sacrifice is good—but one would like it to be in a somewhat nobler cause than that of a diabolical law which chains a man soul and body to a putrefying carcase" (quoted by Hardy 495).[26]

This is, of course, missing the point, for all George Eliot's genius. Jane tells us herself why she leaves Rochester: "... faith was blighted—confidence destroyed! Mr. Rochester was not to me what he had been; for he was not what I had thought him" (260). In other words, she has discovered that her idol has feet of clay, and, more importantly, as is predicted from the title and the very opening of the novel, she must find her identity as Jane Eyre, with a family and independence, and assert her selfhood. She recognizes that, if she chooses to remain with him, "There was a heaven—a temporary heaven—in this room for me, if I chose" (282), but for Jane who, like Pamela and like Charlotte Brontë herself,[27] always remains within Christian confines, there is another heaven beyond, which she is in danger of forgetting.

By the end of the novel Rochester has been chastened—some would say over-punished—and himself accepts the framework of Christian marriage. Jane has, in fact, moderated the extreme positions represented by Rochester and Rivers, and this is her triumph.

*Jane and Rochester: "Elective Affinities"*

The Jane that Rochester meets is already fully formed—all that she lacks is experience of social intercourse. If he deceives or disappoints her, she will move on, for she is young and resilient: "I can advertise again," she thinks (82).[28] Rochester is attuned to her sufficiently to see her social nature: "I saw you had a social heart ..." (277). Until Rochester begins to cultivate her, she is inclined to underestimate her claims to society's interest. When she first arrives at Thornfield, still under the illusion that Mrs. Fairfax, the housekeeper, is the proprietor, she looks at another of the many mirrors in the text as she dresses to meet her supposed employer: "I ever wished to look as well as I could, and to please as much as my want of beauty would permit" (86). Jane is pleased to discover that the amiable Mrs. Fairfax, who is related to Rochester (his middle name is Fairfax)—is a dependent like herself; therefore, that they are equals. Mrs. Fairfax is very conscious of class, and later warns Jane that "Equality of position and fortune is often advisable in such cases; and there are twenty years of difference in your ages. He might almost be your father" (232). Jane obviously has no snobbishness about her for all her own superior education; she and the housekeeper speak on equal terms.[29]

---

25   Eliot lived common-law with George Henry Lewes, who could not divorce his wife Agnes because he had condoned a love affair she was having with his best friend, Thornton Hunt, while still living under his roof.

26   Apparently Eliot was not yet living with Lewes when she made this comment.

27   About Emily, as we shall see, I am not so sure ...

28   Helene Moglen sees Jane's decision to leave Rochester as her first step towards independence (485), but actually her first step is her decision to advertise at Lowood for a position, and her decision to leave Rochester is couched in the same terms.

29   Terry Eagleton, however, sees Charlotte Brontë as somewhat of a snob, and has difficulty reconciling snobbery wih feminism (492–3).

It is this same equality Jane must establish with Rochester. When he first enters the novel, it is as the man on a horse, almost the fantasy figure of the sexually experienced male confronting the young innocent female. But, as has been noted, Charlotte Brontë completely upsets our expectations. Rochester is not the prince on a charger riding to the rescue of the damsel in distress, nor is he the figure out of folk-tale Jane first supposes (Bessie Lee was the spinner of that tale, as she was the singer of Jane's childhood)—Jane at first takes his dog, Pilot, for the Gytrash, a North-of-England spirit out of Bessie's tale, but the man breaks the spell when man and horse slip and fall on a sheet of ice (98). It is Jane, then, who must come to Rochester's rescue and support him. This scene foreshadows the conclusion when Jane must support the maimed and partially blinded Rochester after Bertha's revenge. His horse's name is Mesrour, out of the Arabian Nights, and Charlotte Brontë deliberately sets out to subvert Jane's (and our) book-conditioned expectations of what should be happening in a novel of romance, courtship, and marriage.[30]

When Rochester has his first interview with Jane as the master of Thornfield—he has not identified himself after the accident—he addresses her as a spirit from fairy land, and is tempted "to demand whether you had bewitched my horse" (107).[31] They become accustomed to addressing each other as spirits or fairies, or possessors of strange powers over each other. There is, for instance, the wonderful "Janian reply," as Rochester calls it, when she returns from the Reeds: "I have been with my aunt, sir, who is dead." Rochester comments, "She comes from the other world"—a world of which he has been at times not sufficiently aware (215). Similarly he senses her presence in the orchard in the Midsummer Eve scene. She is lurking behind him when "he said quietly without turning:—'Jane, come and look at this fellow [an insect].'" Jane thinks, "I had made no noise: he had not eyes behind—could his shadow feel?" (218). All this foreshadows her sense of his need when, at the Rivers', she hears his voice calling her at the moment that Bertha has finally succeeded in setting fire to Thornfield. This experience occurs, not coincidentally, when she is most being pressed into a loveless, but not sexless, marriage by Rivers, who is willing to sacrifice them both to his missionary zeal in India.[32] She realizes that "it was the voice of a human being—a known, loved, well-remembered voice—that of Edward Fairfax Rochester; and it spoke in pain and woe wildly, eerily, urgently" (369). Jane denies that it is superstition or the supernatural, but rather "the work of nature" pushed to the utmost (370). All this is in accord with Charlotte Bronte's "New Gothic," as Heilman calls it, whereby she takes a literary convention and then twists and shapes it to her own very different (more realistic?) ends. Like Jane Austen, she tries to create a romance that is consonant with everyday reality.

---

30   This comic deflation is comparable to Jane Austen's comic deflation of Emma Woodhouse's romance-inpired "plots" in *Emma*, or Anne Elliot's refusal to be "rescued" by her cousin, the heir to her father's estate, William Walter Elliot in *Persuasion*.

31   Robert K. Martin and P. Sullivan have both written about the importance of fairy-tale elements in *Jane Eyre*.

32   The exchange between Rivers and Jane concerning the voice she hears also suggests a sharp contrast between Rivers' God of duty and Jane's of human ties and compassion.

Rochester asserts that Jane is not his equal, but his "superior"—because of his moral shortcomings—"I don't wish to treat you like an inferior: that is (correcting himself), I claim only such superiority as must result from twenty years' difference in age and a century's advance in experience." His credentials as a fair and generous landlord to his tenants have already been established by Mrs. Fairfax (9), as the housekeeper establishes Darcy's in *Pride and Prejudice*. So Rochester is not really seen as tyrannical or snobbish—though certainly representative of the patriarchy. "I was your equal at eighteen—quite your equal," he tells her. However, that equality does not deter him from inviting her to give command performances in a whole series of interviews. In the first, he has commanded her to show her accomplishments, after first interrogating her about the ordeal of Lowood. She plays the piano, and then he demands to see her sketches. As Mr. B. begins to fall in love with Pamela because of her writing, Mr. Rochester begins to fall in love with Jane because of her drawings. The first depicts a stormy sea, a shipwreck, a bird, and a drowned corpse (perhaps Jane at Lowood?). There is a suggestion of Noah's Ark. The second shows a hill (perhaps Thornfield?), a star, and "a woman's shape to the bust," a "vision of the Evening Star"—perhaps Jane's yearning for a mother she has never known? The last picture is of an iceberg (Rivers?) and a colossal head resting on it with a crescent, "the likeness of a Kingly Crown," probably foreshadowing Rivers' death in India, but also reflecting back on Helen Burns (110–11).[33] What they all have in common is the breaking of boundaries between nature and humanity, confirming Jane's insistence on human ties. Like Charlotte Brontë, she was "tormented by the contrast between my idea and my handiwork" (11), but Rochester recognizes a genuine, if undisciplined, artistic talent in her. The reader may well be reminded of Mr. Knightley's mentoring of Emma, again the much older, experienced male not dominating but in a sense encouraging the heroine by giving her access to the "male" world.

In the next interview, he confesses his relationship with little Adèle's mother, Céline Varens, the French opera-dancer, but is careful to exculpate himself of Adèle's paternity.[34] He describes himself as a "spoonie" with Céline, a term recently applied by Thackeray to "faithful Dobbin" in *Vanity Fair*. Rochester is consistently frank with Jane, and tells her nothing but the truth—but never *all* of the truth. This series of mock-confessions is designed to ease his conscience, but he never makes the main confession, that he has a mad wife locked in the attic. Jane should be warned at times by his tone: "I will break obstacles to happiness, to goodness" (125). Jane realizes that in him there are "excellent materials," though somehow warped, distorted. She even senses that he is "alienated" from the house (129), and a few pages later Bertha sets fire to his bed, which is both symbolically and literally appropriate.[35] When Jane

---

33   See Jane Millgate's and Alan Bacon's articles on the drawings. Bacon detects a Miltonic influence.

34   I am inclined to trust him (and Charlotte Brontë) on this matter, but both Sandra Gilbert and W.A. Craik refer to Adèle as Rochester's illegitimate daughter.

35   The television drama *The Burning Bed*, based on the actual case of an abused wife who burned her husband to death, suggests how pervasive the mythic dimensions of *Jane Eyre* have been.

once again rescues him (it is becoming a habit), he addresses her as "witch, sorceress" (131), stressing their "natural sympathies" (133). When he dangles Blanche Ingram before her, like Céline, as a surrogate for Bertha, she speaks again of their "elective affinities" (to borrow Goethe's term): "He is not to them [Blanche *et al.*] what he is to me ... he is not of their kind. I believe he is of mine" (154). By this point she confesses her love, if not to him, at least to the reader, since she lacks any other confidante: "I had not intended to love him: the reader knows I had wrought hard to extirpate from my soul the germs of love there detected ... He makes me love him without looking at me" (153).

*Bertha and Blanche as Jane's "Doubles"?: The "Madwoman in the Attic" Thesis*

Again, he commands her to speak to him and to appear every night at the house-party with the Ingrams and others. Thus Jane witnesses the charades in Chapter XVIII—charades indeed, as Blanche angles for Rochester's hand, and Rochester plays his own game of making Jane jealous. One might compare Jane Austen's use of verbal (not theatrical) charades in *Emma*, or, by extension, of the Kotzebue play, "Lovers' Vows," in *Mansfield Park*, or Thackeray's charades in *Vanity Fair*, where Becky Sharp revealingly appears as a murderess. Rochester and Blanche pantomime a marriage, yielding the first syllable, "Bride." In the next the pantomime is of Rebekah at the "Well" (the second syllable), courted by Mr. Rochester in Eastern garb—later Jane is to resist being added to his harem. We might also think of Rivers heading to the Far East (India) with the project of taking Jane there in tow in a loveless marriage, as a human sacrifice to his fanaticism (in part male egoism). Bertha Mason, moreover, is a Creole woman, dark, exotic, and sensual, we are told, a true Rebecca who is only acted out, performed, by the cold Blanche, who physically resembles her, as her unwitting surrogate (160–61).[36] When "the tableau of the Whole" is performed, it is clear that Rochester has stage-managed the performance into yet another veiled confession to Jane of the truth of his situation: that he is shackled to a mad wife. Interestingly, he himself, not Blanche, appears in the role of the desperate, shackled inmate of Bridewell, a prison for the criminally insane (162). Is he assuming responsibility, symbolically, for Bertha? Is Bertha a double for Rochester, as Gilbert and Gubar suggest she is a double for Jane? Terry Eagleton, in *Myths of Power*, suggests this is true: "... the Bertha who tries on Jane's wedding veil is a projection of Jane's sexually tormented subconsciousness, but since Bertha is masculine, black-visaged and almost the same height as her husband, she appears also as a repulsive symbol of Rochester's sexual drive" (495). Cynthia Ann Linder also notes that Bertha could be modeled on a man, Branwell Brontë, and not on a woman at all: Branwell had once set fire to his bed while drunk (61). Everything is possible, as Jane's "ire" or anger appear dangerously often in Rochester himself, not just in the uncontrollable Bertha.

---

36  Richard Chase claims that "Bertha represents the woman who has given herself blindly and uncompromisingly to the principle of sex and intellect," a reading that seems to be derived mainly from Fanny Ratchford's sense that the model for Bertha was Lady Zenobia Ellrington, a character from Charlotte Brontë's juvenilia (466).

Jane recognizes that he is not in love with Blanche: "Miss Ingram was a mark beneath jealousy: she was too inferior to excite the feeling ... She was very showy, but she was not genuine ... her mind was poor, her heart barren by nature ... tenderness and truth were not in her" (163). Jane is so attuned to Rochester that she knows he shares her dim view of Blanche, but fears he would marry her anyhow, for political or financial reasons. Rochester has, in fact, reenacted, and even staged, his marriage of convenience to Bertha, using Blanche as a surrogate.[37] One might compare Emma Woodhouse's use of the unlikely Harriet Smith as a surrogate for herself in the portrait she paints.

In the third *long* interview with Jane, Rochester appears in the guise of a female gypsy. This is the third instance, at least, where our cosy expectations of appropriate gender roles have been overturned, upended. First, Jane rescues him, instead of the other way around, when he is thrown from his horse; second, in the Bridewell charade he appears as a *male* version of Bertha (the madman in the attic?). And third, here he is disguised as a female, a "Mother Bunch" (168). But before addressing Jane, the gypsy woman (Rochester) disillusions Blanche about his fortune (171). That exchange is only a prelude to his interview with Jane, where he hints at an offer to be made to her if she is not too "cold," too "sick," too "silly" to accept it. He deliberately, and rather ungallantly, draws her out about Blanche, and then concludes "the play is played out," a line the Norton Critical Editor, Richard J. Dunn, thinks is echoed by Thackeray in the last installment of *Vanity Fair*.[38] Finally, Rochester echoes the mad King Lear when he doffs his disguise: "Off, ye lendings!" (178). *Lear* was evidently a favorite Shakespearean play for the Brontës: Jane's sufferings overnight on the moors after she leaves Thornfield replicate the mad Lear's on the heath; and Emily Brontë makes even more pervasive use of images from *Lear*—notably the ferocious animal imagery—in *Wuthering Heights*. Jane's directness and

---

37  It is worth noting that the charade, a verbal and theatrical game, is rooted in Rochester's masculine discourse of power and authority. Jane remains silent in this scene, but is later to write out what she has only been thinking as a young girl. The interplay of masculine (public) and feminine (private, subjective) discourse is effectively depicted by Charlotte Brontë in this episode. It can be read as portraying Jane's quest for a liberated language, as can the novel as a whole. I am indebted to my former research assistant Dunja Baus for suggesting an Audre Lord quotation about the female quest for language: "... you cannot dismantle the master's house by using the master's tools." Rosemarie Bodenheimer, in "Jane Eyre in Search of Her Story," also stresses Jane's use of autobiographical materials as a means of gaining control over her life. Barbara Gates discusses Jane's movement from artist to writer. Carol Bock has written on Scott's influence on Brontë's "storytellers," but again, Brontë seeks to free her writing from masculine discourse.

38  As noted previously, *Vanity Fair* started to appear before *Jane Eyre*, but because it was published periodically, we cannot be certain who influenced whom. Because of her dedication to Thackeray, when *Jane Eyre* appeared, there was much speculation that its author had been a governess in Thackeray's household and had had an affair with the master (whose wife was insane). In fact, Charlotte Brontë never met Thackeray until after the publication of *Jane Eyre*, and at her publishers', but the dedication was a source of intense embarrassment at the time for all concerned.

honesty seem at times modeled on Cordelia's plain, blunt speech—Cordelia (*cor /* heart), who speaks the language of the human heart.

Rochester's attitude towards Blanche Ingram needs to be carefully scrutinized. Granted that Blanche is presented as shallow, vain, and materialistic, she is neither madwoman nor criminal, and he shamelessly manipulates her. The treatment of Bertha / Blanche has long been a sticking-point for critics who want to make Charlotte Brontë into an ardent, convinced feminist. Gilbert and Gubar argue that Bertha is a kind of double for Jane, symbolizing Jane's "ire," the anger and hatred contained socially in all women, until at times it threatens to burst forth in madness. There is a partial truth in this, but Bertha also doubles Rochester's sensuality and passion. More importantly, many readers are disturbed by Charlotte Brontë's obvious dislike of, and contempt for, large, voluptuous, sensual, "exotic" females, not only in *Jane Eyre* but also in *Shirley* and especially *Villette*, where the Belgian schoolgirls are presented as large, stupid, and cowlike.[39] I suspect that Charlotte put the diatribes against Blanche / Bertha in Rochester's mouth, rather than Jane's, so that she could vent some of her own spleen with impunity.

Not only does Rochester treat Blanche shabbily, he also describes her physicality in most ungallant, even gross terms: "A strapper—a real strapper, Jane: big, brown and buxom; with hair just such as the ladies of Carthage must have had" (193). Dido, Queen of Carthage, abandoned by her lover Aeneas, kills herself on a funeral pyre—no need to underline that the epic tragedy foreshadows Bertha's death. St. John Rivers would be willing, later, to have Jane suffer a similar fate, but for a different cause. Rochester also torments Jane by insisting she sit up with him the night before his marriage—when the real bride is to be the unknowing Jane herself. He manipulates Jane, as he has Blanche, to be absolutely certain she will have no choice but to marry him. He exhibits a kind of sexual horror, a scorn he cannot avenge on Bertha, but does on Blanche. Charlotte Brontë, we know, saw herself as small and rather mousy, like her heroine Jane. The Brontë Parsonage Museum in Haworth contains Charlotte's tiny slippers and mittens in a showcase, and we are told Charlotte was proud of her tiny feet and hands; but the evidence of her texts suggests she was deeply ambivalent about her insignificant physique. When Jane sets the situation up by suggesting that Adèle must be sent to school after the marriage, Rochester stresses Blanche's weight. The necessity, he recognizes, is "To get her out of my bride's way; who might otherwise walk over her rather too emphatically" (197). And later he refers to Blanche as "an extensive armful" (220). Obviously, this is in very poor taste, but one cannot help suspecting that some of Charlotte's own feelings of inadequacy are reflected here. When the large Thackeray (Sydney Greenstreet, the "Fat Man" of *The Maltese Falcon* fame, played him in the 1940s Brontë biographical film *Devotion*) met Charlotte Brontë, he said he had just met Jane Eyre, and that she came up about to the height of his watch chain (Gérin 405).

If Jean Rhys had not published *Wide Sargasso Sea* in 1967, completing the novel *Jane Eyre*, as she thought, from Bertha Mason's point of view, I doubt if Gilbert and Gubar and others would have been able to promulgate the "Madwoman in the

---

39  My graduate exchange student from Germany, Marian Jaekel, did a paper focusing on Brontë's "Anglocentric," narrow vision of the female predicament.

Attic" thesis that Bertha doubles Jane. Rhys, a Caribbean woman, undoubtedly took umbrage at the treatment of Bertha and determined to depict the situation of women from a non-Eurocentric twentieth-century point of view. It is important to remember, however, that *Wide Sargasso Sea* is *not* the completion of *Jane Eyre*, but the product of a twentieth-century sensibility trying to fill in the gaps or literary spaces the author perceives in Brontë's vision. Ellen Friedman writes that Rhys is "Breaking the Master Narrative."

It is a three-part novel, like *Jane Eyre*. Unlike *Jane Eyre*, the middle section is told from Rochester's point of view, I and III from Bertha's, Part I presenting Bertha as a young girl in the Caribbean, Part III Bertha as the mad wife in the attic. Rhys establishes parallels between Bertha and Jane to arouse our sympathies for the former. Bertha / Antoinette (her own name) has a convent upbringing comparable to Jane's at Lowood. Voodoo is the Caribbean version of Brontë's nature stretched to the utmost, if not the supernatural, in *Jane Eyre*. Antoinette's plantation is set on fire during a slave rebellion, foreshadowing the conflagration at Thornfield. The analogy between the female condition and slavery is overtly explored by Rhys, only hinted at by Charlotte Brontë (as by Jane Austen in *Mansfield Park*, where Fanny Price, the domestic "slave," is the only one interested in hearing Sir Thomas Bertram talk about slavery in the West Indies).[40] Caribbean tropical gardens are haloed by Edenic symbolism, like the Midsummer Eve scene at Thornfield. The novel ends with Bertha / Antoinette, locked in the attic in Part III, escaping and rending a young girl's (Jane's) bridal veil, then setting forth with candle in hand to set fire to Thornfield. Parts I and III are compelling and poignant, but the Rochester section is less persuasive. In her efforts to create sympathy for Bertha / Antoinette (whom we never really get to know in *Jane Eyre*), Rhys rewrites Mr. Rochester completely, blackening his character far beyond what Brontë ever contemplates. He sleeps with Bertha / Antoinette's maid in the very room adjoining his new bride's, adding sadism to infidelity. As Charlotte Brontë (and many readers) might say, "*My* Mr. Rochester would never do that"—his various peccadilloes with Céline, Clara *et al.* show Brontë's racial stereotyping of French superficiality, German phlegm, Italian fire, and so on, but she is also making it clear that these episodes all *follow* Bertha's madness, are never committed on site at Thornfield, and essentially harm Rochester more than the professional kept women.

Brontë's Rochester comes close, often, to confessing to Jane, but he always holds the essential back. He initiates Jane in blood, as previously in fire, when Bertha escapes from the attic—Grace Poole, as Craik remarks, is a terrible keeper (93–4)—and it is evident that he would *like* to share his burden with her, but for the fear of losing her. That Jane is the physical antithesis of Bertha / Blanche is a great source of attraction to him—but also, one suspects, it is gratifying to Charlotte Brontë.

---

40    R.J. Dingly, however, places Rochester in the slave position, on the basis of Rochester's referring to himself as "a man and a brother," while speaking to Jane. Dingly notes that the phrase "a man and a brother" refers to the seal of the Slave Emancipation Society which depicts a Negro kneeling and surrounded by the plea, "Am I not a man and a brother?" However, if Rochester is a slave to anything, it is to his own passions.

Perhaps he wants Jane to suspect the truth, and we begin to wonder whether Jane is not *willing* herself to blindness, for so usually perspicacious an observer.

We suspect that Jane is using denial, repression, even more strenuously at Midsummer Eve, when nature again seems in sympathy with Jane and Rochester, and a nightingale sings (221). We see Jane's and Rochester's "elective affinities" when both admit that "the cord of communion" between them will be snapped if, as Rochester hypothesizes, Jane must be sent away from Thornfield to Ireland, presumably to avoid Blanche (221). The scene takes place under the chestnut tree, emblematic of the Tree of Knowledge in Eden.[41]

When Jane asserts her equality—"I have as much soul as you,—and full as much heart!"—in confessing her love to Rochester (222), he embraces her, and she struggles to be free "like a wild, frantic bird that is rending its own plumage in its desperation" (233). Her resistance anticipates her integrity in fleeing from him when she learns that the "bride" who "stands between us" (223) is not Blanche, as he has pretended, but Bertha. Even now, she asserts, "I am a free human being with an independent will; which I now exert to leave you" (223). Despite her independence, Jane is all too eager to believe her suitor is finally telling the whole truth. She never stops to wonder why he has hitherto been taunting and controlling her through Blanche. As one critic comments, the Midsummer Eve scene proves, if nothing else, that it is ill-advised to consent to marriage with a man whose proposal ends with the words, "God pardon me! … and man meddle not with me: I have her, and will hold her" (224). Moreover, as if in warning, the chestnut tree writhes in the wind. It is later struck by lightning (the first Norton Edition cover picture) in a further exertion of nature's sympathy. Jane recounts, "I faced the wreck of the chestnut-tree; it stood up, black and riven: the trunk, split down the centre, gasped ghastly. The cloven halves were not broke from each other, for the firm base and strong roots kept them unsundered below, though community of vitality was destroyed—the sap would flow no more; …—as yet, however, they might be said to form one tree—a ruin, but an entire ruin" (243). There is no need to labor the point that the cloven tree foreshadows Jane's and Rochester's pending physical separation, but continued spiritual union (almost a Jungian animus-anima). But the shattered tree is also a warning of Rochester's scorched and shattered state when they are finally reunited.

Jane makes it clear to Rochester early on that she stands on principle for human salvation, preferring to wander ("errer") than to depend for salvation on another person (192). Immediately after this dialogue she dreams of "a wailing child" (one is reminded of "Cathy's ghost" in *Wuthering Heights*). She has this dream for seven nights, foreshadowing Bessie Lee's husband's appearance with the news of John Reed's death—again, nature stretched to the utmost. But she may also be regressing to her own younger self in the red room at Gateshead, as well as anticipating the potential frustration of her relationship to Rochester. The night before her wedding

---

41   As Ellen Moers first noted, this scene will be reworked by George Eliot in the Red Deeps passage of *The Mill on the Floss*, with Maggie Tulliver as a heroine also apparently doomed to the governess-trade; but the would-be lover Philip Wakem, who may be Maggie's soulmate, nevertheless does not attract her romantically (or physically?).

she dreams she is "burdened with the charge of a little child," again wailing (247)—herself? The child she may never have with Rochester?

When she returns to Thornfield from Mrs. Reed's deathbed, she pretty directly confesses her love to Rochester, as he has indirectly confessed his sins to Jane. She says to him, "wherever you are is my home—my only home" (216). From this position she is never to deviate. After Midsummer Eve, she comes close to making him into a God: "He stood between me and every thought of religion, as an *eclipse* intervenes between man and the broad sun. I could not, in those days, see God for his creature: of whom I had made an idol" (241). He is, moreover, associated with the pagan god Vulcan. If Rivers is associated with the sun, Rochester with the moon, by making of the latter a false idol, she produces an eclipse—total darkness. It is clear that her subsequent decision to leave Thornfield is well-prepared by Charlotte Brontë—she must learn to mediate the two men's extreme positions and somehow combine Eros and Agape. She recognizes that with a guilty Rochester she would share only a *temporary* heaven (282). She chastizes him: "Mr. Rochester, I will *not* be yours" (267), even here, in her Cordelia-like toughness, desperately trying to save his soul as well as her own. Rochester wants her to "become a part of me" (267). When Jane gives herself, she must give herself entirely; she expects the same of her partner, and Rochester has betrayed her faith in the integrity of his character.

*Escape from Thornfield: Towards Independence?*

The night before she leaves Thornfield, she dreams of "the red-room at Gateshead," calling up this time not the ghost of Mr. Reed, but that of her mother, appearing in love, "as never *moon* yet burst from cloud" (281; underlining mine). The ghost says, "My daughter, flee temptation!" and Jane answers, "Mother, I will" (281).[42] Appropriately, her departure occurs at sunrise, and after the pain and suffering of her flight, she arrives ultimately at a warm family scene at the Rivers', where she sees her two soon-to-be recognized "good" cousins, Diana and Mary Rivers, perusing a book in a foreign tongue (German), a tongue which Jane will later learn as she acquires a voice (292–3). It has been noted that Diana and Mary are named respectively for the pagan (Greek) goddess of chastity / virginity (but, who, as Annis Pratt reminds us, as the triple goddess, and goddess of the moon, also presides over maternity and aging), and for the Christian Virgin Mother.[43]

When St. John appears on the scene, almost the first thing he says is that Jane is "not at all handsome" (299), whereas his sisters feel that she becomes quite pretty when happy and cared for. Jane seeks only independence as a schoolmistress (as Lucy Snowe wins in *Villette*), together with a congenial family, not romantic love, which has deceived her. She sees that Rivers' only passion is his ambition

---

42   I am tempted to speculate about the ghostlike presence of Maria Branwell Brontë in her daughter's life—Maria, a writer herself, whose interest in the poor, as evidenced in her religious tract, "The Advantages of Poverty in Religious Concerns," may have been reflected in her daughter's view of the Industrial Revolution in *Shirley*.

43   I am indebted to my former student, Professor Jo-Ann Wallace (Alberta) for tracing this pattern of symbolism.

(313). He stifles his attraction to Rosamond Oliver, the "Rose of the World," and, unlike Rochester whom we first meet as the man on a horse, metaphorically reins in his passion as "a resolute rider would curb a rearing steed" (321). He ignores his "elysium," even as Jane thinks of the elysium she would have shared with Rochester (324). Rivers loves Rosamond enough not to sacrifice her to the harsh Indian climate, but is perfectly willing to sacrifice the less (to him) sexually attractive Jane: "God and nature intended you for a missionary's wife ... you are formed for labour, not for love ... You shall be mine: I claim you—not for my pleasure, but for my Sovereign's service" (354). As a proposal, this is even less tempting to its object than Darcy's first proposal to Elizabeth Bennet in *Pride and Prejudice* where he says he *cannot* contain his passion for her, to the point that he will even put up with her abominable, vulgar family![44]

Rivers admits to Jane that he is "cold," and she retorts, "Whereas I am hot, and fire dissolves ice" (338)—ostensibly with reference to her desire to share with him and his sisters her inheritance from John Eyre, but reflecting their personal emotions as well. Her statement, "fire dissolves ice," makes it clear that there is "no contest" between the fiery Rochester and the icy Rivers. She tells Rivers that, even though no one else may ever love her (so low is her view of herself), she scorns his idea of marriage. She echoes what Rochester has said to her, in telling Rivers, "I cannot marry you and become a part of you" (359).

Some readers wonder why Jane could not accompany him to India with a form only of marriage—the kind of companionate marriage Virginia Woolf had. But Rivers makes it clear that, little as she attracts him sexually, he will demand of her all the conjugal duties. Jane thinks, "Can I receive from him the bridal ring, endure all the forms of love (which I doubt not he would scrupulously observe) and know that the spirit was quite absent?" (356). She is absolutely correct in her estimate of him, for he refers to "our *physical* and mental union in marriage" (358; emphasis mine), and Jane fears him most when he adds, "undoubtedly enough of love would follow upon marriage to render the union right even in your eyes" (359).[45] Jane does indeed fear that she might arrive at a "strange, torturing kind of love for him." He would demand her conjugal duties as a sure means of riveting her to him—an unconsummated marriage could be dissolved on legal grounds. There is an unconscious nastiness in Rivers—he does not treat Jane as an equal, but would mistrust her as a sister were she to accompany him only in that capacity. She insists on freedom, and he presses her: "... a sister might any day be taken from me. I want a wife: the sole helpmeet I can influence efficiently in life and retain absolutely till death" (397). Not Rochester, but Rivers, is the tyrant, a monster of male egoism. Jane sees, as he admits, that he is "cold, hard, ambitious," and Jane it is who compares him to "a cold, cumbrous column" (346).

Jane does not question his missionary zeal, as a twentieth-century writer like Jean Rhys might have done had she dealt with that portion of the work. Charlotte

---

44   Lest we miss the point, Austen parallels Darcy's proposal to that of the manifestly absurd Mr. Collins, also directed to the unlucky Elizabeth.

45   W.A. Craik is right in commenting that, among his defects, he shows poor taste in women, preferring Rosamond to Jane (99).

Brontë, and Jane herself, remain within Anglocentric and Christian boundaries.[46] As the daughter of a clergyman, living in his household, any reservations or criticisms she had about the Church had to be expressed obliquely. Perhaps through Rivers, she is able to hint at some of her misgivings.[47] Misery and poverty are everywhere in evidence in *Jane Eyre*, especially at Lowood, and surely Charlotte Brontë, and one would hope Jane Eyre, are aware that there is enough to do in England without imposing Christianity on people with religions of their own.

Jane recognizes full well that Rivers' missionary zeal is a sublimation of his libido. She associates him with "ice" and "avalanche." One thinks of Robert Frost's poem "Fire and Ice":

> Some say the world will end in fire,
> Some say in ice.
> From what I've tasted of desire
> I hold with those who favor fire.
> But if it had to perish twice,
> I think I know enough of hate
> To say that for destruction ice
> Is also great
> And would suffice.

She fears "to rush down the torrent of his will into the gulf of his existence, and there lose my own" (368).

*The Ending: Ambiguity*

One can only assume that the concluding paean to Rivers in the last two paragraphs of the novel reflects an uneasy Charlotte Brontë who fears she has taken her love story too far, beyond Christian bounds, and probably wishes to placate her traditional, thoroughly Victorian father. Her father, Richard Chase tells, is supposed to have "fired pistols out of the back door, ... and torn to bits the only silk dress of his wife as she lay dying of cancer after bearing her sixth child in seven years," and her brother Branwell, "dying of alcohol and opium, ... sank down among the tombstones of

---

46   Charlotte does not hesitate later, however, to criticize the Church of England quite virulently through her comic portrait of the three young curates in *Shirley*: "Let England's priests have their due: they are a faulty set in some respects, being only of common flesh and blood, like us all; but the land would be badly off without them: Britain would miss her church, if that church fell. God save it! God also reform it!" (298). She does, however, temper this criticism with portraits of devoted clergymen to offset those of the curates and of the tyrannical Reverend Helstone.

47   Charles Dickens, in *Bleak House*, was to point a finger of scorn at the ludicrous attempts of a supposedly benevolent Christian like Mrs. Jellyby to "civilize" the supposed savages in Africa, while her own family tumbles downstairs, the children get their heads stuck in the railing, the cook gets drunk and serves raw food, and envelopes fall into the gravy.

Haworth Churchyard, armed with a kitchen knife in case he should meet the Devil" (463).[48]

The other difficulty with the ending resides in Rochester's maiming which some critics have seen as not only a punishment inflicted by the author, but a symbolic castration. Jane is now in power, these critics argue, and Rochester is abased, humiliated. As Jane hears from the former butler at Thornfield, "… one eye was knocked out, and one hand so crushed that Mr. Carter, the surgeon, had to amputate it directly. The other eye inflamed: he lost sight of that also. He is now helpless indeed—blind and a cripple" (378).[49] Earlier, in Chapter XXVII, when Jane is trying to tear herself away from Rochester, she alludes to the Biblical punishment for adultery: "… you shall, yourself, pluck out your right eye: yourself cut off your right hand: your heart shall be the victim; and you, the priest, to transfix it" (261). While Jane is engaged in a dialogue with her own soul, and is foreseeing her own punishment were she to remain with Rochester, it is Rochester who is to enact the Biblical prophecy of doom. He admits to Jane after she returns from the Rivers', "I am no better than the old lightning-struck chestnut-tree in Thornfield orchard" (391). G. Armour Craig recaps the castration theory, only to refute it: "The destruction of Rochester's strong hand and volcanic eyes, which has been called, no doubt rightly, a castration symbol, is monstrously prepared for in the paraphrase of a passage from the Sermon on the Mount with which Jane decides what she must do after learning that Rochester is married …" (477). Craig notes that, whatever the sexual implications, Jane is finally in power, "but the price of her mastery is absolute isolation," and that the novel illustrates "the demon of the absolute" (478).[50]

I would underline the fact, however, that Charlotte Brontë has deliberately modified the Biblical punishment, for it is Mr. Rochester's *left* eye and hand,[51] not his *right*, which are injured (though Jane does describe herself as "his right hand") (397).

---

48   Juliet Barker's 1994 biography, *The Brontës*, does, however, cast considerable doubt on this popular reading of the Reverend Patrick Brontë as Victorian domestic tyrant. Barker quotes his defense of himself to Mrs. Gaskell, saying, "He made an interesting defence which, incidentally, reveals him to have been a reader of Mrs. Gaskell's novels and to have shared his children's delight in satire." The Reverend Patrick writes, "The Book-making gentry whose little works I have seen, appear to make me a somewhat extraordinary and eccentrick personage I have no great objection to this, admitting they can make a penny by it. But the truth of the matter is—that I am, in some repects, a kindred likeness to the father of Margaret, in 'North and South.' peaceable, feeling, sometimes thoughtful—and generally well-meaning" (792).

49   See, for instance, Ralph Ellison's *Invisible Man* (1952) with its pun on eyeballs–balls—male genitals. He refers at one point to "balling the jack" when his hero fantasizes about the castration / blinding of the black race as emblematic of genocide by the white majority culture. Ellison is, to be sure, very consciously influenced by Freudian psychology, and blinding was the Oedipal punishment for incest.

50   Robert B. Martin argues that the movement of the novel is towards religious redemption, not sexuality: "It does not seem to me too revolutionary to feel that sin, suffering, and redemption may loom larger than sexual rivalry in Christian thought" (488). Barbara Hardy, however, feels that "*Jane Eyre* … is not a novel about religious conversion, and perhaps this is to be regretted" (490).

51   In heraldry the bend sinister is a sign of illegitimacy, so perhaps the maiming on the left side signals Rochester's earlier promiscuity.

And it is his *right* eye which is eventually salvageable (384)—in partial mitigation of his punishment, for he has not really committed adultery (at least not with Jane)? Moreover, while blinded, Rochester is certainly not rendered impotent. Much is made of his hard muscularity and virility, just as when he first appears to Jane on his horse, and Brontë seems to be, rather, striking a balance between male and female power by showing Jane as the rescuer in both instances (and elsewhere). Rochester remains strong, far from emasculated, a blinded Samson perhaps: "The muscular hand broke from my [Jane's] custody; my arm was seized, my shoulder—neck—waist—I was entwined and gathered to him" (382). His physical strength is emphasized—Jane sits on his lap. But Charlotte Brontë *is* reversing the reader's expectation of the usual romance novel. The first thing Jane announces to Rochester is "I am come back to you," but the second is "I am an independent woman now" (382). Not for Jane the reward of an upward-mobile marriage like Pamela's, but rather a marriage based on independence and free choice. The scales are evenly balanced, and the marriage is a partnership. This would not have been the case earlier, when he tries to dress her "like a doll" (236), or wants to attach her to a chain (figuratively speaking) and wear her in his bosom (238). At that point, like Mary Wollstonecraft before her, she protests, "I'll not stand you an inch in the stead of a seraglio" (236). Again, he refers disparagingly to the hypothetical "tons of [female] flesh" he will purchase, and Jane threatens "to go out as a missionary to preach liberty to them that are enslaved" (237). Jane's threat also curiously foreshadows Rivers' attempt to co-opt her into a missionary role with him, and she refuses again the "pagan" role (as she sees it) of the Hindu wife who would be burned on her husband's funeral pyre (the suttee).[52]

*Jane's Art: From the Heart*

Jane does not write her book to master her world, to break out of total isolation, like Lucy Snowe. Rather, she is freed to write only when she can share her painful journey towards happiness and Christian reconciliation with those of us who may be *Jane's* doubles, not Bertha's: "Reader, I married him." If the novel begins with Jane Eyre's book being flung as a weapon at John Reed's head, it ends with Jane Rochester's book, the book that she has written, directed more gently and compellingly at the reader, at a more appreciative and receptive public that will be complicitous, rather than compelled against its will.

While Jane Eyre's sketches were products of a solitary imagination, private, yearning for human intercourse, her verbal art, her manuscript, is grounded in social intercourse, in her movement from solitude towards integration. George Eliot's Dorothea Brooke was to speculate that "if she had written a book she must have done it as Saint Theresa did, under the command of an authority that constrained her conscience" (*Mid.* 64). According to the convention in which Charlotte Brontë creates, her heroine writes a book out of the constraints of her conscience *and* her

---

52  Adrienne Rich sees Jane as marrying into a radical marriage for her time (469). Walter Allen notes Jane's "triumph in the battle of the sexes" (216). Charles Burkhart and John Maynard associate Jane's sexuality with Charlotte's in their psychobiographies, while Tom Winnifrith, on the other hand, tends to downplay the autobiographical elements.

heart. In so doing, she emerges from the private sphere and speaks to other women over a span of many generations, and that is the triumph of the book, for its heroine's creative consciousness surpasses that of Richardson's Pamela, while borrowing from it, integrating the personal and the "universally" human.

## Charlotte Brontë: Only a Women's Novelist?

For those like Lewes and Cecil who criticize Charlotte Brontë's vision as *too* feminine, it is worth noting her probable influence on that American celebrant of male bonding and brotherhood, Herman Melville (1819–91). His conscientious Captain in the posthumously published *Billy Budd* (1891) is named Edward Fairfax Vere (after Edward Fairfax Rochester). "Vere" is usually taken to imply "verity" or truth, but it is also the name of Georgiana Reed's suitor, Lord Edwin Vere, in *Jane Eyre* (208). As Melville writes:

> Captain the Honorable Edward Fairfax Vere, to give him his full title, was a bachelor of forty or thereabouts, a sailor of distinction even in a time prolific of renowned seamen. Though allied to the higher nobility his advancement had not been altogether owing to influence connected with that circumstance. He had seen much service, been in various engagements, always acquitting himself as an officer mindful of the welfare of his men, but never tolerating an infraction of discipline; thoroughly versed in the science of his profession, and intrepid to the verge of temerity, though never injudiciously so. (306–7)

We are told that Vere had "a marked leaning towards everything intellectual. He loved books, never going to sea without a newly replenished library, compact but of the best" (308). He must hang the young impressed sailor Billy Budd,[53] who has inadvertently struck out at, and killed, the demonic first mate Claggart, even though Billy is "angelic" in Vere's eyes (364). Billy is compared to Adam before the Fall, "ere the urbane Serpent wriggled himself into his company" (299). Billy strikes the serpentine first-mate only because he stutters under pressure and cannot respond verbally to a charge of treason (300). Vere is aristocratic in origin and, like Rochester, has sown some wild oats in his time. It is implied that one of these could be Billy, whose parentage is unknown: "Yes; Billy Budd was a foundling, a presumable bye-blow, and, evidently, no ignoble one. Noble descent was as evident in him as in a blood horse" (298). There was in him, too, "something suggestive of a mother evidently favored by Love and the Graces; all this strangely indicated a lineage in direct contradiction to his lot" (298). But the angel, possibly Vere's son, must hang in the name of naval discipline.

At one point, when Billy is speechless faced with Claggart's accusation of treason, Vere encourages the young man with "words so *fatherly* in tone" (344; emphasis mine). After Claggart's death the Surgeon notes that Vere's reaction is "unwonted agitation … and his excited exclamations so at variance with his normal manner. Was he unhinged?" (346). We are also reminded that Vere "was old enough to have

---

53   Billy is impressed from a merchant ship called the *Rights-of-Man* with its explicit reference to Thomas Paine and the American Revolution (295).

been Billy's father," and he is compared to an Abraham rescuing "young Isaac on the brink of resolutely offering him up in obedience to the exacting behest" (359). When Vere dies of his wounds in a naval engagement, his last words are "Billy Budd, Billy Budd": "That these were not the accents of remorse, would seem clear from what the attendant said to the *Indomitable*'s senior officer of marines who as the most reluctant to condemn of the members of the drumhead court, too well knew though here he kept the knowledge to himself, who Billy Budd was" (373).

That Melville had been reading *Jane Eyre* seems clear, and it explains an otherwise extraneous passage in *Billy Budd* on the Gothic, and specifically the "female Gothic" of Mrs. Radcliffe. This passage also embodies a critique of society's false morality:

> Now to invent something touching the more private career of Claggart, something involving Billy Budd, of which something the latter should be wholly ignorant, some romantic incident implying that Claggart's knowledge of the young blue-jacket began at some period anterior to catching sight of him on board the seventy-four—all this, not so difficult to do, might avail in a way more or less interesting to account for whatever enigma may appear to lurk in the case. But in fact there was nothing of the sort. And yet the cause, necessarily to be assumed as the sole one assignable, is in its very realism as much charged with that prime element of Radcliffean romance, the *mysterious*, as any that the ingenuity of the author of the *Mysteries of Udolpho* could devise. For what can more partake of the mysterious than an antipathy spontaneous and profound such as is evoked in certain exceptional mortals by the mere aspect of some other mortal, however blameless he may be? if not called forth by this very harmlessness itself. (319)

Melville could almost be describing Brontë's "New Gothic," a Gothic consonant with reality.[54] Already in 1852, the Enceladus Stone-Titans episode of his novel *Pierre* echoed Shirley Keeldar's invented mythology, in Charlotte Bronte's *Shirley* (1849), of female Titans trying to storm heaven.[55]

Another perhaps surprising possible influence Charlotte Brontë had on a male writer usually perceived as quintessentially masculine is that on the slightly younger (than Brontë and Melville) Count Leo Tolstoy. The story with a *Jane Eyre* plot

---

54   It is perhaps not too surprising to anyone who recognizes the influence of female writers on Melville that his wished-for relationship with the older Nathaniel Hawthorne (wished for by Melville, not Hawthorne) should be a subject for queer theory (like the relationship between Ishmael and Queequeg in *Moby Dick*). Edwin Haviland Miller's 1975 biography of Melville discusses this subject at length. Claggart's attraction / repulsion towards Billy, whose beauty is described in "female" terms, may stem from Claggart's sexual ambivalence.

55   The Titans were turned to stone, imprisoned in earth, as their punishment. Charlotte and Emily Brontë's pervasive use of stone imagery reflects the realities of Yorkshire life, whose primary building material is the plentiful stone. But the stone also affords a suggestive symbol of emotional starvation and petrification, to be combatted by the writing of women who dip their pens into their hearts. In Melville it is a *male* artist, also alienated by definition, who identifies with the Titans trying to storm heaven only to be buried in the earth. The hero's name, Pierre, literally means stone and echoes Saint Peter, the "rock" on which Christ built his church. Both male and female novelists, interestingly, have had to blend Christian and pagan mythology to develop an appropriate symbology—both, because of exclusions—of the female from the traditional chruch, of the artist from society. Thus the female artist suffers a double exclusion.

imbedded in it is *Happy Ever After* (1859), not coincidentally the only Tolstoy work which employs a female narrator. The narrative is actually split between two female voices, the narrator-heroine and her governess, but the latter's is for the most part silenced; both of these characters evoke Jane Eyre.

I have found no direct evidence of Tolstoy's reading of *Jane Eyre*,[56] but he claimed that the best novels were English.[57] And certainly *Jane Eyre*, with its governess theme, was much in the air at the time.

*Happy Ever After* was written about a decade after *Jane Eyre*, and is therefore very early Tolstoy. Masha, the heroine, resembles the young Jane, and the governess Katya's situation is close to Jane's. The novella starts with an attempt at *integration—* ideal marriage for Masha and Sergei. This attempt leads to *disintegration—*of

---

56   Some of his correspondence does suggest his familiarity with Victorian literature. A.N. Wilson mentions in his biography *Tolstoy* that his cousin Alexandra served as a kind of mentor to him in the winter of 1857–58. On his moral aspirations, she quoted to him a sentence of Charlotte Brontë's: "Do not think I am good: I only wish to be so" (151). R.F. Christian notes that Tolstoy read *The Contemporary*, which offered in translation a number of autobiographical works from European literature:

> Tolstoy, as a regular reader of *The Contemporary*, must have read many of the numerous works of an autobiographical nature which appeared in the original or in translation in that journal during the late 1840s and early 1850s. Translations from West European literature included Goethe's *Wilhelm Meister*, Lamartine's *Confessions*, Charlotte Brontë's *Jane Eyre*, Andersen's *Story of My Life*, Chateaubriand's *Mémoires d'outre-tombe* and Dickens's *David Copperfield*. Of the two best accounts of childhood in nineteenth-century English fiction, *Jane Eyre* and *David Copperfield*, Tolstoy certainly read the latter before his own *Childhood* was published. (27–8)

Christian does not discuss the possibility that Tolstoy may also have read *Jane Eyre*, nor does he connect it to *Happy Ever After*, but certainly the catalogue of autobiographical texts supports the possibility. John Bayley is the only critic I have found who does mention a possible borrowing from *Jane Eyre* in *Family Happiness*:

> There are often disproportionate elements in Tolstoy's tales, as if a sculptor had had to add diminutive limbs to a great torso. This "making it small" is one of the troubles in *Family Happiness*. The other is Tolstoy's notion of borrowing from *Jane Eyre*, which he had read and admired, a female narrator. The vitality of Jane Eyre comes from her being so powerfully and exclusively herself; no imaginative transposition is involved. Tolstoy compels his narrator and centre of consciousness to be the kind of ideal girl whom he feels would suit him, while he himself takes up, as it were, the position of Rochester. (288)

He makes no further mention of *Jane Eyre* or of Brontë. I had not read Bayley before noticing the resemblance between the two texts, and working them up in this form. Bayley does not explore the governess theme, nor the undermining of the far from ideal female narrator. I have so far been unable to locate where Tolstoy makes overt reference to *Jane Eyre*.

57   He felt that the best of these was George Eliot's *Middlemarch* (1870–71), which was available in Russian translation in the 1870s. Eliot's biographer-critic Gordon Haight has argued that there is room for a full-length study of the influence of *Middlemarch* on Tolstoy's domestic tragedy *Anna Karenin* (1875–77).

romantic love in the case of Masha (about Sergei I am less sure). It ends on a note of *re-integration*, or regeneration—in the case of Masha, of a happiness that lies beyond romantic love, in Christian marriage and maturity. The pattern is that of *Jane Eyre*: love, disillusionment, Christian marriage. It is a story which concerns families, and one thinks of Tolstoy's remark in *Anna Karenin*, "all happy families are alike but an unhappy family is unhappy after its own fashion" (13). Anna and Karenin, Masha and Sergei constitute two unhappy families, each in its own way. Is there such a thing as happiness in this story? Certainly, *Happy Ever After* uses the word in its title, and the words "happy" and "happiness" recur frequently in the text. Tolstoy the romantic idealist wants to believe in the possibility of happiness on the human level. Tolstoy the Christian mystic tends to treat marriage rather as Samuel Richardson does in *Pamela* or Charlotte Brontë in *Jane Eyre*: as a way-station, a temporary resting-place on the way to the ideal love: that of human beings for their Creator. We might compare Masha's idealized notion of romantic love with that of Anna Karenin or of Flaubert's Emma Bovary. Love and death in *Madame Bovary* or *Anna Karenin* and *Happy Ever After* seem to be at opposite ends of the scale. But are they really? Both imply absolute union, and Pamela, Jane, Emma, Anna, and Masha, each in her own way, discover that human love is not, and cannot be, the ultimate reality, whether the result is fusion with God, as in the case of Pamela and Jane, or dissolution, as in the case of Emma and Anna, who have throughout confused Christian ecstasy and carnal desires.

The title is usually rendered as *Family Happiness*, or *Domestic Happiness*, but *Happy Ever After*—shouldn't it be "Happily Ever After"?—suggests the fairy-tale vision of Masha at the inception of the narrative. This is the only Tolstoy narrative to be told from a first-person *female* point of view (though certainly we are planted inside Anna Karenin's mind at moments when she becomes the central consciousness, but never the narrator). The technique is that of the quintessential subjective novel, *Jane Eyre*.[58]

The date of the tale is 1859, a crucial year in the western world. The United States was about to be plunged into the Civil War of the 1860s, and Russian writers were quick to detect the analogy between the plight of the serfs in their own land and the slaves in the United States. Britain's role in the slave trade had been already underlined by Jane Austen in *Mansfield Park* (1814). In *Jane Eyre* the context is colonization of the West Indies, based on slavery, the world Jean Rhys was to reveal from the inside in *Wide Sargasso Sea*. In Britain—and Tolstoy was an Anglophile

---

58 Tolstoy's experiment brings to mind the novelist Reynolds Price's article in the *New York Times Book Review* in which he claimed that *male* writers, such as Flaubert, Tolstoy, and Henry James, succeed much better at creating great female consciousnesses than *female* writers—such as Charlotte Brontë, George Eliot, Willa Cather, Toni Morrison—do in creating *male* consciousnesses. He goes on to claim that male writers are more successful because they know what female sexuality is, whereas female writers are clueless as to the male sex drive. He seems to be assuming the double standard: males sleep around with impunity, and females do not. The nature of Flaubert's and James's sexuality has long been problematic, and Tolstoy is not exactly the best example of a role model for the sexually active male. We are entitled to ask whether Tolstoy's "psychology is brilliant" in creating Masha, as Rosemary Edmonds suggests in her introduction to the Penguin edition, or whether it is sentimental.

in his literary and intellectual tastes—1859 was the year of publication of Darwin's *Origin of Species* whose theory of evolution was to rock the foundations of traditional Christian faith and which was soon to be applied to the social organism as well by Herbert Spencer's "Social Darwinism" in *First Principles* (1862).[59]

The social and intellectual ferment of 1859 is reflected in the background of Tolstoy's novella, but it is not foregrounded as it will be later in the panoramic novels, *War and Peace* (1862–69) and *Anna Karenin* (1875–77). Tolstoy's title page, however, describes *Happy Ever After* as a novel. Why? Was it intended as a mini-*Anna Karenin* before Tolstoy was ready to write such a vast social panorama? Particularly the second part is peopled with characters from the great world "out there," who are described only as Princess D, the Prince, Lady S., an Italian marquis, who are never fleshed out or fully developed but seem to wander in and out at random. At times it seems more of a notebook entry for a novel than a novel itself. Did Tolstoy simply tire of it? Or had he not fully assimilated as yet the intellectual currents of the 1850s and '60s throughout Europe in order to weave them into a vast social canvas? In *Anna Karenin* Sergei was to become Alexei Karenin the cuckolded husband, the Italian marquis the seductive Vronsky, and so on, as the social canvas expanded. Or perhaps the point of view technique restricting it to the consciousness of a heroine who is only 17 years old at the outset confines it within psychological bounds, whereas the older Sergei's perspective, who deals with the serfs and matters of government, remains enigmatic as he presses Masha to educate herself. Yet the *Jane Eyre*-ish first part is more successful than the second part in which Sergei is given to lengthy moralizing and editorializing, and becomes only a spokesman for Tolstoy. Perhaps the real problem is not the psychological limitations of the opening part, but the fact that Masha, who has led a charmed existence, lacks the complexity of a Jane Eyre who has had to struggle to survive. Here the governess-figure, Katya, is essential to complete the picture.

In Part One Masha introduces herself as a lonely girl of 17 at Pokrovskoe; she is now completely orphaned and mourning her mother. We can compare her to Jane Eyre, or to Emma Bovary, who is also raised without a mother's influence, or to James's Isabel Archer. Her only companions are a younger sister, Sonya, still a child, and the older Katya, her governess, who can function as a mother surrogate only

---

59   On the literary scene, Darwinism, and particularly Social Darwinism, was to lead to the Naturalism of Émile Zola in France and of Gissing and, to a certain extent, Hardy in England, Crane, Dreiser, and Frank Norris in the United States. In 1959 the Victorian Studies group at Indiana University published a book called *1859: Entering an Age of Crisis*, that "age of crisis" being the world we face today. It also happened to be the year of publication, in England, of George Eliot's first full-length novel, *Adam Bede*, looking back at the end of pastoral England and the beginnings of industrialization; of J.S. Mill's classic essay *On Liberty* asserting the rights of man; and the aptly named Samuel Smiles' *Self-Help* which offered a rationale for "rugged individualism" and self-reliance, of which the flip side, of course, is no charity and no philanthropy for the factory workers and lower classes who are unable to "raise themselves by their bootstraps." All this gives the context of the novels of Turgenev, Dostoyevsky, and Tolstoy, all very aware of changing social concerns elsewhere in the world, and of the plight of the serfs, peasants, and, at least in the case of Dostoyevsky, of the urban poor at home.

up to a certain point as she is, after all, an upper servant with no real influence or disciplinary powers.

Almost the first thing Masha tells us about herself is that she is pretty—or so everyone tells her—"wasting a second winter in the solitude of the country" (13). Like Richardson's Pamela, and unlike the self-reliant plain Jane Eyre, she needs to report the praise of others to establish her qualifications as a heroine. Like *Jane Eyre*, this is a *Bildungsroman*, a novel of an education (as *Madame Bovary* is perhaps a *Bildungsroman* turned inside out, or upended). The hero who is to release her from "that lonely backwater" (14) is a kind of mentor, a much older man, 36 to her 17, Sergei Mihailovich. He is, in fact, her guardian, and therefore in a position of power over her. Their relationship bears a distinct similarity to that of Jane Eyre and Mr. Rochester, 37 to her 18, her employer if not her guardian, but also with complete power over the orphaned girl. Rochester, too, is a burly, not very attractive man, but with considerable animal magnetism. Masha admits from the start that Sergei is not the man of her dreams, that the latter is obviously derived, like Emma Bovary's, from her readings of popular romances: "... the hero of my dreams was quite different. My hero was slight, lean, pale and melancholy, whereas Sergei Mihailovich was no longer in his first youth, was tall and thickset and, it seemed to me, always cheerful" (14). Her love for him seems to stem more from their situation than from any preconceptions of romantic love—whereas we need to read between the lines to guess at the source of his "love" for her. She is to ask later, was he only in love with her youth and beauty? ... and he never quite answers.

Her early uncertainty about him, his failure to conform to her romantic preconceptions of the White Knight or Prince Charming, valorizes his hesitation in courting her, his insistence on not putting pressure on her. But it also foreshadows their on-and-off relations in Part Two when Masha demonstrates what Marcel Proust, in the twentieth century, was to call "*les intermittances du cœur*," the vacillations of the heart, or what Stendhal earlier, in "*De l'Amour*," refers to as the "crystallization" and "decrystallization" of romantic love, exemplified in his own Julien Sorel and Mathilde de la Mole in *Red and Black* (1832) who, as Martin Turnell remarked, are almost never in the same mood at the same time (163). These vacillations are particularly noticeable in the Masha and Sergei of Part Two.

Not only is their love at first situational, but it is also closely linked to the cycle of the seasons and to plant imagery, suggesting something natural and intuitive that is perhaps bound to change with time. As we have seen, Charlotte Brontë also parallels nature and the passions of her characters, but perhaps in the final analysis more mystically and positively. Sergei addresses Masha as "my young violet that smells of melting snow and spring grass" (31), suggesting her shyness and naivety. But this image contrasts with his greeting to her after seeing her for the first time as an adult; she is "a rose in full bloom" (15). I would raise the question whether he is any wiser than she in these initial dealings, whether he really knows what he is after, any more than Rochester does when he tries to dress Jane as a doll. He wants *her* to make decisions, yet she is only capable of them after being shaped by him. He is a kind of Pygmalion who falls in love with his own creation: I am reminded of Rochester's playacting and manipulations in *Jane Eyre*.[60] Sergei talks "like a father or an uncle" (18), but she also sees him as "this good man who was not a member of the family" (16)—indeed, the only outsider she encounters at Pokrovskoe, just as Rochester is the first male "outsider" Jane meets after Lowood.

He takes himself off to Moscow, presumably to escape temptation, saying only "don't mope" (19). But, in keeping with the cyclical nature of their romance he returns in spring, indeed the merry month of May, the month of courtship, the month of Mary. His arrival is unexpected, like Rochester's return in *Jane Eyre*, and is associated with the moon—we can compare to Tolstoy's both Charlotte Brontë's and D.H. Lawrence's use of the moon, symbol of the female, the White Goddess of Robert Graves, sexuality.[61] Masha has impressed him earlier by playing the Moonlight Sonata to display her "women's accomplishments," and will play it again later to effect their reconciliation. Jane Eyre also displays her sketches and plays piano at Rochester's request. In retrospect, now, Masha is "looking back" to understand, defining the narrative as a retrospective autobiography like *Jane Eyre*, analyzing the dreams of her younger self, "so strange and so far removed from reality" (20).

One of the ways in which Tolstoy succeeds in presenting a convincingly female narrative is in his descriptions of food, the cream tart and special spinach sauce Katya prepares for Sergei's dinner (15), the hissing samovar with "cracknel biscuits, cream and cakes" (20). When Virginia Woolf's *A Room of One's Own* makes a point of contrasting the delicious food served at the men's college with the women's college's tough beef and yellowed brussels sprouts, her subtended "message" is that the men get to eat the fabulous food, but only a woman knows how to describe it! Tolstoy may be a notable exception to the rule, along with Proust and E.M. Forster.

But Tolstoy also seems at times to have adopted a female narrator only to undermine her, and to imply that the cryptic male, Sergei, modeled on himself, has all the final answers, and is indeed rather sententious about them.[62] But another way

---

60    I am also reminded of the old James Mason, Ann Todd film, *The Seventh Veil*, in which the much older guardian tyrannizes over his charge, relentlessly training her to be a concert pianist, only to fall in love with her.

61    See Robert B. Heilman's article on Charlotte Brontë's use of the moon as symbol; he feels that her treatment of it is inconsistent in *Jane Eyre*.

62    The only critical article I found on *Domestic Happiness* (the alternate translation), Renato Poggioli's "Tolstoy's *Domestic Happiness*: Beyond Pastoral Love" (1975), seems to lend credibility to my view. In 1856, while waiting for his army discharge, Tolstoy met a wealthy orphan, Valeria Arseneva, near Yasnay Polyana. He became her legal tutor (398). Their relationship became, in Poggioli's words, "less than a troth and more than a flirt" (399). He considered marriage, and when the plans never materialized, he tried to exculpate himself for his involvement with a much younger woman. As Poggioli writes, "… he sought both solace and revenge by composing a story to prove to his and everyone else's satisfaction that, had he wed the girl, the marriage would have ended in failure, or turned out to be a mistake, and that the bride alone would have been responsible for such an outcome" (399). It was composed in 1858 and published in 1859. He once described it as "a shameful abomination" and thought of destroying the manuscript (399). The French novelist Romain Rolland evidently confused the heroine with Sonia Bers, Tolstoy's future wife. His biographers, A.N. Wilson and Martine de Courcel, have discussed his less than gallant treatment of Sonia. During their engagement he evidently showed

he has of undermining not only Masha's narrative but also and especially Sergei's point of view, is through the character of Katya the governess, who is a foil to Masha and might have her own tale to tell, like the underestimated Jane Eyre. If *Jane Eyre* is the master narrative, the tale is as much the governess's as Masha's. It is Katya who suggests to Sergei, "You would make a fine husband" (22).[63] He is 36 years old, as Katya also seems to be. We surmise that they are much of an age when he replies to her, "No, Katerina Karlovna, too late for you or me to marry" (22). Does she live vicariously through Masha by promoting the marriage? Katya and Masha even sleep in the same room. If Bertha is in some ways a double for Jane Eyre, Katya may well be a double for Masha. At some point Masha realizes that Katya "was under no obligation to be the mother, friend and slave to us that she was" (27). The word "happy" has a different meaning for Katya than for her: "… she always told me that she, too, wished for nothing and was very happy, and she kissed me" (27). It is also Katya who may be uttering a personal lament, as well as expressing general received wisdom, when she asserts, "A man can say that he is in love, but a woman can't" (33). We remember Jane Eyre's recourse to sketching Blanche Ingram and herself in order to keep silence and remember how the world disregards her. Katya is a Jane Eyre whose love story never happens, because Sergei, unlike Rochester with Jane, never really sees her, despite similarity of age, taste, and shared interests. In fact, Sergei constantly looks at Masha, but talks to Katya.[64]

This debate on the silencing of women takes place between Katya and Sergei; the younger Masha is only a silent observer, sensing that "this banter contained something serious relating to me" (34). Sergei makes fun of romance heroes, but Katya defends them (34). We must recall that Katya has been Masha's first official mentor(ess?), but now the dominant male takes over. Masha seems to see Katya aging before her eyes as the latter witnesses Masha's happiness: "Poor thing, why

---

her explicitly sexual passages in his bachelor diary. Michael Ignatieff remarks that "she never really recovered" (22). Ignatieff also calls *The Kreutzer Sonata* an "unpardonable jeremiad against married love" (22). In 1910, at the age of 82, he ran away from home, abandoning wife and family, and died in a railway station 150 kilometers from home.

Poggioli refers to *Domestic Happiness* as "a little masterpiece," but "an ambiguous creation" (399). He reads the first part as "pastoral romance," the second as "realistic fiction" (400). Although Masha remains the narrator of Part Two, it nonetheless "may seem to present the outlook of the masculine partner," for, according to Poggioli, "Tolstoy took on in this story the mask of his heroine to proclaim the rights of man" (400). While this may have been the author's conscious intention, I would argue that there is an unconscious subtext in which, in both Parts One and Two, it is the male outlook which is being undermined, and that this is being done through the "ghost novel" of the governess, combined with the naive point of view of Masha. Such a reading also helps explain why, for most readers, Part One is far more successful, while Part Two has a sketchy, improvised air, as though Tolstoy simply wanted to be finished with it.

63   Poggioli discounts Katya, saying that the sister Sonya and the governess, "who is an elderly woman, count for little in the story" (401). This is a serious error about Katya's age: governesses were generally retired long before they became elderly, and whether or not they could afford it. If we overestimate her age, we also miss her importance in the narrative.

64   Jane Austen's Colonel Brandon, in *Sense and Sensibility*, similarly, comes to visit Marianne Dashwood with whom he is supposedly in love, and sits staring at her in dumb admiration, but talks instead to her older sister Elinor.

doesn't she feel the way we do? ... Why isn't everyone young and happy, like this night and like him and me?" (38). Ironically, Sergei is not young, any more than Katya is. If Masha's name is Marya, the Virgin Mary, whose holiday is the Feast of the Assumption, Katya's is Katerina, Saint Catherine, the patron saint of spinsters.[65]

Masha thinks Katya wants to delay the wedding for a trip to Moscow in order to assemble a proper trousseau (47), and considers that Katya believes that Sergei's and Masha's "future happiness" was contingent on the stitching of underwear and hemming of table linen. But Katya may be herself in love with Sergei, and also prolonging her own youth by delaying, recollecting painfully that she herself will never have a trousseau. Why exactly *are* "the tears rolling down her [Katya's] cheeks" at the wedding? (54). Not only is she losing a surrogate daughter, but perhaps also her own last chance at happiness.

Katya also marks the passage of time in the novel. We meet her again in Part Two, but only briefly at the end with Sonya: "... Katya has grown wrinkled and yellow, her eyes no longer sparkle with joy and hope ..." (89). This is true of the older Sergei as well, but also of Masha who has recently heard herself compared somewhat unfavorably to the blooming English rose, the 19-year-old Lady S.

Once Sergei takes over Masha's education from Katya—or her re-education—he "teaches" her to fall in love with himself, not with a romance hero. He brings out her religiosity and desire for self-sacrifice—one thinks of Emma Bovary's charitable excesses with the beggars when she is frustrated in love. Masha donates anonymously for the funeral of the serf Simon's daughter (41), fixates on "the two angels with stars" and "the dove with the golden halo" (40), as Emma Bovary does on the Host and the crucifix. She reads the Gospel and asks her enemies to forgive her. She asks about all her servants, "Why are they all so good to me? What have I done to deserve their love?" (42). The old woman "with her toothless gums" and Christian faith appears like a chorus figure, reminiscent of the blind beggar in Flaubert (40).

Sergei has begun by developing her taste in music and in reading. Presumably, none of the books he recommends are romances! He teaches her to develop a social conscience about " the people who worked for us, our serfs and servants, and maids ... it had never once occurred to me that they had their affections, longings and sorrows just as I had" (27). We note that this new empathy of hers is never extended to Katya's inner life.

She is at first attracted to Sergei by her own exclusion from the "man's world." But does he ever seek to include her in that world, ranging from the management of the affairs of both the Pokrovskoe and Nikolskoe estates, to local government concerns? Rochester, for different reasons, seeks to keep Jane within the confines of Thornfield. Sergei simply promotes Masha's taste and accomplishments in the women's sphere. He does not, however, praise her appearance, "to be sure that I was devoid of vanity" (25). But she is already vain and only awaits her entrance into the world at the capital, St. Petersburg, to rediscover it. We do not know if Tolstoy thinks Sergei has understood her all along, or whether Tolstoy is reproaching himself for an early mistake in love where he had been manipulative and demanding.

---

65    In France, the ceremony to "*coiffer Sainte Catherine*," to don a special hat in church, officializes the title of old maid.

At one point in her "education" Masha claims to have no thoughts of her own: "I did not know then that this was love ..." (28). Well ... it isn't—it is infatuation, or romantic love (Eros) as defined by De Rougemont in *Love in the Western World* in which two beings try to become one—usually the stronger one!—thereby cancelling out individual will and, in De Rougemont's opinion, leading only to death. We can compare Jane's recognition that she has made Rochester into a false idol.

This "education" is accompanied by a series of love scenes, or near-love scenes, in which appear such leitmotifs as lilacs, the moon, flowers, the Moonlight Sonata. One major scene occurs at harvest time, the season of fertility, and the sexual overtones are unmistakable. Tolstoy shows a strong pictorial sense in describing the peasants bringing in the grain. Manet's "The Gleaners" springs to mind. The haystacks resemble houses with pointed roofs, a foreshadowing of Masha's and Sergei's domesticity. There is a feeling of thunder in the air, charged with heat and lightning. The peasants are perceived idyllically. Sergei says, "The peasants everywhere are such a first-rate lot. The more one knows them, the better one likes them" (31). (One might compare Turgenev's skepticism on this subject in *Fathers and Sons* (1862).) "Work is a holy thing," says Sergei, and Tolstoy agrees with him, as will his alter ego Levin in *Anna Karenin*. Some biographers suspect that Tolstoy's treatment of his wife Sonia is directly traceable to his setting work as his highest priority.

We are told "the cherries shone so juicily and black on the plate" (30), and later Sergei sits in a cherry tree, in a subtly sexual scene. Tolstoy's description is evocative of the garden proposal at Midsummer Eve in *Jane Eyre*. The scene climaxes—and I mean in a sexual sense—when Sergei jumps over the wall of the "walled-in garden" (31). In the medieval Court of Love romance, especially the twelfth-century *Roman de la Rose*, the *hortus clusus*, or "walled-in garden," symbolizes the virginity of the loved one, the "rose." He leaps over the wall to pick some cherries, while Masha stands "on an empty barrel so that the top of the wall was on a level with my waist" (32).[66] Therefore he is not—yet—seeing her figure below the waist.[67]

This scene marks Masha's sexual awakening, as Midsummer Eve does Jane's. Indeed, Sergei later uses the rose image to describe Masha: "You are a child still, a bud that has yet to open" (50). Does he love her youth or her self? she asks. Do they each deceive the other? With her woman's wisdom, she knows he loves her. But in what way? "He was no longer the fond old uncle who spoiled or lectured me," she thinks (32), as Rochester is no longer simply Jane's employer. She notes his mood of "wild delight," a phrase signalled by quotation marks which recurs often in Part One, only negatively (by its absence) in Part Two. Her mood is one of total self-surrender. This is a *"moment privilégié"* in the Sartrean existential sense, or a Stendhalian "crystallization": "... all this must be *crystallized* for ever in its beauty" (37; emphasis mine). But this transformation of reality is by definition ephemeral,

---

66  Poggioli mistakes the movement of this scene, claiming that "the girl climbs on the cherry tree to pick its fruits, while the man watches from below" (405). Actually, just the reverse happens.

67  Henry James was to do something similar in *The Turn of the Screw* (1898) where the governess reports several sightings of the ghost of the corrupt Peter Quint, but never sees him below the waist, always on a rampart or only half-visible.

transitory, subjective. For Jane Eyre, in contrast, it may be permanent, but only after suffering and a difficult passage through to Christian marriage. Tolstoy also makes good use of what Sartre was to call *sous-conversation* to show Masha so attuned to Sergei that she reads his thoughts, as Jane and Rochester do, especially during the garden proposal. He says, "You aren't afraid," "but the words I heard him say were: I love you, darling girl!" (38). At this point the horse, symbol of male sexuality, becomes restless, and the cocks crow three times as if to mark the marriage sacrament forthcoming (or to warn of the demise of love?). She imagines her father at the wedding; has she married a father surrogate? The moon is "frosty" this time, perhaps an ill omen (54). Part One ends, "I was *happy* in his power over me," an ominous sign (55; emphasis mine).

Part Two marks an inevitable disintegration, a challenge to that power and to happiness. It is, however, sketchier and more cursory, perhaps naturally, than Part One. Charlotte Brontë merely summarizes Jane's ten years of marriage. Masha discovers that "There was none of the unremitting toil, the doing of one's duty, the self-sacrifice and living for others" she had pictured before marriage, but only "an entirely absorbing and selfish affection for one another" (56). She spends time with her mother-in-law, has her music and reading, or teaches in the village school (again like Jane at Marsh End), but her only motivation is to please Sergei: "... he was the only being on earth" (56). Obviously, this is a frame of mind that cannot continue. She has no sense of self, and mentions "an old pier-glass, which I was almost too shy to look into at first" (57). We can compare Charlotte Brontë's use of mirrors in *Jane Eyre*.

Sergei warns Masha to be content, that "*le mieux est l'ennemi du bien*" (61), but her dreams and reveries are natural to the young. Sure enough, according to the cycle of the seasons, "winter came with its cold and snow" (61). Is her ennui motivated? Or is Tolstoy suggesting that women are more subject to natural triggers and intuition? In any case boredom sets in because neither of them has anything new to disclose. As the snow piles higher, she discovers that "Loving was not enough for me after the happiness I had known in falling in love" (62). In other words, she was in love with love. She begins to feel "youth and a craving for activity" (62). She wants "a life of challenge." Again, this sounds like Jane Eyre pleading for action, and asserting she can always advertise again.

Sergei is content—"You are my life" (65)—whereas she says, "I don't care to play at life ... I want to live" (65). Warning her, as he has earlier about youthful dreams, he quotes Lermontov:

... and in his madness prays for tempests,
Dreaming in tempests to find peace! (67)

And again he says to her, "If you only knew what you are doing" (66). But in a sense, what else can he expect of a much younger wife?

Following the cycle of the seasons, they spend Christmas in St. Petersburg, where the gulf widens between them. She finds people "nice" whom he criticizes (68). Like Balzac's Rastignac in Paris, in *Père Goriot* (1834), she is a naive stranger in "a new and delightful world" (68).[68] She anticipates Anna Karenin as "the most sought-after woman in society" (68). The ball can be compared to that in *Anna Karenin*, or at La Vaubyessard in *Madame Bovary*, where Emma becomes dizzy, or, in a different sense, the formal party at Thornfield. Sergei tends to sententiousness about society, as Tolstoy's spokesman: "Society in itself is no great harm … but unsatisfied social aspirations are a bad and ugly business" (69). But this is a truth the naive Masha must discover for herself. Masha begins to reinterpret her marital experience: "I endured boredom for his sake in the country," which does not happen to be true, because nothing she does is particularly for his sake—she has little choice. Jane Eyre and Rochester are to end up happy, but in rural isolation at the unhealthy Ferndean, apart from the larger society. Sandra Gilbert argues that their union excludes them from society.

The irony is that St. Petersburg values Masha for "a kind of rural simplicity and charm" (70) which she will soon lose in the city—and indeed has lost by the time of going to the watering-place at Baden. The cycle of the seasons also parallels the religious calendar, and at Easter they are still in St. Petersburg. She thinks Sergei "had always to be a demigod on a pedestal for me [compare Rochester as false idol]" (73)—is the male ego being attacked, or the female? The major rupture occurs over the Prince. She accuses Sergei of jealousy. Her worst betrayal of Sergei, however, is not with the Prince, but with Princess D when she criticizes him to her. She judges now: "In a word he was my husband—and that was all" (79), as in an arranged marriage, which this was not. The births of her two sons (again, like Jane's) are almost presented as an aside, along with the death of her mother-in-law. Death and birth are presented simultaneously with the birth of her first child.

Summer is spent at the spa in Baden, where she learns, by overhearing the Italian marquis and his French friend, that, at 21, she may be taking second place to the 19-year-old English Lady S. The bloom is off the rose. She is tempted to commit adultery with the Italian marquis, like Emma with Rodolphe and Anna with Vronsky, but escapes to her husband who is in Heidelberg.

At the conclusion, Sergei redefines happiness: "perfectly happy I am" (92). What has happened to Masha is called growing up: "Each stage in life has its own kind of love" (94). The dialogue between them does not seem to me much of a resolution. He begins to seem "an old man," "an old friend" to her (96). Yet he utters words of wisdom: "I don't ask for impossibilities … You envy the leaves and the grass because the rain wets them, and you want to be the grass of leaves and the rain" (92). This sounds remarkably like an echo of Flaubert's letter to Louise Colet where he describes himself as becoming the horses, the leaves, the lovers in the forest, when he composes the forest love scene between Emma and Rodolphe. For Flaubert, however, such empathy is a positive and for Sergei romantic nonsense.

Sergei does have the insight to blame himself in part: "Either I ought not to have allowed myself to love you at all, or I ought to have loved you in a simple way" (96). What does he mean? That he really left her no choice after all, and it would have been better to renounce? He (or Tolstoy?) is also condescending when he says,

---

68    Dostoyevsky's "Underground Man" is not so charmed with St. Petersburg, that artificial city dominated by government functionaries.

"... all of us, and *especially you women*, must discover for ourselves all the futilities of life in order to come back to life itself" (95; underlining mine). But what *is* life itself? What are we to make of this? And is maternity supposed to be the answer to a woman's youthful dreams when Masha concludes:

> That day ended the romance of our marriage; what was past became a precious, irrecoverable memory, while a new kind of love for my children and the father of my children laid the foundation of a new life and a quite different *happiness* which I am still enjoying at the present moment ... (97; emphasis mine)

The passage, like the novella, ends in an ellipsis, and begs the question of what <u>is</u> the "present moment"? How old is Masha now? What will she and Sergei do when the children leave the nest?

The contrast is sharp between the woman novelist's, Charlotte Brontë's, knowing, complex use of a female narrator, and Tolstoy's use of a female narrator to support a male point of view, undermining Masha with Sergei. Tolstoy, however, perhaps wrought better than he knew by showing the complementarity of the two female characters, Masha the narrator and the silenced Katya, the ghost-heroine, both of whom interrogate male dominance. The comparison of *Jane Eyre* and *Happy Ever After*—as, in a different way, the comparison of *Jane Eyre* and *Billy Budd*—does show how pervasive the Jane Eyre- and Rochester-figures are in the consciousness of even the apparently unlikeliest novelists to follow in Charlotte Brontë's "tiny" footsteps leaving their imprint on the world stage.

Chapter 4

# Cathy's Book: The Ghost-text in Emily Bronte's *Wuthering Heights*

When I am from him, I am dead till I be
with him. United souls are not satisfied with
embraces, but desire to be truly each other; which
being impossible, these desires are infinite, and
must proceed without a possibility of satisfaction.
    Sir Thomas Browne, *Religio Medici* (1642)

## Wuthering Heights *and the Critics*

Emily Brontë's *Wuthering Heights* (1847) is one of those literary icons that is—or should be—daunting to critics. I always think of it in the same context as, not Charlotte Brontë's *Jane Eyre* which, rich and dense as it is, nonetheless remains accessible to existing tools of criticism, but Nathaniel Hawthorne's *The Scarlet Letter* (1850), which I sometimes think is also best approached creatively, and which lends itself to inexhaustible layers of interpretations and readings. *The Scarlet Letter* has inspired a balletic interpretation by Martha Graham, highlighting Rudolf Nureyev as the Reverend Arthur Dimmesdale, rather than Hester Prynne, the wearer of the scarlet letter, in addition to a fine PBS television production and the awful Demi Moore film. *Wuthering Heights* has inspired a song by Kate Bush; a sequel, *Heathcliff*, purporting to examine the missing years in Heathcliff's life when he flees Wuthering Heights after overhearing Cathy Earnshaw say to Nelly Dean that he is not good enough for her, meaning socially and materially; a novel supposedly written by Cathy; and several film and television versions, as well as biographical films such as *Devotion* and *Les Soeurs Brontë*,[1] even a Cliff Richards project to play a musical Heathcliff.[2]

---

[1]    There is a fascinating article by John Collick comparing and contrasting William Wyler's classic 1939 film version with a recent (1988) Japanese film, Yoshida's *Arashi ga oka*. He notes that, typical of its time, the Wyler film foregrounds class consciousness, while the Japanese film focuses on a heroine who can be seen as a radical feminist in a time when "changes in Japanese society are causing many women to assume a more active role in politics. Yoshida's *Wuthering Heights* suggests that the radical avant-garde, in allying itself with feminism, may be finding a more valid and interventionist means of expression than the traditional angst of the crazy rebel" (47).

[2]    My personal favorite among the creative tributes is Robert Barnard's detective novel, *The Case of the Missing Brontë*, concerning the discovery of a manuscript of a supposed second novel by Emily Brontë. When the manuscript is stolen, Detective Superintendent

Cathy's and Heathcliff's love story, in some ways like that of Hester Prynne and Dimmesdale, seems to me best summarized by Sir Thomas Browne's classic description of friendship in *Religio Medici* (1642), which I have used as an epigraph to this chapter. Although he was describing *male* friendship, the scholar / detective novelist Dorothy Sayers was quick to pick up on the possible romantic implications when her heroine, Harriet Vane, uses it to describe her love for Sayers' detective hero, Lord Peter Wimsey, in *Gaudy Night* (1935). Browne's definition comes close to Denis de Rougemont's of Eros, or romantic, passionate love, in *Love in the Western World* (1939), a consummation which can only be attained through death.

Emily Brontë has been much appreciated by other artists. That kindred idealistic spirit Emily Dickinson once wrote of *Charlotte* Brontë, "Oh, what an afternoon for heaven, / When Brontë entered there!" But G.F. Whicher suggests that her strongest affinity was for her fellow poet from Yorkshire, the other Emily: "During the last decade of her life, however, Emily Dickinson spoke less of Charlotte and more of 'gigantic Emily Brontë'" in whom she may have sensed a similar mysticism (213). At Emily Dickinson's funeral, Thomas Wentworth Higginson had Emily Brontë's "No coward soul is mine" read (213–14).

Most critics approach *Wuthering Heights* with awe and trepidation, and perhaps its very openness or permeability to multiple angles of vision makes readers eager to add to the total picture, without detracting from the constructions of others—not that it hasn't generated critical intolerance. J. Hillis Miller refers to essays on *Wuthering Heights* as themselves "metafictions," "fictions spun about fictions" (368).[3]

---

Percy Trethowan of Scotland Yard takes the problem of both locating and authenticating the manuscript to a local university which has no Brontë expert, but does have a George Meredith scholar, who has evidently built his reputation on the Meredith works which practically no one else has read. The university itself was the brainchild of a "great man" (former Prime Minister) whose train stalled in the town and who declared that what it really needed was a university. As Trethowan comments wryly, "Other new universities had made their mark: you went to one because you were bright, to another because you were revolutionary, to a third because you were over-sexed. You went to Milltown because it was there" (45–6). As he adds later, "Vegetation was sparse in Milltown as a whole, but it looked as if that was what was going on in its English Department" (54).

3     Among older, classic critics, Walter Allen calls *Wuthering Heights* "the most remarkable novel in English" (223), closer to a lyric poem than a conventional work of fiction. E.M. Forster places Emily Brontë in the category of the "prophetic" novelists, including the American Herman Melville and the English D.H. Lawrence. Forster writes that *Wuthering Heights* is "filled with sound—storm and rushing wind" (145). Lord David Cecil, to the contrary—more perceptive with Emily than with Charlotte—sees it as moving from the local to the universal. It was Cecil who first claimed that the novel presents the two principles of storm and calm, embodied physically in the Heights and its inhabitants, and Thrushcross Grange and its inhabitants. Cecil sees the characters as "elemental forces," which means that Cathy's love for Heathcliff is essentially "sexless" (146). Like Allen and Forster, he is awestruck: Emily Brontë possessed "the most extraordinary imagination that ever applied itself to English fiction" (158). He notes that Emily Brontë's complex narrative technique of boxes-within-boxes, or "Chinese boxes," as Q.D. Leavis (307) and Hillis Miller (323), among others, have called it, was not to reappear until some eighty years later, with Joseph Conrad and Henry James. Cecil pays Emily Brontë a glowing tribute, calling *Wuthering Heights*

Predictably, and necessarily, most critics have dwelt on the relationship between the two narrators, the "outside" Lockwood and the "inside," the housekeeper Nelly Dean. The English Queenie D. Leavis is most amusing and acerbic on the subject of an unnamed American academic "who had discovered that 'The clue to *Wuthering Heights* is that Nelly Dean is Evil'" (306). *Pace* Mrs. Leavis's battles with the American literary establishment, and overstated as the American professor's case

---

"the one perfect work of art amid all the vast varied canvasses of Victorian fiction," and adds that, "Against the urbanized landscape of Victorian fiction it looms up august and alien, like the only surviving monument of a vanished race" (182).

Cecil has been enormously influential on the critics who succeeded him, whether they agree or disagree with his reading. Thomas A. Vogler, in a 1968 essay, notes three patterns of conflicting interpretations of the sexuality in the text: 1. Early readers focused on the shocking "violent sexuality" of the principal characters; 2. Following Cecil's reading, many have seen the text as sexless and elemental, because Cathy and Heathcliff really wish to return to an innocent pre-sexual childhood; 3. With the more recent influence of psychoanalytic, and particularly Freudian, criticism of the Brontës, critics have pointed out that children are far from asexual beings, and that Cathy and Heathcliff are approximately 12 or 13 when they are still sharing the same bed (78). In fact, in a 1959 essay, Eric Solomon sees Heathcliff as an illegitimate son of Mr. Earnshaw, and therefore Cathy's half-brother, experiencing an incestuous desire for her that can never be acted out. David Daiches notes the Thomistic link between incest and avarice, a fear of the outside. Sheila Smith traces the possible influence of the ballad form on *Wuthering Heights*, noting that the ballads celebrate sexuality, and Cathy and Heathcliff seek "the joy of shared sexual passion" (509).

Jungian critics, on the other hand, displace the sexuality or incest themes with a reading of the complementarity of Heathcliff and Cathy as *animus* and *anima*. Terence Dawson, in a variation on this, applies the theories of Jung and Lévi-Strauss to detect a pattern of "struggle for deliverance from the father" (both Mr. Earnshaw and, later, Heathcliff). Philip Wion gives a psychoanalytic interpretation in which Mrs. Brontë's death traumatized young Emily. He claims that Heathcliff takes on a "mother" role for the similarly alienated Cathy (317–28). This theory runs counter to all those critics who see Heathcliff as a would-be patriarch.

Margaret Homans gives an interesting and influential reading, borrowing from both French and American feminist theory. She takes off from Lacan's theory that the son separates from the mother and enters the "Law of the Father," or "the symbolic order ... of figurative language" (343), while "A daughter is never encouraged to abandon her mother in the way that a son is ..." (343). She summarizes the fate of the two Cathys: "The first Cathy's story is about a girl's refusal to enter something very like the Lacanian symbolic order, while the second Cathy's story revises the mother's, by having the girl accept her entry into the father's law" (344). She goes on, however, to suggest that Emily Brontë writes "as a son," the only way nineteenth-century women novelists *could* write. She even puns on "Penis / tone Crags," to refute Gilbert and Gubar's theory that nature is somehow female in *Wuthering Heights* (348, n. 14). Similarly, she claims that Cathy could not write a novel, that she "regards writing merely as an antidote to boredom, and she prefers to go outside" (349). But Cathy tells us that it is Heathcliff who is impatient, and it is she who keeps the diary which is a microcosm of Emily Brontë's novel. I would argue that nineteenth-century women novelists, like twentieth-century, could make the leap to verbal creativity *not* by imitating male discourse but by moving from the private, domestic sphere to the public. Emily Brontë is what Cathy Earnshaw *could* have become had she not been tamed, domesticated, socialized, by marriage and the influence of Thrushcross Grange.

may be, the character within the text who suspects Nelly Dean is evil is Cathy Earnshaw, although she is hallucinating at the time in a deathbed fever. Others argue that Nelly Dean is not evil, but is a limited narrator who cannot comprehend the enormity of the drama she perceives.

Generally speaking, however, most critics have tended to blame, not Nelly, but either Cathy or Heathcliff, forgetting, as the characters concerned never do, that Cathy *is* Heathcliff, and Heathcliff *is* Cathy. Richard Chase saw *Jane Eyre* as "a feminist tract" as early as 1957 (468)—amazing some feminist critics today—though he obviously did not altogether consider that a compliment—whereas he saw *Wuthering Heights* as something more than that. Carolyn Heilbrun, too, recognizes that, if *Jane Eyre* "vibrates to the Equal Rights bill," Emily Brontë is truly androgynous as a creator—it is amazing that Virginia Woolf never thought so!

Arnold Kettle, in a pre-Terry Eagleton Marxist reading, sees the theme of *Wuthering Heights* as deeper than sex or romantic love—it is about social rebellion. Our acceptance or rejection of this thesis depends on our view of romantic love. But he does make an important contribution in recognizing that Heathcliff is "a conscious rebel," whereas Cathy accepts culture (34). He does not go on to explore what Cathy's gender and family identification have to do with her acculturation. The book may indeed be about the "stresses of nineteenth-century capitalist society," but surely that is not *all* it is about. In an essay published in the Bedford / St. Martin's *Case Study in Contemporary Criticism*, J. Hillis Miller deconstructs his own early position, in a 1963 essay, that the novel focused on reconciliation to God,[4] and instead views the text as fragmented, ungraspable. Tom Winnifrith agrees that *Wuthering Heights*, in the final analysis, is "incoherent."

It seems that any number of systems may apply to this convoluted text, as Vogler says, and they are not mutually exclusive (13).[5] But C.P Sanger's classic 1921 essay on the entail and the exact genealogy of the Earnshaws and Lintons refuted forever any notion that Emily Brontë was not also a realist who rooted her fantastic imagination in facts.[6]

---

4    Another "Christian" reading is that by J. Frank Goodridge. Despite the many good things in his 1964 article, he comes up with a rather outlandish interpretation, placing old Joseph at the center of the text, insisting that he instills pride in young Hareton, protests Hindley's beating by Heathcliff, and, in short, represents "a way of life fit to survive" (75). We have only to look at Cathy's diary and Lockwood's report of Joseph's dialogue for the refutation.

5    Subsequent casebooks and collections on *Wuthering Heights* invariably begin with updated critical surveys. See, for instance, Richard Benvenuto's 1982 *Emily Brontë* in the Twayne English Authors Series. He mentions such approaches as the Marxist, Heathcliff and Cathy as a divided whole, and the cyclical nature of the novel as a unifying device. Linda Peterson's introduction to the *Case Study in Contemporary Criticism*, a critical edition, provides a very useful summary of past and present trends in criticism.

6    Nancy Armstrong, however, argues that Emily Brontë rejects *both* Romanticism and realism, to focus instead on the tradeoff between psycho-sexual and economic power.

*Cathy and Emily: The Author-itative Voice*

I have chosen to focus on one particular aspect of the text, and one particular character—Catherine Earnshaw, dead 18 years before the start of the novel, dead in childbirth, but refusing to be silenced. Cathy is the most author-itative voice within the text. She is the author of the "hidden"or "ghost-text" of *Wuthering Heights*, even though she speaks from beyond the grave—an extraordinary, extreme example of a woman's voice moving from the private to the public sphere, for the grave is "a fine and private place." She leaves behind a daughter, Catherine Linton, and a "text" which we enter through Lockwood—the ledge on which Cathy has scratched her name, trying on various roles to be enacted—or not—in her life. And, perhaps equally importantly, "a Testament," appropriated by the child Cathy for her own use. As *Jane Eyre* begins with a book being hurled at the heroine's head, *Wuthering Heights* opens with a book written by its long-dead heroine—not a retrospective, like *Jane Eyre*, but a voice whose present *is* the past, and which refuses to die. Catherine's book is a marginal commentary "covering every morsel of blank that the printer had left" (8). The Brontës knew how precious a commodity paper and ink were in the nineteenth century and earlier; Richardson's Pamela hoarded her stock as a secret drinker hoards bottles! If Lockwood is the ignorant reader's representative in the text, the effect on him—the dream of the returned ghost-child Cathy—is to be the effect on all of us—that the dream is real.

William Wyler had the right intuition in the famous, if truncated, 1939 film version of *Wuthering Heights*, to have Merle Oberon (Catherine Earnshaw) made up, including hairdo, exactly like the famous profile of Emily Brontë by Branwell which appears on the cover of Winifred Gérin's biography. Though the live Heathcliff appears to dominate the text, in death as in life it is Cathy who leads, proposes, goes before. Theirs is a love that incorporates, but at the same time transcends, the earthly, the sexual. Or, as Georges Bataille writes, "*L'érotisme est ... l'approbation de la vie jusque dans la mort*" (12).

*Charlotte's Introductions*

Even Charlotte's introductions to her sister's text reveal uneasiness about Emily's authorship. Charlotte's "Biographical Notice" to the second edition of *Wuthering Heights*, dated September 19, 1850, over a year after Emily's death on May 28, 1849, shows that Emily's complexity could scarcely be comprehended even within her own close-knit family. In fact, Charlotte sounds faintly uneasy about her sister's art, even while recognizing that all three sisters published under male pseudonyms because "our mode of writing and thinking was not what is called 'feminine'" (xviii). She sees her sister's literary powers as "immature but very real" (xx). On her deathbed Emily was, according to Charlotte, "stronger than a man, simpler than a child" (xxi).

Her second "Editor's Preface" sounds frankly more alarmed after she had read and edited the text and seen, as she supposed, its faults. She claims that "Having formed these beings, she [Emily] did not know what she had done," and goes on to assert that "Heathcliff, indeed, stands unredeemed" (xxvii). In contrast, she tries to present Nelly Dean as "a specimen of true benevolence and homely fidelity," and the rather vapid Edgar Linton as "an example of constancy and tenderness" (xxvii).[7] No wonder, then, that generations of critics have been unable to agree on the book, or on Heathcliff, or Catherine. But if Cathy refuses to be silenced, even from beyond the grave, Emily's book itself becomes almost a message from the hereafter.

In order to focus on Catherine Earnshaw as would-be female artist, or as a Portrait of the Artist as a Young Woman, I will, of necessity, have to frame the discussion by examining the role of place or setting, and the two narrations of Lockwood and Nelly.

*"The Spirit of Place"*

Unlike Charlotte Brontë's *Jane Eyre* and *Shirley*, but like Charlotte's last completed novel *Villette*, Emily Brontë's *Wuthering Heights* has as its title a place name; indeed the novel would fit very well into D.H. Lawrence's formulation of "The Spirit of Place" in his *Studies in Classic American Literature* (1923).[8] In fact, the characters identify strongly with place, and cannot be separated from it. What we are confronting is a whole series of perceptions, by all the principal characters, of the space they inhabit, and I will argue that 12-year-old Cathy's perceptions, read by Lockwood and the inspiration for his dream or nightmare, come closest to a truth that will be diluted, almost lost, in the complexity of adulthood and socialization.

As C.P. Sanger noted, *Wuthering Heights* begins not only with a date—1801—but also two contrasting places. Thrushcross Grange is named before the Heights, but it is the Heights to which Lockwood, the new tenant of the Grange, goes to pay his respects to his landlord Heathcliff. And it is the Heights, far more than the Grange or the generally wild Yorkshire countryside, that is "a perfect misanthropist's Heaven" (1)—though Lockwood's "misanthropy," as I have suggested, cannot bear comparison with Heathcliff's. So filled with sibilants and aspirates is it that Thrushcross Grange does not fall trippingly off the tongue. As Lord David Cecil noted long ago, the Grange is perceived as civilized, tame, polished, as "Thrushcross" suggests birdsong and music. It should be noted, though, that it is low-lying, a less healthy situation than the Heights with its pure air and buffeting, fierce winds (as Ferndean was less healthy than Thornfield). One associates a "Grange" with shepherds, prosperous farm country, the Heights with rocks, stony soil, a hard life. Is the "Heights" partway to Heaven? Emily Brontë, through Lockwood, explains "the name of Heathcliff's dwelling": "'Wuthering' being a significant provincial adjective, descriptive of the atmospheric tumult to which its station is exposed, in stormy weather. Pure, bracing ventilation they must have up there, at all times, indeed ..." (2).[9] Emily Brontë poetically describes the effect of the north wind on "a range of gaunt thorns all stretching their limbs one way, as if craving alms of the sun"—like the inhabitants of

---

7    Mary Visick does try to make a case for Edgar, who is, after all, largely seen from outside.

8    Carol Siegel, in fact, notes a possible influence of Emily Brontë on D.H. Lawrence.

9    Steven Vine notes that "wuther" can also mean "an attack" (340), and he sees *Wuthering Heights* as "a house under stress" (339). Taking off from Eagleton, he continues that some of that stress is a matter of class for the upward-mobile Cathy and the new capitalist Heathcliff (345).

the Heights (2). It has been remarked that we have a strong architectural sense of the Heights: "Happily, the architect had foresight to build it strong: the narrow windows are deeply set in the wall; and the corners defended with large jutting stones" (2).

From William Wyler on, directors of successive film, television, and theatrical versions of the novel have had no difficulty with set design, for Emily Brontë has given them virtually an architect's blueprint. We can picture the Heights vividly from its door where, as Lockwood says, "among a wilderness of crumbling griffins and shameless little boys, I detected the date '1500,' and the name 'Hareton Earnshaw'" (2), to its kitchen with benches arranged almost in a circle where the young Heathcliff overhears Cathy's recognition of his unsuitability as a marriage partner, to the upstairs room with its bed set in a cabinet with a window to the moors (or the spirit world), where Lockwood thinks he encounters the ghost of the dead Cathy. It scarcely matters whether Emily modeled it on Top Withens, the now ruined farmhouse on the moors. She has conjured up a precisely realized house which seems almost to have a life of its own.

Of the Grange, on the other hand, we have no sense of structure, of the relative location of the rooms or the kitchen.[10] Wyler's set designer did well to give us simply an overall impression of drawing rooms, lights, wealth and luxury. We can picture the Earnshaws in their kitchen, the heart of the house, but the Lintons only in a nonfunctional drawing room. Who were these Earnshaws anyhow? A race of yeoman farmers, rough around the edges but risen to prosperity? The elder Earnshaws die young, but so do the elder Lintons (partly thanks to Cathy's illness which she passes on to them). "Earnshaw," it has been mentioned, means "eagle's *cliff*" in Old English, as "Eyre" evoked "eyrie" or "the eagle's nest" in *Jane Eyre*. Is Heathcliff the eagle in this novel, as Rochester is in *Jane Eyre*?[11]

Heath / cliff's name is itself a place name, composed of two rather opposed settings (an oxymoron?). But he is grafted onto the heath, and indeed is named for a lost Earnshaw son who died as a baby.[12] The Heights also motivates Heathcliff's acquisitiveness. Albert Guerard seems to intuit that William Faulkner could have been influenced by Emily Brontë, as I have argued Herman Melville was by her sister Charlotte.[13] Thomas Sutpen, in Faulkner's *Absalom, Absalom!*, is the outsider,

---

10   Although it is supposedly based on Ponden Hall, we have no sure sense of interior.

11   Sheryl Craig examines the bird imagery in *Wuthering Heights*, associating Heathcliff with the "cuckoo."

12   Stevie Davies sees the dead Cathy as well as the "mother beneath the earth."

13   Linda Peterson, in her "Critical History" attached to the Bedford / St. Martin's *Case Study*, gives a good, succinct account of a possible real-life model for Heathcliff, one Jack Sharp, who was adopted by a John Walker, and who supplanted Walker's sons, like Heathcliff, robbing the estate (293–4). Albert Guerard, like Forster, implicitly recognizes Emily's affinities with the *American* prophetic novel, in this case William Faulkner's *Absalom, Absalom!* (1936), which also builds on a strong sense of identification with a geographical place, on themes of heredity and ownership, and which exploits images of locks, keys, and windows. There is, even more conspicuously, a strong resemblance to Faulkner's earlier *The Sound and the Fury* (1929), of which *Absalom, Absalom!* is the prequel: Candace Compson (Caddy) and her daughter Quentin seem to be twentieth-century reworkings, in a different time and place, of Cathy Earnshaw and her daughter Cathy Linton (whom I refer to as Cathy I and Cathy II).

the poor boy of unknown but lowly origins, who comes down from the Tennessee hills to a Mississippi plantation, where, as "poor white trash," he is sent to the back door by a slave / house servant. He then spends his entire life trying to graft himself onto a Southern plantation tradition by acquiring what he perceives as the essentials: land, slaves, and a legitimate white male heir in order to create a dynasty. Ironically, the "survivors" of his dynasty are female or partly black, and therefore cannot inherit, according to his "grand design."[14] Instead of questioning the ethics of a nefarious system, or attempting to overthrow it, he focuses only on his own role within it, and not on the suffering of women and blacks (and the most suffering, the black women). Faulkner maintains that he is, in a peculiar sense, "innocent"—because he neither belonged to, nor ever understood, the patriarchal system. Like Heathcliff, he is neither "hero" nor "villain," but a tragic figure. Heathcliff, too, "succeeds" in a material sense—and only in a material sense—by exploiting those with whom he should be identifying: the hapless orphan Hareton Earnshaw whose name echoes that of the very founder of the Earnshaw "dynasty," Cathy's daughter Cathy II, and perhaps worst of all, his own son by Isabella Linton, the peevish, spiteful Linton.

Like Sutpen's, Heathcliff's acquisitiveness is at least as metaphysical as it is physical. If Sutpen tries to affirm his own identity, and to seek justice for other poor boys like himself, for Heathcliff Cathy *is* the Heights, *is* the land. His most fervent wish—and hers, before socialization at the Grange—is for the two of them to dissolve into dust and return to earth together in a fusion both literal and spiritual. Cathy also recognizes Heathcliff's identity with the land. In her diatribe to the smitten Isabella, her sister-in-law, she describes him as "an arid wilderness of furze and whinstone" (86)—an apt description of her own heart too at this point.

*Wuthering Heights*, as title and as house, could be compared to Dickens's *Bleak House* (1853) for its realistic architectural detail and its symbolic resonances. Both novels concern families destroying each other for the sake of property. Appropriately, if *Bleak House* opens with the fog of Chancery, *Wuthering Heights* opens with sleet and black frost (6). The sheltered valley of Thrushcross and exposed hilltop of the Heights are constantly contrasted. A storm parallels Heathcliff's heartbroken departure from the Heights after Cathy confesses to Nelly why she cannot marry him: "It *was* a very dark evening for summer: the clouds appeared inclined to thunder, and I said we had better all sit down; the approaching rain would be certain to bring him home without further trouble ..." (72). The storm, in fact, seems to attack the house itself: "About midnight, while we still sat up, the storm came rattling over the Heights in full fury. There was a violent wind, as well as thunder, and either one or the other split a tree off at the corner of the building; a huge bough fell across the roof, and knocked down a portion of the east chimney-stack, sending a clatter of stones and soot into the kitchen fire" (72). The effect is not unlike that of the tree cloven by lightning after the Midsummer Eve scene in *Jane Eyre*. Nelly almost approaches old Joseph's superstitions in interpreting the storm as an ill omen: "I felt some sentiment that it must be a judgment on us also" (72). Indeed, Nelly may well have reason to feel uneasy, as she is guilty of *not* having warned Cathy, as soon

---

14   My 1974 article, "Women, Blacks, and Thomas Sutpen's Mythopoeic Drive in *Absalom, Absalom!*," explores this subject more fully.

as she perceived him, that Heathcliff was behind the settle listening—one of many notable omissions on Nelly's part.

During Cathy's final illness at the Grange, Nelly compares the sound of "the beck in the valley," while Gimmerton chapel bells ring, at the Grange and at the Heights: "It was a sweet substitute for the yet absent murmur of the summer foliage which drowned that music about the Grange when the trees were in leaf. At Wuthering Heights it always sounded on quiet days, following a great thaw, or a season of steady rain" (134), again images of freeze and thaw—and Catherine is mentally transported to her real home at the Heights. After Cathy's death, appropriately, "the wind shifted from south to north-east, and brought rain, first, and then sleet, and snow" (144).

Earlier, in Chapter XI, Nelly notes the signpost which signifies the three directions of the novel, serving "as a guide-post to the Grange, Heights, and village" (92). The village, apart from Dr. Kenneth, does not loom large in the novel, but it could connote the outside world, the world beyond the two houses. But the village is also part of Yorkshire, the birthplace of all the characters except Heathcliff (and Lockwood), and, as Nelly stresses, Yorkshire is exclusive of foreigners: "We don't in general take to foreigners here, Mr. Lockwood, unless they take to us first" (37), a statement which could apply equally to Heathcliff and Lockwood. Lockwood mentions Yorkshire provincialism: "They *do* live more in earnest, more in themselves, and less in surface change, and frivolous external things. I could fancy a love for life here almost possible ..." (52). But Nelly also denies that the Yorkshire people are different, except in degree, from the majority of human beings: "Oh! here we are the same as anywhere else, when you get to know us" (52). If her creator agrees with Nelly, then Emily has forestalled the critics who argue the local versus the universal in her text: like Faulkner's, her work is both local and universal, and the most provincial of texts frequently address the most universal human issues.

*Narrative Technique: "Chinese Boxes"*

*Lockwood*
Lockwood is probably the easier narrator to deal with. Dorothy Van Ghent's famous diagram is definitive (see Figure below), with Lockwood as outside narrator / frame talespinner, Nelly as inside narrator / confidante to all the principals. Van Ghent further divides the novel into the two-generation plots with Heathcliff as the link between the two, as lover in the first part, and "father" in the second.

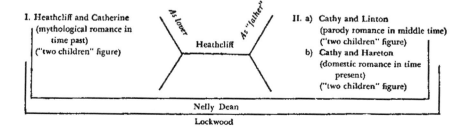

Both parts contain what she calls a "two children" figure, Heathcliff and Cathy in the first part, and two pairs, Cathy II and Linton as a parody romance, and Cathy II and Hareton as a realistic romance in time present in the second (156). She does, however, get the "gold" and "dark" pairings wrong (168): Cathy, like Heathcliff, is dark, not golden, emphasizing the similarity of their natures, whereas Edgar and Isabella are both fair. Cathy is therefore *not* the conventional blonde heroine of romance, any more than Jane Eyre is. Cathy II is a combination of both the Earnshaws and the Lintons, with her mother's expressive dark eyes, but blonde like her father. Hareton also has his Aunt Cathy's eyes, which prevent Heathcliff from doing more harm than he does to the lad.

In Wyler's film version, Lockwood is an older man, because there *is* no second generation theme, and therefore no wistful would-be love story between Lockwood and Cathy II. He remains the viewer's, as he is the reader's, means of entry into the script / text. In keeping with the house imagery, his name indicates that he is to aid us in "unlocking," finding the key to, the secret of, Wuthering Heights. His very obtuseness—he begins by mistaking a pile of dead rabbits for puppies—makes us more willing to accept the strangeness of the household—if it can be called that—in which he intrudes. He tends to project himself on Heathcliff, but adds, "I bestow my own attributes over liberally on him" (3). His first inkling of the gulf between them occurs when he realizes that "It is astonishing how sociable I feel myself compared with him" (6). We learn that Lockwood is rather vain and considers himself somewhat of a ladykiller: "I knew, through experience, that I was tolerably attractive" (10). He seems to have exiled himself in order to avoid commitment to a woman.

He does, however, have the relative objectivity of the outside observer stunned and astonished by this ménage in which he first takes Cathy II for Mrs. Heathcliff, a role her mother should have played. She is, in fact, Mrs. Linton Heathcliff, Heathcliff's daughter-in-law. His naive blundering prepares us to accept the "reality" of Cathy's ghost in Lockwood's dream.[15] The dream occurs, after all, on the basis of very little evidence—Cathy's trying out various names scratched on the window ledge, and the Testament with its scribbled marginalia on all the blank spaces. Admittedly, this is more evidence than he confesses to Heathcliff when the latter bursts in on Lockwood's terrified outcry. Thus Lockwood's "reading" is quite literally that, based on texts either scratched, printed, or handwritten. As Craik writes, "We believe very firmly in a ghost that must reveal itself to so unpromising a young man as Lockwood" (42).[16]

---

15   Carol Jacobs is on a somewhat similar track to mine when she argues that Lockwood permits the novel to speak of its textuality. T. McCarthy, on the other hand, sees him as just plain "incompetent." David Galef perceives Lockwood and Isabella as "doubles," but only the artist (Lockwood) survives to tell the tale. I suspect this interpretation gives too much importance to Lockwood.

16   She disagrees with those critics who feel that he is "foppish" (the Penguin Introduction) or a "dandy" (Mark Schorer). She notes the debt to Sir Walter Scott's frame-tale narrator, Jedediah Cleishbotham, in *Tales of My Landlord*, and indeed Scott seems to have been a major influence, in terms of both narrative technique and his use of history, on the Brontës, as he was on Elizabeth Gaskell and George Eliot.

Lockwood can be seen as the "misreader," the less-than-ideal reader or critic. That it should be he who dreams the dream which contains the microcosm of the text authenticates the narrative. His dream is to be verified by the remainder of the tale told by Nelly and others. Lockwood's perceptions are based on "Cathy's book," the ghost-text of *Wuthering Heights*. Cathy *is* the text, and the text is Cathy. But Lockwood tries to superimpose another, less realistic, frame which just does not fit the circumstances. He tries desperately to make what he has heard conform to a conventional romance, or to a fairy tale. Indeed, the two are not far apart, as Richardson, Charlotte Brontë, and Dickens knew. Nelly ends the first part of her narrative with Cathy's marriage to Edgar Linton, and Lockwood admits that, "In truth, I felt rather disposed to defer the sequel of her narrative, myself ..." (76). He constantly uses literary terms, such as "sequel," to recount Nelly's version, and "edits" his own narrative to Heathcliff of the dream in the coffin / bed. His acceptance of Nelly's closure of the first part of her narrative bears a striking resemblance to Wilkie Collins's famous advice to writers of "cliffhangers": "Make 'em laugh, make 'em cry, make 'em wait."

When he decides to ask her to resume, it is clear that he is perceiving Heathcliff and Cathy as the conventional hero and heroine of romance: "Why not have up Mrs. Dean to finish her tale? I can recollect its chief incidents, as far as she had gone. Yes, I remember her hero had run off, and never been heard of for three years: and the heroine was married" (77). We also learn at this point that there is a human side to Heathcliff, despite Isabella's, Cathy II's, and often Nelly's attempts to demonize him. When his tenant, Lockwood, is ill—admittedly a result of his near-expulsion by Heathcliff into the snow outside the Heights—Heathcliff nonetheless has the conscience to visit the invalid and chat with him.

Lockwood soon, out of fear, withdraws from any attempt to play the role of knight in shining armor with Cathy II, and, typically, expresses his reservations in "bookish" terms: "I should be in a curious taking if I surrendered my heart to that young person, and the daughter turned out a second *edition* of the mother!" (132; emphasis mine). We more or less trust that, as he is restored to health, and nearer spring, he is, insofar as possible, keeping to Nelly's "own words," as he claims, "only a little condensed." He also testifies to her narrative skills: "... I don't think I could improve her style" (132). Thus, the reader is induced, more or less, to accept the good intentions and veracity—insofar as they know the facts—of both narrators.

Lockwood's distillation of Nelly's narrative ends at the conclusion of Chapter XXX: "Thus ended Mrs. Dean's story ... I would not pass another winter here, for much" (252–3). At this point Nelly is still housekeeper at the Grange, Zillah at the Heights, and Nelly sees no way of helping the young Cathy II: "I can see no remedy, at present, unless she should marry again; and that scheme, it does not come within my province to arrange" (252). If she intends this as a strong hint to Lockwood to try his hand, it has the reverse effect—as, indeed, do many of Nelly's well-intentioned (or not?) efforts: Lockwood decides to decamp. He pays one last visit to the Heights, and shows his fear (probably justifiable) of Cathy II: "'She does not seem so amiable,' I thought, 'as Mrs. Dean would persuade me to believe.

She's a beauty, it is true; but not an angel'" (253).[17] Indeed, milder version of her mother as she is, she is fully capable of eating Lockwood for breakfast! Cathy II and Hareton are already quarreling over—what else?—her books, and his illiteracy. The very literate Lockwood misses his chance with her, and is already waxing nostalgic even as he rides away from the Heights: "What a realization of something more romantic than a *fairy tale* it would have been for Mrs. Linton Heathcliff, had she and I struck up an attachment, as her good nurse desired, and migrated together, into the stirring atmosphere of the town!" (258; emphasis mine). Lockwood remains, as ever, without a clue to what animates Cathy II: she can no more be transplanted from the Yorkshire Dales than her mother before her, who is literally absorbed by the moors.[18]

Thus Lockwood is an absentee for the dénouement, as he has been for all the major events of Nelly's narrative. A passive observer at best, he is destined to return only the next year, having missed the climaxes of Heathcliff's death (and reunion with Cathy?) and the engagement of Cathy II and Hareton. Chapter XXXII begins, as Chapter I did, with a date: "1802.—This September, I was invited to devastate the moors of a friend, in the North; and, on my journey to his abode, I unexpectedly came within fifteen miles of Gimmerton" (258). Lockwood is, in fact, talented at "devastation," as has been remarked. He therefore decides to pay a visit to Thrushcross Grange, finds that Nelly is now housekeeper at the Heights, and hears the end (or is it?) of the first generation story, and the new beginnings for the second generation.

### Nelly Dean

The more important, and more complex, of the two narrators is Nelly Dean. She takes over at Chapter IV, where she begins telling the tale to Lockwood. A favorite critical "game," as Mrs. Leavis and others have noted, is the attempt to determine Nelly's share of responsibility for the events she recounts. "Unreliable narrators" may seem familiar to us today, but Emily Brontë was perhaps the first to foreground the "unreliability."

Perhaps Nelly is less unreliable than inconsistent. Although she is Hindley's foster sister—sister by milk, not by blood—she is not really a member of the family, but an upper servant (somewhat like Mrs. Fairfax in *Jane Eyre*).[19] Her loyalties are due to whoever employs her at the moment. When Mr. Earnshaw initially introduces the foundling Heathcliff to his family, Nelly takes her cue from the wild, spirited Cathy's first response: "… Cathy, when she learnt the master had lost her whip

---

17   Coventry Patmore's *The Angel in the House*, which promoted a popular Victorian ideal of domesticated womanhood, did not appear until 1854, but the un-Victorian Emily Brontë seems to show her resistance to it already through her unangelic Cathy II.

18   Lockwood's snobbishness about rustics clearly demonstrates that he would never be the man for her: "Living among clowns and misanthropes, she probably cannot appreciate a better class of people, when she meets them" (258).

19   I once had a graduate student who assumed that Nelly was in love with Hindley, but married someone else, missing the point that Nelly is Hindley's foster sister. "Mrs." was, of course, short for "Mistress," the term used until the beginning of the nineteenth century for *all* women, whether married or not, beyond marriageable age.

in attending on the stranger, showed her humour by grinning and spitting at the stupid little thing …" (30–31). Fourteen-year-old Nelly, old enough to know better, refers to the future "Heathcliff" as a sexually indeterminate "it," or object, and is complicitous with Hindley's and Cathy's brattiness: "They entirely refused to have it in bed with them, or even in their room, and I had no more sense, so, I put it on the landing of the stairs, hoping it might be gone by the morrow" (31). Cathy soon changes her mind, but Nelly does not. Soon Cathy and he *are* to share a bed, the coffin / bed which Lockwood is to lie in many years later. At this point Nelly sees Heathcliff as a discord in the house, as the Reeds see Jane Eyre in Charlotte Brontë's novel. Mr. Earnshaw, Nelly reports, favored Heathcliff, now "christened" (but not Christianized?) with "the name of a son who died in childhood, and it has served him ever since, both for christian and surname" (31).

If, in fact, it is his Christian name, there can be no "Mrs. Heathcliff," nor can Heathcliff create a patriarchal dynasty since he has no patronym.[20] The "patriarch" of Nelly's tale, indeed, Mr. Earnshaw, while no domestic tyrant, does set up a situation which is bound to destroy his family, "petting him [Heathcliff] up far above Cathy, who was too mischievous and wayward for a favourite." "So," Nelly concludes, "from the very beginning, he bred bad feeling in the house," implicitly blaming Heathcliff, the victim, and not Mr. Earnshaw, her patriarchal employer. Joseph calls the dead man "a saint in Heaven," but the reader may well entertain doubts. One can understand how some critics (Solomon for one) have seen in Heathcliff Mr. Earnshaw's illegitimate son,[21] but it suffices that he has supplanted the older Hindley in his father's heart, perhaps as a result of Mr. Earnshaw's attempt to compensate for the dead son. Nelly, on Mr. Earnshaw's death, already expresses a death wish that is ominously prophetic of both Cathy's and Heathcliff's deaths: "I could not help wishing we were all there [in Heaven] safe together" (36). The feeling is one of "all passion spent," or "After life's fitful fever he sleeps well." The Nelly of the ending does not believe in ghosts; she says: "I believe the dead are at peace …" (286), and Lockwood, finally, "wondered how anyone could ever imagine unquiet slumbers, for the sleepers in that quiet earth" (287). Nonetheless, the Romantics among us want to believe the "little boy with a sheep and two lambs before him" (285) who says to Nelly, "They's Heathcliff, and a woman, yonder, under t'Nab … un'Aw darnut pass 'em" (286).[22]

Later Nelly is to take an older Heathcliff's part against Edgar Linton. Says Nelly to Heathcliff, "… I'll steal time to arrange you so that Edgar Linton shall look quite a doll beside you: … you could knock him down in a twinkling; don't you feel that you could?" This is yet another example of Nelly's bad advice: Heathcliff will later

---

20   I will return to this theme later.

21   William Goetz looks at the closed community of *Wuthering Heights* in terms of Lévi-Strauss's definition of the incest taboo.

22   Among the believers were those responsible for the 1939 film—though Wyler himself was apparently a dissenter—who actually show the ghosts of Cathy and Heathcliff on Peniston Crag at the end. The ghost sighting is reported not by a little boy, but by the reliable Dr. Kenneth (Donald Crisp), and believed by a formidable Nelly (Flora Robson), contrary to the Nelly of the novel.

show only too ready a tendency to violence. Here, however, even he recognizes the ineffectiveness of Nelly's counsel: "But, Nelly, if I knocked him down twenty times, that wouldn't make him less handsome, or me more so" (47). She feeds him a romantic fairy tale to "frame high notions of [his] birth": "You're fit for a prince in disguise. Who knows, but your father was Emperor of China, and your mother an Indian queen, each of them able to buy up, with one week's income, Wuthering Heights and Thrushcross Grange together?" (48). It is Nelly who first plants in Heathcliff's head the idea of acquiring the two properties as the means to Cathy's heart.

Heathcliff has earlier rebuked Nelly for her pious homilies when she tries to tell him that the spoiled Edgar and Isabella "are good children": "'Don't you cant, Nelly,' he said: 'nonsense!'" (39). Nelly is indeed guilty of "cant" through much of the novel. As Thomas Vogler emphasizes, Nelly is as conventional as a poor man's daughter can be: she is "trapped in schedules and tangled in time" (84). She is careful to cite her qualifications as storyteller to Lockwood, having read all the English language books in the library (53). These seem to be the same books that Hareton later "steals" from Cathy II in a vain, frustrated effort to access literacy. We become increasingly aware that this is, among other things, a book about books, about readings and misreadings. What Nelly has been reading is evidently romantic, the frame tale for a potential Lockwood–Cathy II marriage. Nelly it is who presents us with the details—of dates, ages, sequence, Yorkshire nature—while Lockwood edits and condenses. As Nelly continues, about Hareton's birth and his mother Frances's death, "However, if I am to follow my story in true gossip's fashion, I had better go on; and instead of leaping three years, I will be content to pass to the next summer—the summer of 1778, that is, nearly twenty-three years ago" (53).

It soon becomes clear that Nelly dislikes the grown Cathy, as she never showed much tolerance for the child Catherine with her "wicked," wild ways: "At fifteen she was the queen of the countryside; she had no peer: and she did turn out a haughty, headstrong creature! I own I did not like her, after her infancy was past; and I vexed her frequently by trying to bring down her arrogance; she never took an aversion to me though" (55). We learn later, however, when Cathy is on her deathbed, that she does see Nelly as her "hidden enemy." At this point, when Edgar is courting Cathy, Nelly cannot comprehend what Edgar finds attractive in her: "… I marvelled much how he, with a mind to correspond with his person, could fancy *my idea of Catherine Earnshaw*" (56; emphasis mine). From this point on we begin to see Nelly's allegiance shifting to Edgar Linton, her future employer, for all her previous negative comments about him to Heathcliff.

Nelly's courage is undeniable; Pritchett notes the way she stands up to a drunken Hindley in defense of the helpless little Hareton: "He held the knife in his hand, and pushed its point between my teeth: but, for my part I was never much afraid of his vagaries. I spat out, and affirmed it tasted detestably—I would not take it on any account" (62; Pritchett, x). But Hindley is her foster brother; when class complicates the issue, Nelly is often more deferential.

We continue to find evidence of her misreadings of Cathy's character. When the young Heathcliff hurls a tureen of apple sauce at Edgar and is beaten by Hindley, Nelly sees Cathy as uncaring and selfish. On this occasion, at least, Nelly learns to re-read Cathy, who, in fact, climbs along the roof into the skylight of the garret where he is confined, foreshadowing the "ghost's" attempt to reenter the Heights through their old room with the coffin / bed. Nelly's subsequent misreadings of Cathy are not so readily corrected and amended by Cathy herself, who keeps her thoughts secret and seems increasingly to mistrust her old confidante.

After Cathy's marriage, Nelly, predictably, comes to prefer Edgar to Cathy: "My heart invariably cleaved to the master's, in preference to Catherine's side ..." (91). By this time, too, Heathcliff, taking advantage of the heartbroken, drunken Hindley at the Heights, has become to Nelly "an evil beast [which] prowled between it [Hindley as 'stray sheep'] and the fold, waiting his time to spring and destroy" (92). It is no wonder that Charlotte, whose first-person narrator is always the heroine and for the most part trustworthy, should accept at face value Nelly's reading of Heathcliff as "unredeemed" and Edgar as a model of virtue. It is always necessary to keep track of Nelly's "chops and changes." We never quite know what to make of her comment about Cathy's increasing dominance in the marriage: "... they were really in possession of deep and growing happiness"; but "It ended" with Heathcliff's return in September, at harvest time: "Well, we *must* be for ourselves in the long run; the mild and generous are only more justly selfish than the domineering" (78). Is she talking about Edgar? About herself? Both? In any event, she makes a case for our acceptance that there is a ruling passion in every human being.

To be fair, Nelly does defend Cathy to Isabella when Cathy tries to warn her sister-in-law not to fall in love with the manipulative Heathcliff, newly returned with a polish and a fortune acquired no one knows how or where: "'Banish him from your thoughts, miss,' I said. 'He's a bird of bad omen; no mate for you. Mrs. Linton spoke strongly, and yet, I can't contradict her. She is better acquainted with his heart than I, or any one besides; and she never would represent him as worse than he is'" (88).

In trying to warn Hindley about Heathcliff, Nelly comes to the aforementioned stone signpost to the Heights, the Grange, and the village, and "all at once, a gush of child's sensations flowed into my heart. Hindley and I held it a favourite spot twenty years before" (92). Nelly and Hindley, we are reminded, were once children together, as Cathy and Heathcliff were, and there is throughout the novel a drive to return to that pre-civilized, intuitive, irrational world of nature and childhood. But Nelly does not make the connection between these two pairs of children, and is shortly after preoccupied with warning Edgar against Heathcliff. And again, Nelly edits, holds back information, to put all the blame on Heathcliff, none on Cathy—not because she cares for Cathy, but to placate Edgar.

When an altercation ensues between Edgar and Heathcliff, and Cathy is, as she says, "nearly distracted," Nelly is careful to conceal her role in alerting Edgar. More seriously, Nelly, having seen Cathy's previous manifestations of what we call today psychosomatic illness, is cynical about her current threat to become ill: "A thousand smiths' hammers are beating in my head! Tell Isabella to shun me—this uproar is owing to her; and should she or any one else aggravate my anger at present, I shall get wild. And, Nelly, say to Edgar, if you see him again to-night, that I'm in danger of being seriously ill—I wish it may prove true" (99). And indeed, Cathy's threat becomes a self-fulfilling prophecy. When Edgar insists that Cathy choose between himself and Heathcliff, Cathy cries, "I require to be let alone! ... I demand it! Don't you see I can scarcely stand? Edgar, you—you leave me!" (101). She then has a fit, grinds her teeth, and beats her head against the sofa until her lips become bloody, as Edgar sees: "In a few seconds she stretched herself out stiff, and turned up her eyes, while her cheeks, at once blanched and livid, assumed the aspect of death" (101). Some critics have suspected that Cathy, like Dostoyevsky and, possibly, Flaubert, is subject to epileptic fits. But the obtuse Nelly fails to see the gravity of the situation, or to acknowledge that psychosomatic illness can be very serious. Instead, she reassures Edgar, telling him not to worry about the blood on her lips: "'Never mind!' I answered tartly. And I told him how she had resolved, previous to his coming, on exhibiting a fit of frenzy" (101). Cathy proceeds to lock herself in her room for three days (a mystic number?), while Nelly says, "I went about my household duties, convinced that the Grange had but one sensible soul in its walls, and that lodged in my body" (102). When Cathy finally unbars the door, she tells Nelly she thinks she is dying, and Nelly still does not alarm Edgar (103).

Cathy is burning with fever and desires to open the window, undoubtedly thinking of herself and Heathcliff as children escaping out of another window to scamper over the moors to Thrushcross Grange (104).[23] The reader recognizes in this scene an echo of Lockwood's dream of the dead Cathy trying to get *in* a window, rather than escaping out of one. Cathy later threatens to leap out the window (as Emma Bovary also considers after Rodolphe abandons her) when Edgar presses her as to whether she loves Heathcliff: "Hush, this moment! You mention that name and I end the matter, instantly, by a spring from the window! What you touch at present, you may have: but my soul will be on that hilltop before you lay hands on me again" (109). Unlikely as it seems, Heathcliff takes Nelly back as housekeeper at the Heights, after

---

23   Cathy's containment in her illness, and her wish to escape, can be seen as a trope of desire. Susan McKinstry uses René Girard's notion of "triangular desire" to argue that desire is not finally contained in the novel, whose characters seek to return to a childlike state where desire is unlimited: "The novel does not celebrate the containment of desire but, rather, the power, overthrowing the traditional obstacles of love—family, status, misinterpretation, marriage to rivals, and even death. Desire turns lovers into mimetic demons, it transforms houses into prisons, and it translates romantic conventions into children's fairytales" (145). Anita Levy, on the other hand, says that Cathy II's tale makes of the second half of the novel domestic fiction by containing "desire" within domestic space: "The undifferentiated landscape that Catherine and Heathcliff roamed gives way to a park, an enclosed and organized space par excellence" (429). Carol A. Senf also emphasizes containment, but sees it as positive because it enables Emily Brontë to create her own "version of feminist history": "Thus she concludes her novel with a vision of what might happen if the relationships between the sexes … so familiar to patriarchal history were replaced by something both more feminine and more egalitarian … she also chooses a realistic heroine, the younger Catherine, to embody her feminist vision, the final stage in her history" (203). Senf notes that only George Eliot among Victorian novelists shows this sense of modernism as a historian (206). She takes off from Cecil, contrasting the "primitive, violent, elemental," and often "cruel" love of Heathcliff and Catherine to the "more conscious and mature" love of Hareton and Cathy II (21). The problem with this, however, is that it is a teleological reading which privileges the latter pair because they represent the future. Cecil balances them more evenly, if anything tilting the scales towards the elder pair. And for most readers (and filmmakers) the second generation theme simply does not have the power of the first.

Lockwood's departure. Nelly knows he is refusing food, and yet never considers calling in Dr. Kenneth, fatalistically letting nature take its course.

Cathy's mad scene seems a deliberate echo of Ophelia's in *Hamlet*, in a not dissimilar situation: being crossed in love. As noted briefly, like her sister Charlotte, Emily makes great use of images of birds found on the Yorkshire moors. Cathy is fantasizing that she is out there, on the moors, with a young Heathcliff. Pulling the feathers from her pillows, she says,

> "Ah, they put pigeons' feather in the pillows—no wonder I couldn't die! Let me take care to throw it on the floor when I lie down. And here is a moor-cock's; and this—I should know it among a thousand—it's a lapwing's. Bonny bird; wheeling over our heads in the middle of the moor. It wanted to get to its nest, for the clouds touched the swells, and it felt rain coming. This feather was picked up from the heath, the bird was not shot—we saw its nest in the winter, full of little skeletons. Heathcliff set a trap over it, and the old ones dare not come. I made him promise he'd never shoot a lapwing, after that, and he didn't." (104)[24]

Is it Cathy's gentler spirit which also prevents Heathcliff from harming her young (Cathy II) and her brother's (Hareton)? It is only in the next chapter, XIII, that we learn almost casually and coincidentally that Cathy is pregnant with Cathy II (115). Unfortunately, the child is not to be an heir, but an heiress, and the estate would pass first to Isabella's offspring if she bore a male heir. The relationship between Cathy's illness and her pregnancy is never clarified.[25]

Cathy's accusation during her illness that Nelly is her enemy is the basis for those analyses that suggest Nelly bears full responsibility for the tragedy. But Nelly means well; she simply cannot comprehend the transcendence towards which Heathcliff and Cathy are striving, only the day-to-day acceptance of an Edgar Linton. Cathy says to Nelly, "I see in you, Nelly, ... an aged woman—you have grey hair, and bent shoulders. This bed is the fairy cave under Peniston Crag, and you are gathering elf-bolts to hurt our heifers; pretending, while I am near, that they are only locks of wool. That's what you'll come to fifty years hence; I know you are not so now" (105). In effect, she denounces Nelly as a witch—or future witch.

Edgar also berates Nelly for concealing the seriousness of Cathy's condition: "You knew your mistress's nature, and you encouraged me to harass her. And not to give me one hint of how she has been these three days! It was heartless! months of sickness could not cause such a change!" (109). Nelly tries to defend herself, but Cathy makes matters worse: "Nelly is my hidden enemy—you witch! So you

---

24   One critic reads the episode as prefiguring Heathcliff's sadism, but I would add it also helps explain how an abused child can try to become part of the system that oppresses him.

25   Although Thomas Moser finds the second-generation plot boring, he does note that both Linton and Cathy II are born just about nine months after Heathcliff's reappearance, and comments on Emily Brontë's "woman's sense of the biological rhythms of life," although Heathcliff is not literally Cathy II's father (196). (The 1970s film version with Timothy Dalton implied that he was.) At any rate, Emily Brontë may have been suggesting Heathcliff's potency, even by his mere presence.

do seek elf-bolts to hurt us! Let me go, and I'll make her rue! I'll make her howl a recantation!" (110).

When Cathy dies, Heathcliff removes Linton's hair from a locket to be buried with her and replaces it "by a black lock of his own" (144). Nelly tries to have it both ways, and refuses to choose up sides: "I twisted the two, and enclosed them together" (144). At times she demonizes Heathcliff, but she is also capable of defending him to the furious Isabella: "'Hush, hush! He's a human being,' I said. 'Be more charitable; there are worse men than he is yet!'" (147). Speaking to young Cathy II in Chapter XXII, Nelly gives her age as 45 (196). Hindley was the same age, Heathcliff and Cathy a few years younger, so Emily Brontë is careful with her details, as Sanger notes.[26]

Heathcliff, like Cathy earlier, accuses Nelly of duplicity: "Worthy Mrs. Dean, I like you, but I don't like your double dealing" (198). In this case, however, Nelly is better motivated, by the desire to protect her charge, Cathy II. Perhaps Nelly's worst tactics occur when she attempts to disgust the young Cathy with Linton: "'Like him?' I exclaimed. 'The worst tempered bit of a sickly slip that ever struggled into its teens!'" (206). Nelly's knowledge of psychology is fairly rudimentary; she does not realize that Cathy II is as rebellious and stubborn as her mother before her, and her kindness predisposes her to the sickly Linton. She finds herself in the same dilemma as with Cathy I: to tell, or not to tell, Edgar about Cathy II and Linton, "for I hardly knew what to hide, and what to reveal" (224).

### "Cathy's Book": The Microcosm of Wuthering Heights

"Cathy's Book," or the ghost-text of *Wuthering Heights*, is only one of several narratives that supplement those of the principal "outside" and "inside" narrators, Lockwood and Nelly Dean. The others include Heathcliff's own verbal account to Nelly of the two children's visit to the Grange, and Isabella's long letter to Nelly after her marriage to Heathcliff. Heathcliff's tale, in fact, is the sequel to Cathy's diary, which ends with Heathcliff and herself planning to escape the Heights and run across the moors. It thus fills the gap, or "*espace littéraire*" (Blanchot's term) in Cathy's text. She introduces the name of "Linton"—presumably at a later date when she scratches her alternative last-name identities on the window-ledge—but it is Heathcliff's narrative to Nelly that solves the mystery by introducing the two spoiled Linton children, Edgar and Isabella, witnessed by him in the act of pulling a puppy apart—a motif repeated later by Heathcliff himself, who hangs Isabella's little spaniel, and, less believably, by Hareton, who hangs puppies, as witnessed by Lockwood.[27]

---

26   Between Nelly's narrative and Lockwood's pinpointing of 1801 and 1802, it is possible to produce a genealogical chart, as Sanger has done, yet another device William Faulkner may have learned from Emily Brontë as a means of surveying the history of a region and its families.

27   J. Weissman, in an article entitled "Like a Mad Dog," comments on Brontë's analogy between human and dog natures. There is also the famous story of Emily's dog Keeper, which

The third major narrative intervention is the long letter from Isabella Linton, now Mrs. Heathcliff—or can she be, when Heathcliff is only a first name?—that occupies the better part of Chapter XIII, which affords the only "inside" view of their marriage, a bitter, enraged one. It is, presumably, not edited by Nelly. This is followed in Chapter XVII by Isabella's verbal account to Nelly, after she has "escaped" to the Grange, of a scene involving Heathcliff's abuse of her—a scene from which Nelly has been necessarily absent.

Beth Newman has studied the text with reference to the Lacanian "gaze," characters observing and reifying each other—I would argue both male and female.[28] But Emily Brontë also seems to be playing with "intertextuality," before the term was invented (as she played with the "unreliable narrator" before the term was invented). But much of the "intertextuality," apart from the literary allusions to Shakespeare, Milton, Byron, *et al.*, is generated by the characters themselves, whose "documents" and oral narratives complement and supplement each other. These are in turn read and misread, interpreted and misinterpreted, critiqued and re-critiqued by themselves, with the inscrutable "Sphinx," as Gérin calls Emily, refusing to solve the riddle or conundrum she poses, in a technique anticipatory of Wallace Stevens' "Thirteen Ways of Looking at a Blackbird." But what exactly *are* we looking at? Heathcliff? Cathy? The second generation?

I would like to argue that the center of the text is "Cathy's Book." It is, in fact, a microcosm of Emily Brontë's allusive, elusive narrative technique with its silences and literary spaces. Everything we need to know is in Cathy's "narrative," yet we can only understand it in hindsight through Lockwood's and Nelly's accounts, Heathcliff's and Isabella's supplements. Like *Jane Eyre* it is a retrospective. But unlike *Jane Eyre* it is only part of a larger whole, *Wuthering Heights* itself, which is a divided and again subdivided retrospective privileging no single narrative voice over another (except the voice from the dead). Moreover, Jane's vision of herself as a ten-year-old child is filtered through 30-year-old Jane's consciousness (and unconscious). With Cathy's narrative we are plunged directly into Cathy's and Heathcliff's childhood world, with no mediation other than the uninitiated, ignorant Lockwood's, who is in the reader's position.

---

she at one time almost beat insensible, but which mourned at her bedroom door for days after she died.

28   Newman quotes Clara Kaplan on the "'masculine' position" of "the gaze" (1029). Newman summarizes Teresa de Lauretis's analysis of the gaze of the Medusa: "That is, Medusa defies the male gaze as Western culture has constructed it" (1031). She quotes Stephen Heath's summary of Lacan's seminar on the gaze: "If the woman looks, the spectacle provokes, castration is in the air, the Medusa's head is not far off; thus, she must not look, is absorbed herself on the side of the seer" (92). Cathy II "looks" at Lockwood, and the mild flirtation is over. Like Gilbert and Gubar, but from a different angle, Newman notes that "looking as telling"—Nelly's function as narrator—"works in the service of regulating the family ... to preserve order for the male head of the house" (1035). She seems to borrow from Ian Watt in remarking that the rise of the novel coincides with the rise of the bourgeoisie, adding that the latter creates "the gendered gaze in which each member is constituted as a subject" (1036).

I will examine first Cathy's childhood narrative, and then Heathcliff's and Isabella's relatively unmediated (by Nelly) supplements.

When Lockwood is led to his room for the night by Zillah, then housekeeper at the Heights, the first thing he (and we) learn is that, like the Red Room in *Jane Eyre*, it is a room with a secret, a mystery that lies at the heart of *Wuthering Heights* the text, as at the heart of Wuthering Heights the old farmhouse. Zillah notes that "her mother had an odd notion about the chamber she would put me in; and never let anybody lodge there willingly" (14). She is, in fact, ignorantly violating Heathcliff's orders, for to him the room is a shrine where Cathy and he had their ideal union— Nelly Dean would never have made this mistake, but Nelly now works at the Grange. As the furnishings of the Red Room convey the multi-layered symbolism attached to that color, the furnishings of this bedchamber at the Heights convey a mystery within a mystery, for the bed itself is hidden behind a screen, in "a large oak case, with squares cut out near the top, resembling coach windows" (15). This detail of the "coach windows" associates the bed-closet subtly with movement, perhaps the children's wish to escape Hindley's tyranny through their scamper on the moors, and much later, after Cathy's death, Heathcliff's obsession with joining Cathy's spirit on the moors. Emily Brontë's description of this "little closet" is, in fact, a reworking of a Gothic convention, one borrowed originally from Richardson's *Pamela*, whose heroine is always scribbling in the closet, out of everyone's sight. In *The Poetics of Space*, Gaston Bachelard associates drawers, closets, locks with mysteries to be decoded or decrypted.

Emily Brontë puts another spin on the convention by having the place of dreams also be the place of verbal creativity, as it was for Pamela: "In fact, it formed a little closet, and the ledge of a window, which it enclosed, served as a table" (15). Again, the prophetic Emily anticipates the focus of modern psychoanalytic critics on the relationship between the oneiric and the creative impulse. Much has been written, notably by Dorothy Van Ghent, about the window as the barrier, and, at the same time, the opening, to the world "out there," the world of spirit, of imagination, as opposed to the domestic world of reality, the room itself and the house. The closet, moreover, serves, ultimately, as a coffin for Heathcliff, and he and Cathy achieve consummation in love / death.

I am most interested, however, in the ledge / table as the site of Cathy's creativity.[29] Like schoolgirls and schoolboys before and since, Cathy has inscribed her name—in various alternative forms—on the paint on the wooden ledge: "This

---

29   Carol Jacobs and Stevie Davies have written probably the most insightful pieces on the function of Cathy's text. Jacobs sees Lockwood's reading of the diary and subsequent dream(s) as "the text's mode of elaborating on its own textuality" and as "a pre-figuration of the narrative to come" (53). Davies uses autobiographical materials to connect Cathy's diary with Emily Brontë's diaries. Davies writes of Emily's diaries:

The Diary paper is secret. It was never meant for our eyes. The sensation we receive in viewing its faded and mottled paper is not so very different from the poignant thrill registered in "Wuthering Heights" as Lockwood, rifling through Catherine Earnshaw's book, reads the child's diary of a quarter of a century back, scribbled all down the margins and blank pages of a New Testament and other pious books. (5)

writing, however, was nothing but a name repeated in all kinds of characters, large and small—*Catherine Earnshaw*; here and there varied to *Catherine Heathcliff*, and then again to *Catherine Linton*" (15). We have already met Heathcliff, but, as I have said, must await his narrative of the Grange to meet Edgar Linton. The Poet is the Namer, writes Ralph Waldo Emerson, and Cathy Earnshaw is a kind of poet trying to create her self. She is, in effect, signing her text, moving away from female anonymity, but, like Nathaniel Hawthorne, implying a technique of "multiple choice" (as Hawthorne critic F.O. Matthiessen calls it). Such, in brief, is Emily Brontë's technique throughout the novel. Cathy's creativity succeeds with Lockwood—and the reader—for the drowsy near-dreaming Lockwood feels that "the air swarmed with Catherines" (15)—to paraphrase Norman Mailer, will the real Catherine Earnshaw please stand up?

The window-ledge constitutes not only a writing table, but also a library, symbol— and reality—of both Cathy's and Emily's allusiveness, or use of intertextuality. Cathy has been formed by books, as well as by life—but she resists the books as much as she resists the "socialization" of the child by Hindley and Frances.[30]

---

She explains that Emily "well understood the appetite of readers for 'deciphering hieroglyphics'" (6). Unlike Jacobs, who sees Cathy's self-naming—"I *am* Heathcliff"—as a "willed dispossession of self-unity" (61), Davies claims it transcends gender distinctions:

> While "Wuthering Heights" is an account of female and male sundering and self-division, centralizing woman and making man secondary, it is also a holistic account of male-and-female bonding and identity with one another which at once opens and closes the breach between the sexes ...

> The novel seems to speak at the genderless level of "soul" and it speaks for both sexes in the same scintillating but strangely neutral voice of the spirit at fullest stretch: "I am Heathcliff" annihilates the significance of biological and cultural gender distinctions. (76)

She further notes that the secret diary is a female challenge to the patriarchy:

> Cathy's diaries are the annals of a counter-culture, the secret testament of repressed women and children to whom organized religion is just another name for ill-usage and who (because they have no paper and no authorized public voice) are reduced to inscribing their rebellious testaments all down the margin and on the blank pages of pious books. "Wuthering Heights" foregrounds these marginalia, sidelong the patriarchal text in favour of a transgressive writing recording transgressive actions. The ink from Emily's pen licenses the sacrilege of Cathy's trespass against "good books" which are useful only for defacing with your own story ... Hand-writing (and of course "Wuthering Heights" itself began as a handwritten manuscript, in those days before typewriters) uniquely signs and affirms the self. Its vivacity challenges the authority of sermonical print. (151)

I would add that Cathy's diary moves from private to public status only when the outsider Lockwood reads it, and that Emily Brontë is subtly establishing a parallel to her own movement from private writer of diaries to "public" writer of poetry and a novel whose center is a diary.

30   Gilbert and Gubar note that Isabella Linton has also been formed by books, but by romances that set her up as a potential victim for Heathcliff: Isabella "is victimized by the

Emily, like Charlotte, has begun her novel with a window ledge and a library, where books may represent, ambiguously, both an escape from tyranny, and a means of oppression: John Reed throws a book at Jane, and old Joseph drums the teachings of the Testament into the reluctant Heathcliff and Cathy.

Lockwood's detective work gives the beginnings of the tale a date: if *Wuthering Heights* begins with a date, "1801," the Testament is inscribed (again by Cathy) "'Catherine Earnshaw, her book,' and a date some quarter of a century back," taking us back, approximately, to the mid-1770s. Like Jane Eyre, Cathy Earnshaw does not simply accept what the books tell her; she adapts them to her own imaginative purposes. As an older Jane will borrow bird imagery from Bewick's Birds, and images of oppression by size and power from *Gulliver's Travels*, Cathy, already as a child, *appropriates* the Testament by asserting it is "*her* book," and proceeds to rewrite its pages, wherever space permits, on her own terms: "Catherine's library was select; and its state of dilapidation proved it to have been well used, though not altogether for a legitimate purpose; scarcely one chapter had escaped a pen and ink commentary, at least, the appearance of one, covering every morsel of blank that the printer had left" (15). Cathy seems, in fact, to have created a kind of palimpsest which, I am suggesting, is one way of reading Emily Brontë's text as well with its profusion of documents inherited from the old epistolary novel.

Cathy's "select library," presumably inherited by her daughter, in the second generation part of the novel, also becomes the means for Cathy II to "edu-cate" (lead forth) and civilize young Hareton. If the mother is writer, the daughter is teacher.

Cathy's art is fragmented, elliptical, like Emily's: "Some were detached sentences; other parts took the form of a regular diary, scrawled in an unformed, childish hand" (16).[31] Both Charlotte and Emily are inscribed in the broad tradition of women's writing, taking off from the private forms of letters, diaries, and journals.[32] Cathy is not above illustrating her own text, as well; she provides "an excellent caricature" of old Joseph, as Emily affords us a verbal caricature of him. All of the Brontës, especially Charlotte and Branwell, were visual as well as verbal artists.[33]

Lockwood occupies the reader's position as he begins to decrypt, to decode, "to decypher her [Cathy's] faded hieroglyphics" (16). This is also to be his position throughout the novel. Like George Eliot in *Adam Bede*, Emily Brontë is referring obliquely to the decoding of the Rosetta Stone, which had been discovered by Napoleon's armies in Egypt, and which opened up a whole ancient civilization to the world.

---

genre of romance" (288).

31   Emily was evidently thinking of the Brontës' childhood worlds of Gondal and Angria.

32   Gilbert and Gubar also note the importance of reading to the Brontës: "... it was the habit in the Brontë family, as in the Wollstonecraft–Godwin–Shelley family, to approach reality through the mediating agency of books, to read one's relatives, and to feel related to one's reading. Thus the transformation of three lonely yet ambitious Yorkshire governesses into the magisterially androgynous trio of Currer, Ellis, and Acton Bell was a communal act, an assertion of family identity" (250).

33   In fact, Charlotte had an exhibition of her work, which is more than Branwell ever did.

Then Cathy speaks for two whole pages in her own voice—and a forceful, compelling voice it is, with a genuine novelist's gift for dialogue and rich textures. In these two pages the relatively pre-civilized, pre-socialized (pre-Linton) Cathy is more vividly realized than anywhere else in the novel, with the possible exception of her dialogue with Nelly (again relatively unmediated) when Heathcliff is hidden behind the settle, and she is experiencing the push-pull of socialization / marriage versus wilderness / freedom.[34] Cathy's picture of Joseph preaching to his captive "congregation in the garret," while Hindley and his wife bask downstairs before a comfortable fire, doing anything but reading their bibles, "I'll answer for it," shows a rare comedic strain for a 12-year-old. She elaborates later on Hindley's and Frances's relationship when she and Heathcliff finally "descend" from their "devotions" in the garret, and are promptly dismissed: "Frances pulled his [Heathcliff's] hair heartily; and then went and seated herself on her husband's knee, and there they were, like two babies, kissing and talking nonsense by the hour—foolish palaver that we should be ashamed of" (16). And yet the parallel is there—Hindley will later drink himself to death when Frances dies, as Heathcliff eventually starves himself to rejoin Catherine in death. But Cathy's point is well taken; Heathcliff's and her feelings for each other do escape all bounds of conventional romantic love or sexuality.

The two children put up a curtain over the arch in Cathy's dresser, reinforcing the motif of curtains, cupboards, closets, secrets, hiding. But old Joseph soon rousts them out, unveiling their "cave," and tries to send them back to "*good* books" (17; emphasis mine), as opposed to the kind Cathy likes to read—and write. As John Reed hurled a book at Jane Eyre, inciting *her* act of rebellion, Cathy and Heathcliff "hurl" their "good" books "into the dog-kennel," Cathy "vowing I hated a good book" (17). Does this epitomize *Emily's* quiet—or not so quiet—rebellion? Gérin remarks of Emily's only pronouncement on religion: "Mary Taylor spoke of Emily lying on the hearthrug 'while the other friends discussed questions of religion'; Emily's only contribution was a laconic 'that's right' when Mary claimed that it concerned merely God and oneself" (cited by Gaskell 140–42). It is noteworthy that Cathy's is almost always the first act of rebellion; then Heathcliff follows suit, as Cathy will be first to die, with Heathcliff anxious to follow his "leader." Cathy shows as keen an ear for Yorkshire dialect—which, after all, Lockwood would not understand—as her creator:

"Maister Hindley!" shouted our chaplain. "Maister, coom hither! Miss Cathy's riven th'back off 'Th' Helmet uh Salvation,' un' Heathcliff's pawsed his fit intuh t'first part uh 'T' Brooad Way to Destruction'! It's fair flaysome ut yah let 'en goa on this gait. Ech! th' owd man ud uh laced 'em properly—but he's goan!" (17)

*Pace* Frank Goodridge on Joseph as the conscience of the novel, but the "old man's" failure to discipline Cathy and Heathcliff was what caused the older Hindley's resentment in the first place. Joseph is, in fact, guilty of child abuse. He would, if he could, turn them both into haunted children, like little Miles and Flora in Henry James's *The Turn of the Screw*: "... Joseph asseverated, 'owd Nick' would fetch us

---

34   Craik sees Cathy as "the driving force" of the novel (14), and "the true Catherine" as 12 years old.

as sure as we were living …" (17). (Miriam Allott thinks James may indeed have been influenced by *Wuthering Heights*.) In fact, the first talk of diabolical possession in the novel comes from the "religious" / superstitious old Joseph.

At this point Cathy and Heathcliff cleverly separate momentarily—so the devil will have a harder time finding them. And Cathy turns to "her book," writing on the window ledge / table in the coffin / bed closet. Heathcliff, ever the boy / man of action, becomes "impatient," and rousts her out, proposing "that we should appropriate the dairy woman's cloak, and have a scamper on the moors, under its shelter" (17). This stage of escape—and doubtless many others like it, but this is the last Cathy writes of—is taken up by Heathcliff's narrative in Chapter VI, beginning,

> "Cathy and I escaped from the wash house to have a ramble at liberty, and getting a glimpse of the Grange lights, we thought we would just go and see whether the Lintons passed their Sunday evenings standing shivering in corners, while their father and mother sat eating and drinking, and singing and laughing, and burning their eyes out before the fire. Do you think they do? Or reading sermons, and being catechised by their man-servant, and set to learn a column of Scripture names, if they don't answer properly?" (39)

Heathcliff's question will be answered later, but we should first look at Lockwood's dream(s), triggered by Cathy's creative imagination.

Cathy is the writer of the two, not Heathcliff, though he does compose and dictate his son Linton's letters to Cathy II, borrowing the conventional language of romance (which he has also, presumably, exploited in courting Linton's mother, Isabella). Does writing presume a certain stillness, which Heathcliff habitually rejects? Or does the female's conditioning to readier socialization produce a kind of creative tension between wildnesss and civilization that may be conducive to art? At any rate, as I have said earlier, the male, Heathcliff, remains a "wild child," like Truffaut's hero / anti-hero in *The Four Hundred Blows* and *The Wild Child*, unchanneled by society, and like Sir Walter Scott's Whistler in *The Heart of Midlothian* (1818), or William Golding's boys who revert to savagery in *Lord of the Flies* (1954). Cathy Earnshaw, on the other hand, and Hawthorne's little Pearl in *The Scarlet Letter*, both "wild children" at the start, ultimately try—one (Cathy) fruitlessly, the other (little Pearl) successfully—to reconcile nature and civilization.[35]

But what of the "civilization" they are being conditioned to accept? It appears ambiguous in both Lockwood's dream and in Lockwood himself. In fact, Lockwood's dream splits neatly into the Joseph-driven religious conditioning part, and the Cathy-driven escape / freedom part. Lockwood makes the mistake of falling asleep over a sermon title, "Seventy Times Seven, and the First of the Seventy First. A Pious Discourse delivered by the Reverend Jabes Branderham, in the Chapel of Gimmerdon Sough" (18). Lockwood comments that he cannot remember another such night "since I was capable of suffering"—a rather ironic comment in that we are invited to compare his suffering with Heathcliff's, which takes on a whole different dimension. Lockwood imagines Joseph as his guide in this skewed Pilgrim's Progress, also the source of the ending of *Jane Eyre*. Old Joseph's religion confuses "a pilgrim's staff"

---

35   See my article, "'A Wild Child': A Cross-Cultural Literary View," in *Existere* for a more detailed analysis of the "wild child" theme.

with "a heavy-headed cudgel"; *his* "religion" is used as a weapon of fear. Lockwood recollects "Gimmerton Sough" which he has passed, and one little detail about it is destined to be used later: the chapel "lies in a hollow, between two hills—an elevated hollow—near a swamp, whose peaty moisture is said to answer all the purposes of embalming on the few corpses deposited there" (18).[36] One of those corpses is Cathy's, and we learn later that Heathcliff, with an obsession verging on necrophilia, has the sexton "remove the earth off her coffin lid" and opens it: "I would have stayed there, when I saw her face again—it is hers yet—he had hard work to stir me; but he said it would change, if the air blew on it …" (244). Heathcliff bribes the sexton to loosen one side of the coffin and remove it when Heathcliff is buried beside her, and one side of Heathcliff's, so that their dust will mingle and they will finally attain the fusion of flesh and spirit they sought so desperately in life. They will, in fact, become part of the wild landscape, of the heath. Linton, Cathy, and Heathcliff are to rest finally together, but Linton's coffin remains sealed.[37]

Lockwood's dream triggers a Hawthornesque phenomenon: the search for "the unpardonable sin," carried out by Hawthorne's Ethan Brand.[38] Had Hawthorne read Emily Brontë? I suspect as much. Lockwood speculates on "odd transgressions that I never imagined previously," and finally he stands to "denounce Jabes Branderham as the sinner of the sin that no Christian need pardon" (19). Jabes in turn denounces him: "*Thou art the Man*" (19). Indeed, each of us conceives of ourself as the worst sinner, committing transgressions we can only imagine. Lockwood, identifying with Cathy and Heathcliff, makes an imaginative leap into their drama of passion, jealousy, and revenge. And the reader takes the same trip. Lockwood moves from dream to reality in hearing "a shower of loud taps on the boards of the pulpit," which turns out to be "only the branch of a fir-tree that touched my lattice" (20). Cathy II later climbs down that tree to meet Heathcliff and his son Linton. The effect is similar to that of Emily Dickinson's poem, "'Twas like a Maelstrom," composed of three stanzas based on similes, with the subject of the poem being the "It" in "'Twas"—death? Something else? The persona awakens from a dream—or does she?—only to find the reality is worse. The whole poem poses the question, "Which agony was the utterest, then,—to perish or to live?"

> 'Twas like a Maelstrom, with a notch,
> That nearer, every Day,
> Kept narrowing its boiling Wheel
> Until the Agony
>
> Toyed coolly with the final inch
> Of your delirious Hem –
> And you dropt, lost,

---

36   Inga-Stina Ewbank mentions the significance of the embalming peat.

37   I am reminded again of Hawthorne's *The Scarlet Letter*, where Hester, Chillingworth, and Dimmesdale are buried under one headstone, with the epitaph, "On a field, sable, the letter A, gules."

38   Peter Allen Dale notes that in real life all the Brontë children "agonized over the unforgiveable sin" (281).

When something broke –
And let you from a Dream –

As if a Goblin with a Gauge –
Kept measuring the Hours –
Until you felt your Second
Weigh, helpless, in his Paws –

And not a Sinew – stirred – could help,
And sense was setting numb –
When God – remembered – and the Fiend
Let go, then, Overcome –

As if your Sentence stood – pronounced –
And you were frozen led
From Dungeon's luxury of Doubt
To Gibbets, and the Dead –

And when the Film had stitched your eyes
A Creature gasped "Reprieve"!
Which Anguish was the utterest – then –
To perish, or to live?
c. 1862

Lockwood awakens only to dream again, "if possible, still more disagreeably than before"—the famous, powerful "Cathy-dream." This time the setting is not transposed: "I remembered I was lying in the oak closet" (20). He imagines he is trying to silence the fir-tree branch, but is unable to open the casement: "The hook was soldered into the staple, a circumstance observed by me, when awake, but forgotten" (20)—a realistic dream indeed! So Lockwood breaks the glass with his knuckles, reaches through it for "the importunate branch; instead of which, my fingers closed on the fingers of a little, ice-cold hand!" The entire passage is compellingly dramatized:

> The intense horror of nightmare came over me; I tried to draw back my arm, but, the hand clung to it, and a most melancholy voice, sobbed,
>
> "Let me in—let me in!"
>
> "Who are you?" I asked struggling, meanwhile, to disengage myself.
>
> "Catherine Linton," it replied, shiveringly, (why did I think of *Linton*? I had read *Earnshaw* twenty times for Linton) "I'm come home, I'd lost my way on the moor!"
>
> As it spoke, I discerned, obscurely, a child's face looking through the window—Terror made me cruel; and, finding it useless to attempt shaking the creature off, I pulled its wrist on to the broken pane, and rubbed it to and fro till the blood ran down and soaked the bed clothes: still it wailed, "Let me in!" and maintained its tenacious gripe, almost maddening me with fear.

"How can I?" I said at length. "Let *me* go, if you want me to let you in!"

The fingers relaxed, I snatched mine through the hole, hurriedly piled the books up in a pyramid against it, and stopped my ears to exclude the lamentable prayer.

I seemed to keep them closed above a quarter of an hour, yet, the instant I listened, again, there was the doleful cry moaning on!

"Begone!" I shouted, "I'll never let you in, not if you beg for twenty years!"

"It's twenty years," mourned the voice, "twenty years, I've been a waif for twenty years!"

Thereat began a feeble scratching outside, and the pile of books moved as if thrust forward.

I tried to jump up; but could not stir a limb; and so, yelled aloud, in a frenzy of fright. (20–21)

I see the dream as technicolor, and it is worth noting that Lockwood, who dreams he has broken the glass, must also be bleeding in his dream.[39] He tries to use Cathy's books as a barrier against her, and it does not stretch the point too much to see him as a representative of that civilization which separated her from Heathcliff.

His unfortunate scream awakens Heathcliff, who imagines that Cathy has indeed returned. Lockwood says, "It is only your guest, sir," but "guest" and "ghost" are unmistakably homonyms. Zillah's impropriety in assigning Lockwood the room— "It was your servant, Zillah"—introduces obliquely Nelly Dean and foreshadows the long tale of Nelly's and Heathcliff's checkered relationship. Lockwood proceeds to make matters worse by ranting of "ghosts and goblins," and continues to guess at Cathy's role in all this: "If the little fiend had got in at the window, she probably would have strangled me! ... that minx, Catherine Linton, or Earnshaw, or however she was called—she must have been a changeling—wicked little soul! She told me she had been walking the earth these twenty years: a just punishment for her mortal transgressions, I've no doubt!" (22). Having put his foot in it, Lockwood suddenly recollects that Cathy had linked her name with Heathcliff's in the testament / diary. At this Lockwood edits himself, to conceal the fact he has been reading private diaries, and claims that the whole dream was suggested by "spelling over the name scratched on that window-ledge" (22). Lockwood's concealment of the whole truth ministers to Heathcliff's superstition that Cathy has indeed revealed all this past history in the dream alone:

"Come in! come in!" he sobbed. "Cathy, do come. Oh do—*once* more! Oh! my heart's darling, hear me *this* time—Catherine, at last!" (23)

---

39  I am indebted particularly to Derek Traversi—not surprisingly, a Shakespearean scholar—for focusing my attention on the dream which, according to Traversi, produces on Lockwood and the reader "a sense of physical pain that borders on the intolerable" (52–3).

Later we learn that Heathcliff has *wanted* Cathy to haunt him. As she is dying, he exclaims:

"... And I pray one prayer—I repeat it till my tongue stiffens—Catherine Earnshaw, may you not rest, as long as I am living! You said I killed you—haunt me then! The murdered *do* haunt their murderers. I believe I know that ghosts *have* wandered on earth. Be with me always—take any form—drive me mad! only *do* not leave me in this abyss, where I cannot find you! Oh, God! it is unutterable! I *cannot* live without my life! I *cannot* live without my soul!" (143)

Even James Joyce, in *A Portrait of the Artist as a Young Man*, never surpassed Emily Brontë in her introduction of all the leitmotifs and major themes of the novel through an opening microcosm. The scratched and bleeding hand motif recurs twice. Cathy, now Mrs. Linton, has a catfight with Isabella who is being "courted"—if "courting" is the right word for it—by Heathcliff for revenge and her estate. Cathy clutches Isabella's arm in an effort to persuade her of the danger she is incurring, and Isabella scratches her in an effort to free herself:

"There's a tigress!" exclaimed Mrs. Linton, setting her free, and shaking her hand with pain. (90)

And, finally, as has long been noted, Heathcliff dies in the coffin / bed, the window open to the moors—and Cathy's ghost—and his hand scratched:

"I [Nelly] could not think him dead—but his face, and throat were washed with rain; the bed-clothes dripped, and he was perfectly still. The lattice, flapping to and fro, had grazed one hand that rested on the sill—no blood trickled from the broken skin, and when I put my fingers to it, I could doubt no more—he was dead and stark!" (284)

The tree image itself affords continuity with the second generation. Young Cathy II grows "like a larch" (160). She is agile, like her mother, and loves to climb trees: "In summer, Miss Catherine delighted to climb along these trunks, and sit in the branches, swinging twenty feet above the ground ..." (195). Like the older generation, Cathy II and Hareton are at least in part associated with the Yorkshire landscape. We are told, "Catherine's face was just like the landscape" (225). Cathy II compares her idea of happiness to young Linton's:

"... He said the pleasantest manner of spending a hot July day was lying from morning till evening on a bank of heath in the middle of the moors, with the bees humming dreamily about among the bloom, and the larks singing high up over head, and the blue sky, and bright sun shining steadily and cloudlessly. That was his most perfect idea of heaven's happiness—mine was rocking in a rustling green tree, with a west wind blowing, and bright, white clouds flitting rapidly above; and not only larks, but throstles, and blackbirds, and linnets, and cuckoos pouring out music on every side, and the moors seen at a distance, broken into cool dusky dells; but close by great swells of long grass undulating in waves to the breeze; and woods and sounding water, and the whole world awake and wild with joy. He wanted all to lie in an ecstasy of peace; I wanted all to sparkle and dance in a glorious jubilee." (210)

And when her father dies, Cathy II, now Mrs. Linton Heathcliff, escapes her prison at the Heights by climbing down the very same tree whose tapping branch triggered Lockwood's dream (241–2).[40]

Heathcliff tries to turn Hareton, metaphorically, into a crooked tree, as Hareton's father Hindley tried to do with Heathcliff: "Now, my bonny lad, you are *mine*! and we'll see if one tree won't grow as crooked as another, with the same wind to twist it!" Heathcliff has previously used a similar metaphor to describe his beloved Cathy I's position as Mrs. Edgar Linton at the Grange: "He might as well plant an oak in a flower-pot, and expect it to thrive, as imagine he can restore her to vigour in the soil of his shallow cares!" (131).

*Heathcliff's and Isabella's Supplements*

Heathcliff dies with his grazed hand on the ledge, Cathy's former writing table. His own narrative contributions are not written (apart from the letters, previously mentioned, to Cathy II which he dictates to his son Linton). Heathcliff lives out the text Cathy creates, to the bitter end. He fills in the gap at the end of Cathy's diary, recounting their first visit to the Grange. He corrects Nelly's reading of the Lintons as "good children," depicting them as spoiled brats, trying to pull a dog apart between them. According to Heathcliff, he and Cathy equally scorned "the petted things"—but then the first major event of the past narrative occurs—*another* dog, the family bull dog, seizes Cathy by the ankle: "She did not yell out—no! She would have scorned to do it, if she had been spitted on the horns of a mad cow" (41). But thus begins Cathy's socialization, her five-week separation from Heathcliff while her ankle mends at the Grange—and, to all intents and purposes, thus ends her writing career. The fact that she is female, that she was somewhat more socialized than Heathcliff to begin with, makes her more vulnerable to social ambition and material concerns. From Lockwood's evidence, her "writing" thereafter consists simply of the trying on of potential marital surnames scratched on the ledge. But is it not also possible that early on, her female-ness (she is less active than Heathcliff) and her partial socialization were enabling factors for her writing? The "essential" Cathy, at any rate, as Craik has said, is the 12-year-old.

A second female writer is the adult Isabella Linton, now Mrs. Heathcliff, whose long letter in Chapter XIII is a cry for help, addressed to Nelly, but really directed at Edgar, who has cast her off after her marriage to the hated Heathcliff. Her epistolary style can be compared to Cathy's: "Inform Edgar that I'd give the world to see his face again—that my heart returned to Thrushcross Grange in twenty-four hours after I left it" (116)—as Cathy's returns to the Heights. The friendliest presence at

---

40  Like Faulkner in *The Sound and the Fury*, Emily Brontë may be implying the Tree of Knowledge: Caddy Compson climbs down a tree at her window to enter the world of adult sexuality. In this instance, at least, Cathy II enters the world of death.

the Heights is, once again, a dog, "Throttler, whom I now recognized as a son of our old Skulker" (123). Isabella idealizes her old home, but her nostalgia should be compared to Heathcliff's initial perceptions of it. From Heathcliff's point of view, it was the home of sloth, indulgence, and spoiled children.

Isabella does validate Lockwood's initial perception of the Heights as a terrifying setting. She also validates Heathcliff's recognition that Hareton has "a look of Catherine in his eyes, and about his mouth" (117), as does his father Hindley: "… *his* eyes, too, were like a ghostly Catherine's …" (118).

The demonization of Heathcliff probably reaches its apogee, understandably, with Isabella: "Is Mr. Heathcliff a man? If so, is he mad? And if not, is he a devil?" (116). She also calls him "a tiger, or a venomous serpent" (124). Isabella proves her total inadequacy in the kitchen, and, unlike Cathy, defends herself only by stealth. She sees herself almost as a kidnapped bride in a melodrama, a victim, or Pamela abducted and imprisoned by Mr. B—but if so, it is a situation more like Austen's Catherine Morland, who is thrown out of Northanger Abbey and sent home when General Tilney thinks that her fortune is inadequate to marry his son. Heathcliff has, in fact, been clever enough to push the button of romance or melodrama in Isabella: "She abandoned them [her family] under a delusion, … picturing in me a hero of romance, and expecting unlimited indulgences from my chivalrous devotion. I can hardly regard her in the light of a rational creature …" (128).[41] Heathcliff calls Isabella "an abject thing," a "brach" (again, a dog) (129).

He is taking revenge for her childish contempt for him, "Isabella lisping," noting his resemblance to the fortune-teller's son. It is not so much Isabella, as her dishonoring him in front of Cathy, that Heathcliff cannot forgive. He speaks of "their [Edgar's and Isabella's] vacant blue eyes" (42), and he clearly hates Isabella for resembling Edgar, their blue eyes contrasted to the dark eyes of Cathy and Heathcliff.

As children, Isabella and Edgar are spoiled, whereas Cathy and Heathcliff are neglected or abused. But there is a parallel: both sets of children (the dark and the fair) grow up fancying "the world was made for their accommodation" (83). Even Nelly admits that Edgar "wanted spirit in general" (56), and he dies easily at 39 whereas Heathcliff must actively will himself to die.

*Cathy's Verbal Gifts*

Although the interest is pretty equally divided between Cathy and Heathcliff—they see themselves, after all, as one—Cathy is given all the best speeches, despite the fact she dies at the beginning of Chapter XVI, about midway through the text, and is dead nearly twenty years for the better part of the narrative.

Heathcliff, we are told, has a clipped speech, a "laconic style of chipping off his pronouns, and auxiliary verbs" (5)—ergo, he is not verbally skilled. As a boy, mistreated by Hindley, he gives up books, slouches, loses ground, forgets "any curiosity he once possessed in pursuit of knowledge, and any love for books, or learning" (57). This is the pattern he tries to impose later on Hindley's son Hareton.

---

41   One thinks again of Austen, and of Mrs. Croft's distinction, in *Persuasion*, between "fine ladies" and "rational creatures."

But he and Cathy always understand each other, even on a non-verbal level. He would allow Cathy whatever she wants, even if it's Linton: "I never would have banished him from her society as long as she desired his. The moment her regard ceased, I would have torn his heart out, and drunk his blood!" (127)—Heathcliff as vampire! Indeed, like the dog imagery, there is a great deal of blood imagery in the novel, the most vivid of which is imaginary—or is it?—in Lockwood's dream. Heathcliff sees his love is greater than Linton's: "If he loved with all the powers of his puny being, he couldn't love as much in eighty years, as I could in a day. And Catherine has a heart as deep as I have; the sea could be as easily contained in that horse trough, as her whole affection be monopolized by him ... It is not in him to be loved like me, how can she love in him what he has not?" (127). Critics have noted, moreover, that they always tell the truth to each other. Heathcliff does not deny that she is dying: "Oh, Cathy! Oh my life! how can I bear it?" (135). And again, "oh God! would *you* like to live with your soul in the grave?" (138).[42]

Cathy, for obvious reasons (she has not been rescued from a Liverpool slum) is much more articulate than Heathcliff. At first she shares the family's contempt for the little dark orphan, especially angry because her father was supposed to bring her a riding whip, not an orphan boy. A whip, indeed!—Catherine's character is immediately sharply defined, and her father prefers Heathcliff to both Catherine and Hindley. Heathcliff, however, comes to prefer the spirited Cathy to her father. When her father asks her why she cannot always be good, her quick, prescient reply is, "Why cannot you always be a good man, father?" (36). Immediately thereafter he dies—which does problematize his relationship to Heathcliff—just favoritism? Love for the dead son of the same name? Disappointment in Hindley? Or something else?

After his death both Heathcliff and Cathy are abused by Hindley, but especially Heathcliff, who is utterly degraded and treated like a servant or stable hand. Even Jane Eyre was not utterly deprived of books and letters. Following the excursion to the Grange, Cathy is apparently—only apparently—transformed by the supposedly well-bred Lintons. The surface politeness and luxury of the Grange awaken her social drives. She becomes "the queen of the countryside" at 15 (55), "full of ambition" (56). Nelly realizes, moreover, her isolation—that she becomes Cathy's confidante for want of anyone with more authority or maturity. She wants "to be the greatest woman of the neighbourhood," she confides to Nelly (66)—an ambition she might have transcended if the hurt Heathcliff, who has overheard her revelations to Nelly, had not taken himself off in search of a fortune.

But the deepest Cathy—like the "serious self" of Emma Woodhouse, as Mr. Knightley calls it—never really changes. Edgar has one warning of her unregulated passion when she slaps him for trying to protect young Hareton from her wrath (60). Cathy claims she meant no harm, but she can get her own way by crying herself sick: "I did nothing deliberately—Well, go, if you please—get away! And now I'll cry—I'll cry myself sick!" (61). This scene foreshadows her self-induced illness

---

42  The Wyler film is much more conventionally romantic. Cathy dies in Heathcliff's arms when he carries her to the window. This scene, I believe, inspired the equally romantic *Wake of the Red Witch* in which John Wayne carries a dying Gail Russell to the window.

when Heathcliff runs off, and later when he returns and conflict arises between him and Edgar, now her husband.

In the crucial dialogue with Nelly, where Heathcliff is hidden behind the settle, but Nelly at first thinks he has gone to the stable and she is "alone" (65), Cathy has some of the most powerful dialogue in the novel, and makes it clear her physical / spiritual union to the point of identification with Heathcliff remains intact: as for marrying Edgar, "In whichever place the soul lives—in my soul, and in my heart, I'm convinced I'm wrong!" (67). Cathy warns us she would be unhappy in heaven: "If I were in heaven, Nelly, I should be extremely miserable," and she continues, making it clear that Heathcliff's absence from heaven would be the crux:

> "I was only going to say that heaven did not seem to be my home; and I broke my heart with weeping to come back to earth; and the angels were so angry that they flung me out, into the middle of the heath on the top of Wuthering Heights; where I woke sobbing for joy ... I've no more business to marry Edgar Linton than I have to be in heaven; and if the wicked man in there [Hindley], had not brought Heathcliff so low I shouldn't have thought of it. It would degrade me to marry Heathcliff, now; so he shall never know how I love him; and that, not because he's handsome, Nelly, but because he's more myself than I am. Whatever our souls are made of, his and mine are the same, and Linton's is as different as a moonbeam from lightning, or frost from fire." (68)

Emily Dickinson's poem, "I cannot live with you," expresses a similar transcendent (or Transcendental) desire for fusion, where she would choose damnation, over "sordid excellence / As Paradise," were the lover damned:

> And were You lost, I would be –
> Though My Name
> Rang loudest
> On the Heavenly fame –
>
> And were You – saved –
> And I – condemned to be
> Where You were not –
> That self – were Hell to Me –
> c. 1862

Cathy's speech foreshadows the hypothetical ghostly reunion of Cathy and Heathcliff at the end which is reported, significantly, by a child—these two were most united as children.[43] At this point in the dialogue, "Ere this speech ended," Nelly becomes conscious of Heathcliff's presence and sees him "steal out, noiselessly" (68). She fails to stop Cathy's speech before the end, and though she knows he departed *after* Cathy's statement that it would degrade her to marry him, and *before* her final affirmation of love, Nelly fails to alert Cathy that he has overheard most of their

---

43  As Ewbank remarks, when the dying Cathy dreams in delirium of "the first time she was 'laid alone,'" "At this stage in the novel, the bed and its window has grown into a symbol of the time when Heathcliff was Cathy's 'all in all.' After Heathcliff's death, perhaps neither of them is laid alone? We do not know ... Emily Brontë stops short of the final mystery" (333).

exchange. Especially, Heathcliff misses the poetic similes in which Cathy compares her passing attraction to Linton and her deep, abiding passion for Heathcliff to the landscape:

> "... My love for Linton is like the foliage in the woods. Time will change it, I'm well aware, as winter changes the trees—my love for Heathcliff resembles the eternal rocks beneath—a source of little visible delight, but necessary. Nelly, I *am* Heathcliff—he's always, always in my mind—not as a pleasure, any more than I am always a pleasure to myself—but, as my own being—so, don't talk of our separation again—it is impracticable; and—" (70)

Heathcliff, of course, has unfortunately already left the room, and never hears Cathy's confession. Nor does Nelly help matters much by keeping Heathcliff's presence during the earlier part of the interview a secret. It is also at this point that Cathy speaks probably the most important line in the novel: "What were the use of creation if I were entirely contained here?" (70). That question may be answered by the little boy who thinks he encounters Cathy's and Heathcliff's ghosts at the end. That would confirm Cathy's creative authority. But it should be noted that it is no orthodox heavenly hereafter she seems to envisage, but an absorption into nature.[44]

After marriage to Linton, Cathy's sense of identity with Heathcliff and with nature remains intact. In the climactic scene in Chapter XV just before Cathy II's almost parenthetic birth and her mother Cathy's death, Cathy is dressed in white for her final earthly reunion with Heathcliff as if, although bearing Edgar's child, she were Heathcliff's bride (133). Thus Heathcliff can almost be seen as the father of both Linton and Cathy II.

*Patriarchy and Art*

Cathy II is more than a parenthesis in the text, however—her tale occupies the whole latter half of the book.[45] In an important sense, she completes her mother's work, and biological and textual creativity merge (as they do in *The Scarlet Letter*). I still find compelling Cecil's focus on the second generation as providing a necessary continuity in *this* life, whereas Cathy and Heathcliff seek an unattainable—except in death—ideal of fusion. If the second generation's love story is diachronic—therefore tellable by Nelly—the first generation's is synchronic—timeless, encompassing all time—and therefore recoverable only by the reader. The artist's speech (Cathy's) is clearly synchronic, whereas the second generation story, dealing with the attainable, belongs more to the world of Charlotte Brontë.[46] But I would like to return to Lockwood's dream of Cathy again, and her Emersonian poetic naming of herself.

---

44   Cathy's view may also account for the frequent association of the characters with the landscape, or with animals.

45   Mary Burgan and others have taken a cue from Cecil in focusing on the second generation theme.

46   Juliet McMaster deals with the sexual imagery in the Linton–Cathy II marriage as an expansion of the theme of juvenile sexuality. She argues that Cathy II is "symbolically raped by a father-and-son team," though it is implied she never literally loses her virginity in this

Catherine Earnshaw becomes Catherine Linton, bears a daughter named Catherine Linton who marries to become first Mrs. Catherine Heathcliff (if we accept that as a surname), and finally, after widowhood, Mrs. Catherine Earnshaw—the circle is complete, and the first Cathy seems also, through her daughter, to revert to her original strong childhood identity.

In a sense, the two youngsters, Cathy II and Hareton, redeem Heathcliff, who is never as much of a villain as he tries to be. (One critic, at least, expresses disappointment at his lack of will!) But the spirit of the first Cathy animates the two youngsters, and Heathcliff is never as bad as he seems. From the moment he instinctively saves the baby Hareton dropped over the balustrade by his drunken father Hindley, we know that he will never mistreat any kin of Catherine's but Hindley, who had abused them both.

Heathcliff betrays his own nature, his "deepest self" (meaning Cathy), when he plays the role of cruel, tyrannical patriarch with Cathy's daughter and nephew. Their eyes, he says, are Cathy's, and rebuke him. Heathcliff is the principal male figure in the novel who, by definition, seems to escape patriarchal roles, in that he does not know who his father is, and his surname and "Christian" names are identical. Hareton also, to a certain extent, is raised without a father—at least a responsible one—although he knows his identity. These two "free" males are the ones beloved by both Cathys.

To be "free" is to deny, or be outside, the patriarchy (the two Cathys, Heathcliff and Hareton). Cathy and Heathcliff both succumb at one point, the former to social ambition, the latter to revenge.[47] The patriarchy is based on one kind of document—legal (the entail, genealogical charts, inheritance).[48] Counterpointed throughout are literary works—Nelly is well-read for a poor man's daughter; Cathy I and II are both constantly seen with book in hand. Cathy I writes a book or journal in which she sounds most, of all the characters, like her creator Emily Brontë. Cathy II's relationship with Hareton is triggered first by his theft of her books, in a desire to improve himself. By the time Lockwood returns, after Heathcliff's death, in 1802, young Cathy is teaching her "handsome young rustic" fiancé, Hareton, how to read, in a charming scene:

"And now, kiss me, for minding so well."

"No, read it over first correctly, without a single mistake."

---

first marriage (11). She also quotes Patricia Yaeger that "The novel runs with a river of female blood" (4; Yaeger, 220), and, like Gilbert and Gubar, notes that in Cathy I "the bleeding wound" signals menstruation, but McMaster adds that in Cathy II it symbolizes "defloration." Clearly, one could associate this imagery with that of the Red Room in *Jane Eyre.*

47   Eagleton argues that Heathcliff, like the others, cannot maintain integrity with capital (395). Society has produced "a pitiless capitalist landlord out of an oppressed child" (407).

48   The mistake, we recall, that Faulkner's former poor boy, Thomas Sutpen in *Absalom, Absalom!*, makes is a repetition of Heathcliff's: to become part of the system, rather than rebelling against it.

The male speaker began to read—he was a young man, respectably dressed, and seated at a table, having a book before him. (260)

Thus a book begins and ends the novel, both in defiance of patriarchal structures, one written by the first Cathy, the other taught by the second Cathy, a pattern comparable in some ways to that of *Jane Eyre*, which begins with the heroine as a reader of books, and ends with her as a writer. The ghosts of Wuthering Heights are, in a sense, both animated and freed (exorcised?) by the literary word, a word which seems to come from beyond the graves of both Catherine Earnshaw and her creator Emily Brontë.

Have I solved the Sphinx's riddle in *Wuthering Heights*? I doubt it; I keep thinking of Henry James's remark about Hawthorne's cryptic "Young Goodman Brown": "If it means anything, it means too much." But perhaps the emphasis on female literariness versus patriarchal discourse in *Wuthering Heights* may shed some light.

# Chapter 5

# "The Iron of Slavery in Her Heart": The Literary Relationship of Elizabeth Gaskell and Harriet Beecher Stowe

Mentioning Elizabeth Gaskell (1810–65) and Harriet Beecher Stowe (1811–96) in the same breath may seem like an arbitrary juxtaposition. Perhaps the most obvious common element in their two careers is that both are women novelists who, despite tremendous popularity in their own era, have until recently suffered benign critical neglect in ours.[1]

Even when she is incorporated in the canon, Elizabeth Gaskell is often described as a "major-minor" or "minor-major" Victorian novelist, somewhat overshadowed by the four unqualifiedly major British women novelists of the nineteenth century, Jane Austen, her friends Charlotte and Emily Brontë, and her younger contemporary George Eliot. We tend to forget that the comparison is unfair in that the other four were groundbreakers who experimented with the young, flexible form of the novel more daringly than their British male contemporaries; and that Mrs. Gaskell's substance and technique were far more typical of her period.

Mrs. Stowe, on the other hand, was certainly not overshadowed during her own period. We have all heard the story that President Abraham Lincoln is supposed to have said, on being introduced to her, "So this is the little lady who made this big war" (480).[2] Her *Uncle Tom's Cabin* is usually cited as the most striking example of a literary work that has changed the course of history. But there is always a slight malaise or embarrassment when we mention Mrs. Stowe's triumph. Since the 1950s, both her artistry—in particular, her alleged sentimentality and her propagandizing—and her ideology have fallen into disrepute.

---

1    Whether or not they are currently regarded as "canonical" depends on one's historical perspective. Sue Roe, the Editor of the Indiana University Key Women Writers Series, which includes Patsy Stoneman's *Elizabeth Gaskell*, asks whether mainstream women writers, among whom she includes Gaskell, can be regarded as feminists. For some feminist critics, mainstream means malestream. But perhaps some of these mainstream writers have been canonized for the wrong reasons, coopted by the malestream, when in their own day they may have been subversive. Roe suggests that they too may have been misread, and that it is time for revisionist readings of the canon.

2    Quoted by John William Ward, "Afterword," Harriet Beecher Stowe, *Uncle Tom's Cabin*.

In the 1950s the novel became an acute source of embarrassment to Civil Rights activists in the United States.[3] As a result of the "consciousness-raising" effected in part by the Supreme Court decision to desegregate the public schools (*Brown vs. Board of Education*, 1954), to be labelled an "Uncle Tom" was to be accused of collaborating with the oppressor. Still today, only the few who have read the book recognize that Mrs. Stowe's Uncle Tom was by no means an "Uncle Tom" in the 1950s sense; he was self-sacrificing, while a contemporary "Uncle Tom" was guileful.[4]

The neglect of both women writers has resulted not only from shifting historical perspectives, but also from shifting critical trends. In her 1929 *A Room of One's Own*, Virginia Woolf describes being invited to give a lecture on Women in Literature. Outlining the usual topics, she says that she will be expected to make "a passing reference to Mrs. Gaskell"—and indeed that is the one and only reference she does make. She proceeds to develop a theory that the great women novelists effected a tradeoff of biological for artistic creativity. Her failure to highlight Gaskell's achievements seems to result not so much from a negative assessment of her talent as from her inability to fit Gaskell into the pattern of singleness / childlessness, a pattern Mrs. Stowe also violates.[5]

Criticism is coming back to Mrs. Gaskell, and it is beginning to do so with Mrs. Stowe as well. Edgar F. Wright's *Mrs. Gaskell: A Reassessment* (1965), was an early sign of this revival of interest in Gaskell, pursued today by writers like Patsy Stoneman whose 1987 book places Gaskell in relation to critical ideologies ranging from Marxism in the 1950s to socialist feminism today.[6]

---

3    The most famous voice attacking Stowe's "message" was James Baldwin in his essay, "Everybody's Protest Novel," in *Notes of a Native Son*. Baldwin objected strenuously to Stowe's alleged "racism": her mulatto couple, Eliza and George Harris, are able to escape via the Underground Railroad to Canada because they can pass for white, whereas her "Uncle Tom," African to the core, "jet-black, wooly-haired, illiterate ... and ... phenomenally forbearing" (17), cannot escape by disguising himself and is therefore sold down river to die ultimately at the hands of the archetypal villainous slaveowner, Simon Legree.

4    Moreover, Alice Crozier, in *The Novels of Harriet Beecher Stowe*, reminds us that Uncle Tom dies as a result of courage, not cowardice: "Uncle Tom was killed by Simon Legree because he would not inform on his escaped fellow slaves, Cassy and Emmeline ... The reason that Tom is today regarded as a symbol of the cowardly, bootlicking slave is that he forgives Legree" (vii).

5    Lord David Cecil, in *Victorian Novelists*, has been much lambasted for his condescending view of Mrs. Gaskell—"... her work was wholly lacking in the virile qualities. Her genius is so purely feminine that it excludes from her achievement not only specifically masculine themes, but all the more masculine qualities of thought and feeling" (185)—but he was only repeating a critical commonplace first served up by Virginia Woolf a few years earlier.

6    Stoneman's Preface asks whether women writers like Gaskell have been adopted into the canon at the expense of being misread as women. In her useful historical overview of Gaskell criticism, Stoneman notes that the eminently sensible, tolerant Gaskell is often deemed irrelevant or marginal by those critics who see Charlotte Brontë's *Jane Eyre* as the central document in nineteenth-century women's literature (see Gilbert and Gubar, *The Madwoman in the Attic*). She continues, Gaskell has been "colonized up to a point by Marxists [Arnold

Ironically, as well, Mrs. Stowe is neglected by readers and critics today because in her own time she was so popular. *Uncle Tom's Cabin* started the best-seller era.[7] In the mid-nineteenth century the neglected authors were those now seen as giants, Hawthorne and Melville. The assumption seems to be that what was seen as popular in the nineteenth century cannot be taken seriously today. Yet in the nineteenth century Heine called *Uncle Tom's Cabin* "the greatest book since the Bible" (quoted by Gerson 72), and Tolstoy compared it to *A Tale of Two Cities* and *Les Misérables*. Even Henry James paid a somewhat bemused tribute to her composition, saying that it was "as if a fish, a wonderful 'leaping' fish, had simply flown through the air" (quoted by Foster 13).

Many postmodernist critics, both feminist and others, now reject the New Critical (Old New and New New / structuralist) tendency to devalue social commitment in favor of formal experimentation à la Flaubert. The kind of literature Gaskell and Stowe wrote can now be situated referentially, and without apology, in its socio-historical context. Moreover, Woolf's theory of the biological tradeoff has been increasingly disputed by the experience of contemporary writers like Alice Munro, who claims that writing is "just something I did, like the ironing."[8]

---

Kettle, John Lucas, Raymond Williams], but almost ignored by feminists" (1). Yet Gaskell may, in fact, have been more politically radical and committed than her more frequently critiqued literary "sisters", such as Charlotte Brontë, whose heroines plumb psychological depths but whose resolutions remain individual.

Stoneman does not deal with Winifred Gérin's fine biography, *Elizabeth Gaskell*, from a theoretical standpoint, but actually Gérin affords many fresh insights into Gaskell's character and writings, and forces one to rethink Gaskell's feminism. Aina Rubenius, author of *The Woman Question in Mrs. Gaskell's Life and Works*, should also be mentioned as a major contributor to Gaskell scholarship; she pioneered a feminist approach in the 1950s. Poststructuralist theory, Stoneman thinks, could point the way to a reevaluation of Gaskell: women writers are by definition alienated, marginalized, since writing is seen as a male prerogative.

Ruth Bernard Yeazell examines the linkage between strong heroines and politics in a 1985 article, "Why Political Novels Have Heroines: *Sybil, Mary Barton*, and *Felix Holt*." Recent doctoral dissertations, I note, have focused on Gaskell's Unitarianism as a major motivation for her social activism. Jane P. Tompkins' 1981 article, "Sentimental Power: *Uncle Tom's Cabin* and the Politics of Literary History," is symptomatic of a feminist revival of interest in Stowe. Tompkins argues that the critical-scholarly neglect of the book stems from the fact that it was a sentimental novel, a subgenre written mainly by women whom Hawthorne castigated as a "damned mob of scribbling women"—women, moreover, who were perceived as shoring up the existing social order (80–82). Tompkins, however, sees the novel as both conformist and subversive. While she is a persuasive apologist, she completely omits references to the racial stereotyping which distressed Baldwin, as do other feminist apologists for the sentimental novel.

7    Unfortunately, as John R. Adams remarks in *Harriet Beecher Stowe*, Mrs. Stowe passed up an offer of 50 percent royalties in return for an investment in the publication, and received only 10 percent royalties from sales (55).

8    Interview in *The Globe and Mail*, Saturday, December 11, 1982: E1. Indeed, echoing *A Room of One's Own*, but inverting its viewpoint, Munro waxes eloquent on the subject of

Ellen Moers underlines the importance of a feminine tradition in literature, and mentions some major links between Gaskell and Stowe: not only were they "two of the rare Victorian women writers who were also mothers" (147), they also knew each other and corresponded, affording a fascinating example of female literary networking. In an important sense, they create a spiritual network with the Alice Munros, Margaret Laurences, and Margaret Atwoods of today, preparing the way for artists who feel capable of melding life and art seamlessly, without conflict. Both did, however, anticipate Virginia Woolf's view of the special problems of a woman writer. As Gaskell said:

> When a man becomes an author, it is probably merely a change of employment to him. He takes a portion of that time which has hitherto been devoted to some other study or pursuit; ... and another merchant or lawyer, or doctor, steps into his vacant place, and probably does as well as he. But no other can take up the quiet, regular duties of the daughter, the wife, or the mother ... ; a woman's principal work in life is hardly left to her own choice; nor can she drop the domestic charges devolving on her as an individual, for the exercise of the most splendid talents that were ever bestowed. (Quoted by Moers 22)

Despite these obstacles, her productivity was really enormous. We are told that "in 20 years she produced seven novels, five 'nouvelles' ... 22 short stories, uncounted short essays (and several long ones), magazine articles, as well as her major work, 'The Life of Charlotte Brontë.'" She accomplished all this without "a room of [her] own." As she described her activities in a letter:

> In the hour since breakfast I have had to decide on the following variety of important questions: Boiled beef—how long to boil? What perennials will do in Manchester smoke? Length of skirt for a gown? Salary of a nursery governess? Read letters on the state of the Indian army lent me by a very agreeable neighbor, and returned them with as many wise remarks as will come in a hurry. Settle 20 questions of dress for the girls. See a lady about a MS story of hers, and give her disheartening but very good advice. Arrange about selling two poor cows for one good one—and it's not half past ten yet![9]

Mrs. Stowe is equally vivid on the subject of her difficulties finding a plumber. In this 1850 letter she finally finds rest only in the pain of childbirth:

> These negotiations extended from the first of June to the first of July, and at last my sink was completed ... Also during this time good Mrs. Mitchell and myself made two sofas, or lounges, a barrel chair, divers bedspreads, pillow cases, pillows, bolsters, mattresses; we painted rooms; we revarnished furniture; we—what *didn't* we do?

---

the poor *male* writer, fully equipped with private study and obliging wife and children, who goes blank with terror at the thought that he has no excuse *not* to produce:

> "I can't tell you how horrified I feel when I go to a male writer's house and see *the Study*, you know, the entire house set up for him to work, with a wife acting as a buffer zone. I just can't help thinking, *poor bugger*. What a load to carry, it's really got to work that novel, if everybody else is sacrificing for it."

9    Quoted by Beverly Gray, "Mrs. Gaskell's home town drab and not the world of the novels," *The Globe and Mail*.

Then on came Mr. Stowe; and then came the eighth of July and my little Charley. I was really glad for an excuse to lie in bed, for I was full tired, I can assure you. (Quoted by Moers 4)

There are a number of other curious biographical similarities between the two women. Both turned to writing novels largely as a result of losing a beloved son. Gaskell's only son, Willie, died of scarlet fever at the age of ten months, and her husband encouraged her to throw herself into her writing. Stowe's son Charley, her sixth child, died of cholera in 1848 (she named a later son for him), and she took up the pen to describe families separated by slavery, as well as by death. In an 1853 letter to Mrs. Follen, she wrote that "much that is in that book ('Uncle Tom') had its root in the awful scenes and bitter sorrows of that summer" (quoted by Foster 27). As Foster remarks, Mrs. Stowe, Puritan that she was, determined "to kiss the rod."

Mrs. Stowe seems to have been the more vigorous of the two. Born to a New England Brahmin family, her father, the Reverend Lyman Beecher, was a militant evangelist. Her sister Catherine was a feminist concerned with equal education for women. As George Frisbie Whicher writes, "Any of the Beechers, if cast away on a cannibal island, would have been capable of organizing a church, a school, a temperance movement, and a ladies' aid society before help could arrive"—for the cannibals, presumably![10]

Both women supplemented the family income by their writing, and Ellen Moers comments that "there might never have been an *Uncle Tom's Cabin* had the Reverend Calvin Stowe been a better provider for his wife and many babies" (129). Winifred Gérin reports that the Reverend William Gaskell was somewhat sulky when his wife's fame far exceeded his. Without his knowledge, Mrs. Gaskell attempted to provide for her daughters after her death by investing the money she earned from writing in a house.[11]

Despite their bereavements, hardships, and complaints about the many demands on their time, both were twice the age of Mary Shelley at their babies' deaths, Moers reminds us, and "both were respectably settled middle-class women, wives of ministers" (129). Gérin recounts how Mrs. Gaskell, far removed from the *Sturm und Drang* of the Brontës' private lives, simply tumbled off the couch, dead of a heart attack at 55, and characteristically in mid-sentence. Mrs. Stowe lived to 85.

In addition to having, for the most part, parallel lives, Gaskell's and Stowe's paths occasionally intersected. The two women had several mutual friends, acquaintances, and correspondents. Both had their portraits painted in England by Henry Richmond, Gaskell in 1852, Stowe in 1854. Charlotte Brontë, the subject of Mrs. Gaskell's biography, was an admirer of Mrs. Stowe and wrote: "I doubt not Mrs. Stowe had felt the iron of slavery enter into her heart, from childhood upwards" (quoted by Moers 27), a statement almost equally applicable to Mrs. Gaskell and her empathy

---

10   George Frisbie Whicher, "Harriet Beecher Stowe," *Literary History of the United States*.

11   Dickens, who admired her, may have reflected some of her husband's occasional aggravation with her stubbornness: he commented acerbically when she refused to go back to work on *Cranford*, "If I were Mr. Gaskell, Oh Heaven how I would beat her!" (quoted by Gérin 126).

with factory workers in the Manchester slums of *Mary Barton* and *North and South*. Furthermore, if we look at Gaskell's correspondence, we discover that she and Mrs. Stowe did actually meet during the latter's triumphal tour of Europe. In a letter to Charles Eliot Norton, dated June 3, 1857, following Mrs. Gaskell's return to smoky Manchester from Italy, she wrote, "Mrs. Stowe comes to us today for one night and tomorrow I shall go for the first time with her."[12]

Despite the well-documented, if unexplored, personal and literary relationship of these two women, no one seems to have noted the remarkable similarity in narrative structure of Stowe's 1852 anti-slavery novel, *Uncle Tom's Cabin*, and Gaskell's 1848 factory novel, *Mary Barton* (perhaps because American Studies and Victorian scholarship rarely join forces). Specifically, the Eliza and George Harris plot of Stowe's novel has resonances of the Mary–Jem Wilson plot of *Mary Barton*.

Stowe detected the analogy—perceived today as essentially false—between the conditions of American slaves and British factory workers. Her failure to see the limits of her analogy provides a convincing explanation of some serious gaps in her treatment of slavery.[13]

In the twentieth century Mrs. Stowe has been accused of lacking any visceral sympathy with, or real knowledge of, the condition of slavery. No one, on the other hand, has ever charged Mrs. Gaskell with lacking sympathy with the working classes of Manchester. Indeed, her husband's parish was there, and she assumed many of the duties of his parish visits, freeing up his time to compose sermons. Many critics have commented that, of all the Victorian novelists, she lived closest to the world she described, unlike Dickens, who tended to treat the working class in an overly sentimental, if not downright maudlin, manner, as in *Hard Times*.[14] Living in the Manchester created by Ricardo, Say, Adam Smith, and the laissez-faire policies of Manchester economics, Mrs. Gaskell early learned to cast a sympathetic but realistic eye on the virtues and defects of the factory workers and owners, the seamstresses, and even the fallen women (*Ruth*). As Gérin writes, "her work was the handmaid of her conscience" (10). In fact, her picture of Manchester life is so accurate that Kathleen Tillotson and others have compared it to Engels' analysis of the city, in which he emphasizes its 60 percent rate of infant mortality.[15] Tillotson claims that

---

12   Jan Whitehill, ed. *Letters of Mrs. Gaskell and Charles Eliot Norton, 1855–65*.

13   My claim does not deny that there are numerous possible literary influences on Stowe, in additon to those she names herself in the *Key to Uncle Tom's Cabin*: the 1849 autobiography of the Reverend Josiah Henson as the source for Uncle Tom, and Theodore Weld's *American Slavery As It Is* (1839) and the *Narrative of the Life of Frederick Douglass, An American Slave* (1845) as the source for George Harris (Foster, 18). Foster mentions, for instance, Richardson's sentimentality, Defoe's blend of authentic sources with fiction, Scott's historical accuracy and journey motif (14–16). But the two-plot novel was characteristically Victorian (see Adams, 46), and Stowe is recognizably a novelist of her period.

14   See, for instance, Stephen Gill, "Introduction," *Mary Barton*.

15   Adams makes a similar claim for Stowe, whose Augustine St. Clare makes a statement that might have come from Marx and Engels' recent *Communist Manifesto*: "... there is a mustering among the masses, the world over; and there is a *dies irae* coming on, sooner or later. The same thing is working in Europe, in England, in this country" (52).

Gaskell was "drenched in her subject" (222)[16] and applies a line from Carlyle's *Past and Present* to her vision: "sooty Manchester, it too is built upon the infinite abysses!" (Tillotson 222).

Where Mrs. Gaskell is most often found wanting by modern readers is in her lack of sympathy for trade unions. Like Mrs. Stowe, she is often labeled resolutely middle-class, burdened with a "small-l liberal middle-class bias" which makes her uneasy about organized labor. In fairness to Gaskell, we would do well to remember that even such an advanced thinker as George Eliot was later to betray a deep suspicion of the use of systems to reform systems—a suspicion that may have been rooted in a womanly sense of disenfranchisement. Why should a woman intellectual trust an organization to reform political economy, when neither the radical organization nor the government acknowledged her right to full citizenship, in the form of the vote? Nor were many trade unions open to women. This sense of disenfranchisement is also what Charlotte Brontë had in mind in recognizing that Mrs. Stowe, as a woman, had some sense of what it must mean to be a slave. If Gaskell and Stowe leave us with a final "message" that the world would be a better place if only people were nicer to each other, they were only working on a variation of the theme George Orwell ascribed to their male contemporary Charles Dickens, who never imagined an alternative political system either.

A more serious criticism of both Gaskell and Stowe relates to the *facture* of both novels, which split around two principal plots. Gaskell, we are told, originally planned to call her novel "John Barton" and to focus on the psychology of a good man driven by desperate social conditions, as well as by a certain lack of personal moral strength, to the commission of a crime of violence. Some readers ask, in fact, how it can be read as a feminist novel when the focus is on John, not Mary. I will argue, however, that the Mary–Jem plot is more central and less conventional than has been recognized. Gaskell has created a working-class heroine whom she must make palatable to the middle class, her intended audience for implementing reforms. But, as we shall see, Mary is an active heroine, unlike most female characters in the genteel tradition but like Scott's Jeanie Deans (1818) or, later, Eliot's Dinah Morris (1859) (who also works in a factory when she is not preaching Methodism).

All things are not as they seem. Mary is not really a traditional heroine, and Gaskell's appeal to the middle class is subversive. One detects a similar dire warning to James Baldwin's in *The Fire Next Time*: if not voluntary reform on the part of the power structure, then "the fire next time." Gaskell's narrative strategies are subtly subversive; at times the narrative voice that cajoles the middle class into sympathy with the workers sounds maddeningly naive, moderate, and understated. Yet surely the subtext is a veiled threat, and the author seems conscious that she is evoking as strong an audience reaction as the rhetorical Carlyle, not by frontal assault, but rear-guard action.[17]

---

16   Kathleen Tillotson, *Novels of the Eighteen-Forties*.

17   In another vein, Robyn Warhol's 1986 article, "Toward a Theory of the Engaging Narrator: Earnest Interventions in Gaskell, Stowe, and Eliot," argues that the so-called "sentimental," naive narrative voices of certain mid-nineteenth-century English and American women novelists were, in fact, breaking with a male tradition of "distancing" in order to

An example of this "double speak" occurs in her Preface, when Gaskell states, "I know nothing of Political Economy, or the theories of trade" (38). Surely, as Stoneman suggests, the subtext is not that of a naive middle-class housewife but of an astute Unitarian social activist who implies that she *wants* to know nothing of Political Economy, because to know of it would somehow valorize it, or justify the existing system (Stoneman 68–9). As one of my graduate students, Sheila Greene, who is herself a lawyer, remarked, Jem Wilson is finally freed not by the legal system but by a jury of sympathetic individuals.

Gaskell undermines her narrator subtly, so that we, as readers or *"narrataires"* (Gerald Prince's term), sympathize more with the working class than with the middle class. As in the case of her later novel, *North and South*, the most violent critiques of the middle class are put in the mouth of a working-class character, John Barton in *Mary Barton*, Nicholas Higgins in *North and South*. It is John who makes the Dives / Lazarus comparison, who asks whether God isn't the masters' father too (104), whether the Dives / Lazarus parable haunts the rich as it does the poor, and who says "it's the poor, and the poor only, as does such things for the poor" (45). The tone is far from that of the apparently moderate narrator, notably in her descriptions of the well-intentioned but selfish Carson family (one daughter reads Emerson—perhaps "Self-Reliance" ungenerously interpreted?—while the poor starve to death around them) (254).

Yet the dramatic scenes composed of dialogue convey a far more desperate "message" than the narrator's voice. At the same time, that narrator does quietly document the despair of the poor with facts, thereby supporting John Barton's anger. She or he notes, for instance, that Davenport is buried in a pauper's grave covered by "a raised and handsome tombstone; in reality a wooden mockery of stone respectabilities which adorned the burial-ground ... But little they recked of this who now gave up their dead" (112–13). Lest we miss the point, Gaskell's own anger is revealed in the factual footnote: "The case, to my certain knowledge, in one churchyard in Manchester. There may be more" (113). She must be aware that the impact on her reader is going to be closer to John's fury than to the narrator's calm benevolence.

A trope for this subtext, the dire warning, or Carlylean prophecy of doom, takes the form of the crumpled Valentine from Jem to Mary, on which John Barton has had Mary copy a poem by Samuel Bamford, a radical weaver-poet (verbal art). John finally abandons words, as well as the love / nurturing implied by the Valentine, for violence when he crumples it up to use as the wadding for the bullet that kills Harry Carson. Moreover, the Valentine both unites and divides the three central characters and is expressive of Mary's dilemma, torn between father and true love. Discovered by Esther, the Valentine can be mistakenly used as evidence against Jem, its author, not John, its betrayer. What was intended as a verbal and artistic declaration of love is turned into an instrument of hate.

As a two-plot novel, the title of *Uncle Tom's Cabin* also points to the older man as the central figure, persecuted and driven by slavery rather than poverty; but in fact the

---

"engage" the "narratee" (Gerald Prince's *narrataire*, the person to whom the tale is supposedly told), and thereby "extend the referentiality of their fiction" (817).

Eliza–George Harris plot probably occupies more space in the novel. It is possible that both John Barton and Uncle Tom lack the articulateness to narrate their own stories, or to attain full awareness of their significance. But in the process, Mary, Jem, Eliza, and George sound frequently like the author's mouthpieces, somewhat undermining the realism of their respective novels. As Tillotson notes, Mary Barton was probably more "marketable" than her father, and that is why she, of all the working class characters in the novel, is the only one to speak standard, educated English.

Stowe may actually be more accurate in her treatment of Eliza and George. As mulattoes, they would have been descended from a white plantation owner and a female slave. In the antebellum South, such children were often raised as house servants, rather than field servants, and educated with their white half-brothers and - sisters (see, for instance, Faulkner's *Absalom, Absalom!*). As Franklin Frazier points out in *The Black Bourgeoisie*, after the Civil War the black middle class was naturally recruited from these mulatto house slaves who were educationally advantaged for upward mobility.

The subtitle of *Mary Barton* foregrounds the social context: "A Tale of Manchester Life." Stowe's subtitle, similarly, "Life Among the Lowly," suggests a focus on the poor and powerless.

Gaskell's wedding of writing and social commitment comes out of an impressive tradition of "factory novels" written by women in the Britain of the 1840s and 1850s. Many of these women were wives and daughters of Unitarian ministers. Among the basic tenets of the Unitarian Church were equal education for women, and the notion that the husband does not exercise authority over the wife, but is an equal partner in marriage. Not surprisingly, Unitarians and Quakers were later in the forefront of women's rights movements in both Great Britain and the United States, as formerly they had pioneered factory reform in England and abolitionism in the United States. Coral Lansbury says of Gaskell's Unitarian background, "... to be born a woman and a Unitarian was to be released from much of the prejudice and oppression enjoined upon other women." (11). Gaskell shared this background with Harriet Martineau, Florence Nightingale, and Barbara Bodichon (13).[18]

Gaskell and Stowe were both aware of the popular analogy between factory workers and slaves. One of the most famous factory novels was *Michael Armstrong, the Factory Boy* (1839–40) by Mrs. Frances Trollope, mother of novelist Anthony Trollope. Mrs. Trollope and Harriet Martineau also wrote novels about slavery. Indeed, Foster sees Mrs. Trollope's *The Life and Adventures of Jonathan Jefferson*

---

18   Moreover, in Stowe's United States, abolitionism and feminism both had strong historical ties with Unitarianism and with Transcendentalism, itself both a logical extension of, and a form of rebellion against, the more structured Unitarian church. Despite the common liberal stances of Gaskell and Stowe, to be sure, Stowe, taught by a suspicious father, did feel that Unitarianism was too extreme and, as Crozier puts it, "beyond the pale of the Christian faith" (118). Stowe belonged to the liberal northern wing of the Presbyterian Church, then torn by dissension with the southern branch over the northern antislavery stand. Stowe shows a missionary zeal in claiming that "The Lord Himself wrote" *Uncle Tom's Cabin* (Crozier 69). A Unitarian would have seen the divine as immanent in all of us, not as a God pulling strings from above. With these predictable differences, both novelists share a Christian view of the human condition, though Stowe's is more deterministic (Calvinistic).

*Whitlaw*, written 15 years earlier, as a possible source for *Uncle Tom's Cabin*. In 1843–44 another woman writer, Mrs. Tonna (known as Charlotte Elizabeth) wrote a novel called *The Wrongs of Women*, about the factory system in Britain. Aina Rubenius feels that Gaskell was well acquainted with her work and influenced by her.[19] Stowe, we know, not only read Mrs. Tonna but wrote, in 1844, an introduction to the American edition of *The Wrongs of Women* (Moers, 39). Gaskell seems not to have read Disraeli's *Sybil; or The Two Nations* (1844) before writing *Mary Barton*, but had probably read Mrs. Tonna, so Moers educes the impact of a female tradition in literature from this evidence.

The British public was quick to detect resemblances between Stowe's moving depiction of the condition of slaves and the situation of the English working class. Her second novel, *Dred* (1856), sold 100,000 copies in four weeks; and both *Dred* and *Uncle Tom's Cabin* were used by the British to build support for the Reform Bill of 1867, which paved the way for the emancipation of British labor. But no one seems to have realized that Stowe herself was indebted to, and inspired by, the tradition of the British factory novel.

This nineteenth-century perception of the analogy between blacks and the working class breaks down in our day, as Baldwin puts it, because the black man always wears his badge upon his face. The working man, on the other hand, if liberated in other ways, can move upwards socially through education if he polishes his accent and manners and acquires the tools of capitalism. When Stowe seems to patronize her Uncle Tom and to "favor" her mulattoes with a "happy ending," she may, in fact, have simply drawn a mistaken or inexact analogy between slaves and British factory workers, and underestimated the obstacles to success for former slaves. By the same token, Chartism scarcely presented a direct parallel to the flight of slaves, or a slave rebellion, but it may have been perceived as such in the nineteenth century.

Both Gaskell and Stowe see employed and employers, slaves and masters, as "so bound to each other by common interests" that it is madness for them to commit violence against each other. The capitalist does not abuse his tools or destroy his own property. For Gaskell, such abuse can arise only out of ignorance. Stowe, perhaps less sentimentally than one might expect, recognizes that the relatively benign and conscientious Shelbys of Kentucky permit the existence of the Simon Legrees of Mississippi—in a word, that the system itself is evil, far more evil than the individuals caught up in it. Stowe uses as her spokesman a nameless young man:

> "... in my opinion, it is you considerate, humane men, that are responsible for all the brutality and outrage wrought by these wretches; because, if it were not for your sanction and influence, the whole system could not keep foothold for an hour. If there were no planters except such as that one," said he, pointing with his finger to Legree, who stood with his back to them, "the whole thing would go down like a mill-stone. It is your respectability and humanity that licenses and protects his brutality." (365)

Both women are also sharply perceptive about the links between power and sexual abuse. Gaskell's frame tale concerns Mary's Aunt Esther, the "fallen woman." Mary's mother, the virtuous woman, suffers an equally grievous fate as the result

---

19   Noted by Moers (39).

of the complications of a very late pregnancy. But Esther, the "pretty woman," serves as a negative role model to Mary, who resembles her, and keeps her on the "straight and narrow" when she is tempted by Harry Carson, the millowner's son. Esther is a kind of *deus* (*dea*?) *ex machina* in the plot. Gaskell does not condemn her melodramatically, or treat her fate with Dickensian bathos; rather, she indicates that only drink makes life tolerable for a prostitute with a strong ethical sense. But the same can be said for John Barton, who, after his act of violence, takes to drink and drugs. Esther is finally buried in the same grave with John (compare Hester Prynne and Arthur Dimmesdale in *The Scarlet Letter*), in seeming acknowledgment not only of complicity, but also, I think, of his half-conscious sexual attraction to his sister-in-law. Gaskell was subsequently to present an even more sympathetic, controversial portrait of the fallen woman in *Ruth*.

For the slave woman, of course, virginity was even more at risk than for the British working-class girl. Eliza is described from the beginning as a "sex object," a possession, "a fine female article." As in Faulkner, the black women were seen as virgin fields ready for the planting. With reference to Bon's quadroon mistress in *Absalom, Absalom!*, who combines the white man's standard of beauty with a supposed African passion and warmth, Faulkner writes, "We, the white men, created them"—that is, a hereditary class of mistresses. Similarly, Stowe's Eliza was "a petted and indulged favorite" (21). As one of the mercenaries capturing fugitive slaves comments, "gals allers is the devil to catch"—because they have the most to lose. The sexual exploitation even includes perversion, as the slavetrader Haley "wants to buy up handsome boys to raise for the market" (15).

Perhaps the greatest evil of slavery, from Stowe's point of view, and perhaps also from that of modern sociology, was the separation of families, which was only made acceptable to whites by the reification of blacks, echoed in one of Stowe's discarded subtitles, "The Man That Was a Thing." As Mr. Haley says, echoing the logic of Swift's *A Modest Proposal*, "Tain't, you know, as if it was white folks, that's brought up in the way of 'spectin' to keep their children and wives and all that" (17). In case the reader is in danger of accepting this dehumanization, Cassy, Eliza's real mother, kills her last child to save it from the white world. Stowe also describes in some detail the woman who throws herself from the boat when her baby is stolen from her.

Escape from sexual exploitation precipitates the major action of both plots, though Harry Carson's attempted seduction of Mary Barton is essentially a red herring: he is murdered by her father not for having attempted to seduce his daughter, but for having mocked the rag-tag Chartist delegation of which John was a member. In fact, Mary's head is turned only briefly by the owner's son. Ambition alone feeds her attraction to Harry Carson: she "did not favour Mr. Carson the less because he was rich and a gentleman" (121). But her innate good sense, bolstered by the warning example of her Aunt Esther, almost immediately causes her to reject the temptation. The moment after she refuses Jem Wilson's proposal, she realizes that it is he whom she truly loves:

> What were these hollow vanities to her, now she had discovered the passionate secret of her soul? She felt as if she almost hated Mr. Carson, who had decoyed her with his baubles. She now saw how vain, how nothing to her, would be all gaieties and pomps,

all joys and pleasure, unless she might share them with Jem; yes, with him she harshly rejected so short a time ago ... She had hitherto been walking in grope-light towards a precipice; but in the clear revelation of that past hour, she saw her danger and turned away resolutely, and for ever (176–7).

Gaskell refuses to let her heroine become a Cinderella (or a Pamela); indeed, if Mary keeps finally to her class, it is because Jem Wilson is more deserving, worthy, and gifted than the idle, thoughtless Harry. Moreover, in Gaskell's England, Harry was only one generation removed from being a factory worker himself, as John Thornton in *North and South* is an ex-worker become millowner. Unhappily, the newly rich Harry seems to have lost all the working-class virtues in his upward move.

Eliza is not even momentarily tempted by a "master" or owner. She is already married to George Harris, who belongs to a neighboring slaveowner and is the father of her son, little Harry. Eliza is to be sold by Mr. Shelby only because, kind owner as he is, he is also financially irresponsible and a gambler. Although "good natured and kindly," he had "speculated largely and quite loosely" (19). Stowe suggests that treating human beings as property automatically dehumanizes both master and slave. The Kentucky Shelbys are implicitly compared to the St. Clares who purchase Uncle Tom. Augustine St. Clare is a kind man, with a spoiled, selfish, petulant wife, Marie, who is narcissistic and hysterical. When he is killed in a duel, his wife sells Uncle Tom down-river. In contrast, in the Shelby ménage, Mrs. Shelby is the more liberal and sensible. For Stowe, unlike Gaskell, individual kindness is inadequate to combat a nefarious system. The subtended benevolence of "patriarchy" is only apparent, not real, and soon disappears in case of need; the cash nexus is primordial.

Shelby tries to turn a blind eye to Eliza's potential fate, but her marketability is based on her beauty. As Margaret Mead and James Baldwin have pointed out in *Rap About Race*, white women, as well as black women and black men, were victims of white males—the slavemasters or plantation owners. As in Faulkner's *Absalom, Absalom!*, the white wife was expected to produce (but without giving or experiencing sexual pleasure) legitimate white male heirs to found a dynasty. Black concubines were expected to gratify the master's appetites and to produce house slaves. Faulkner ironically underlines that it is the black and female side of the Sutpen dynasty, and of the McCaslins in *Go Down, Moses*, that survives. Thomas Sutpen, in *Absalom, Absalom!*, is finally dispatched by Wash Jones' rusty scythe, in revenge for his treating Wash's daughter, Milly, the last hope of Sutpen's aging loins, worse than a mare in his stable because she has produced yet another girl instead of a son. Yet Sutpen has refused to acknowledge as his a mulatto son, Charles Bon, and simply discounts the white child closest to his own nature, Judith, because she is female. Faulkner may, in fact, through the instrument of death, the scythe, be referring obliquely and sardonically to the Biblical warning, "As ye sow, so shall ye reap." Sutpen has sown liberally the seeds of his own destruction.[20] The white man early learned to divide and conquer, as white and black women, split by status and, more importantly, by sexual jealousy, were unable to make common

---

20  For a further discussion of Faulkner's linkage of women and blacks, see my article, "Women, Blacks, and Thomas Sutpen's Mythopoeic Drive in *Absalom, Absalom!*" in *Modernist Studies* I.

cause. When Malcolm X cried, "Give us back our manhood," he was referring to the emasculation, or cuckolding, of black males by the white slavemaster. After the Civil War, the emasculation was to continue as black women were forced to become the family breadwinners because they were often separated from their husbands by poverty, the senseless quirks of the welfare system, and the greater availability of jobs, albeit menial, for black women than for black men.

Eliza flees with her child, little Harry, to save her marriage from such a forced separation. She is, moreover, struggling against her own inevitable dishonor at the hands of white men as yet unknown. Love of George Harris and of little Harry precipitates her great act of "heroinism": the famous set-piece of "Eliza Crossing the Ice" into free territory. Love for Jem Wilson prompts Mary Barton's act of "heroinism": giving her fate into the hands of the rough watermen to reach the ship on which Will Wilson, Jem's cousin and only defense witness in the Harry Carson murder trial, is due to set sail. Finally, it motivates her even greater heroinism in confessing publicly her love for Jem during the trial, which she has not been able to do heretofore, privately to him, because of the convention of female reticence. She can admit her love only to save her lover, not to win another proposal from him. Caught in the Freudian dilemma of having to choose between saving father or lover, she manages to rescue the latter without betraying the former.[21] The slave and the working-class women in some ways suffer far fewer restraints than the middle-class or genteel girls such as Lucy Snowe in Charlotte Bronte's *Villette*, who is easily swindled by comparable watermen to those Mary Barton encounters so fearlessly.[22]

The vocations of Mary's and Eliza's young men complete the plot parallelisms. Jem Wilson is an engineer in an international firm "who send from out their towns of workshops engines and machinery to the dominions of the Czar and the Sultan" (65). He first proposes to Mary when he rises to foreman in the works. Although she initially turns him down, she almost immediately regrets her decision. He subsequently makes his fortune as an inventor, though his master owns the patent. As Mary's friend Margaret tells her, Jem has informed her of his rise in the world: "... he told me all about his invention for doing away wi' the crank, or somewhat. His master's bought it from him, and ta'en out a patent, and Jem's a gentleman for life wi' the money his master gied him" (189).

George Harris, similarly, is a self-made man, a young man who rises by his bootstraps during the Industrial Revolution. He invents a hemp-cleaning machine, which "displayed quite as much mechanical genius as Whitney's cotton-gin" (22). Stowe notes the factual basis of this story, that "A machine of this description was really the invention of a young colored man in Kentucky" (22). Black history was not altogether submerged, apparently, in pre-Civil War times. The white man's evaluation of this major contribution, however, reveals his blindness: "... a machine

---

21  Lansbury disagrees with most critics that John Barton was ever intended as the center of the novel, and claims that the original title was "A Manchester Love Story", thus foregrounding the Mary–Jem plot (22).

22  To be sure, Mary does suffer a nervous collapse after confessing her love for Jem during the trial. But the act of heroinism is unblemished, and we are expected to admire her modest gentility (or perhaps sympathize with her continuing bondage to "feminine"custom?).

for saving work, is it? ... let a nigger alone for that" (23). Stowe's description of George is patronizing, indeed racist: "From one of the proudest families in Kentucky he had inherited a set of fine European features, and a high, indomitable spirit. From his mother he had received only a slight mulatto tinge" (123). His mother has suffered the fate now threatening his wife: she was "marked out by personal beauty to be the slave of the passions of her possessor, and the mother of children who may never know a father" (123). George is a free-thinker about both religion and politics. As in the case of Jem Wilson, his views illustrate a clever and practical mind at work. As he protests about the supposed Biblical rationale for slavery, "to quote Bible to a fellow in my circumstances is enough to make him give it up altogether" (124). While Stowe is herself, like Gaskell, a minister's daughter and wife, she issues a warning to the Christian churches about institutionalized racism and hypocrisy. Similarly, George, as one of the excluded, questions the validity of "knee-jerk" patriotism: "Haven't I heard your Fourth-of-July speeches? Don't you tell us all, once a year, that governments derive their just power from the consent of the governed? Can't a fellow *think*, that hears such things?" (125).

The rebuilding of the extended family, separated in the one instance by the Industrial Revolution and in the other by slavery, is a central theme in both novels. The consequences of this breakdown include physical disabilities and deformities often noted in twentieth-century post-colonial writings such as Rachid Boudjedra's *La Répudiation* (Paris: Denoel, 1969). Margaret, Mary's seamstress friend in Gaskell's novel, is going blind as a consequence of her occupation, and Alice Wilson, the aged white witch, is rapidly losing her hearing. The literal deformities symbolize the spiritual distortions effected on the oppressed, the colonized, the enslaved. Alice Wilson expresses a Wordsworthian nostalgia for the countryside, and for the mother from whom she has been separated by time, space, and history. In many ways she reflects Mary's quest for a mother. The poor fill the gap by serving as parent-surrogates for each other when the old extended family structure is exploded and fragmented into nuclear families by the factory system. Thus old Job Legh and the other grandfather, old Jennings, rescue the infant Margaret from London after the death of her parents. To clinch the point, old Jennings even pretends to be a woman, disguising himself with a chambermaid's cap, to substitute for the child's dead mother (149). Similarly, John Barton and George Wilson, Jem's father, take care of the Davenports when their father dies.

It should be noted that Gaskell identifies strongly with this working-class proclivity for nurturing. As well, she stresses, especially in the Job Legh / Margaret subplot, their ability to articulate their sufferings and grievances. Margaret in some ways reflects Gaskell's biography, as well as her role as artist. Gaskell, like Margaret, was born in London; she was half-orphaned, and taken north to Manchester by her father. Margaret's blindness forces her to make singing, her hobby, a vocation, and she specializes in working-class songs such as "The Oldham Weaver":

Oi'm a poor cotton-weyver, as mony a one knoowas,
. . . . . . . . . . .
We lived upo' nettles, whoile nettles wur good,
An' Waterloo porridge the best o' eawr food,
. . . . . . . . . . . (72)

Gaskell incorporates, often in their entirety, working-class songs and poems, such as "The Oldham Weaver" and Samuel Bamford's "God help the poor!" (the text inscribed on the back of the Valentine-clue), in her own work, unpatronizingly, and signaling her admiration for their verbal skills and artistry. Job Legh, moreover, is a working-class encyclopaedia of information, and there is some indication that he is aware all along of John Barton's guilt.

Lord David Cecil accuses Charlotte Brontë of stretching the long arm of coincidence, in *Jane Eyre*, until it is dislocated (108). Stowe, however, manages to outdo Charlotte Brontë in the ingeniousness of her plot coincidences. Madame de Thoux, who happens to be travelling on the same steamboat as young George Shelby, who has arrived too late to rescue Uncle Tom from Simon Legree, turns out to be George Harris's sister Emily, and Cassy, escaped from Legree and travelling on the same boat, to be Eliza's mother. George Shelby is thus able to reunite a family separated by his father's reckless speculation. In a somewhat similar vein, Gaskell effects a reconciliation between John Barton and the former "exploiter," the millowner Carson, just before John's death. Again, however, Stowe may be the more realistic, despite the multiple coincidences. As Herbert G. Gutman has demonstrated, in *The Black Family in Slavery and Freedom, 1750–1925*, black families both during and after slavery "invented" family networks to compensate for the disruption of normal family life. Hence, aged "Uncles" and "Aunts" (usually honorific titles only) would supply parental love to the young if their parents were sold, under slavery, or out working, after the Civil War. Rather than destroying black family life, the white man succeeded only in enhancing its value, in any possible form.

Jem's and George's inventiveness, finally, equips them both to create a new life for their families in Canada. If local attachments are lost in town in *Mary Barton* (158), perhaps the answer is to create a new structure elsewhere. As in the case of Susannah Moodie and her Captain, the solution to a lack of fortune in England was to seek it in the "colonies," and Canada becomes a kind of Promised Land for Jem and Mary. Jem's old master, Mr. Duncombe, well aware of his innocence but also of the difficulties Jem's checkered past will create for him in England, is asked "to recommend an intelligent man, well acquainted with mechanics, as instrument-maker to the Agricultural College they are establishing at Toronto in Canada" (probably Guelph) (446). Job Legh, the amateur entomologist, eventually decides to visit them "to try and pick up a few specimens of Canadian insects" (466); Gaskell, as we have seen, constantly underlines the intellectual curiosity of the working class, exemplified both in Jem's inventiveness and Job's scientific hobby.

Edgar Wright sees the escape to Canada as an unrealistic Wordsworthian return to nature (96), but in fact the ending is realistic in the sense that Gaskell knowingly focuses on the great period of British emigration to the New World, seen as the land of promise for the working classes, as for Crèvecoeur's American farmer a little earlier: "*Ubi panis, ibi patria.*"

By the same token, George and Eliza Harris, together with little Harry, can escape the Fugitive Slave Law only by means of the Underground Railroad to Canada. They and the Wilsons are among the earliest of a long line of fugitives, dissidents, and poor people to choose Canada as a refuge, later to include the Vietnam War draft-resisters and Americans fleeing urban rot. George subsequently spends four years at a French university to complete his education, and ends up going back to Africa to help "his own people." The "solution" is more expeditious and naive on Stowe's part than we would find acceptable today; Stowe seems to be exiling the issue rather than confronting it. Baldwin and others have felt that such a return to Africa is an evasion: "Negroes are Americans and their destiny is the country's destiny. They have no other experience besides their experience on this continent" (Baldwin, 42). Frazier has said that the American black must find a "motive for living under American culture or die" (quoted by Baldwin, 170). It would be fairer to say, rather, that North American society must recognize the unique contributions of its "native sons"—and "daughters"—to use Baldwin's double-edged term—or die.

The Canadian presence is also felt in *Uncle Tom's Cabin* in another way: the St. Clare family is originally of Acadian stock and has been itself expatriated from Nova Scotia to Louisiana's "Cajun" country (168). Little Eva's full name, Evangeline St. Clare, suggests that she was named for the heroine of Longfellow's poem "Evangeline" (1847). The one branch of the family, Miss Ophelia's, landed in Vermont, the other in Louisiana. It is Miss "Feely," the Northern liberal, who must be taught how to feel viscerally, as opposed to intellectually, with the blacks. And Simon Legree, the most villainous, indeed demonic, slaveowner, is also a Northerner.

One plot of both novels, that focusing on, respectively, John Barton and Uncle Tom, is so unrelievedly bleak that a conventional romantic subplot seemed necessary to lighten the gloom. Arguably, however, the conventional romance is at least equally important because, like the second generation plot in *Wuthering Heights*, it provides continuum, a means of survival. Unfortunately, Stowe fails to perceive that her real and best survivor is Topsy, black as Uncle Tom, but a female picaro who lives by her wits. She presents the extreme case of a lack of family ties, having been raised by a speculator as if on a chicken farm: "I spect I grow'd. Don't think nobody never made me" (262). She serves as a foil to little Eva, who is all soul and no body. Stowe may not have intended this reading, but Eva's passive religiosity reflects a death wish in the entire St. Clare family, similar to that which Mark Twain was later to parody in Emmeline Grangerford, in *Huckleberry Finn*,[23] whereas Topsy, like Faulkner's blacks, endures and prevails, by constructing her own surrogate extended family.

It is difficult to arrive at any final value judgment about Stowe's use of racial stereotypes. Certainly, on balance, she is more open than Baldwin suggests. But she is guilty of seeing her black characters as "impassioned and imaginative" (40), "not strictly honest" (albeit out of necessity) (231), and as having "peculiarly strong" "instinctive affections" (109). Dinah, the cook, is "a self-taught genius" creating order "out of chaos and old night down there" in the cave-like kitchen (239). The image is both positive and negative, connoting as it does the African-American's power of creativity, of bringing light out of darkness, in a variation on Plato's

---

23    As Huck describes the morbid Emmeline, who is given to writing odes to the dead, "Every time a man died, or a woman died, or a child died, she would be on hand with her 'tribute' before he was cold. She called them tributes. The neighbors said it was the doctor first, then Emmeline, then the undertaker ..." (97). Initially, Huck mourns her own death, but finally concludes, "But I reckoned that with her disposition she was having a better time in the graveyard" (95).

parable of the cave. But Stowe gives with one hand and takes away with the other by implying that this creativity is purely instinctual and domestic.

On the other hand, Stowe puts in the mouth of her sympathetic white drover the line, "... the Lord made 'em men, and it's a hard squeeze getting 'em down into beasts" (121). Discussing heroism, she compares the applauded actions of a hypothetical Hungarian refugee helping others flee from Europe to America to a black man's, and asks why we hold back our praise "when despairing African fugitives do the same thing" (216).

I am not trying to suggest that Stowe's depiction of "Life Among the Lowly" is realistic and accurate, but only that she may have further confused the race issue by using a wrong and incompatible model, that of the working-class Jem and Mary, for her young couple, George and Eliza, and thereby projecting for them a more immediately hopeful future than most blacks could realistically expect. Whatever her faults on the matter of racial stereotyping, however, Stowe's contribution is genuine and more nuanced or complex than has generally been recognized. It is time for a reassessment of her thinking from a feminist perspective. She was clearly working in an already existing feminine tradition of social commitment in fiction. Moreover, both she and Gaskell detected the analogy between the female condition—passive, receptive, suffering—and the powerlessness of the American slaves and the English factory workers.

In the final analysis, both novels have perhaps too small an exit. Both writers posit a solution in human kindness and brotherhood; neither focuses on political or legal action. But the same criticism has been levelled at, for instance, Dickens's *Bleak House* by Barbara Hardy, and indeed at Dickens's work in general by George Orwell. Gaskell modestly admits that it would take a Dante to describe the Manchester scene. If Manchester did not get a Dante, we may be glad that at least it found a Gaskell, as slavery found a Stowe. If *Mary Barton* was "the first great factory novel" (Moers 25), Stowe may have been the first to perceive its connection with other conditions of servitude.

Arthur Schlesinger, Jr., calls *Uncle Tom's Cabin* "a great repository of history"; and Gaskell's novels present a clear-eyed panorama of the Victorian period, its politics, economics, and religion. Neither novel would stand up under close structuralist analysis, and some deconstructionists might suggest that the "realism" of both texts represents an attempt to "sell" bourgeois ideology. But critics like the deconstructionists, and like Edward Saïd (see *The World, the Text, and the Critic*), are coming back to referentiality. They remind us that the text is, after all, worldly, in and of the world, as well as being a structure of words. A Sartrean or Marxist or deconstructionist or feminist critic would find in both novels ample materials for a historical-literary analysis, whether that material supports or subverts bourgeois ideology.

Neither Gaskell nor Stowe ever pretended to a Jamesian concern with form and experimental techniques; both are preoccupied with social texture, with life as it is lived, and not with theory. As Gaskell writes at one point, "So much for generalities. Let us now return to individuals" (223). An almost mythic journey or quest motif permits both women to bind together all elements of their given society at a particular moment in history. Stowe's contrast between North and South corresponds in some ways to Gaskell's contrast of the industrial North of England and the agrarian South, genteel and static, in her later novel of the same name (*North and South*, 1854–55). The same dualistic vision informs the contrast of country and city, of worker and owner, of Dives and Lazarus—of what Disraeli referred to as the "Two Nations" (*Sybil*, 1844)—in *Mary Barton*. In keeping with the dialectical tendency, the willingness to show the humanity of characters who, in more melodramatic hands, would be cardboard villains,[24] both women writers focus on individual attitudinal change as the path to social justice:

> But, what can any individual do? Of that, every individual can judge. There is one thing that every individual can do,—they can see to it that *they feel right*. An atmosphere of sympathetic influence encircles every human being; and the man or woman who *feels* strongly, healthily, and justly on the great interests of humanity, is a constant benefactor to the human race. See, then, to your sympathies in this matter! (472)

Stowe's peroration may belong in the realm of the pious hope, but she intends to leave it to the reader to complete the action. Her appeal is directed to all our consciences, as is Gaskell's summary of the reforms instituted by the repentant Carson:

> Many of the improvements now in practice in the system of employment in Manchester, owe their origin to short earnest sentences spoken by Mr. Carson. Many and many yet to be carried into execution, take their birth from that stern, thoughtful mind, which submitted to be taught by suffering. (460)

Like the factory workers and the slaves, Gaskell and Stowe emphasize the connectedness of quasi-familial relationships as the chief means of alleviating human suffering.[25] By expanding their compassion from their own families to embrace the entire human race as a family, both writers are "maternal feminists" whose not-so-naive solution to the evils of the factory system and slavery is a new version of the "extended family."[26] Both women, while remaining resolutely middle-class,

---

24  Legree is, of course, cardboard, but his function is symbolic or mythic rather than realistic.

25  Stoneman suggests that the ethics of the working class are based on "caring," or "nurturing," and are therefore essentially "female" (69). She argues that *Mary Barton* is not "a flawed industrial novel," but a novel embodying a working-class female ethic based on the survival of children. Stoneman, however, sees the ending of the novel as patriarchal. Mary's "role ends with this enablement of her menfolk" (specifically Jem) in the "world of technology," whereas "Mary's life is as private as her mother's" (85). I would suggest, rather, that the ending celebrates Mary's active role as the promoter of the ideal community, of the extended family Gaskell envisages. The very expatriation of this particular family implies a radical break with the "masculine" revenge or violence tradition represented variously by the owners, the desperate strikers, and John Barton himself when he lapses tragically from his earlier role as nurturer of his own family and of the wretched Davenports.

26  Some critics, like Rosemarie Bodenheimer, in "Private Griefs and Public Acts in *Mary Barton*," see the public sphere as threatening for Gaskell, and consider her locked into the private sphere. It seems to me, however, that Gaskell is consciously trying to bridge the gap. As Crozier describes Stowe's themes as well, "The dramatization of the evils of slavery through its destructive effect on families in the novel implies that the rehabilitation of the nation should come about through a recognition of the sacred ties of family love" (33). Foster

nonetheless escape the prison of womanhood—genteel womanhood—by a kind of maternal "heroinism" that transcends that of their creations, Mary and Eliza.

---

notes that "the theme of mothers separated from children" appears with relation to the whites as well, to Augustine St. Clare and even Legree (39).

Chapter 6

# George Eliot's *Daniel Deronda*:
# "A Daniel Come to Judgment"

In *The Great Tradition*, F.R. Leavis was not the first—but was perhaps the most influential—critic to note an unsatisfactory split between the two major character-driven plots of George Eliot's *Daniel Deronda*: the Gwendolen–Grandcourt material, and the Deronda–Mirah–Zionist material. Before him, Henry James had also deplored the unconvincing, rather thin characterization of Deronda. Leavis was later—in 1960, in an essay published first in *Commentary* and a little later as an introduction prepared for the Harper Torchbook edition—to recant his earlier view. Since the Harper edition is long out of print, many readers are unaware of the shift in Leavis's position and continue to quote his earlier assertion that *Daniel Deronda* is a two-plot novel whose two plots are never—as Eliot intended them to be—integrated.[1]

## Kadosh: *A Modern Analogue*

An Israeli film released in the summer of 1999, and the official Israeli entry at the 1999 Cannes Film Festival, unwittingly sheds light on the enigma of more than a century earlier that is Eliot's *Daniel Deronda*. The film is called *Kadosh* (*The Rite*), directed by Amos Gitaï. It was shown in Paris in the original Israeli version, with French subtitles which may or may not have been entirely accurate. Set in Mea Shearim, the Orthodox Jewish quarter of Jerusalem, it begins at dawn in the bedroom of Rivka and her husband Meir, Hasidic Jews who have been married ten years and are childless. The husband is praying, thanking God every Sabbath that he was not born a woman. Not only does this prayer play a major role in *Daniel Deronda*, but in 1963 Betty Friedan quoted the same Jewish prayer in *The Feminine Mystique* as one of the motivations behind her feminism.

Rivka is a beautiful, passionate, sensual woman, and they are obviously as much in love as when they first married. But he is refusing to sleep with her because, if they have not had a baby in ten years, the situation is obviously hopeless. The director has

---

1    The Zionist plot was, be it said, a tremendous success at the time in the United States, with an increasing number of Jewish immigrants. However, an American work inspired by *Daniel Deronda*, *Gwendolen: A Sequel to George Eliot's 'Daniel Deronda'* (1878)—by an anonymous, but apparently non-Jewish author—killed off Mirah and her child in Palestine, leaving Daniel free, after various plot convolutions, to marry Gwendolen. As Sara Putzell summarizes, "The *Sequel* thus contracts Daniel's ecumenical vision within the safer confines of romance in which he and Gwendolen come to care only for each other" (43).

no need to underline the circularity of this reasoning: they are not going to produce a baby if they are not having intercourse. They are both suffering, but Rivka moreso because—as the prayer also suggests—in the Hasidic tradition (at least according to the film), it is inevitably the wife's "fault" if *she* fails to become pregnant!

Her younger sister Malka is the victim of an arranged marriage to Youssef, who is constructed comically—only the consequences are anything but funny—as a religious fanatic who rides through the streets with a megaphone exhorting liberal Jews to return to the fundamentalist fold before the arrival of the millennium. We also witness him working himself into a frenzy at prayer, seeking the special blessing of God. That this is a compensation for all his inadequacies as a male is made clear when he brutalizes Malka on the wedding night with the same "religious" fervor. Malka is more overtly rebellious than her sister, and has an affair with the young man she has loved since childhood—also Jewish, but not Orthodox, and a rock musician.

This is the 1990s, and Rivka goes to a female gynecologist, who informs her that she *is* fertile, and that her husband should come in for a sperm count. He will never come, she says hopelessly, knowing that, in their tradition, it has to be the wife's failing, no matter what modern science says. The gynecologist suggests taking a lover, which is equally out of the question for Rivka, not only for religious reasons but because she loves her husband. The film, however, is not about solutions, but about arousing anger in its audience at a fixed, static, unchanging system—analogous in some ways to the class- and gender-structured English society Eliot deplored at the end of the nineteenth century.

The girls' mother is also trapped in the situation. She is a kind of elder wise woman, whose task it is to purify the brides (after their menstrual period presumably) and prepare them for sexual intercourse. When her husband repudiates Rivka for her supposed infertility, her own mother must prepare the new virgin bride, ducking her 12 times in a kind of purification bath.[2]

A more plausible alternative offered by the gynecologist is artificial insemination. After the repudiation Rivka is discarded in a small cell-like apartment without comfort or honor. Her husband comes to her once—drunk—because he cannot resist her, but she recoils. When her sister visits her, Rivka imagines she is carrying a baby, and for the moment, the viewer begins to wonder if she had taken the gynecologist's advice about artificial insemination. But for her husband to accept the baby as his own, she would need to sleep with him at least one more time. She goes to him, offers herself sensually, and he resists, like a rock. In the morning she has died of love, and only then does he let his natural feelings take over—too late.

The film ends with a stunning long shot of an ideal Jerusalem, seen through the audience's eyes, but also through those of Malka, standing at a distance. Is she about to flee her tradition, escape her sister's fate? The ending is deeply ambiguous.

What is not ambiguous is the film's evaluation of the female condition among the Hasidim: men are freed to study the Torah; they are the scholars; they have sole access to the word of God. The women must cover their crowning glory, their hair,

---

2    One might compare the *bains maures* of the Moslems, in which women are sequestered and immersed during their menstrual periods.

and serve only as "baby factories." In other words, woman's "choice" is "Hobson's Choice"—no choice at all: one is either born a male, or, if female, becomes a mother or, failing that, dies.

## The Ambiguity of *Daniel Deronda*: George Eliot, Zionism, and Feminism

George Eliot, writing in 1876, has been both praised for her prophetic powers, and criticized (by Leavis among others) for her naïveté about Zionism. She did see the only hope for Utopian experiments as *outside* rigid, class-structured England. Dorothea Brooke and Will Ladislaw at one point contemplate setting up a Utopian community in the "Far West"—presumably of the United States or, less likely at the time, Canada.[3] But Eliot was not as politically naïve as either her creation, Dorothea (whom her skeptical sister Celia persists in referring to as "Dodo"!), or the somewhat more sophisticated, though less appealing, Deronda. She problematizes the role of women in the Jewish tradition by juxtaposing the portraits of Mirah, the ideal, submissive wife who is a professional concert singer (with a small, pure voice) only until she marries, and of the Alcharisi, the Princess Leonora Halm-Eberstein, Deronda's mother, with a big voice and a big talent to match her personal ambition.

George Eliot's ambivalence about the relationship between Zionism and feminism extends to the Judaeo-Christian tradition in general. The depiction of Mirah and Leonora inevitably leads us back to Gwendolen, as a Gentile and a lady, who cannot escape bondage, or what I have called elsewhere "the prison of womanhood." Book titles like "Maidens Choosing" and "Gwendolen Gets Her Choice" are unmistakably ironic and bitter as to "maidens" having any "choices" at all, unless, like the Alcharisi, they rebel against their culture.

## "O Wise Young Judge": Deronda as a "Womanly Man"

The key to the unity of *Daniel Deronda*, which lies in its Judaeo-Christian feminist theme, is, I think, a hidden allusion to Shakespeare's *The Merchant of Venice*.[4] There have been important articles written on the Book of Daniel and its relation to the text: Daniel in the Lions' Den, perhaps alluding to Deronda's moral and religious dilemma, caught between two worlds; the author of the Book of Daniel as the first church historian. But more pervasive than these in Eliot's text are references to her Daniel as a learned judge, a sage or wise man. Even in the field of music, he "is a musician himself, and a first-rate judge" (442). It is this aspect of the Biblical Daniel that Shakespeare had in mind when his Shylock, a Jew, cries out to the lawyer

---

3     Eliot was well acquainted with Ralph Waldo Emerson and American Transcendentalism, including, presumably, offshoots like Brook Farm or Bronson Alcott's Fruitlands.

4     In fact, I was so convinced of this intertextuality that I mistakenly remembered the relevant Shakespearean passage as an epigraph to one of the chapters. Adrian Poole notes a number of allusions in *Daniel Deronda*, but feels that these play a much larger part in Gwendolen's story than in Deronda's, which consequently weakens the Deronda plot. I believe, however, that *The Merchant of Venice* allusion opens up the Deronda plot.

who determines that he shall, after all, have his pound of flesh from his debtor, the Christian Antonio: "O wise young judge—a Daniel come to judgment." The "wise young judge" is, in fact, the heroine, Portia, disguised as a male lawyer to empower her to act legally: although she is the wealthiest of heiresses, Venetian law, like that of most of the then-known world—and like George Eliot's much later—allowed only male professionals. And she has not yet rendered the rest of her judgment: that Shylock is entitled to his pound of flesh only if he can collect it without spilling one drop of Christian blood. If I am correct, Eliot has in mind the most problematical of Shakespeare's texts, one which has been seen, on the one hand, as virulently anti-Semitic, and, on the other, as sympathetic to the psychology of an oppressed race. At any event, it is clear in the play that there is a curious linkage of female power with racial issues, and an equally curious ambiguity as to both Shakespeare's and Eliot's stands on these issues.

If the "Daniel" of *The Merchant of Venice* is actually female, is it possible that Eliot intended to present her hero, Daniel Deronda, as "feminine" in some ways?[5] Certainly it is Deronda, not poor Gwendolen, who has the imagination and constructive vision of such earlier Eliot heroines as Dinah Morris (who also envisions a religious Utopia), Maggie Tulliver (who dreams at first of the "out there" of such Walter Scott novels as *The Pirate*), and Dorothea Brooke (with her project of founding a Utopian community in the New World).

In his revised 1960 interpretation of *Daniel Deronda*, Leavis intuits this "feminine" aspect of Eliot's hero, though he does not link him with the "Daniel" apostrophized in *The Merchant of Venice*. As Leavis comments, "There is no dangerous heroine [i.e.

---

5    In an interesting article, "Resisting Gwendolen's 'Subjection': *Daniel Deronda*'s Proto-Feminism," Eileen Sypher does glance at the reader's need "to find a potential female hero, an unsubjected subject," but she does not really see it in Deronda. She considers the novel to be dominated "by the icon ... of the nearly drowned woman ( a dubious improvement from *Mill on the Floss*) clinging to the benevolent patriarch: her male savior hero" (506). Sypher seems, in fact, more than subtly hostile to Deronda, and, perhaps, to Eliot's "protection" of her titular hero. Gwendolen, on the other hand, she sees as "an enigma," "that shadowy signifier waiting to be a 'character,' a 'subject,' in a new discourse and a new social system" (509). But *what* new social system can that be? She opines that Deronda's disapproval of Gwendolen's gambling does not stem from, as Wilfred Stone thinks, Eliot's distrust of Chance and Fortune in favor of a religion of humanity, but rather because "Deronda somewhere knows that gambling offers Gwendolen the potential freedom of a man" (511). Moreover, she twists Eliot's motivation, I think, more than a little, in seeing Grandcourt not as the villain of the piece but as "Deronda's foil and his double, the decoy to siphon off any anxieties the reader feels about Deronda" (511). Although the reader is in a more privileged position than "either Deronda or Grandcourt, in terms of knowing more about Gwendolen's thought and needs" (514), Eliot remains evasive about her, providing none "of the framing summaries" she offers in other novels (516). Sypher concludes that "Eliot's strategy for allowing a potentially powerful and desiring woman character in a world inhospitable to such qualities in a woman is to construct her as changeable and so unknowable" (517). This sounds remarkably like Freud throwing up his hands in despair: "What *does* a woman want?" If Deronda is paired with Grandcourt, Gwendolen is paired with the Alcharisi to "[highlight] her powerful unmapped regions" (520), to suggest the Gothic, the uncontrollable. Thus Sypher seems to view *Daniel Deronda* as "A Novel in Search of a Heroine."

Maggie, Dorothea] in *Daniel Deronda*" (xvi). Gwendolen is "dangerous," but not as a creative imaginist: she curls in upon herself "like a sea anemone"; she suffers, resents, and retaliates. Leavis continues:

> … There is, however, a significant agreement that the hero is not a man. … But it registers something positive at the same time: the constatation that Deronda, though he cannot be called a creation, is very positively feminine—very positively a feminine expression. Who, contemplating the ardors, the emotional intensities, the idealistic exaltations that are focused in him can think "cold" an apt word for this failure of the creative writer? The high-powered intellectual, with her disinterested and clearsighted humanity, is certainly very much engaged in the Zionist part, but when we contemplate Deronda we cannot ignore the presence in it of something strongly, and very questionably, emotional; a powerful, but equivocal, element of inspiration … (xvi)

Leavis recognizes that Deronda's ardent longings are very much of a piece with Maggie's and Dorothea's (and Dinah's, I would add). Citing Daniel's "sweet irresistible hopefulness that the best of human possibilities might befall him—the blending of a complete personal love in one current with a larger duty," Leavis comments that "Deronda here indulges himself in a more inclusive hopefulness than Maggie or Dorothea in their exalted moods—or Deronda himself—tends to cultivate in full consciousness" (xvi). But Leavis goes on to argue that Deronda *does* realize "his 'sweet hopefulness' to the full," for in marrying Mirah, he "is able to identify 'the larger duty' … with a 'complete personal love'" (xvi).

Like other critics of the novel, such as Henry James, Leavis seems to attribute lack of conviction, or lack of psychological realism, to this "happy" resolution of Deronda's plight. In fact, to understand Eliot's predicament as an artist, I would argue that we need to view Deronda and Gwendolen together, as alter egos, as the male and female, or Yin and Yang, of the same dilemma. Having tried throughout her career to attribute agency to her heroines, only to find it, in the final analysis, drastically reduced, muted in impact, in her last novel Eliot reverts to giving agency to a man who, however, is at the outset in a "feminine"—that is, powerless—position. But by granting only negative agency to the other principal character, Gwendolen, she illuminates the tension and paradox resulting from her own role as a passionate, caring woman who is trying to survive in the "man's world" of art.[6]

Her gifted, imaginative heroines never conceive of fulfilling their destinies alone, but only through men of talent and intelligence. But Eliot is clearly ironic about this predisposition, when her heroines consistently choose men who are disappointing,

---

6    It is tempting to speculate (as others have) on the nature of Eliot's very late marriage to the much younger J.W. Cross, after the death of the love of her life, George Henry Lewes. They were married in May, and she died in December. One hears anecdotes about Cross jumping into the canal in Venice on their honeymoon, and certainly he rushed his biography of his wife into print not long after her death. Did she marry him out of a continuing drive to conform outwardly to societal expectations of woman, as her father had made her conform outwardly by attending church when she had begun as a young woman to question her old faith? Speaight, indeed, notes the split in her, suggesting that "George Eliot's most insidious foe was her imaginative and emotional femininity, divorced from the guidance of reason" (111). But he also adds, "Before writing of this quality [*Daniel Deronda*] criticism is silent" (114).

who are less gifted than themselves. Did she herself fall into the same trap? Or does this last completed novel express a final disillusionment and bitterness as to the possibility of a woman's finding any outlet beyond the domestic—unless, like the Alcharisi, she severs all human, affective ties in favor of art?

While Leavis sees Deronda as a distinctly female creation, he means that he is the ideal man created by a woman: "the beau idéal of masculinity" (xvi). He says that the "imagined life of sustained and wholly satisfying intensity George Eliot now conceives as a man's ..." (xvi). But it seems to me that Deronda is not only a woman's conception of the ideal man, but a "womanly man," androgynous, not in the sexual sense, perhaps, but in both intellectual concerns and emotional responses.

## A Two-Plot Novel: Daniel and Gwendolen

Society views Deronda as a man who is too emotional and vulnerable, Gwendolen as a woman who is too "frigid" and inexpressive. Like *Middlemarch*, *Daniel Deronda* is a two-plot novel growing out of the philosophic dialectic of Eliot's mind. Originally, Leavis, in *The Great Tradition*, following James, saw the Gwendolen Harleth section as so compelling that the entire novel should have been devoted to her, with the Deronda-Zionist plot dropped. But by 1960, his rereading reinforced his "already growing sense that the surgery of disjunction would be a less simple and satisfactory affair than I had thought ..." and that one "will demand the whole book that she wrote, and will be right" (xiv).

If we first examine Deronda's development and his awakening consciousness of the role he is to play, we can then better understand why his outlets are closed to Gwendolen, firmly entrenched in the status quo, and therefore the domestic sphere. Gwendolen, moreover, unlike Maggie and Dorothea, has no dreams beyond anything she has ever personally experienced. The dichotomous fates of the two principal characters help to explain the choice of title—Daniel belongs to a larger, more public world than Gwendolen, even when he is not sure what that world is.

If we apply the image Eliot uses in *Middlemarch* of "the systole and diastole of the human heart," Deronda's would be the expansion, Gwendolen's the contraction. As there is between Lydgate and Dorothea in *Middlemarch*, a wistful thread of a would-be romance exists between Gwendolen and Deronda; but it seems to me that the latter are more alter egos than potential lovers. Deronda, unlike Lydgate who is all too masculine, is constantly described in terms Eliot uses elsewhere to delineate her aspiring, imaginative heroines. Eliot's contemporary Thomas Henry Huxley remarked that she "depicts not the superiority of women, but the inferiority of men" (quoted by Beer, lecture); thus the androgynous Deronda is seen as superior to Lydgate, whose "spots of commonness" blind him to the female virtues.[7]

---

7    Carole Robinson sees Deronda's "precursors" as female, but faults Eliot for not showing convincingly that he has a feminine—that is affective—sensibility.

### Daniel's Awakening Conscience: A "Female Quest"?

Daniel is orphaned—or semi-orphaned, as it turns out—like Dinah and Dorothea; Maggie, too, loses her father, the parent most appreciative of her. As it turns out, Daniel and Gwendolen both have mothers, but no living father. Mirah, too, is searching for a family, and has no mother, but a father (abusive) and a brother, Mordecai (almost ideal).[8] There is a quest motif in the novel, a quest for the mother, and sometimes the father. Deronda's situation is misleadingly first set in a Christian context. As a boy, he asks his tutor, "Mr. Fraser, how was it that the popes and cardinals always had so many nephews?" —and the tutor has to reply, "Their own children were called nephews" (120). Thus Daniel is led to believe that he is the illegitimate product of a Christian liaison, whereas he is the legitimate heir of a traditional Jewish marriage. He has vague sensory memories of a mother: he "had a dim sense of having been kissed very much, and surrounded by thin, cloudy, scented drapery, till his fingers caught in something hard, which hurt him, and he began to cry" (121). The image is similar to that used to delineate Hetty Sorrel's character in *Adam Bede*: a downy peach with a hard stone at the center. On the other hand, the fact that his mother "kissed [him] very much" suggests a warmer side to Leonora's character than she presents herself in her interview with her son.

Hoping that Sir Hugo Mallinger, his guardian, is his real father, Daniel compares his looks to the portraits in the Mallinger gallery. He resembles them not in the slightest, but is handsomer, "and when he was thirteen might have served as model for any painter who wanted to image the most memorable of boys"—in other words, a prepubescent boy who resembles a girl. His intellect, moreover, "showed the same blending of child's ignorance with surprising knowledge which is oftener seen in bright girls" (123)—such as Maggie and Dorothea. He is implicitly compared to Dorothea in an echo of *Middlemarch*: "... he had never brought such knowledge into any association with his own lot" (123). Witnessing the Featherstone funeral, Dorothea wants to establish a connection between the "rich Lowick farmers" and herself, to include them in her "lofty conception of the universe." As with Eliot's heroines, "... there was hardly a delicacy of feeling this lad was not capable of" (124). Eliot emphasizes about Daniel, as she does earlier about Maggie Tulliver, that a child's education originates in life experiences more than in "book learning": "It is in such experiences of boy or girlhood, while elders are debating whether most education lies in science or literature, that the main lines of character are often laid down" (126).

Despite the Alcharisi's apparent lack of maternal instinct, he resembles his mother. As Sir Hugo's estate bailiff says to his wife, "He features the mother, eh?" (126). We never meet the father, but Daniel and his mother are linked by looks, talent, musicality, intelligence, and ambition. She, however, being a woman, is

---

8     Barbara Hardy, in her study of imagery in Eliot's novels, compares Mirah, who is "a half-reared linnet, bruised and lost by the wayside" (Chapter XXXII), to Gwendolen who is "like a lost, weary, storm-beaten white doe, unable to rise and pursue its unguided way" (Chapter SVI) (206). There is not much hope in either case, and reading between the lines Gwendolen seems to have had an abusive stepfather, if not an abusive father.

accused of a lack of female feelings for following her ambitions, while the son is free to accomplish what he wants. Curiously, he resents the possibility of a singing career, which had been his mother's means of escape: "... the lad had seemed angry at the notion of becoming a singer" (128). His ambitions are not mimetic or aesthetic, but political and legal: "I would rather be a greater leader, like Pericles or Washington"—in other words, a lawgiver or founder of a country. Later he also sees Columbus as a genius, who does not *found*, but *finds* a country. His role models have to be masculine; it is important to remember that women in England, however brilliant or well-educated, did not receive the suffrage until after the First World War, nor even the right to own property, if married, until the passage by Parliament of the Married Women's Property Acts between 1870 and 1882. But his quest for a vocation uniting deep feelings and intellect is closest to the female quests of Maggie and Dorothea—and Eliot herself.

Daniel is reserved, like a woman (126); he is hurt when Sir Hugo ends his bachelorhood by marrying a Miss Raymond, and never acknowledges Daniel as his son. Unlike Gwendolen, however, he is free from "moral stupidity" and does not resent Lady Mallinger and her three daughters (129), whereas Gwendolen marries Grandcourt, although she is fully aware of the existence of his former mistress, Mrs. Lydia Glasher, and her children by him. Since Sir Hugo does not have a son, legitimate or illegitimate, his nephew Grandcourt is, ironically, his heir. Similarly, Grandcourt has no legitimate male heir, but Mrs. Glasher's son should be in that position, as Daniel originally imagined himself to be Sir Hugo's illegitimate son. What saves Daniel, and not at least the early Gwendolen, is his ability to transcend "the personal": "It was his characteristic bias to shrink from the moral stupidity of valuing lightly what had come close to him, and of missing blindly in his own life of to-day the crises which he recognized as momentous and sacred in the historic life of men" (382).

Sir Hugo has, in fact, been partly benefiting from the double standard: "No one was better aware than he that Daniel was generally suspected to be his own son. But he was pleased with that suspicion; and his imagination had never once been troubled with the way in which the boy himself might be affected ... by the enigmatic aspect of his circumstances" (129). That "enigmatic aspect" is comparable, we are told, to "Byron's susceptibility about his deformed foot" (128).[9] Sir Hugo advises him to "make yourself a barrister—be a writer—take up politics," but within England (130). Daniel is already sensing that there is not much hope within class-structured England, but he has as yet no conception of what the outside world is.

Daniel is not a grind at school, not an Eton scholar, because he exhibits that "meditative yearning after wide knowledge which is likely always to abate ardour in the fight for prize acquirement in narrow tracks" (132). Eliot shows some of the same sarcasm towards (male-dominated) university education, and academia generally, that Virginia Woolf was also to show in 1929 in *A Room of One's Own*: "(Deronda's undergraduateship occurred fifteen years ago, when the perfection of our university methods was not yet indisputable)," she comments parenthetically

---

9    We might compare the Alcharisi's reference to Jewish law for women as being analogous to Chinese foot-binding.

(133). He would become "an Ishmaelite," Eliot warns us, foreshadowing the Judaic context. But Ishmael was also the founder of the 12 tribes of Islam, as Melville reminds us in *Moby Dick* (1851), so Eliot is positioning Daniel cross-culturally and cross-religiously, as well as across genders. If he is Daniel in the lion's den, and a Daniel come to judgment, he is also, as has been remarked, related to the author of the Book of Daniel, the first church historian, with "his boyish love of universal history, which made him want to be at home in foreign countries ..." (133).[10] Ultimately, he will make the "foreign" country—Palestine—his own.

He is reading law when he rescues Mirah from drowning herself in the Thames, near Kew Bridge; Gwendolen will be unwilling or unable to rescue her villainous husband, Grandcourt, when he is drowning towards the end of the novel.[11] Moreover, Mirah's rescue occurs in July, the same date as the archery meeting when Gwendolen begins her relationship with Grandcourt, so it is "too late" for both Gwendolen and Daniel by the time they meet on the continent at the gambling tables. In Mirah he sees "the girl-tragedies that are going on in the world, hidden, unheeded, as if they were but tragedies of the copse or hedgerow," and begins to connect them, for once, with his usual telescopic vision of "wide-sweeping connections with all life and history" (139). He thinks, significantly, "perhaps my mother was like this one" (141). She is searching, in fact, for her own good mother, who, unfortunately, is dead; there remains only her brother Mordecai to represent the good of her family.[12]

Eliot compares Sir Hugo's and Daniel's attachment to that between man and woman (238). Sir Hugo remembers the mother's attractions in the son. Eliot elaborates on what we would call today Daniel's androgyny: he "was moved by an affectionateness such as we are apt to call feminine, ... while he had a certain inflexibility of judgment, an independence of opinion, held to be rightfully masculine" (238). He is, in other words, a judge embodying both male and female traits: judgment and affectiveness—a Daniel who is really a Portia, moving easily between public and private spheres. Like many Eliot heroines—notably Dinah, Maggie, and Dorothea—he exhibits "a many-sided sympathy," which makes him

---

10 Mary Wilson Carpenter reminds us that the author of the Book of Daniel was the first to distill a philosophy of history, and argues the unity of the two plots from its Old Testament basis, the 70 chapters deriving from the prophecy of the Seven Weeks, which are 70 weeks of exile: the major characters are all exiled in one way or another. Eliot herself said of the textual unity (as she also did of the two-plot *Middlemarch*) that "she meant everything in the book to be related to everything else there" (Letter 6, 290). Eliot is trying to reconcile the two streams of Western history, Jewish and Gentile. Carpenter claims that she reads the Book of Daniel as the Apocalypse of the Old Testament. Haight and others have remarked on Eliot's friendship with Emanuel Deutsch, who was educated by an uncle who was a rabbi. She wrote to Harriet Beecher Stowe about "the Jewish element in *Deronda*" (183), and denounced "in plain English, the stupidity—which is still the average mark of our culture" (quoted by Bennett, 184). There was no Zionist Movement until 1900. Both Eliot and Stowe may have seen the outward journey as the only outlet for people oppressed in different ways.

11 H.M. Daleski also notes that the drowning image links Mirah and Gwendolen (84).

12 Bernard Semmel sees the Jew as "the superego" in the novel, an epithet most suited to Mordecai (121). He also notes the resemblance to Scott's *Ivanhoe*, with Mirah in the Rebecca role, but a Rebecca who marries the hero (123).

"fervidly democratic in his feeling for the multitude," yet, perhaps paradoxically, "intensely conservative" in his reluctance "to part with long-sanctioned forms" (271). Eliot could well be describing her own ambivalence: on the one hand, she is almost Whitmanian in her desire to embrace the universe, and had to protest at one point, "In spite of what some caustic people may say, I fall not in love with every one" (quoted by Paterson viii); on the other hand, she is driven back to forms and structures (including conventional marriage?) seemingly valorized by history, as she had been to the forms of the Church of England.

Again like many Eliot heroines, Deronda tends to embrace the defenseless, and "suspected himself of loving too well the losing causes of the world" (271). Like Dorothea's, his sympathy is sometimes too reflective and diffusive (272), and distracts him "while he was reading law"—or the purest attendance to forms! Again like Dorothea, he feels poetry within him, without having the self-confidence—or stupidity, like Mr. Brooke and Will Ladislaw—to declare himself a poet: "... he had a fervour which made him easily feel the presence of poetry in everyday events ..." (273). Society, like Sir Hugo, might see him as "Quixotic" if they knew what he was thinking and feeling; Eliot had earlier used a passage from *Don Quixote* to bring out Dorothea's true qualities as a "Female Quixote."[13]

Along with his love of all oppressed humanity goes a certain blindness to individual passions; one thinks of the nearsighted Dorothea, so obsessed with reforming the universe that she is apt to trample on small animals that get underfoot. Sir Hugo tells him early on that he is "a kind of Lovelace who will make the Clarissas run after you instead of your running after them" (269). It is Sir Hugo, again, who says alliteratively that he has "a passion for people who are pelted" (541). The gossipy Mr. Vandernoodt recognizes in Daniel "one of the historical men—more interested in a lady when she's got a rag face and skeleton toes peeping out" (325). He does retain sympathy for the obviously suffering live ladies such as Mrs. Glasher: "... Deronda had naturally some resentment on behalf of the Hagars and Ishmaels"—who were, in fact, alienated and exiled from the Jewish community because of sexual jealousy, as Mrs. Glasher is from the Gentile.

All this makes one wonder about the basis of his love for Mirah: she is certainly one of the discarded, the "people who are pelted." She in turn hero-worships him, regarding him as a "Lord Chancellor" (562).

But Gwendolen, too, is in need of salvation from drowning. First, the threat is figurative: "It was as if he saw her drowning while his limbs were bound" (341). Later it is only too real: Grandcourt really drowns, but something of Gwendolen dies in the process, and Daniel's "rescue," while well-intentioned, comes too little and too late. Gwendolen's fate, however, arouses his pity, not love, because something in her (her class, her Englishness) has proven to be alien to him: "It had lain in the course of poor Gwendolen's lot that her dependence on Deronda tended to rouse in him the enthusiasm of self-martyring pity rather than of personal love, and his less

---

13   This epithet can be used to describe all four heroines treated in my earlier book, *The Prison of Womanhood: Four Provincial Heroines in Nineteenth-Century Fiction*: Austen's Emma Woodhouse, Flaubert's Emma Bovary, Eliot's Dorothea Brooke, and Henry James's Isabel Archer.

constrained tenderness flowed with the fuller stream towards an indwelling image in all things unlike Gwendolen" (561). In other words, Mirah, completed by her theological brother Mordecai, gives concrete shape to what had hitherto been a vague yearning. As he says to Mordecai, "It is you who have given shape to what, I believe, was an inherited yearning—the effect of brooding, passionate thoughts in many ancestors—thoughts that seem to have been intensely present in my grandfather" (565). Later, about Gwendolen, he considers that "I should have loved her, if—: the 'if' covering some prior growth in the inclinations, or else some circumstances which have made an inward prohibitory law as a stay against the emotions ready to quiver out of balance" (466). Gwendolen is not competing on a level playing field.

*Daniel and the Alcharisi*

The Cohens, who lead Daniel to Mordecai, quote the Jewish prayer: "A man is bound to thank God, as we do every Sabbath, that he was not made a woman; but a woman has to thank God that He has made her according to His will. And we all know what He has made her—a childbearing tender-hearted thing is the woman of our people" (433).[14] This prayer is offered in dialogue by one of the less intelligent characters, and Eliot offers no direct commentary on it. But the indirect critique comes from one of those Jewish women, Deronda's mother, the Princess Leonora Halm-Eberstein, a.k.a. the Alcharisi. It implicitly helps motivate her artistic rebellion against her culture: she chooses to be an operatic diva rather than a wife and mother.[15] It is difficult to resist hearing the poignant notes of George Eliot's own musical voice in the Alcharisi's defense to her son of her choices:

> "You are not a woman. You may try—but you can never imagine what it is to have a man's force of genius in you, and yet to suffer the slavery of being a girl. To have a pattern cut out—'this is the Jewish woman; this is what you must be; this is what you are wanted for; a woman's heart must be of such a size and no larger, else it must be pressed small, like Chinese feet; her happiness is to be made as cakes are, by a fixed receipt.' That was what my father wanted. ... He hated that Jewish women should be thought of as a sort of ware to make public singers and actresses of. As if we were not the more enviable for that! That is a chance of escaping from bondage."(474)

Daniel, ironically, emulates his grandfather in "silencing" Mirah, albeit with the best of intentions. The Alcharisi's impassioned apologia anticipates contemporary feminist critiques which use Chinese footbinding as a trope for the female condition.

---

14   Gillian Beer does suggest, however, that Eliot was taking notes from the Kabbalah in which it was suggested that the soul was originally androgynous (216)—some support for my reading of Daniel himself, I think, though not for the status quo.

15   William Baker notes that the Princess is based on a Jewish actress, not singer, Rahel Lewin (53). He also adds that George Henry Lewes "was a philo-semite, fascinated by Jewish life and ideas" (53). He, in fact, wrote about the actress Rachel (variant spelling) (Beer, 209). Beer also notes Ellen Moers' reference in *Literary Women* to the powerful role of female opera singers, and raises the question of Eliot's keen interest in public performance. Beer speculates that singers, in contrast to the "Silly Novels by Lady Novelists" Eliot excoriated early in her career, have "the absolute safeguards that technique afforded against self-delusion" (205).

The title of Book VII invites us to compare "The Mother and the Son"—so alike in physique, in aspirations and talent, but one female and one male. Only one has to transgress social conventions—Jewish *and* European—to realize her aspirations. As a great singer, she says, "I was living myriad lives in one. I did not want a child" (470).[16] Victim of an arranged marriage, she nonetheless sees it as *relative* freedom from patriarchal law: "I was forced into marrying your father—forced, I mean, by my father's wishes and commands; and besides, it was my best way of getting some freedom. I could rule my husband, but not my father. I had a right to be free. I had a right to seek my freedom from a bondage that I hated" (470–71).[17] The Alcharisi sees the Jews as a hard people, and remarries only when, fearing the loss of her talent, she begins to lose her voice (480). She is dying, presumably of cancer, before she contacts her son. But love is also a talent, one which she admits she lacks (501).[18]

---

16   Eliot herself never had a child, but there is no indication that she did not want to, and indeed she supported Lewes's son even after her common-law husband's death.

17   We might be back in the world of Jane Austen, and the theme of marriage as relative independence through an establishment.

18   Several critics try to foreground Mirah, comparing her favorably to both the Alcharisi and Gwendolen. Amanda Anderson considers that "the Jewish question" for George Eliot represents a movement beyond cosmopolitanism towards rootedness: "... Daniel's history functions more generally as an allegory about cosmopolitanism, which for Eliot is a condition of Judaism, Jewish nationalism" (45). Anderson sees Leonora "as a willfully cosmopolitan woman who has renounced her cultural heritage," and who represents "the more extreme dangers of modern detachment." She fails to transmit "the affective bonds of the community." On the other hand, Anderson idealizes Mirah, who "represents just such ideal femininity": "Unable to achieve the higher-order, mediated cultural affirmation associated with Deronda, Mirah nonetheless represents what Deronda comes to recognize and avow: the importance of a deeply felt connection to family and culture" (53). This is a rather surprising statement coming from a woman critic, seemingly favorably disposed towards the Jewish prayer offered by men each Sabbath. She adds, moreover, that "... Leonora aligns herself with the transitional force of art, and seeks to divorce herself entirely from the trifling confinement of a tradition-bound cultural heritage" (53–4). But does George Eliot see art as a merely "transitional force," or as a kind of religion of humanity?

Oliver Lovesey also focuses on Mirah, seeing her as "The Other Woman in *Daniel Deronda*." I would be inclined to see *Gwendolen*, rather, as "the other woman" in the sexual sense, in terms of the love triangle. Lovesey seems to be thinking of the marginalized status of Mirah as Jewish performer: "*Daniel Deronda*'s representation of the female Jewish artist as other encapsulates its critique of Englishness and designates the Jewish woman as signifier of freedom, integrity, and agency: however, this designation is accomplished through the construction of a racial dialectic that reproduces the ideological constraints it attempts to critique" (505). It is Mirah who "channels Deronda's diffuse anxieties into a quest for personal and collective myths of origin" (505). Gail Marshall also considers that Mirah embodies "a redemptive hope for the female performer, and by extension for all female art ..." (134). The problem is, once again, that she ceases performing when she marries. Marshall does contrast her professionalism to Gwendolen, who acts in real life, "mistakenly seeking to enthrall the male gaze" (119). She compares actresses to Ovid's Galatea as "objects and products of their spectators" (118). Marshall notes the possible etymological linkage of "speculation"—the gambling of the opening scene, and the speculators who lose Mrs. Davilow's money—and "a spectacle," in which Gwendolen performs in the opening scene: "Gwendolen is from the start

Since Eliot was notoriously an ardent, loving, expansive woman, she manages to allow the Alcharisi the most explicitly feminist plea in all her fiction, while at the same time distancing herself from the character articulating it. Leonora is a tortured woman, but so is Gwendolen, and in Chapter LIV we move straight from the Alcharisi's confession to Gwendolen's "purgatorio" on the yacht with Grandcourt.

*Daniel and the Jewish Community*

Deronda's development is traced not only through his discovery of his own genealogy, but also through his shifting perspectives on the Jewish community.[19] At first he is faintly repelled when he meets the then-unknown Mordecai in a bookstore, who takes his arm and asks anxiously, "You are perhaps of our race?" Deronda's response is awkward, somewhat embarrassed, but he quickly denies it (289). He then begins to contrast the slim, scholarly man he has met with the "glistening," heavy Ezra Cohen. Deronda is partly amused at Ezra's mixture of kindness and "calculation" (300). From this position he moves to embracing the dream of the Promised Land. He says to Mordecai at last, "And you were right. I am a Jew," and he continues, "we have the same people. Our souls have the same location. We shall not be separated by life or by death" (563). Deronda is, moreover, a Spanish, or Sephardic, Jew, who are direct descendants of the original Semitic tribes. Eliot's constant linkage of Zionism and the role of women, however, suggests that her position is much more ambivalent than her hero's.

## Gwendolen Harleth: A Woman Come to Judgement

Certainly more of the text is devoted to Gwendolen's story, but it would be a dead end without Deronda and the Jewish material.[20] Her fate must be placed in the context of that of the other women in the novel: Mirah, a minor singing talent with a major talent

---

engrossed in, and enclosed by, her desire to be seen, and her theatrical self-exhibition itself becomes part of the gambling and speculation in the casino" (13). She is at the same time the statues Galatea and Hermione, and an actress living a "life of pretense" (4). Wilfred Stone also notes that, though there is "no etymological connection between the word 'speculation' and (by way of 'speculum') the act of looking in mirrors ... there ought to be, for gamblers tend to be narcissists, and Gwendolen is a brilliant representative of the species" (49). As he notes, Gwendolen "looks continually in her mirror and entices others to look into it, and she even kisses her own image in the cold glass" (50).

19   In an influential article, Cynthia Chase presumes that Daniel was circumcised, which should have led to his recognition of his Jewish identity, rather than the other way around. Thus she considers that the narrative deconstructs history. Judith Wilt, however (like myself), finds this reading "Problematic in view of his strong anti-Jewish mother's desire, and ability, to control her mild-mannered husband" (316).

20   Sara Putzell, in an article with the inspired title, "The Importance of Being Gwendolen," explores a number of possible sources of the heroine's name, including Sir Walter Scott's *The Bridal of Triermane* (1813), the anonymous *The Legende of St. Gwendoline* (1867), and James Payn's *Gwendoline's Harvest* (1870), all of which "describe the fate of willful heroines who meet disappointment" (33). It is somewhat of a letdown, however, to see no reference

for loving; the Alcharisi, a major talent with little gift for loving; Gwendolen, the somewhat talented amateur without discipline or training; the literary women—Mrs. Arrowpoint and her daughter Catherine; the visual artists in the Meyrick family.[21]

### Gwendolen's Anti-Quest: Her Awakening Conscience

The inevitability of Gwendolen's separation from Deronda is suggested from the beginning by her sarcasm about "these Jew pawnbrokers." At the end she is dumbfounded to discover Deronda is himself a Jew. Finally, they are speaking not only across class, race, religion, and gender, but in two different languages (605). Unlike Dinah, Maggie, Dorothea, but like the much less agreeable, less sympathetic Rosamond Vincy, Gwendolen is the perfect, conditioned product of a system whch values women's appearance, trivial accomplishments, and marketability over intrinsic worth. Unhappily for Gwendolen, however, unlike Rosamond but like Edith Wharton's Lily Bart in *The House of Mirth* (1905), she has innate intelligence and taste that make her constantly come up short, bridle when she confronts the patriarchal system.[22] She is capable of development, but Eliot leaves her with an awakened conscience and no visible outlets; marriage to Rex Gascoigne is surely a red herring. She is, in effect, condemned to live. Deronda offers the "comfort that serves in a whirlwind" when he gives his farewell salute: "Now we can perhaps never see each other again. But our minds may get nearer" (608). She can in no way participate in his dream "of restoring a political existence to my people, making them a nation again, giving them a national centre, such as the English have, though they too are scattered over the face of the globe" (606). The difference, of course, is that the English have been the colonizers, not the colonized, and the patriarchy in which Gwendolen has been inscribed is largely responsible for that colonization.

---

beyond the title to the most famous other heroine named Gwendolen, in Oscar Wilde's *The Importance of Being Earnest* (1895). Was Wilde inspired by Eliot?

21   Judith Wilt links Gwendolen and the Alcharisi through the theme of "The Fathers of Daughters," including Leonora's and Mirah's, as well as Gwendolen's father and stepfather, and through the "search for origins" which is also a search "for original sin" (316). She notes the link between Captain Davilow, the stepfather, and Grandcourt's "languid authority," and the violence of Gwendolen's reactions to both (327). She nonetheless tries to end on a note of hope for a female community, following from Gillian Beer's statement that "Gwendolen survives her marriage, does not bear children to a hated husband, and so avoids becoming a part of that genealogical world of succession ..." (337). But such a dream of a Charlotte Perkins Gilman's *Herland* or Sandra Gilbert's "No Man's Land" seems doomed by Gwendolen's continued entrapment in the man's world with its corollary, female conditioning. It is also implicit in Wilt's reading that Daniel cannot be "feminine" in sensibility, since she feels that "Daniel's decison [about her innocence] deprives Gwendolen of an achievement" (335). Deirdre David also points to a Freudian reading, noting Gwendolen's "fixation upon her mother": "... her fits of spiritual dread ... are a manifestation of her guilt for having wished both her father and her step-father dead so that she may have her mother to herself ... " (177).

22   Stuart Hutchinson also detects a possible influence of *Daniel Deronda* on *The House of Mirth* some quarter of a century later.

Gwendolen's "awakening conscience"[23] is far more concretely detailed than Deronda's because, while he has a gap of yearning to fill, Gwendolen must divest herself of the cumbersome baggage of patriarchal England. That Deronda fills his gap with patriarchal Judaism leaves Eliot's own position, at the very least, obscure, enigmatic.

### "A Problematic Sylph"

Gwendolen, like Deronda, is introduced on the very first page of the novel, gambling on the Continent as she is literally gambling with her life.[24] No harlot (Harleth),[25] we learn later that her desperation in this scene is motivated by her need to escape marriage to Grandcourt, which has appeared the only alternative to what she would consider abject poverty (Wharton's Lily Bart calls it "dinginess"). She is seen from the start as "a *problematic* sylph" (emphasis mine), and we are invited to guess what the "problematic" is, or a "Nereid in sea-green robes and silver ornaments," an image reinforced later at the archery meet when she again appears attired in green, as Diana the Huntress, Goddess of Chastity.[26] Eliot from the outset conjures up a beggar image, but negatively, as being the polar opposite to Gwendolen, and a role which she resists: she is gambling "not in the open air under a southern sky, tossing coppers on a ruined wall, with rags about her limbs, but in one of those splendid resorts which the enlightenment of ages has prepared for the same species of pleasure at a heavy cost of gilt mouldings, dark-toned colour and chubby nudities, all correspondingly heavy ..." (1). Nonetheless, Gwendolen's dread is of being reduced to a state she, at least, if not Mirah, would consider a "beggar's": that of a governess, also reduced to "beg" and live as a humble dependent.[27]

---

23 There is a famous Pre-Raphaelite story painting by William Holman Hunt that is almost an icon of the period: called "The Awakening Conscience," it depicts a young woman sitting at a piano, beginning to rise from the stool, with a new light in her eyes while a suave villain looks on. Her state of déshabillé and lack of a wedding ring suggest that she is a kept woman beginning to suffer pangs of conscience.

24 E.A. Hobbs relates the opening scene to Schopenhauer's pessimistic secularization of religious myths. Gambling for Eliot, Hobbs argues, was the opposite to her Comtean religion of humanity, representing a faith in chance, and therefore a hell of moral irresponsibility. I am not sure, however, whether Gwendolen's "ennui" is attributable primarily to Schopenhauer or to Baudelaire: it is also one of the Seven Deadly Sins. Joan Bennett notes that the genesis of the book was an 1875 journal entry, but she had originally written from Homburg in October 1872 about the vice of gambling (181). Ashton also remarks that Lydgate, in *Middlemarch*, loses control partly through gambling.

25 Semmel does note the similarity in sound.

26 But the description also evokes Hetty Sorrel, another "problematic" Eliot heroine who suffers because she is *not* chaste, and whose green clothing contrasts sharply with that of the virginal Dinah Morris, dressed in white, during their bed-chamber interview when Dinah tries to help the younger woman.

27 Jane Austen, in *Emma*, refers to the " governess-trade" as the "slave-trade," implying white slave trade.

The novel opens with Gwendolen, and a question: "Was she beautiful or not beautiful?" (1). But her beauty is not finally the central question: it is, rather, why the onlooker feels compelled to continue gazing (1). The silver and green dress also suggests a serpent to the onlookers, and Eliot deliberately compares Keats's Lamia: "Woman was tempted by a serpent: why not man?" (5). There are echoes of another dangerous, clever, fatal woman, Becky Sharp in Thackeray's *Vanity Fair* (1848), but also of Eliot's own dangerously stupid Rosamond Vincy with her swan-like or serpent-like neck which she twists about. Yet throughout the novel Gwendolen, for all her faults, is intended (like James's Isabel Archer) to awaken the reader's understanding, tenderness, and sympathy.[28] Eliot reminds us that her motive for winding her neck about is not public display but observation: "Tonight she wound her neck about more than usual ... But it was not that she might carry out the serpent idea more completely: it was that she watched for any chance of seeing Deronda ..." (16). She seeks to be the gazer, not the object of the gaze. To pursue *The Merchant of Venice* analogy, the play turns on a wedding between Jew and Gentile, which is not a relationship destined to bear fruit in this novel.

Gwendolen is seen by the dowagers and other onlookers as "headlong" (6), though they cannot know her motivation. She puts on an act of being "always bored," and is a better actress or performer in real life than she could ever be on the stage, contrary to the Alcharisi and Mirah. It is not surprising to read that the novel was originally conceived as a play (Hughes, 443). Certainly the dramatic scenes are the most powerful and effective, and the shadow of *The Merchant of Venice* lurks behind both intertwined plots. The cash nexus is central in Gwendolen's life, as it is in Shylock's and Antonio's, and finances are controlled by the man's world. Instead of meeting Deronda that evening when she seeks him, Gwendolen finds instead a letter from her mother, Mrs. Davilow, informing her that Grapnell and Company have gone bankrupt, and what little fortune they had is lost.[29] The guilt of the man's world parallels Gwendolen's reckless gambling: as her mother writes, "... it is hard

---

28   Baruch Hochman surmises that "in Gwendolen George Eliot conflates qualities of the two kinds of girls on which her work centres: the active, aspiring ones like Maggie, Romola and Dorothea, who desperately crave love, but generally can't find it, and the passive man-traps, like Hetty and Rosamund [sic], who are loved, but end up destroying the man who loved them" (126). Dorothea does, of course, find love, though she and Maggie are looking for more; and to be a man-trap is not to be passive: Hetty destroys herself, not the man she loves (Arthur—Adam marries his soulmate Dinah). Gwendolen's tragedy is that she does not know what to seek, and is a far more sympathetic character than Rosamond. Grandcourt does not love her—or anyone except, perhaps, himself.

29   One is reminded of the bank failure in Gaskell's *Cranford*, where the world of Drumble (Manchester) proves anything but a solid support for the elderly ladies of Cranford (Knutsford). As Wilfred Stone comments, "... public speculation and private gambling are but two sides of the same coin. It takes [the] author to point out that Grapnell and Company were gamblers pure and simple who, like Gwendolen, also thought of reigning in the realm of luck, and were also bent at amusing themselves, no matter how!" (54). Hughes discusses interestingly Eliot's increasing disillusionment with modern greed: "*Daniel Deronda* is George Eliot's only novel to be set in the near-present, around 1875. There is no galloping coachman or historian-narrator taking us back to the England of 1820s or beyond." In February 1874

to resign one's self to Mr. Lassman's wicked recklessness, which they say was the cause of the failure" (8). Eliot does not comment on Mr. Lassman's racial origins, but she is surely playing with some stereotypes reinforced by Gwendolen's thoughtless remark about "these Jew dealers," with Gentiles apparently scapegoating Jewish financiers, moneylenders, and pawnbrokers for their own greedy market speculations. Progressively throughout the text Daniel is stripping off the mask, seeing what lies behind the stereotypes, as he recognizes the spirit of Mordecai behind the Cohens *et al.* The character of Shylock, with all its ambiguities, seems to haunt Eliot's vision.

Jessica, in Shakespeare's play, makes off with her father's money: "O my ducats! O my daughter!" cries Shylock, not knowing which to mourn the most. Gwendolen pawns her turquoise necklace, which "had belonged to a chain once her father's; but she had never known her father ..." and, as we soon learn, she detested her stepfather. The absence of a father to admire, to look up to, is a crucial lack in Gwendolen's upbringing, and her mother helps to make her "the spoiled child" she is. The mother's conditioning, social programming, of her is given away inadvertently in her letter: "I always felt it impossible that you can have been made for poverty" (8). But the only way out she envisions for her daughter is marriage—as the epigraph to Chapter X reminds us, "Our daughters must be wives" (71), and Eliot comments cynically, "... perhaps it is not quite mythical that a slave has been proud to be bought first ..." (72). Gwendolen complains, "Can nobody be happy after they are quite young?" and her mother replies, "Marriage is the only happy state for a woman, as I trust you will prove" (18). Fanny Davilow is scarcely the outstanding example of the happiness and freedom to be found in marriage. Her own sad fate undermines her attempts at any wholehearted support of the institution; she fears that Gwendolen's response would resemble "that of the future Madame Roland": "when her gentle mother urging the acceptance of a suitor, said, 'Tu seras heureuse, ma chère.' 'Oui, maman, comme toi'" (67–8).[30]

Gwendolen is the most valued of her family because apparently the most suited to the marriage market; her younger sisters are seen as "superfluous." Because she is spoiled, "her will was peremptory" (9). She seems to be sitting for "a portrait" (10).[31] She is at this point naively self-satisfied, but Eliot does at least foreshadow a necessary change in her consciousness.

---

she complained about the modern "'eager scrambling after wealth and show' and in *Daniel Deronda* she shows this process at work" (448).

30   Catherine Belsey (incidentally one of the critics who seems not to realize that Leavis recanted his views expressed in *The Great Tradition*), argues that the novel is about sexual power relations and "the social production of femininity," and that the central question is not Deronda's identity, but what has produced Gwendolen. She concludes that the novel challenges the "classic realism" of *The Great Tradition* by rejecting romantic closure.

31   In this respect she resembles James's Isabel Archer in *The Portrait of a Lady*, for whom she may be one model ( though I think Eliot's other great heroine, Dorothea Brooke in *Middlemarch*, who literally sits for a portrait by Naumann in Rome, is the more significant one).

*The Quest for Origins: Gwendolen's Beginnings*

The epigraph to the opening chapter points to Eliot's concern with origins: "Men can do nothing without the make-believe of a beginning … Nought really sets off *in medias res*. No retrospect will take us to the true beginning; and whether our prologue be in heaven or on earth, it is but a fraction of that all presupposing fact with which our story sets out" (1).[32] *Middlemarch* starts out with Dorothea's mother's jewels (as *Daniel Deronda* does with Gwendolen's), which she Puritanically refuses to wear but keeps beside her as "fragments of heaven," a metaphor which applies to Eliot's own sense of structure. *Daniel Deronda* also seems to start off *in medias res*, in that we are left to wonder about Gwendolen's and Deronda's circumstances until later, when we realize why what seems to be starting as a romance between these two is already "too late."

Origins further account for the heroine's psychology. It is suggested that Gwendolen is spoiled and self-centered not only because she is the most "interesting" of her family, but also because she has been raised in isolation, is rootless.[33] Gwendolen, half-orphaned, moves with her family[34] from one watering-place to another. Eliot writes, "Pity that Offendene [near the Gascoigne relatives at Pennicote Rectory] was not the home of Miss Harleth's childhood, or endeared to her by family memories! A human life, I think, should be well rooted in some spot of a native land …" (12).[35] This sense of rootedness sustains the Tullivers throughout their sufferings in *The Mill on the Floss*, as it does many of Hardy's characters.

But Offendene is "rather too anxiously ornamented with stone at every line," and has no view: "One would have liked the house to have been lifted on a knoll, so as to

---

32   In *Darwin's Plots*, Gillian Beer writes significantly and philosophically about Eliot's concern both with origins and the future. She writes that "*Daniel Deronda* is a novel haunted by the future" (181), and that Eliot once projected a book called "The Idea of a Future Life" (183). She notes the "problematic, cryptic" opening of the book by the author's apparent non-presence, except for the epigraph (191). Both in narrative and substance the novel is elusive: "In *Daniel Deronda* past and future are dubiously intercalated: the order of telling and the order of experience are confused and can never thoroughly be rearranged. The work brings to the centre of our attention the idea of a future life" (185). But what is that future life to be? As Beer says, "Gwendolen's story also, like that of the Zionist state, is still to come, a marriage of fictions, not yet fixed and diminished by the retrospect of history" (193). Most critics have noticed the absence of closure in the text, which many see as moving Eliot's work into the realm of modernism—or beyond?

33   Dorothea, similarly, was raised "on plans at once narrow and promiscuous, first in an English family and afterwards in a Swiss family at Lausanne," a seat of Swiss Calvinism (6), and only comes to Middlemarch as a young woman, where she tries to find connections between herself and the teeming, but formless, life of the farmers, bankers, merchants, doctors, surrounding her.

34   … like James's Archers and Moreens.

35   Offendene is located in Wessex, Hardy country, and Leavis surmises that Hardy "actually did, I think, take the use of the name of the old West Saxon kingdom, Wessex, from *Daniel Deronda*, where also (a congruous fact) he would find that manifest influence of Greek tragic thought which undoubtedly played its part in the suggestiveness that George Eliot's work in general had for him" (xii, xiii).

look beyond its own little domain to the long thatched roofs of the distant villages, the church towers, the scattered homesteads, the gradual rise of surging woods, and the green breadths of undulating park which made the beautiful face of the earth in that part of Wessex" (13). Astronomy, Eliot reminds us, starts "as a little lot of stars belonging to one's own homestead" (13). As it is, Gwendolen has no wish or inducement to look beyond herself: she is "the pet and pride of the household," " a princess in exile" (27). Like Rosamond Vincy, she went to a "showy school" which put her on display; the "Lacanian gaze" early conditions Gwendolen to public—but always amateur—performances.

*Gwendolen the Archer: Her Destructive Tendencies*

If Deronda is caring and sensitive (positively feminine?), Gwendolen shows latent—and sometimes overt—tendencies to violence (negatively masculine?). Is it that Deronda's initial lack of awareness of who he is leads to some constructive "feminine" traits? Whereas Gwendolen's rigid class position and totally "feminine" conditioning lead to "masculine" destructive tendencies? If Eliot's ideal is androgyny, a blending of apparent opposites, she reveals reservations and ambivalences as to some gender crossovers. Gwendolen's maternal grandfather's wealth is suspect in origin: "... he had been a West Indian—which seemed to exclude further question; and she knew that her father's family was so high as to take no notice of her mamma ..." (14). Her wealth is new, not old, based on the same colonization as the Bertrams' Antigua fortunes in Austen's *Mansfield Park*. Moreover, it is somewhat unsavory, probably based, at least at the beginning, on slave labor—in other words, on the oppression of a people by race, analogous to the European treatment of the Jews.

   The patriarchy in Gwendolen's background was doubtless guilty of its own share of violence, which turns up curiously in Gwendolen who "strangled her sister's canary-bird in a final fit of exasperation at its shrill singing which had again and again jarringly interrupted her own" (15). "That infelonious murder" is the first concrete foreshadowing of Gwendolen's later feelings of guilt at having let Grandcourt die. An even clearer foreshadowing occurs when her little sister Isabel opens a panel of the wainscot: "The opened panel had disclosed the picture of an upturned dead face, from which an obscure figure seemed to be fleeing, with outstretched arms" (16). She thinks of marriage as "rather a dreary state," bringing "domestic fetters," and tolerates the idea only for the "social promotion" it could afford. Moreover, domesticity may be the wrong choice, for "this delicate-limbed sylph of twenty meant to lead" (26). She is here linked with the "masculine" ambition for power and authority, with its concomitant tendency to violence.

   Among her sisters, "all of a girlish average," she is "a young race horse in the paddock among untrimmed ponies and patient hacks" (15). Like Dorothea, she is known for her horsemanship, which implies a "masculine" desire for control. She is also proud of her skills at archery:[36] "There is nothing I enjoy more than taking

---

36   This is one of the reasons she is often associated with James's Isabel *Archer*.

aim—and hitting" (22).[37] This activity connects her with the Arrow / points, and Catherine Arrowpoint, significantly, is the better archer of the two. Her dreams of conquest and leadership, however, take place "among strictly feminine furniture, and had no disturbing reference to the advancement of learning or the balance of the constitution; her knowledge being such as with no sort of standing room or length of lever could have been expected to move the world"—unlike George Eliot, or even Dorothea, whose influence is "incalculably diffuse," but still greater than the passage of the First Reform Bill. Her "knowledge" is confined to the usual assortment of female accomplishments designed to bait the Venus fly-trap in the marriage market.

In this context, "no one had disputed her power or her general superiority" (27). There is "a certain unusualness about her" (27), and Eliot remarks on "the iridescence of her character—the play of various, nay, contrary, tendencies" (28). She is compared, not only to "the queen in exile" (the tragic Mary Queen of Scots?), but to Macbeth, another Scot, ambitious of being king, and a murderer many times over (28). We are forewarned that, as in Macbeth's case, Gwendolen will later find in her husband's death that "a moment is room enough for the loyal and mean desire, for the outlash of a murderous thought and the sharp backward stroke of repentance" (28).

When Grandcourt begins to court her, Gwendolen nervously, holding "her whip [like the young Cathy Earnshaw in *Wuthering Heights*], which she had snatched up automatically with her hat," launches into what sounds like a feminist diatribe:

> "We women can't go in search of adventures—to find out the North-West Passage or the source of the Nile, or to hunt tigers in the East. We must stay where we grow, or where the gardeners [male, understood] like to transplant us. We are brought up like the flowers, to look as pretty as we can, and be dull without complaining. That is my notion about the plants; they are often bored, and that is the reason why some often have got poisonous." (98)

The implied reference is to the adventuress-explorer Lady Hester Stanhope, who is mentioned elsewhere:[38] Eliot is reminding us that some women have been fortunate—or self-willed—enough to escape the usual feminine conditioning.

In this same courtship scene, Gwendolen deliberately lets fly the whip, in order to break off the dialogue. The "courtship" is really a battle of the sexes. Grandcourt mistakenly thinks, "It is all coquetting ... the next time I beckon she will come down" (99). Gwendolen, in a kind of silent "*dialogue de sourds*," is thinking only that he may be tolerable, if one *has* to marry: "He seemed as little of a flaw in his fortunes as a lover and husband could possibly be" (99). But, in an echo of, perhaps,

---

37   Later she thinks, underestimating Grandcourt, "My arrow will pierce him before he has time for thought" (68), and again, to Mr. Gascoigne, "If I am to aim I can't help hitting" (76). Bows and arrows are seen as "among the prettiest weapons in the world for feminine forms to play with" (73)—but they are also feminine appropriations of the phallic, the penetrating.

38   Earlier, when Rex is courting her, he asks what she would like to do, and she replies, "Oh, I don't know!—go to the North Pole, or ride steeplechases, or go to be a queen in the East like Lady Hester Stanhope" (49). Her ambitions sound quasi-"masculine"—if we can believe them. She also ignores the fact that Lady Hester did not aspire to be a queen, but to be an explorer, to break new ground.

Racine's Phèdre, certainly of Flaubert's Madame Bovary, "Gwendolen wished to mount the chariot and drive the plunging horses herself, with a spouse by her side who would fold his arms and give her his countenance without looking ridiculous" (98–9).[39] The chariot image recurs when, ironically, "Gwendolen Gets Her Choice": "... it was as if she had consented to mount a chariot where another held the reins; and it was not in her nature to leap out in the eyes of the world" (243). As the walls of matrimony close in on her later, she never gets beyond the outlets of the opening, galloping and gambling.

Gwendolen is often accused of being "unfeminine," not because of her violent impulses, but because she seems a type of the "frigid" woman—uninterested in Mr. Middleton the clergyman, whom she "collects" because he is there, in handsome Rex Gascoigne, repelled by Grandcourt, attracted only to the unattainable Deronda. But it would be surprising to see a passionate woman novelist like Eliot accepting this "masculine" stereotype of female frigidity. In fact, she shows that Gwendolen is ready to love passionately when the moment and the man for loving come together.[40] If Gwendolen is aroused only by Deronda, we should feel somewhat skeptical at the prospect of Gwendolen's ultimately dwindling into marriage to Rex Gascoigne, for want of anyone better.

*Gwendolen's "Talents"*

In the opening scene at Leubronn, Gwendolen is implicitly compared to the handsome Italian gambler who is "probably secure in an infallible system which placed his foot on the neck of chance" (3). The image is of St. George and the dragon—patron saint of both Italy and England, with Gwendolen in the masculine, heroic role. Gwendolen, too, at this point has no reason to question or doubt her place in the "infallible system" which is English class structure. Eliot says she likes to "connect the course of individual lives with the historic stream ..." (64).[41] By the same token, the Gwendolens—and Mirahs—of this world insist on mattering: "In these delicate vessels is borne onward through the ages the treasure of human affections" (90)[42]

---

39   Beer also recognizes allusions to Emma Bovary (223), but I believe not the chariot image.

40   Even Austen's apparently submissive Fanny Price, in *Mansfield Park*, pressed by Sir Thomas Bertram and even by Edmund (whom she really loves) to marry Henry Crawford, protests that a woman is not to love simply in gratitude to a man who loves her:

"I *should* have thought ... that every woman must have felt the possibility of a man's not being approved, not being loved by some one of her *sex*, at least, let him be ever so generally agreeable. Let him have all the perfections in the world, I think it ought not to be set down as certain, that a man must be acceptable to every woman he may happen to like himself." (349)

41   As in *Middlemarch*, Dorothea's small efforts at alleviating human misery reverberate more than the passage of the First Reform Bill in 1832, so in *Daniel Deronda* the arrrival of Sir Hugo Mallinger's nephew, Mr. Mallinger Grandcourt, has more impact that "the results of the American War" (64).

42   This is a line, not coincidentally, quoted by Henry James in his praise of Eliot's heroines in the "Preface" to his *The Portrait of a Lady*. In this "Preface," curiously, he

Thus Eliot is able to connect Gwendolen with the larger history that is Deronda's, but unfortunately poor Gwendolen herself is not good at making connections.

Gwendolen, Eliot admits, is "a deep young lady," but only in aid of her own self-promotion. She uses her wit as a weapon, as the epigraph to Chapter V suggests:

> Her wit
> Values itself so highly, that to her
> All matter else seems weak.
> *Much Ado About Nothing*

That same wit makes her "not quite liked" by other ladies, notably Mrs. Arrowpoint of Quetcham Hall. She "had a keen sense of absurdity in others," but sometimes does not know when to rein it in: "... self-confidence is apt to address itself to an imaginary dulness in others," and Gwendolen "could not escape that form of stupidity" with the sharp Mrs. Arrowpoint. Her wit gets the better of her common sense when she says to Mrs. Arrowpoint, "I wish I could write books to amuse myself, as you can! ... Home-made books must be so nice" (31). Again, Mrs. Arrowpoint quotes "the poet's eye in a fine frenzy rolling," and Gwendolen's less than innocent response is: "But it was not always found out, was it? ... I suppose some of them rolled their eyes in private. Mad people are often very cunning" ((32). When she claims, "I dote on Tasso [the *Gerusalemme Liberata*]," Mrs. Arrowpoint swallows the bait—but only for a time. Gwendolen realizes herself she has gone too far when she avers, "I am sure I often laugh in the wrong place" (31). She also says, "But I always want to know more of the world than there is in the book" (31).[43] Mrs. Arrowpoint finally realizes that "the girl is double and satirical" (35).

At the same party her wit is also turned on the unfortunate Mr. Middleton who is persuaded "to play various grave parts" in the charades (39). Gwendolen's only reaction to him is "that she had no objection to being adored" (40). Even her uncle sees her as a "young witch" (55).

"Floating along in white drapery," she adds insult to injury by also "eclipsing" Catherine Arrowpoint, the daughter of the house, who is "unfortunately also dressed in white" (29). The virginal, bridal white is also contrasted to the deep black of mourning that Gwendolen is later to wear for Grandcourt. Catherine Arrowpoint, however, does not fit into Gwendolen's schemes (no more so than Jane Fairfax fits into Emma Woodhouse's). Catherine is not to be eclipsed in at least one respect, and that is musicianship (32). But Catherine—like Dorothea and unlike Rosamond—does not sing, so Gwendolen can perform unrivalled: "Her voice was a moderately powerful soprano (some one had told her it was like Jenny Lind's), her ear good, and she was able to keep in tune, so that her singing gave pleasure to ordinary hearers, and she had been used to unmingled applause. She had the rare advantage of looking almost prettier when she was singing than at other times ..." (32). But she is singing now before an expert audience, Herr Klesmer, whose name refers to Jewish

---

mentions Gwendolen but not Dorothea, a heroine he praised to the skies in his 1873 review of *Middlemarch*.

43   The two Emmas, Dorothea, and Isabel all turn from books to life.

popular folk music. His love story with Catherine is parallel to the would-be love story of Deronda and Gwendolen. Klesmer lukewarmly characterizes her singing as "acceptable," and adds that she has "not been well taught" (33). The contrast is clear with Mirah, who has a small voice, but has received professional training from childhood so that she can make a living as a singer.

Because she has acted in *tableaux vivants* at school, like Wharton's Lily Bart, Gwendolen wonders if "she should become an actress like Rachel, since she was more beautiful than that thin Jewess" (37). She is always trying to compare herself to professionals, like Jenny Lind or Rachel, but not only is it too late to train for the concert hall or the stage, she also comes from a social sphere where the theater would be considered a disreputable profession. Eliot subtly suggests through Rachel, Mirah, and the Alcharisi the advantages of *not* being "a lady," that is, a middle-class Gentile. Only those marginalized in class-structured England can become professional performers *without* sullying their reputations. James's Miriam Rooth in *The Tragic Muse*, one of his few non-comic portraits of a woman as artist, is also Jewish, and therefore marginalized.[44] Even in the more raffish United States, it is not until 1900 that Dreiser's Sister Carrie works her way *out* of being a kept woman by going on the stage and "regaining" her virtue.

While scarcely as helpless and incompetent as Thackeray's Amelia Sedley or Gaskell's Miss Matty Jenkins when their menfolk go bankrupt, and they must wrack their feeble brains for how to market their women's accomplishments—a little tatting, a little piano-tinkling, and so on—Gwendolen's skills are really no more marketable, nor her assessment of her future any more realistic: "… her horizon was that of the genteel romance … and if she wanders into a swamp, the pathos lies partly, so to speak, in her having on her satin shoes" (37).[45] Discussing tragedy with her mother, however, she anticipates the *real* tragedy to occur in her life, one, unfortunately, which is not simply acted out on stage. Gwendolen says, "… the more feminine a woman is, the more tragic it seems when she does desperate actions" (38).

### Gwendolen: Galatea or Medusa?

In the charades, Gwendolen plays "Hermione as the statue in the Winter's Tale," and indeed Gwendolen is often seen as both statuesque and cold, unfeeling. But the statue comes to life, with a vengeance—vivified by terror, not love (unlike Galatea whom Pygmalion animates, as Deronda is capable of breathing life into Gwendolen):

> … the movable panel, which was on a line with the piano, flew open on the right opposite the stage and disclosed the picture of the dead face and the fleeing figure, brought out in pale definiteness by the position of the wax-lights … all eyes in the act of turning towards the opened panel were recalled by a piercing cry from Gwendolen, who stood without

---

44   Judith Wilt hints that James may have been influenced (once more) by Eliot, since *The Tragic Muse*, written 13 years after his critique ("*Daniel Deronda*: A Conversation"), presents not only "a Jewish woman who becomes a great actress," but who also marries, for "cover," like the Alcharisi, "a non-erotic and controllable man" (320).

45   We might compare Rosamond Vincy's genteel romances, where one need not know anything of the vocational aspirations of Prince Charming!

change of attitude, but with a change of expression that was terrifying in its terror …
Gwendolen fell on her knees and put her hands before her face. (42)

For once, Klesmer is impressed: "A magnificent bit of *plastik* that" (43). Grandcourt
will have the opposite effect from Deronda / Pygmalion: that of turning a living
woman to stone, like the "Old Maids," Miss Mann and Miss Ainley, in Charlotte
Bronte's *Shirley* (1849). Is Gwendolen instead the Gorgon / Medusa figure, turning
men who look at her into stone?

Gwendolen has a curious psychology, a mix of apparent coldness and fear, or "fits
of spiritual dread" (44). Perhaps, in fact, the two are linked. Rex's infatuation with
(love for?) her is like "the unimagined snowstorm" of the Egyptian who has never
seen snow (45). She has "a sort of physical repulsion to being directly made love
to" (49), and, we are told, there is "a certain fierceness of maidenhood in her" (50).
If Gwendolen sees herself as a princess, or queen, in exile, Rex's name, ironically,
means king. Rex's "love" is presented, however, as more Platonic and idealistic than
physical; for him, Gwendolen embodies "the fundamental identity of the good, the
true, and the beautiful" (47). Their debate turns on whether men's or women's lives
are harder. Gwendolen argues that "Girls' lives are so stupid: they never do what
they like," but Rex maintains that men "are forced to do hard things, and are often
dreadfully bored, and are knocked to pieces too" (49). Gwendolen's character is a
mixture of good and evil; some suspect "a trace of demon ancestry" in her (48).
Ironically, of her suitors Rex would give her the most freedom, but, perhaps by
his very physical attractiveness, he poses a threat to her and helps to set her up for
Grandcourt who appeals to her not at all. She rides to hounds with Rex, an apparently
"masculine" pursuit, but "she was never fearful in action and companionship"—only
when her selfhood is threatened (50). The only other woman who rides to hounds
is "Mrs. Gadsby, the yeomanry captain's wife," "with her doubtful antecedents
grammatical and otherwise." Gwendolen's spirited horse leaves Rex far behind, and,
unknown to her, Primrose falls, breaks his knees, and throws poor Rex. Although she
does not directly cause his accident, she is partly responsible for losing him in favor
of joining Lord Brackenshaw.

When she does learn of the accident from his father, she cannot resist (a little like
Emma Woodhouse) making a joke of it: "Now Rex is safe, it is so droll to fancy the
figure he and Primrose would cut—in a lane all by themselves—only a blacksmith
running up. It would make a capital caricature of 'Following the hounds'" (55).
Rex's accident echoes that of her father years earlier, as Mrs. Davilow reminds
Mr. Gascoigne (54). Equally importantly, her attitude anticipates that which she
demonstrates when Grandcourt drowns: she always takes flight. Her uncle also
reminds her (unfortunately), "… if you intend to hunt, you must marry a man who
can keep horses," unwittingly also helping to set her up for Grandcourt (55). Rex's
proffered love "made her curl up and harden like a sea-anemone at the touch of
a finger" (58), an echo of the mermaid / Nereid sea image. Her response to Rex
is fierce: "Pray don't make love to me! I hate it" (58). She thinks, "… the life of
passion had begun negatively in her. She felt passionately averse to this volunteered
love"—in sharp contrast to the earlier Dorothea, whose love goes out to the whole
universe (54). She confesses to her mother, "I can't love people. I hate them," and adds,

"I can't bear any one to be very near me but you" (59). At this point, however, she has not yet encountered Deronda, who will arouse her emotions in a positive way, but without reciprocating them.

### *"The Gaze" and the Battle of the Sexes*

Gwendolen is compared gratuitously to Juliet Fenn at the archery meeting where the relationship with Grandcourt begins. Juliet scores eight points above her, but who can be jealous of a plain woman, "a girl as middling as mid-day market in everything but her archery and her plainness"? (82).[46] In any event, Gwendolen successfully eclipses Juliet Fenn as well at the dance that follows: her arms

> … were bare now: it was the fashion to dance in the archery dress, throwing off the jacket; and the simplicity of her white cashmere with its border of pale green set off her form to the utmost…. Sir Joshua would have been glad to take her portrait; and he would have had an easier task than the historian at least in this, that he would not have had to represent the truth of change—only to give stability to one beautiful moment. (84)

The reference to Reynolds reminds us of the portrait of Dorothea as Santa Clara by Naumann in Rome, and anticipates James's verbal *Portrait of a Lady*—Isabel *Archer* (emphasis mine).[47] Hans Meyrick refers to Gwendolen as a "Van Dyke Duchess." In *Middlemarch*, however, Eliot stressed that words are the finer medium, because closer to human breath. Writing must capture the flux of experience.

Not only does Gwendolen invite Grandcourt's "gaze" while she is dancing; she also affects to be "adorably stupid," thus misleading him as to her malleability (87). When she meets him, she does not find him sexually threatening, and she reflects that "… Marriage would be the gate to a larger freedom" (107). She is to learn to her chagrin, however, that there are worse violations than the sexual.[48] Their misperceptions of each other lead ultimately to a contest, or a battle of the sexes à la Valmont and La Merteuil in Laclos' 1782 novel, *Les Liaisons dangereuses*, when La Merteuil throws down the gauntlet: "*Hé bien, la guerre*" (358; Lettre 153). Not only does Gwendolen feel "physical antipathies" towards Lush (which should be transposed to Grandcourt), but she begins to see Grandcourt as a kind of Merlin or sorceror—the sylvan setting, the green, all evoke Arthurian legend or, as Eliot pointedly remarks, "Robin Hood and Maid Marian" (88). Gwendolen begins "to feel a wand over her that made her afraid of offending Grandcourt" (88).

---

46 Somewhat unnecessarily Eliot goes on to speculate (like Mr. and Mrs. Tulliver) on how their "female offspring" may come to resemble their ugly fathers, rather than their pretty mothers—a theme that seems to haunt her as she demonstrates her awareness of how naive Mr. Tulliver's "genetic engineering" really is. Is Eliot herself bitter?

47 Reynolds' portrait of Mrs. Lloyd is also the source of Lily Bart's *tableau vivant* in Edith Wharton's *The House of Mirth*.

48 As with Jane Austen's Emma Woodhouse and Frank Churchill, part of her interest in him is based on the fact that "her friends thought of him as a desirable match for her ..." (77).

She is also Rosalind in *As You Like It*, but only just before she encounters Mrs. Glasher, Grandcourt's cast-off mistress, at the Whispering Stones, whose message must be decrypted: "They turned their blank grey sides to her: what was there on the other side?" (111). Mrs. Glasher's "message" is terrifying: "… it was as if some ghastly vision had come to her in a dream and said, 'I am a woman's life'" (112)—a life with which Gwendolen can identify. The Puritanical Dorothea and Isabel would have recoiled irretrievably from a Grandcourt—Dorothea would probably have gone further, and tried to aid and comfort Mrs. Glasher! James's Osmond is derivative from Grandcourt,[49] but Isabel is completely ignorant of his prior relationship with Madame Merle until virtually the end of the novel, whereas Gwendolen knows from the start what she is getting into. Gwendolen's response is, "I believe all men are bad, and I hate them"—doubtless thinking of her father and stepfather as well. Gwendolen's readings of fiction had not prepared her for sordid reality (as Eliot's works might have done).

Gwendolen does not take a stand, but flees like "Amaryllis" into the shades—or at least to Leubronn, where she desperately hopes that gambling will preclude the necessity of marriage to Grandcourt. Thus it takes us from Chapter III to Chapter XV to return to the beginning of the book, the gambling scene with Gwendolen and Deronda both present, but now one of them, at least, accounted for. And in Chapter XXI, Gwendolen, having learned from her mother of the family bankruptcy in which the Gascoignes are also implicated, returns from Leubronn to Offendene, and we are finally able to return to the present tense of the narrative, the reader having become acquainted with origins. We are then invited to parallel *that* quest for origins with Deronda's.

### Gwendolen's "Choices"

In Book III, "Maidens Choosing," Gwendolen ironically has no choice at all: marriage to Grandcourt, gambling, hope of Deronda as a savior. Gwendolen fails to see beyond the self, the "me," as the pronouns she uses reveal: "Everything has gone against *me*. People have come near *me* only to blight *me*" (172; emphasis mine). And, adds Eliot, "Among the 'people' she was including Deronda" (172).

She refuses—wrongly—Miss Arrowpoint as a "patroness" (194). Herr Klesmer, whom Catherine (named for the patron saint of spinsters) has definitely chosen, knows that it is "too late" for Gwendolen to become an artist.[50] Catherine's patronage, she thinks, would be "as bad as being a governess" (196).[51] Her mother knows that she is luxurious, and at least as a governess "you will have every luxury

---

49   The name of the Touchett estate, Gardencourt, may well have been an echo of the name "Grandcourt."

50   He is, however, as Gillian Beer comments (reflecting negatively on Deronda), the "only decent father-confessor" in the novel. He can also be seen as the type of the Wandering Jew, though Daleski gives Mirah this role (74); in any event, both are artists in exile, with whom Eliot herself strongly identified.

51   In Wharton's *The House of Mirth*, Lily Bart plays the part of paid companion to a wealthy woman during her downward slide.

about you"—but not to own (198). Gwendolen says her uncle "ought to have taken some other steps"—but she does not know which! She even says, "I would rather emigrate than be a governess" (173)—but emigrate to what? To do what? The last straw is her dawning realization that "even as a governess it appeared she was to be tested and was liable to rejection" (202). She "had read romances where even plain governesses are centres of attraction"—doubtless *Jane Eyre*, which Eliot had also alluded to obliquely in *The Mill on the Floss* (203). She experiences "a world-nausea," and finds herself in a "labyrinth" without an Ariadne's thread to conduct her (unlike Dorothea). Unlike Mirah, she would not consider suicide. Like Emma Bovary, she cries, "I am stifled" (219).

Given Gwendolen's situation and character, the "choice" of marrying Grandcourt is really no choice at all. She wears black to refuse his offer (220), as she earlier resembled a statue in black, white, and marble (Hermione) (187). She might as well be wearing the black of mourning, as she does at the end of the novel. Eliot constantly reminds us of the differences between male and female psychology (and their conditioning). As Eliot writes of Gwendolen, "Her griefs were feminine; but to her as a woman they were not the less hard to bear, and she felt an equal right to the Promethean tone" (206). Gwendolen is also naive in thinking that passion is called for only on the part of the man (222).[52] She prattles, thinking only of "the woman's paradise where all her nonsense is adorable" (226). She expects, following Rosalind's example, that "everything is to be as I like" (227).

*... and After ...*

In the next book, IV, "Gwendolen Gets Her Choice," which is really no choice at all—or Hobson's Choice! She tries to motivate her marriage as support for her mother, but Mrs. Davilow rebukes her, "... I trust you are not going to marry only for my sake" (231). The best she can say of Grandcourt is that "he was likely to be the least disagreeable of husbands" (227), and that "He really is not disgusting" (232). But, in fact, he is. She thinks of handling the situation with Mrs. Glasher administratively, regarding matrimony "as altogether a matter of management ..." (233). She accomplishes her "administrative" task by keeping Grandcourt at arm's length, which suits him fine. Gwendolen, in fact, acts better in real life than she could on stage: "Perhaps if Klesmer had seen more of her in this unconscious kind of acting, instead of when she was trying to be theatrical, he might have rated her chance higher" (234).

After marriage she takes up needlework, which she "had always intensely disliked" (241), and develops "an absent-minded acquaintance with her new ceilings and furniture" (418), preoccupied instead with thoughts of Deronda. Deronda, unfortunately, sees in her "a dreary lack of the ideas that might help her" (309)—rather a harsh judgment for a woman trained like a young race horse to run on only one course, that of matrimony. On the other hand, she certainly cannot comprehend "that Deronda's life could be determined by the historical destiny of the

---

52 One thinks of Henry Tilney's country-dance metaphor for courtship in Austen's *Northanger Abbey*, in both of which the man must please the woman in order to succeed.

Jews ..." (411). Like Emma Woodhouse, or Dorothea Brooke, she lacks the training or background to understand the wider context. Although inspired by Deronda, she adopts no systematic course of reading. Grandcourt's attempts to separate her from her family actually lead her towards them (413). She has "no work to mark off intervals" of her boring life (441). Like James's Charlotte Stant in *The Golden Bowl* (1904), she is "like an imprisoned dumb creature" (443). Indeed, she is treated largely like "a lap-dog" (411). (Eliot is inordinately fond of dogs and dog-images, as in *Adam Bede*). Her situation is not much better than Lush's. Grandcourt trains her as he trains his dogs, horses—and Lush: "He delights in making the dogs and horses quail." Lush, too, is "kickable" (98), and "if his puddings were rolled towards him in the dust, he took the inside bits and found them relishing" (94). "A half-caste among gentlemen," Gwendolen sees him as the worst part of Grandcourt, but he is more like Wilde's "Picture of Dorian Grey," a reverse mirror image of Grandcourt's real venality, as well as a dire warning of his psychological abuse of human beings. Hughes is quite right in saying that Lush pimps for Grandcourt (449).

Gwendolen wears her diamonds, sent vengefully by the wronged Mrs. Glasher, as fetters, or a yoke (304).[53] Mr. Vandernoodt, the society gossip (like Laurence Lefferts and company in Wharton's *The Age of Innocence*), sees the triangle in mythic terms as Lydia / Medea, who kills her own children and feeds them to their faithless father), Gwendolen / Creüsa (the "other woman"),[54] and Grandcourt / Jason (324).[55] Both women are "fiery," sisters under the skin, one undone by passion, the other by the lack of it.

Like Isabel Archer, Gwendolen develops the weapon of sarcasm early in her marriage. As Gwendolen says to Sir Hugo, "Mr. Grandcourt won me by neatly-turned compliments. If there had been one word out of place it would have been fatal" (313). Also like Isabel Archer at Gardencourt, she inspects "the rows of quaint portraits in the gallery above the cloisters" while talking to Deronda. Like Charlotte Stant and Maggie Verver in *The Golden Bowl*, she imagines Grandcourt "threatening to throttle her" (320), as Isabel Archer figures metaphorically Osmond's psychological violence. Later, his death is "the only possible deliverance for her" (456), as Raffles' death is "the image that brought release" for Bulstrode the banker in *Middlemarch*. She projects her own egoism until his death seems to her a form of self-defense: "The thought of his dying would not subsist: it turned as with a dream-change into the terror that she should die with his throttling fingers on her neck avenging that thought" (456).

Before meeting him, Gwendolen speaks prophetic truth in jest when she recounts a hypothetical dream: "I shall dream that night that I am looking at the extraordinary face of a magnified insect—and the next morning he will make me an offer of his

---

53  The diamonds can be viewed as a Lévi-Straussian medium of exchange for the female, as Shylock's "ducats" are in *The Merchant of Venice*.

54  Gwendolen can be viewed, in fact, as the "other woman" in two triangles, with Mirah and Deronda as well as Lydia and Grandcourt.

55  René Girard, in *Mensonge poétique et vérité romanesque*, hypothesizes that the triangle, so central to French literature, actually awakens love, or sexual passion, by way of jealousy.

hand …" (69). Grandcourt is indeed later described as an insect, or an animal of a lower species: he is "a handsome lizard of a hitherto unknown species"—reptilian, like the serpent in Eden (100). At 36 he is completely burnt out, "as neutral as an alligator" (115). He has "a will like that of a crab or a boa-constrictor" (317). He is always associated with snakes, or with rather invidious, slimy water animals in contradistinction to Gwendolen's mythic figuration as a mermaid or a Nereid. The Rector, Mr. Gascoigne, is as responsible for Gwendolen's mistaken choice as Mr. Brooke and the town of Middlemarch are, generally, for Dorothea's choice of Mr. Casaubon. At the end of the novel Mr. Gascoigne realizes his moral turpitude in failing to warn Gwendolen of Grandcourt's previous debauchery. His remorse associates Grandcourt again with insects, "creepy, crawly things," and his "dissipations" with "an array of live caterpillars" (570).

Jane Eyre envisions Thornfield Hall as Bluebeard's Castle, though Rochester is no Bluebeard, despite the mad wife in the attic. But Grandcourt, who keeps his former mistress Mrs. Glasher in a home in the Black Country and discards her carelessly on marriage to Gwendolen, fits the Bluebeard role very comfortably—a Bluebeard who will cancel the existence not only of a former mistress, but of his heir by her.

At dinner with him the newly married Gwendolen prefers "the boiled ingenuousness" of a prawn's eyes to his lizard's eyes—again comparing him to lower forms of animal life. She prefers all the "disgust" in the marriage "to be on her side" (453). Her thoughts and passions are "porous," "mere honeycombs … not always with a taste of honey" (453). At this stage Gwendolen is wandering in a labyrinth. She has no "vocation," such as George Eliot's heroines and heroes always seek. Like Emma Bovary, she has lost control of the chariot she had earlier dreamed of driving.

Gwendolen shudders "playfully" at the ghosts when Sir Hugo shows her the old abbey, and we are reminded of the Ghost Walk in Dickens's *Bleak House* (1853), which resonates in James's *The Portrait of a Lady* whose Isabel must know sadness and loss (Ralph Touchett's death) to see the ghost walk at Gardencourt.[56]

Grandcourt's only "Criterion," like his horse's name, is taste (244). He comes to see Gwendolen as "a mad woman in a play" (336), as dangerous as "gunpowder." Gwendolen hears only "the flavour of bitter comedy" when her uncle advises her to influence her husband to enter Parliament: "A wife has great influence with her husband" (414). One presumes Sir Hugo is against further Reform, unlike Eliot, who is only disgusted with its repeated failures. Deronda, on the other hand, becomes a kind of priest or father-confessor to her.

---

56  The likenesses between *Daniel Deronda* and *The Portrait of a Lady* are striking, all the more so since James wrote a "Conversation" about Eliot's last novel. He admired it, calling it "full of the world" (Hughes, 448), though he was less admiring of the Deronda plot. James also drew a map of Italy linking *The Portrait* with its predecessor (Cook, 41). But, as Barbara Hardy remarks astutely, "… Isabel returns to the world she has left, while Gwendolen's is the isolation of a new beginning" (154).

*"La Pia de' Tolomei": Sinner or Victim?*

If the model for Deronda is Shakespeare's Portia, for Gwendolen it is, above all, La Donna Pia, La Pia de' Tolomei, in Dante's *Purgatorio*, the image of her penultimate fate.[57] In Gwendolen's case the "piety" is ironic, as her marriage is built on another woman's misery—that of Mrs. Glasher, the mother of Grandcourt's rightful, if illegitimate, heir. It is possible that Eliot had in mind the Rossetti painting, "La Pia de' Tolomei," as well as Dante's original text. The finished painting is dated 1880, but Rossetti was working on sketches much earlier, and it seems to have been commissioned in 1869 (see Figure 6.1). His model for La Pia was his favorite model—and sometime mistress—Jane Morris, the unhappy wife of literary figure and socialist William Morris, whose marriage was sexually unfulfilling. So the frustrated wife was to turn for consolation to the somewhat exotic Rossetti, of Italian ancestry, as Gwendolen is to turn to the equally exotic Deronda, of Jewish origin. Given this reading, the novel does not necessarily become a *roman à clef*, but contemporary readers in the 1880s may well have appreciated the richness of the double allusion.[58] Except for the fact that her hair is not that dark—rather light brown or chestnut—the portrait could be of Gwendolen Harleth, who is almost literally imprisoned by her husband.[59]

Contrasted to Dante's version, Eliot's re-visioning of Madonna Pia's story is more ironic than tragic,[60] for she implies that her imprisonment, and eventual death (by poison?) may be a blessing in disguise; it at least relieves her of her husband's company:

> Madonna Pia, whose husband, feeling himself injured by her, took her to his castle amid the swampy flats of the Maremma and got rid of her there, makes a pathetic figure in Dante's *Purgatory*, among the sinners who repented at the last and desire to be remembered compassionately by their fellow-countrymen. We know little about the grounds of mutual discontent between the Siennese couple, but we may infer with some confidence that the

---

57   As it happens, I chose Dante Gabriel Rossetti's portrait of his namesake's *verbal* portrait—without remembering Eliot's reference to la Pia de' Tolomei—as the cover picture for my first book, *The Prison of Womanhood*.

58   I chose the cover picture of *The Prison of Womanhood* because (La Pia) Jane Morris seems tall, queenly, a striking brunette, with strong hands, pensive, tied to her religious / ethical sense, and imprisoned by her womanhood—traits that appear in one form or another in the four provincial heroines—Austen's Emma Woodhouse, Flaubert's Emma Bovary, Eliot's Dorothea Brooke, and James's Isabel Archer.

59   In fact, George Levine sees Gwendolen as an important model for James's *The Portrait of a Lady*—Isabel Archer—and detects affinities between Grandcourt and Gilbert Osmond, though I still think the more important model for Isabel is the quixotic, socially conscious Dorothea Brooke.

60   Laurence Lerner considers that Eliot is recasting the Madonna Pia story in realistic mode: "... Chapter 54 opens with a rewriting in realistic mode of the tragic romance of Dante's Pia so radical that, to the reader fresh from his Dante, it will seem philistine. Such is the completeness with which realism can reject alternative modes" (95). I am not sure that this adds much to our understanding of the tragedy that Eliot always stresses can be found in everyday life.

Fig 6.1    Dante Gabriel Rossetti, "La Pia de Tolomei" (1868–80), reproduction courtesy of the Spencer Museum of Art, The University of Kansas. Lawrence, Kansas. Museum purchase: State funds.

husband had never been a very delightful companion, and that on the flats of the Maremma his disagreeable manners had a background which threw them out remarkably; whence in his desire to punish his wife to the uttermost, the nature of things was so far against him that in relieving himself of her he could not avoid making the relief mutual. (502)

Gwendolen, on the other hand, feels herself locked up, together with Grandcourt, for the rest of their natural lives. Therefore, Eliot emphasizes, we feel more sympathy for Gwendolen, who, given no chance to repent in purgatory, finds herself instead "at the very height of her entanglement in those fatal meshes which are woven within more closely than without" (503).

Rossetti's painting provides a contemporary gloss on Eliot's treatment of the same subject. Rossetti took La Pia's story from the *Purgatory*, Canto V, lines 12–136, and translated these lines on the frame:

> Remember me who am La Pia: me
> Siena, me Maremma, made, unmade.
> This in his inmost heart well knoweth he
> With whose fair jewel I was ringed and wed.

He apparently chose this subject because of its relevance to the life of his model and sometime mistress, Jane Morris, who, like Gwendolen, was imprisoned in an unfulfilling marriage (to William Morris). He may also, apparently, have seen a theatrical version, *Pia dei Tolomei*, by Charles Marenco, performed in London in 1856 and 1857 with Adelaide Ristori as the lead.[61] Rossetti had begun studies for the picture as early as January 1868, and had agreed with Jane Morris to sit as the model. As he proceeded with the sketches, he increasingly emphasized the hands and the wedding ring. It was commissioned in 1869, but completed in 1880.[62] La Pia's rosary and devotional book shed an ironic light on the conspicuously irreverent Gwendolen, who never hesitates to satirize the church in the persons of Mr. Middleton and her uncle, the Reverend Mr. Gascoigne. The painting is also a study of change and disillusionment in marriage, but Gwendolen never loved Grandcourt to begin with, knew that he had a dissolute background and another family, and her only disillusionment stems from her realization that she lacks the "administrative" skills to manage him.

---

61   There is no way of knowing if Eliot may have seen this play, but it is certainly suggestive that it starred one of the great actresses of the day, which would certainly fit Eliot's concern with female singers and actresses in her text. Rossetti's focus on La Pia's wedding ring in his work accords with Eliot's on Gwendolen's jewelry, and particularly her "wedding gift," the diamonds from Grandcourt.

62   The source of my information about the painting is an art history of the Pre-Raphaelite period. The author signs himself simply "A.G.," and unfortunately I can no longer trace the book. The author does, however, cite his own sources: J. Bryson and J.C. Troxell (eds.), *Dante Gabriel Rossetti and Jane Morris*, 1976, p. 1; and Doughty and Wahl, II, p. 702.

*The Flying Dutchman: "A Haunted Ship"*

Far worse than Madonna Pia's husband, Grandcourt has no intention of isolating or murdering his wife; rather, he delights in feeling "that she was his to do as he liked with, and to make her feel it also" (503). The yacht trip is calculated to quell her "growing spirit of opposition," "and, above all, to separate her from what he suspects is the growing influence of Deronda, though he himself is too bloodless to admit the possibility of sexual jealousy. Gwendolen's purgatorial yachting expedition with Grandcourt, and his subsequent death, are recounted in Book VII, "Mother and Son," so the climactic event in each protagonist's life is highlighted. Deronda's departure to meet his mother, with "Gwendolen's face of anguish framed black like a nun's" as he takes his leave (459), is paralleled by Gwendolen's departure from England, devoid of Deronda's moral support. She and Grandcourt experience "dual solitude in a boat" (510), and seem doomed to wander endlessly like the cursed *Flying Dutchman* of legend (513). Grandcourt treats their marriage as a "contract" which he has fulfilled, and which she is trying to abrogate. This is indeed the *reductio ad absurdum* of the marriage market. Deronda at least recognizes her basic humanity. Moreover, Grandcourt's very physical attractiveness makes him more sinister and threatening than Casaubon, with whom one assumes Dorothea's marriage is never consummated, and closer to James's Machiavellian Osmond: "She was under his power," and we feel sure it is sexual as well as spiritual, for she fears becoming a mother. Gwendolen tries to dream herself out of harsh reality; as Eliot remarks humorously, she even cultivates an interest "in sugar-canes as something outside her personal affairs" (505). Increasingly she sees in Deronda, as Lydgate sees in Dorothea, a reflecting mirror. Again dressed in white, she seems frozen as a statue, or "a glacier after sunset" (510).

Grandcourt is usually considered the one unredeemably evil character Eliot has created. In some ways he seems to exhibit the "motiveless malignity" of an Iago, but (as with Iago) it is not really motiveless at all, but animated by his drive towards power and mastery: "... he could manage a sail with the same ease that he could manage a horse"—or, one might add, a woman (512).[63] Gwendolen begins to think

---

63   In a quotation from *Middlemarch*, "The Other Side of Silence" (which I used as a subheading in *The Prison of Womanhood* for my discussion of Eliot's art in that novel), Andrew Dowling compares the "symbolic value of silence" in "the issue of marital breakdown," and "the legal discourse" of the first English Divorce Court. To that end, Dowling focuses on Grandcourt's silence: "In *Daniel Deronda* the husband's silence operates as a sign of some truth beyond itself: of an unspeakable, and specifically sexual, horror" (323). He quotes one of the workers at Grandcourt's wedding: "a quarrel may end wi' the whip, but it begins wi' the tongue" (325). Dowling adds that Grandcourt commands silence with his tongue: "He uses silence to shroud his thoughts and intentions in mystery and menace" (333). Dowling misses the fact that earlier Gwendolen has used her riding whip to command Grandcourt's silence and evade his marriage proposal. Dowling writes, "Throughout the novel, Gwendolen's position of silent acquiescence implies a specifically sexual submission" (335)—but in fact she is constantly rebellious *before* marriage.

of his using instruments of torture:[64] "His words had the power of thumbscrews and the cold touch of the rack" (512). She tries to take refuge in helpless indifference: "I shall like nothing better than this" (514).

Grandcourt's fatal accident is viewed through Deronda's eyes; we do not actually witness it, and he hears of it first through the rumor mill. As Eliot comments ironically, a Frenchman without a telescope to view the accident would doubtless think that "it was *milord* who had probably taken his wife out to drown her, according to the national practice" (516)—many a truth is spoken in jest! She *has* died in a sense—Deronda sees her, supposedly rescued from drowning, covered with a tarpaulin and pea-jackets, "pale as one of the sheeted dead" (516). The rest of the story consists of Gwendolen's recollection of the events. She describes her consciousness in almost a psychological process of dissociation: "I was like two creatures. I could not speak—I wanted to kill—it was as strong as thirst—and then directly—I felt beforehand I had done something dreadful, unalterable that would make me like an evil spirit. And it came—it came" (520). She actually has thought of knifing him. Grandcourt's dead face haunts her like that in the panel at home, and, after his death, the *Flying Dutchman* remains a haunted ship forever in her memory. All she has done finally is let go the tiller, literally and figuratively, but she repents again:

> "… I remember then letting go the tiller and saying 'God help me!' But then I was forced to take it again and go on; and the evil longings, the evil prayers came again and blotted everything else dim, till, in the midst of them—I don't know how it was—he was turning the sail—there was a gust—he was struck—I know nothing—I only know that I saw my wish outside me." (524)

As she recalls, she has vacillated between the destructive impulse and her strong moral sense. She seizes a lifeline, the rope, as he commands, but "my heart said, 'Die!'—and he sank …" The account is elliptical, halting, fragmented, and again she experiences dissociation, almost a fugue state: "I was leaping away from myself—I would have saved him then. I was leaping from my crime, and there it was … there was the dead face—dead, dead" (524). She repeats, "It can never be altered," so that in an important sense she never does escape the incubus of Grandcourt.

If Grandcourt is Eliot's only completely villainous character, it is probably because not only does he have no sense of vocation, but also he does not want one. He loves the "dreamy do-nothing absolutism" of yachting (503). It is too late for him to become an occupationless but naïve, innocent Fred Vincy, and not even a Mary Garth could reshape him. Gwendolen, similarly, has no sense of vocation, but is in vague quest of one, having tried to resist the usual options for women. Because of her resistance, Grandcourt falls rather more in love with her than he expects. He lives in passive grandeur on inherited land (439). Hilariously, his silence is often taken for wisdom. He is in some ways a male Rosamond Vincy, who also resembles

---

64   The imagery is similar to Jane Austen's when Emma Woodhouse realizes she has been torturing Jane Fairfax: "An airing in the Hartfield carriage would have been the rack, and arrow-root from the Hartfield storeroom must have been poison" (316).

his male counterpart, James's Osmond, an interior decorator with a vengeance.[65] His one goal is power—over the helpless. He likes a thrashing horse or kicking dog—or a kicking wife (509). He keeps reminding Gwendolen not to make a fool of herself (446). But at the same time this "white handed man with the perpendicular profile" is himself a moral idiot;[66] he is described wittily as a Mephistopheles "who couldn't really manage his own plots" (449).

Gwendolen does learn tragically from her experience. She becomes ultimately the judge of her own character, assisted by Daniel. The Purgatory she experiences on board the yacht recalls Dante's Paolo and Francesca, the misguided lovers doomed to all eternity—but an eternity together.[67] Did Eliot have the contrast in mind with Dante's other heroine, La Donna Pia?[68] We see Gwendolen lying on the floor all night, like Dorothea, but the latter has no feelings of guilt (529). Her punishment too is Dantesque, but perhaps more the Dante of the *Inferno* than of the *Purgatorio*. Her mother realizes that she knows what she has done, adding to the hellishness of her fate (571). She feels herself on a precipice of despair, and sees herself as a backsliding child (582). She is left with not much consolation from Deronda— a few postcards, perhaps.[69] Deronda's farewell, however, echoes the Biblical "chariots of

---

65   Rosamond's name means "the rose of the world," and Osmond's probably means "the bones of the world."

66   We may note his physical resemblance to Wagner's conception of the hero (anti-hero?) of *The Flying Dutchman*. In Wagner's original production, moreover, the heroine, Senta, throws herself into the sea to be one with her lover. Gwendolen's living death seems an ironic commentary on the Wagnerian opera.

67   Hester Prynne, in Hawthorne's *The Scarlet Letter* (1850), dreamed of just such an eternal punishment, together with Dimmesdale.

68   Andrew Thompson, studying Italian influences "from Dante to the 'Risorgimento'" in *Daniel Deronda*, notes that references to Dante are especially dominant in the second half: "... the Dante allusion in *Daniel Deronda* amounts to an overarching purgatorial metaphor" (145). He concludes that Gwendolen finally "enters a purgatorial condition of 'difficult blessedness,' despite being abandoned by Daniel" (145). He is somewhat puzzled by Eliot's expansion of Dante's tale of La Pia, in that the deaths are reversed. Perhaps Dante Gabriel Rossetti's visual version helps explain Eliot's reading. Deirdre David sees the Purgatory, the yacht, as a symbol for Gwendolen's and Grandcourt's detachment from "their environment" (151).

69   Deirdre David notes that the novel ends in a cul-de-sac as far as England is concerned: "... *Daniel Deronda* ... falls apart under the pressure of offering a moral alternative to its representation of a corrupt upper-class society; Eliot leaves Gwendolen Harleth high and dry with her moral enlightenment and no place to exercise it and sends Deronda off on a Zionist mission whose didactic function is to show the absence of any worthwhile moral life to be had in England" (135). David is, not coincidentally, another of the critics who fails to recognize that Leavis recanted his original notion of the irreconcilable split between the two plots (145).

John Halperin psychoanalyzes Gwendolen without the social context. He sees her egoism as less "subtle" than, for instance, Dorothea's, but admits she *does* develop. He does attribute the "serpent" quotation to Eliot, however—Gwendolen "has got herself up as a sort of serpent"—but in fact this is the Leubronn gossips (164). He also underlines the limits of her perception—she wants to *be* seen, not to see: Eliot writes, she is "apt to think rather of those who saw her than of those whom she could not see." Halperin comments that her "moral

fire" (606), which may reflect ironically on Gwendolen's unfulfilled wish to drive her own chariot.

Thus at the end of the novel one principal character is dead, one is on a quest for an ideal life, and the third is condemned to a living death, in quest of—she knows not what.

What are we to make of this puzzling, enigmatic novel? We began with the Israeli film *Kadosh*, and have ended haunted by the dejected, pensive statue of an apparently fragile George Eliot in the main square at Nuneaton (Newdigate Square, named for the owners of the Arbury estate, where she was born and her father was the estate agent). Unlike the ending of *Middlemarch*, in which Eliot assures us of Dorothea's all-diffusive influence on her mediocre town, the ending of *Daniel Deronda* presents us with a heroine whose consciousness has been refined and subtilized through her ordeal by water, but who is offered no convincing hope for even partial achievement in her circumscribed world.

While it offers no promise to Gwendolen, Eliot has at least chosen to focus on a religion which has two books in the Bible named for women, Esther and Ruth. The fact that Eliot mentions neither would be surprising were it not for the fact that both, while heroic, exemplify the traditional idealized role of the Jewish wife. Esther does indeed save her own race when she marries King Ahasuerus, but she supplants his first wife Vashti, beautiful but rebellious, who has refused to be paraded like a prostitute in front of her husband's guests.[70] Not only could Eliot scarcely have ignored the existence of Vashti, who has become somewhat of a feminist heroine, but two of her slightly older predecessors highlight Vashti's significance. In her last completed novel, *Villette* (1853), Charlotte Brontë's Lucy Snowe is carried away by the tempestuous, explosive performance of an actress she names only as "Vashti," and whose passions externalize Lucy's own (much as the "Madwoman in the Attic" externalizes Jane Eyre's, Rochester's, and the reader's). Elizabeth Gaskell's Margaret Hale, in *North and South* (1854–55), with her latent but violent emotions, is compared to a Vashti. The Biblical Ruth is not only an ideal wife, but an ideal daughter-in-law, for after her husband's death she says to Naomi, her mother-in-law, "Whither thou goest I will go, and thy people will be my people."

If Eliot does not mention Vashti (who could well be a prototype for Leonora Halm-Eberstein, the Alcharisi), one other Biblical heroine (or anti-heroine, depending on your point of view) is featured prominently, by name and by symbolic implication: Hagar the exile, mother of Ishmael by Abraham, cast out when Sarah, Abraham's elderly wife, finally becomes pregnant. Deronda feels tremendous compassion, as we have seen throughout, for the Hagars, including Mrs. Lydia Glasher, Grandcourt's discarded mistress. Implicitly, Eliot's own sympathies belong definitively with the Hagars and the Vashtis, not the conventional Esthers and Ruths. If Gwendolen,

---

stupidity" stems from the fact that what is out of her sight is out of her mind (166). He tends to idealize Deronda, and sees Gwendolen approaching his level: "Gwendolen's story ... is the story of her own expanding psyche, of her acquisition of the moral and spiritual virtues which are embodied in Deronda from the beginning of the novel" (192). But to what end?

70   The role of Mordecai, the elder wise man, needs to be compared to Eliot's character, but that is outside the scope of this analysis.

Mrs. Glasher, and the Alcharisi are Vashtis or Hagars, and Mirah an Esther or Ruth, where then does Eliot leave us with Zionism as a Utopian alternative to English stasis? Do even Utopias marginalize women? As women writers, and their heroines, move from private sphere to public stage, that apparent progress is accompanied by female rage, madness, violence, and is often accomplished by the Hagars and the Vashtis.

# Chapter 7

# Conclusion—and a New Beginning

Looking back at the five nineteenth-century women novelists we have analyzed, I am struck with how undated and timeless they seem—in many ways, how prophetic. Each in her own way simultaneously reflects and critiques her age, but we also witness an evolution in thinking about the female condition from the Regency period of Jane Austen to the mid-(high) Victorian of the Brontës and Elizabeth Gaskell, to the late Victorian / verging on modernism of that "Victorian Sage" George Eliot.

While it is Eliot who is most often credited with highlighting the theme of community, the works of all five take sharper definition when one examines in them the developing consciousness of the interaction of woman and community. If Jane Austen exercises weapons of wit and irony on the social constraints of the marriage market in which her heroines find themselves trapped, she recognizes that for most women during her age there was no outlet in Anglo-Saxon, Protestant England—on the Continent, there was always the convent, if that can be considered an escape—except her own, that of the secret, clandestine artist, hidden behind the generic authorship as "A Lady."

Later, in the early- to mid-Victorian Age, Charlotte Brontë's heroines typically chafe at the restraints, rebel furiously, but finally (like Charlotte herself) accept a rigid order unlikely to alter significantly during their lifetime.[1] Her sister Emily, however, for whatever reason less inclined to submit, creates a double-heroine figure in the two Catherines, mother and daughter, of *Wuthering Heights*. The first Cathy, only temporarily acquiescent to social norms, finds her final release in death (like Charlotte's anti-heroine, the mad Bertha Mason in *Jane Eyre*). It is the daughter Cathy who survives, her rebellion contained within the framework of Christian marriage.

---

1  Polly Teale's 2003 play, *After Mrs. Rochester*, takes off from Jean Rhys's perception, in *Wide Sargasso Sea* (1966), of the sufferings of the first Mrs. Rochester, Bertha Mason. Teale suggests that the twentieth-century novelist saw parallels between her own life and that of Bertha: "Like Jean, *Mrs. Rochester* was a white Creole born in the West Indies who ended her life isolated in the remote English countryside" (Shared Experience Playbill 12). In the play, Bertha appears as a voiceless, dehumanized alter ego to Jean. We are told that the latter was once sent to Holloway Prison "for biting a neighbor who she said had made too much noise and disturbed her writing. *Mrs. Rochester* used a similar method of attack on unwanted intruders into her attic" (12). Jane Austen confined her defense against intruders to the warning of a creaking door. Teale's play does not, however, explore the possible parallels between Jean Rhys and Charlotte Brontë herself, for whom the "Madwoman in the Attic" may be also Jane Eyre's alter ego, as Gilbert and Gubar argue, as well as Charlotte Brontë's. Jean Rhys's heartfelt statement, "When you've written it down it doesn't hurt any more," seems to echo the situation of her nineteenth-century predecessor as well.

The most important factor linking the five women novelists is their movement, however tentative, provisional, and anonymous, from private sphere to public. Their desire to communicate to a public larger than their own families and immediate circles culminates in a female discourse ranging from mild discontent to anger, even rage. The last two novelists in this study, Elizabeth Gaskell and George Eliot, most vigorously and determinedly step across the domestic threshold of women's fiction into the "man's world" of "political economy," laissez-faire capitalism, science and medicine, scientific agriculture, architecture, and—yes—the arts. In so doing, they differ from their male contemporaries in recognizing the major role women can and should play in the larger social world, despite all the Victorian shibboleths relegating them to a domestic prison, "the prison of womanhood."

Gaskell's "maternal feminism," Eliot's metaphor of "this particular web" of community address in different ways what the critic Allen Tate signals, in *The Man of Letters in the Modern World*, as the passage from communication to the transcendent communion: "... men cannot communicate by means of sound over either wire or air. They have got to communicate through love. Communication that is not also communion is incomplete. We *use* communication; we *participate* in communion" (16).

If we "*participate* in communion," in the intricate web of human and social relations, it may seem contradictory to end this analysis with a heroine (or anti-heroine?), Gwendolen Harleth, who is "silenced" both from within (her own severe limitations) and without (social constraints and expectations for women). Mary Barton, the working-class girl, has more options, and a wider sphere of action, than the genteel lady, Gwendolen. Gwendolen cannot move from the private to the public—now we all do, whether by choice or not!

The options presented by Eliot in her last novel seem to be: to be born male, or at least a womanly male like Deronda; to trail in a male wake like Mirah; to die literally, like Rivka, or spiritually, like Gwendolen (or receive postcards); or become a George Eliot, and I suspect even she was not satisfied.[2] George Eliot is not a prescriptive novelist, nor a pamphleteer; she may be urging that if there are answers, they are in all of us.

Gwendolen Harleth has been compared to the heroines of the "sensationalist" novels. Elaine Showalter argues compellingly that female novelists were not "silenced" between the period of George Eliot and that of Virginia Woolf, but

---

2    Deirdre David concludes hopefully, "There appears to be one positive aspect of performance in *Daniel Deronda*, and it lies in Eliot's myth of the artist" (187). However, none of the female artists within the novel can be deemed truly successful: the Alcharisi, to paraphrase Henry James, gives up "too much of life to produce too little of art" ("The Middle Years"), and Mirah will cease to perform (to her great relief, one suspects) as soon as she marries. Alan Mintz notes that for Gwendolen, "vocation is disqualified" (141)—she is not an artist—and Eliot, like her predecessor Jane Austen, places an extremely high value on a sense of vocation. For the two protagonists, "To remain in society is of *necessity* to become a Gwendolen; and to become a Daniel, society—at least English—must be left behind" (Mintz, 140). Mintz continues that George Eliot uses "the motifs of folklore" (142) to point "towards the emergence of the artist and the hegemony of art" in later texts, by other writers (156). Unlike David, he does not see that hegemony emerging yet—in this novel.

that they wrote fictions of revenge against husbands, of desertions of children. Actually, this was not a new phenomenon in female literature. An undercurrent in the nineteenth-century women novelists we have been examining has been female rage, ranging from the "regulated hatred" of Jane Austen against paternal tyranny and the patriarchy, to the Brontës' anger verging on madness and obsession, again against the patriarchy, to Gaskell's and Stowe's moral indignation directed at the exploitation of both working-class women and female slaves. At the end of the nineteenth century, the usually cautiously optimistic, philosophic George Eliot created a vividly destructive, almost self-destructive heroine who is out of control.

Gwendolen, unlike Mirah, cannot move from the private sphere of singing in the drawing room to public performance. And even Mirah, given the choice, opts for the domestic sphere. At this beginning of the new millenium, we may think that we have outgrown all the problems generating female oppression, and its corollary, female self-destructiveness. A Gwendolen of today, with intelligence and some measure of talent, is free to surf the Internet, go public with all her ideas and frustrations. But the World Wide Web, "this particular web" of the twenty-first century, is fraught with perils, is diseased—with spiders and Blaster worms invading our privacy, leading to computer crashes, identity theft, to blocked communication rather than communion. These metaphors of worms and viruses for a diseased web may even make us yearn for an older world where pain was endured and contained, as Alice Munro's Del Jordan, in *Lives of Girls and Women*, dreams at times of a Charlotte Brontë kind of world (one wonders which Brontë novel she was reading!). But emerge women will and must, and the lessons of nineteenth-century Europe, and particularly of British and French imperialism, are not lost on postmodern minority women in Western culture, such as Toni Morrison's Reba in *Song of Solomon*, whose diatribe against men seems to echo (though in more explicit sexual terms) that of George Eliot's wonderful Mrs. Poyser in *Adam Bede*, or women from emerging nations, such as the Moroccan mother in Driss Chraïbi's *La Civilisation Ma Mère* (1976), who moves from traditional wife and mother to leading a march of women seeking freedom, and Hédi Bouraoui's Zitouna in *Retour à Thyna* (1997), who not only liberates herself from male political and sexual / social domination, but takes on the traditional public "male" role of talespinner in the marketplace, and becomes the voice for her countrywomen. Women writers of the nineteenth century were astute in sending letters to the world—a larger, more inclusive world than they could have known—in the form of questions we have yet to answer today.

# Bibliography

**Primary Sources**

Austen, Jane. *Emma.* 1816. Boston: Houghton Mifflin Riverside Edtion, 1957.
—— *Mansfield Park.* 1814. *The Complete Novels of Jane Austen.* New York: Random House Modern Library, n.d.
—— *Northanger Abbey.* 1817. *The Complete Novels of Jane Austen.* New York: Random House Modern Library, n.d.
—— "The Plan of a Novel, According to Hints from Various Quarters." *Discussions of Jane Austen.* Ed. William Heath. Boston: D.C. Heath, 1961.
—— *Persuasion.* 1817. Harmondsworth, Middlesex: Penguin Books, 1965.
—— *Pride and Prejudice.* 1813. Boston: Houghton Mifflin Riverside Edition, 1956.
—— *Sense and Sensibility.* 1811. Harmondsworth, Middlesex: Penguin Books, 1969.
Barnard, Robert. *The Case of the Missing Brontë.* New York: Dell, 1983.
Bouraoui, Hédi. *Retour à Thyna.* Tunis: Editions L'Or du Temps, 1996, 1997.
—— *Return to Thyna.* Trans. Elizabeth Sabiston. Saratoga Springs, New York: CELAAN, Editions les Mains Secrètes, 2004.
Brontë, Charlotte. *Jane Eyre.* 1847. New York: Norton Critical Edition, 1971.
—— *Shirley.* 1849. Harmondsworth, Middlesex: Penguin Books, 1974.
—— *Villette.* 1853. New York: Dutton Everyman, 1957.
Brontë, Emily. *Wuthering Heights.* 1847. Boston: Houghton Mifflin Riverside Edition, 1956.
Chraïbi, Driss. *La Civilisation, Ma Mère!* Paris: Denoël, 1972.
Crane, Stephen. *The Red Badge of Courage.* 1895. New York: Holt, Rinehart, Winston, 1956.
Dickens, Charles. *Bleak House.* 1853. Boston: Houghton Mifflin Riverside Edition, 1956.
Dickinson, Emily. *The Poems of Emily Dickinson.* Ed. Thomas H. Johnson. Cambridge, Mass.: The Belknap Press of Harvard UP. 1951, 1955, 1979, 1983.
Dostoyevsky, Fyodor. *Notes from Underground.* 1864. Trans. Mirra Ginsburg. New York: Bantam Classics, 1974.
Eliot, George. *Adam Bede.* 1859. Introduction by John Paterson. Boston: Houghton Mifflin Riverside Edition, 1968.
—— *Daniel Deronda.* 1876. New York: Harper Torchbook, 1960.
—— *Middlemarch.* 1871–72. Boston: Houghton Mifflin Riverside Edition, 1956.
—— *The Mill on the Floss.* 1860. Introduction by Gordon Haight. Boston: Houghton Mifflin Riverside Edition, 1961.
Faulkner, William. *Absalom, Absalom!* 1936. New York: Random House, 1951.
—— *The Sound and the Fury.* 1929. New York: Random House, 1946.
Flaubert, Gustave. *Madame Bovary: Moeurs de Province.* 1857. Ed. and trans. Paul DeMan. New York: Norton Critical Edition, 1965.

Gaskell, Elizabeth. *Cranford*. 1853. Harmondsworth, Middlesex: Penguin Books, 1976.

—— *Mary Barton*. 1848. Harmondsworth, Middlesex: Penguin Books, 1970.

—— *North and South*. 1854–55. Harmondsworth, Middlesex: Penguin Books, 1970.

Golding, William. *Lord of the Flies*. New York, 1954.

Hawthorne, Nathaniel. *The Scarlet Letter*. 1850. New York: Holt, Rinehart and Winston, 1957.

—— "Young Goodman Brown." 1846. "Ethan Brand." 1851. *Selected Tales and Sketches*. New York: Holt, Rinehart and Winston, 1957.

James, Henry. "The Art of Fiction."1884. *The Future of the Novel*. Ed. Leon Edel. New York: Vintage, 1956.

—— "*Daniel Deronda*: A Conversation." *Discussions of George Eliot*. Ed. Richard Stang. Boston: D.C. Heath, 1960.

—— *The Golden Bowl*. 1904. New York: Grove Press, 1952.

—— *The Portrait of a Lady*. 1881. Boston: Houghton Mifflin Riverside Edition, 1956.

—— *The Tragic Muse*. 1890. New York: Harper Torchbook, 1960.

—— *The Turn of the Screw*. 1898. New York: Norton Critical Edition, 1966.

—— *Washington Square*. 1880. New York: Dell, 1959.

Laclos, Choderlos de. *Les Liaisons dangereuses*. 1782. Paris: Editions Garnier, 1952.

Lennox, Charlotte Ramsay. *The Female Quixote*. 1752. Ed. Margaret Dalziel with an Introduction by Margaret Anne Doody, Chronology and Appendix by Duncan Isles. Oxford and New York: Oxford UP, 1989.

Mailer, Norman. *The Armies of the Night*. New York: Signet, 1968.

Melville, Herman. "Billy Budd, Foretopman." 1891. *Selected Tales and Sketches*. Ed. Richard Chase. New York: Holt, Rinehart and Winston, 1957.

Morrison, Toni. *Song of Solomon*. 1977. New York: New American Library, 1979.

Munro, Alice. *Lives of Girls and Women*. 1971. Scarborough, Ontario: Signet, 1974.

Poe, Edgar Allan. "Ligeia." 1838. *The Portable Poe*. New York: Viking, 1945.

Rhys, Jean. *Wide Sargasso Sea*. 1966. Harmondsworth, Middlesex: Penguin Books, 1968.

Shakespeare, William. *As You Like It*.

—— *The Merchant of Venice*.

—— *The Winter's Tale*.

Stowe, Harriet Beecher. *Uncle Tom's Cabin*. 1852. New York: Signet, 1966.

Tolstoy, Leo. *Anna Karenin*. 1873–76. Trans. Aylmer Maude. New York: Norton Critical Edition, 1970.

Turgenev, Ivan. *Fathers and Sons*. 1862. Trans. Herbert J. Muller. New York: Random House Modern Library, 1950.

Wharton, Edith. *The Age of Innocence*. 1920. New York: Random House Modern Library, n.d.

——. *The House of Mirth*. 1905. New York: Scribner's, 1969.

Wilde, Oscar. *The Importance of Being Earnest*. 1895. *The Portable Oscar Wilde*. Ed. Richard Aldington. New York: Viking Press, 1946.

Wollstonecraft, Mary. *A Vindication of the Rights of Woman.* 1792. Ed. Carol H. Poston. New York: Norton Critical Edition, 1975.

Woolf, Virginia. *A Room of One's Own.* 1929. London: Panther Granada, 1980.


## Secondary Sources


Adams, John R. *Harriet Beecher Stowe.* New York: Twayne, 1963.

Allen, Walter. *The English Novel.* New York: Dutton Everyman, 1958.

Allott, Miriam. "Mrs. Gaskell's 'The Old Nurse's Story': A Link Between 'Wuthering Heights' and 'The Turn of the Screw'." 1961. *The Turn of the Screw.* New York: Norton Critical Edition, 1966: 142–5.

Anderson, Amanda. "George Eliot and the Jewish Question." *Yale Journal of Criticism: Interpretation in the Humanities* 10:1 (Spring 1997): 39–61.

Armstrong, Nancy. "A Cultural and Critical Perspective on *Wuthering Heights.*" *Wuthering Heights.* Peterson 428–49.

Ashton, Rosemary. *George Eliot: A Life.* 1996. Harmondsworth, Middlesex: Penguin, 1997.

Astell, Ann W. "Anne Elliot's Education: The Learning of Romance in *Persuasion.*" *Persuasion.* Ed. Patricia Meyer Spacks. New York: Norton Critical Edition, 1995. 275–85.

Babb, Howard S. *Jane Austen's Novels: The Fabric of Dialogue.* Columbus: Ohio State UP, 1967.

Bachelard, Gaston. *The Poetics of Space.* 1957. Trans. Maria Jolas. New York: The Orion Press, 1964.

Bacon, Alan. "Jane Eyre's Paintings and Milton's 'Paradise Lost'." *Notes and Queries* 229 (1984): 64–6.

Baker, William. "George Eliot and Zionism." Shalvi 47–63.

Baldwin, James. "Everybody's Protest Novel." *Notes of a Native Son.* Boston: The Beacon Press, 1955.

Banfield, Ann. "The Influence of Place: Jane Austen and the Novel of Social Consciousness." Monaghan 28–48.

Barker, Juliet. *The Brontës.* 1994. London: Orion Books, Phoenix, 1995.

Bataille, Georges. *La Littérature et le mal.* Paris, 1957. Qtd. in J. Hillis Miller, "The Disappearance of God: Five Nineteenth-Century Writers." Vogler.

Bayley, John. *Tolstoy and the Novel.* New York: Viking, 1967.

Beer, Gillian. *Darwin's Plots: Evolutionary Narrative in Darwin, George Eliot, and Nineteenth-Century Fiction.* 1983. London: Ark Paperbacks, 1985.

—— *George Eliot.* Bloomington: Indiana UP, Key Women Writers Series, 1986.

—— Lecture, York University, 1985.

Belsey, Catherine. "Re-reading the Great Tradition." *Re-Reading English.* Ed. Peter Widdowson. New York: Methuen, 1982. 121–35.

Bennett, Joan. *George Eliot: Her Mind and Her Art.* Cambridge: Cambridge UP, 1962.

Benvenuto, Richard. *Emily Brontë.* Boston: Twayne, 1982.

Bock, Carol. "Charlotte Brontë's Storytellers: The Influence of Scott." *Cahiers Victoriens et Édouardiens: Revue du Centre d'Etudies et de Recherches Victoriennes et Édouardiennes de l'Université Paul Vale* 34 (October 1991): 15–30.

Bodenheimer, Rosemarie. "Jane Eyre in Search of Her Story." *Papers on Language and Literature* 16 (1980): 387–402.

Boren, Lynda S. "The Performing Self: Psychodrama in Austen, James, and Woolf." *The Centennial Review* 30:1 (Winter 1986): 1–24.

Brownstein, Rachel. *On Becoming a Heroine*. New York: Viking, 1982.

Burkhart, Charles. *Charlotte Brontë: A Psychosexual Study of Her Novels*. London: Victor Gollancz, 1973.

Burlin, Katrin. "The Four Fictions of *Northanger*." *Jane Austen: Bicentenary Essays*. Ed. John Halperin. Cambridge: Cambridge UP, 1975.

Burton, Antoinette. "'Invention is what delights me': Jane Austen's Remaking of 'English' History." Looser 35–50.

Bush, Douglas. *Jane Austen*. New York: Collier, 1975.

Butler, Marilyn. *Jane Austen and the War of Ideas*. Oxford: Oxford UP, 1975. Rev. 1987.

—— "Disregarded Designs: Jane Austen's Sense of the Volume." Monaghan 49–65.

Carpenter, Mary Wilson. "The Apocalypse of the Old Testament: *Daniel Deronda* and the Interpretation of Interpretation." *PMLA* 99:1 (January 1989): 56–71.

Cecil, Lord David. *Victorian Novelists*. 1935. Chicago: U of Chicago P, 1958.

Chase, Cynthia. "The Decomposition of Elephants: Double-Reading *Daniel Deronda*." *PMLA* 93:2 (1978): 215–27.

Chase, Richard. "The Brontës, or Myth Domesticated." 1948. *Jane Eyre*. New York: Norton Critical Edition, 1971. 462–71.

Collick, John. "Dismembering Devils: The Demonology of 'Arashi ga oka' (1988) and 'Wuthering Heights' (1939)." *Novel Images*. Ed. Peter Reynolds. London: Routledge, 1993. 34–7.

Cook, Eleanor. "The Italian Journey: From James to Eliot to Browning." *The Motif of the Journey in Nineteenth-Century Italian Literature*. Ed. Bruno Magliocchetti and Anthony Verna. Gainesville: U of Florida P, 1994. 41–52.

Courcel, Martine de. *Tolstoy: The Ultimate Reconciliation*. Trans. Peter Levi. New York: Charles Scribner's Sons, 1988.

Craft, Catherine. "Reworking Male Models: Aphra Behn's *Fair Vow-Breaker*, Eliza Haywood's *Fantomina*, and Charlotte Lennox's *Female Quixote*." *Modern Language Review* 86:4 (October 1991): 821–38.

Craig, G. Armour. "Private Vision and Social Order in *Jane Eyre*." 1956. *Jane Eyre*. New York: Norton Critical Edition, 1971. 471–8.

Craig, Sheryl. "Brontë's *Wuthering Heights*." *Explicator* 52:3 (Spring 1994): 157–9.

Craik, W.A. *The Brontë Novels*. London: Methuen, 1968.

—— *Jane Austen: The Six Novels*. London: Methuen, 1965.

Crozier, Alice. *The Novels of Harriet Beecher Stowe*. New York: Oxford UP, 1969.

Daiches, David. "Introduction," *Wuthering Heights*. Harmondsworth, Middlesex: Penguin Books, 1965. Rpt. in Vogler.

Dale, Peter Allen. "Varieties of Blasphemy: Feminism and the Brontës." *Review* 14 (1992): 281–304.

Daleski, H.M. "Owning and Disowning: the Unity of *Daniel Deronda.*" Shalvi 67–85.

David, Deirdre. *Fictions of Resolution in Three Victorian Novels: "North and South," "Our Mutual Friend," "Daniel Deronda."* New York: Columbia UP, 1981.

Davies, Stevie. *Emily Brontë: Heretic.* London: The Women's Press, 1994.

Dawson, Terence. "The Struggle for Deliverance from the Father: The Structural Principle of *Wuthering Heights.*" *Modern Language Review* 84:2 (April 1989): 289–304.

Dingly, R.J. "Rochester as Slave: An Allusion in 'Jane Eyre'." *Notes and Queries* 229 (1984): 66.

Dowling, Andrew. "'The Other Side of Silence': Matrimonial Conflict and the Divorce Court in George Eliot's Fiction." *Nineteenth-Century Literature* 50:2 (September 1995): 322–36.

Duckworth, Alistair M. *The Improvement of the Estate: A Study of Jane Austen's Novels.* Baltimore: Johns Hopkins UP, 1994.

Duthie, Enid L. *The Themes of Elizabeth Gaskell.* London: Macmillan, 1980.

Eagleton, Terry. "Jane Eyre's Power Struggle." 1975. *Jane Eyre.* New York: Norton Critical Edition, Second Edition, 1986. 491–6.

—— "Myths of Power: a Marxist Study on *Wuthering Heights.*" Peterson 399–414.

Edwards, Anne-Marie. *In the Steps of Jane Austen.* Newbury, Berkshire: Countryside Books, 1979. Rpt. 1996.

Ewbank, Inga-Stina. "The Structure and Pattern of the Whole Novel." 1966. *Wuthering Heights.* Norton Critical Edition, 1972. 322–33.

Farrer, Reginald. "Jane Austen." 1917. *Discussions of Jane Austen.* Ed. William Heath. Boston: D.C. Heath, 1961. 19–24.

Fergus, Jan. "Sex and Social Life in Jane Austen's Novels." Monaghan 66–85.

Forster, E.M. *Aspects of the Novel.* 1927. Harmondsworth, Middlesex: Penguin Books, 1978.

Foster, Charles H. *The Rungless Ladder: Harriet Beecher Stowe and New England Puritanism.* Durham, North Carolina: Duke UP, 1954.

Friedman, Ellen G. "Breaking the Master Narrative: Jean Rhys's *Wide Sargasso Sea.*" *Breaking the Sequence: Women's Experimental Fiction.* Ed. Ellen G. Friedman and Miriam Fuchs. Princeton: Princeton UP, 1989. 117–28.

Galef, David. "Keeping One's Distance: Irony and Doubling in *Wuthering Heights.*" *Studies in the Novel* 24.3 (Fall 1992): 242–50.

Gallagher, Catherine. "George Eliot and *Daniel Deronda*: The Prostitute and the Jewish Question." *Sex, Politics and Science in the Nineteenth-Century Novel.* Ed. Ruth Bernard Yeazell. Baltimore: Johns Hopkins UP, 1986. 39–62.

Gard, Roger. *Jane Austen's Novels: The Art of Clarity.* New Haven: Yale UP, 1992.

Gates, Barbara. "'Visionary Woe' and Its Revisions: Another Look at Jane Eyre's Pictures." Ariel 7 (1976): 36–49.

Gérin, Winifred. *Charlotte Brontë: The Evolution of Genius.* Oxford: Oxford UP, 1967.

—— *Elizabeth Gaskell.* London: Oxford UP, 1976.

—— *Emily Brontë.* Oxford: Oxford UP, 1971.

Gerson, Noel. B. *Harriet Beecher Stowe: A Biography.* New York: Praeger, 1976.

Gilbert, Sandra M. "From Our Mothers' Libraries – Women Who Created the Novel." *New York Times Book Review*, May 4, 1986: 30.

Gilbert, Sandra M. and Susan Gubar. *The Madwoman in the Attic: The Woman Writer and the Nineteenth-Century Literary Imagination*. New Haven: Yale UP, 1979.

Goetz, William R. "Genealogy and Incest in *Wuthering Heights*." *Studies in the Novel* 14 (1982): 359–76.

Goodridge, J. Frank. "The Circumambient Universe." Rpt. in Vogler. 69–76.

Gray, Beverly. "Mrs. Gaskell's home town drab and not the world of the novels." *The Globe and Mail*, October 23, 1976: 2.

Guerard, Albert. "Preface." *Wuthering Heights*. New York: Washington Square Press, n.d. Rpt. in Vogler. 63–7.

Gutman, Herbert. *The Black Family in Slavery and Freedom, 1750–1925*. New York: Pantheon, 1976.

Haight, Gordon S. *George Eliot: A Biography*. 1968. Harmondsworth, Middlesex: Penguin Books, 1985.

Halperin, John. "George Eliot." *Egoism and Self-Discovery in the Victorian Novel: Studies in the Ordeal of Knowledge in the Nineteenth Century*. New York: Franklin, 1974. 125–92.

Harding, D.W. "Regulated Hatred: An Aspect of the Work of Jane Austen." 1940. *Discussions of Jane Austen*. Ed. Heath. 41–50.

—— "Introduction." *Persuasion*. Harmondsworth, Middlesex: Penguin Books, 1965.

Hardy, Barbara. *A Reading of Jane Austen*. London: Owen, 1975.

—— *The Novels of George Eliot*. 1959. New York: Oxford UP, 1967.

Harris, Anne Leslie. "Psychological Time in *Wuthering Heights*." *International Fiction Review* 7 (1980): 112–17.

Harris, Jocelyn. "Jane Austen and the Burden of the (Male) Past: The Case Reexamined." Looser 87–100.

Heilbrun, Carolyn. *Toward a Recognition of Androgyny*. New York: Knopf, 1973.

Heilman, Robert B. "Charlotte Brontë's 'New' Gothic." 1958. *Jane Eyre*. New York: Norton Critical Edition, 1971.

Hobbs, E.A. "*Daniel Deronda* as Will and Representation: George Eliot and Schopenhauer." *Modern Language Review* 80:3 (July 1985): 533–49.

Hochman, Baruch. "*Daniel Deronda*: The Zionist Plot and the Problematic of George Eliot's Art." Shalvi 113–33.

Hoeveler, Dianne. "Vindicating *Northanger Abbey*: Mary Wollstonecraft, Jane Austen, and Gothic Feminism." Looser 117–35.

Homans, Margaret. "The Name of the Mother in *Wuthering Heights*." Peterson 341–58.

Honan, Park. *Jane Austen: Her Life*. London: Orion Phoenix, 1987. Rev. 1997.

Hopkins, Robert. "Moral Luck and Judgment in Jane Austen's *Persuasion*." New York: Norton Critical Edition. 265–74.

Horowitz, J. Barbara. *Jane Austen and the Question of Women's Education*. New York: Peter Lang, 1991.

Hughes, Kathryn. *George Eliot: The Last Victorian*. London: Fourth Estate Ltd., 1998.

Hutchinson, Stuart. "From *Daniel Deronda* to *The House of Mirth*." *Essays in Criticism* 47:4 (October 1997): 315–31.

Ignatieff, Michael. "His Art Was All He Mastered." *New York Times Book Review*, August 28, 1988: 1, 22, 24.

Jacobs, Carol. "*Wuthering Heights*: A Threshold Interpretation." *Boundary 2* 7:3 (1979): 49–71.

Jerinic, Maria. "In Defence of the Gothic: Rereading *Northanger Abbey*." Looser 137–49.

Johnson, Claudia. *Jane Austen: Women, Politics, and the Novel*. Chicago: U of Chicago P, 1988.

Kelly, Gary. "Jane Austen, Romantic Feminism and Civil Society." Looser 19–34.

Kettle, Arnold. *An Introduction to the English Novel*. New York: Harper Torchbooks, 1960.

Lane, Maggie. *A Charming Place: Bath in the Life and Novels of Jane Austen*. Bath: Millstream Books, 1988.

Lansbury, Coral. *Elizabeth Gaskell: The Novel of Social Crisis*. London: Paul Elek, 1975.

Lascelles, Mary. *Jane Austen and Her Art*. 1939. London: Oxford UP, 1963.

Leavis, F.R. *The Great Tradition*. 1948. New York: Doubleday Anchor, 1954.

Leavis, Q.D. "A Fresh Approach to *Wuthering Heights*." 1969. Rpt. in *Wuthering Heights*. New York: Norton Critical Edition, 1972. 306–21.

Lerner, Laurence. "*Daniel Deronda*: George Eliot's Struggle with Realism." Shalvi 89–109.

Levine, George. "Isabel, Gwendolen, and Dorothea." *ELH* 30:3 (September 1963): 244–57.

Levy, Anita. "The History of Desire in *Wuthering Heights*." *Genre* 19:4 (Winter 1986): 409–30.

Lewes, George Henry. "The Reality of Jane Eyre." 1847. *Jane Eyre*. New York: Norton Critical Edition, 1971. 447–8.

Linder, Cynthia A. *Romantic Imagery in the Novels of Charlotte Brontë*. London: Macmillan, 1978.

Litz, A. Walton. *Jane Austen: A Study of Her Artistic Development*. New York: Oxford UP, 1965.

Looser, Devoney, ed. *Jane Austen and Discourses of Feminism*. New York, 1995.

Lovesey, Oliver. "The Other Woman in *Daniel Deronda*." *Studies in the Novel* 30:4 (Winter 1998): 505–20.

*A Map of Bath in the Time of Jane Austen*. Compiled by E.L. Green-Armytage. n.d.

Marshall, Gail. "Actresses, Statues and Speculation in *Daniel Deronda*." *Essays in Criticism* 44:2 (April 1994): 117–39.

Martin, Robert Bernard. *The Accents of* Persuasion: *Charlotte Brontë's Novels*. London: Faber and Faber, 1966. See also excerpt, "Religious Discovery in *Jane Eyre*." *Jane Eyre*. New York: Norton Critical Edition, 1971. 478–88.

Martin, Robert K. "*Jane Eyre* and the World of Faery." *Mosaic* 10 (1977): 85–95.

Maynard, John. *Charlotte Brontë and Sexuality*. Cambridge: Cambridge UP, 1984.

McCarthy, T. "The Incompetent Narrator of *Wuthering Heights*." *Modern Language Quarterly* 42 (1981): 48–64.

McKillop, Alan D. "Critical Realism in *Northanger Abbey*." *Jane Austen: A Collection of Critical Essays*. Ed. Ian Watt. Englewood Cliffs, N.J.: Prentice-Hall, 1963. 52–61.

McKinstry, Susan Jaret. "Desire's Dreams: Power and Passion in *Wuthering Heights*." *College Literature* 12:2 (Spring 1985): 141–6.

McMaster, Juliet. "The Courtship and Honeymoon of Mr. and Mrs. Linton Heathcliff: Emily Brontë's Sexual Imagery." *Victorian Review* 18:1 (Summer 1972): 1–12.

McMullen, Bonnie. "'The Interest of Spanish Sights': From Ronda to *Daniel Deronda*." *George Eliot and Europe*. Ed. John Ringnall. Vermont: Scholar Press, 1997. 123–37.

Miller, Derek. "*Daniel Deronda* and Allegories of Empire." *George Eliot and Europe*. Ed. Ringnall. 113–22.

Miller, J. Hillis. *The Disappearance of God: Five Nineteenth-Century Writers*. Excerpt in *Twentieth-Century Perspectives on "Wuthering Heights."* 1963. Ed. Vogler.

—— "*Wuthering Heights*: Repetition and the 'Uncanny'." *Wuthering Heights*. Peterson 371–84.

Millgate, Jane. "Narrative Distance in *Jane Eyre*: The Relevance of the Pictures." *Modern Language Review* 63 (1968): 315–19.

Mintz, Alan. "*Daniel Deronda* and the Messianic Vocation." Shalvi 137–56.

Moers, Ellen. *Literary Women*. 1977. London: The Women's Press, 1978.

Moglen, Helene. *Charlotte Brontë: The Self Conceived*. New York: Norton, 1976. Excerpt, "The Creation of a Feminist Myth," in *Jane Eyre*. New York: Norton Critical Edition, Second Edition, 1986. 484–91.

Monaghan, David, ed. *Jane Austen in a Social Context*. Totowa, N.J.: Barnes and Noble, 1981.

—— "Jane Austen and the Position of Women." Monaghan 105–21.

Morrison, Paul. "Enclosed in Openness: *Northanger Abbey* and the Domestic Carceral." *Texas Studies in Literature and Language* 33:1 (Spring 1991): 1–23.

Moser, Thomas. "What Is the Matter with Emily Jane? Conflicting Impulses in *Wuthering Heights*."1962. Rpt. in *The Victorian Novel*. Ed. Ian Watt. Oxford: Oxford UP, 1971. 190–97.

Mudrick, Marvin. *Jane Austen: Irony as Defense and Discovery*. Princeton: Princeton UP, 1952.

Munro, Alice. Interview, *The Globe and Mail*, December 11, 1982: E1.

Nardin, Jane. "Jane Austen and the Problem of Leisure." Monaghan 122–42.

Newman, Beth. "'The Situation of the Looker-on': Gender, Narration, and Gaze in *Wuthering Heights*." *PMLA* 105:5 (October 1990): 1029–44.

Oates, Joyce Carol. "The Magnanimity of *Wuthering Heights*." *Critical Inquiry* 9 (1982): 435–49.

Peterson, Linda H., ed. *Wuthering Heights*. Boston and New York: Bedford Books of St. Martin's Press, 1992.

—— "A Critical History." Peterson 289–302.

Poggioli, Renato. "Tolstoy's *Domestic Happiness*: Beyond Pastoral Love." 1975. *Tolstoy's Short Fiction*. New York: Norton Critical Edition, 1991. 398–413.

Polhemus, Robert. "The Passionate Calling: *Wuthering Heights*." *Heathcliff*. Ed. Harold Bloom. New York: Chelsea House, 1993.

Poole, Adrian. "Hidden Affinities in *Daniel Deronda*." *Essays in Criticism* 33 (1983): 294–311.

Poovey, Mary. "*Persuasion* and the Promises of Love." *The Representation of Women in Fiction: Selected Papers from the English Institute, 1981*. Ed. Carolyn Heilbrun and Margaret R. Higonnet. Baltimore: The Johns Hopkins UP, 1983. 152–79.

Price, Reynolds. "Men, Creating Women." *New York Times Book Review*, November 9, 1986: 1, 16, 18, 20.

Pritchett, V.S. "Introduction." *Wuthering Heights*. Boston: Houghton Mifflin Riverside Edition, 1956.

Putzell, Sara M. "The Importance of Being Gwendolen: Contexts for George Eliot's *Daniel Deronda*." *Studies in the Novel* 19:1 (Spring 1987): 31–45.

Rich, Adrienne. "Jane Eyre: The Temptations of a Motherless Woman." 1979. *Jane Eyre*. New York: Norton Critical Edition, Second Edition, 1986. 462–75.

Robinson, Carole. "The Severe Angel: A Study of *Daniel Deronda*." *ELH* 31 (1964): 278–300.

Rougemont, Denis de. *Love in the Western World*. 1939. New York: Doubleday Anchor, 1956.

Rubenius, Aina. *The Woman Question in Mrs. Gaskell's Life and Works*. Cambridge: Harvard UP, 1950.

Sabiston, Elizabeth. *The Prison of Womanhood: Four Provincial Heroines in Nineteenth-Century Fiction*. London: Macmillan, and New York: St. Martin's, 1987.

—— "'A Wild Child': A Cross-Cultural Literary View." *Existere* 2:1 (November 1979): 18–21.

—— "Women, Blacks, and Thomas Sutpen's Mythopoeic Drive in *Absalom, Absalom!*" *Modernist Studies* 1 (1974–75): 15–26.

Saïd, Edward. "Jane Austen and Empire." *Raymond Williams: Critical Perspectives*. Ed. Terry Eagleton. Cambridge: Polity Press, 1989. 150–64.

Sanger, C.P. "The Structure of *Wuthering Heights*." 1926. Rpt. in *Wuthering Heights*. New York: Norton Critical Edition, 1972. 286–98.

Schorer, Mark. "Fiction and the Matrix of Analogy." 1949. Rpt. in Vogler.44–8.

Semmel, Bernard. *George Eliot and the Politics of National Inheritance*. New York and Oxford: Oxford UP, 1994.

Senf, Carol A. "Emily Brontë's Version of Feminist History: *Wuthering Heights*." *Essays in Literature* 12:2 (Fall 1985): 201–14.

Shaffer, Julie. "Not Subordinate: Empowering Women in the Marriage-Plot: Novels of Frances Burney, Maria Edgeworth, and Jane Austen." *Reading with a Difference*. Ed. Arthur F. Morroth, Renata R. Mautner Wasserman, Jo Dulan, and Suchitra Mathser. Detroit: Wayne State UP, 1993. 21–43.

Shalvi, Alice, ed. *"Daniel Deronda": A Centenary Symposium*. Jerusalem: Jerusalem Academic Press, 1976.

Siegel, Carol. "Border Disturbances: D.H. Lawrence's Fiction and the Feminism of *Wuthering Heights*." *Man Writing the Feminine: Literature, Theory, and the Question of Gender*. Ed. Thais E. Morgan. Albany: SUNY P, 1994: 59–76.

Sisken, Clifford. "Jane Austen and the Engendering Disciplinary." Monaghan 51–67.

Smith, Sheila. "'At Once Strong and Eerie': The Supernatural in *Wuthering Heights* and Its Debt to the Traditional Ballad." *Review of English Studies* 43:172 (November 1992): 498–517.

Solomon, Eric. "The Incest Theme in *Wuthering Heights*." 1959. Rpt. In Vogler.

Southam, B.C., ed. *Critical Essays on Jane Austen*. London: Routledge and Kegan Paul, 1968.

Spacks, Patricia Meyer. "Muted Discord: Generational Conflict in Jane Austen." Monaghan 159–79.

Speaight, Robert. *George Eliot*. London: Arthur Barker Ltd., 1954.

Stone, Wilfred. "The Play of Chance and Ego in *Daniel Deronda*." *Nineteenth-Century Literature* 53:1 (June 1998): 25–55.

Stoneman, Patsy. *Elizabeth Gaskell*. Bloomington: Indiana UP, 1987.

Sulivan, P. "Fairy Tale Elements in *Jane Eyre*." *Journal of Popular Culture* 12 (1978): 61–74.

Sypher, Eileen. "Resisting Gwendolen's 'Subjection'; *Daniel Deronda*'s Proto-Feminism." *Studies in the Novel* 28:4 (Winter 1996): 506–24.

Tandrup, Birthe. "A Trap of Misreading: Free Indirect Style and the Critique of the Gothic in *Northanger Abbey*." *The Romantic Heritage: A Collection of Critical Essays*. Ed. Karsten Engelberg. Copenhagen: U of Copenhagen P, 1983. 81–91.

Tanner, Tony. *Jane Austen*. London: Macmillan, 1986. Rpt. 1993.

—— "In Between – Anne Elliot Marries a Sailor and Charles Heywood Goes to the Seaside." Monaghan 180–94.

Tate, Allen. *The Man of Letters in the Modern World*. New York: Meridian Books, 1955.

Thompson, Andrew. *George Eliot and Italy: Literary, Cultural and Political Influences from Dante to the "Risorgimento"*. Basingstoke, Hampshire: Macmillan, and New York: St. Martin's, 1998.

Thompson, James. *Between Self and World: The Novels of Jane Austen*. University Park: Pennsylvania State UP, 1988.

Tillotson, Kathleen. *Novels of the Eighteen-Forties*. Oxford: Oxford UP, 1954.

Tompkins, Jane P. "Sentimental Power: *Uncle Tom's Cabin* and the Politics of Literary History." *Glyph* 8 (1981): 79–102.

Traversi, Derek. "The Brontë Sisters and *Wuthering Heights*." 1958. Rpt. in Vogler 50–61.

Trilling, Lionel. "Why Read Jane Austen?" *Lionel Trilling: The Last Decade, Essays and Reviews, 1965–75*. Ed. Diana Trilling. Oxford: Oxford UP, 1982.

Turnell, Martin. *The Novel in France*. 1951. New York: Vintage, 1958.

Van Ghent, Dorothy. *The English Novel: Form and Function*. New York: Harper Torchbooks, 1953.

Vine, Steven. "The Wuther of the Other in *Wuthering Heights*." *Nineteenth-Century Literature* 49:3 (December 1994): 339–59.

Visick, Mary. "Catherine Earnshaw and Edgar Linton." 1958. Rpt. in *Wuthering Heights*. New York: Norton Critical Edition, 1972. 358–70.

Vogler, Thomas A., ed. *Twentieth-Century Interpretations of "Wuthering Heights"*. Englewood Cliffs, N.J.: Prentice-Hall, 1968.

Vogler, Thomas A. "Introduction"and "Story and History in *Wuthering Heights*." Vogler 78–99.

Warhol, Robyn. "Toward a Theory of the Engaging Narrator: Earnest Interventions in Gaskell, Stowe, and Eliot." *PMLA* 101 (1986): 811–18.

Watt, Ian. "Introduction." *Jane Austen: A Collection of Critical Essays*. Englewood Cliffs, N.J.: Prentice-Hall, 1963. 1–14.

Weissman, Cheryl Ann. "Doubleness and Refrain in Jane Austen's *Persuasion*." *The Kenyon Review* 10:4 (Fall 1988): 87–91.

Whicher, George Frisbie. "Harriet Beecher Stowe." 1946. *Literary History of the United States*. Ed. Robert E. Spiller and Willard Thorp. New York: Macmillan, 1953.

White-Lewis, Jane. "In Defense of Nightmares: Clinical and Literary Cases." *The Dream and the Text*. Ed. Carol Schreier Rupprecht. Albany: SUNY P, 1993. 48–70.

Whitehill, Jan, ed. *Letters of Mrs. Gaskell and Charles Eliot Norton, 1855–65*. 1932. Folcroft, Pennsylvania: Folcroft Library Editions, 1973.

Wilt, Judith. "'He would come back': The Fathers of Daughters in *Daniel Deronda*." *Nineteenth-Century Literature* 42:3 (December 1987): 313–38.

Winnifrith, Tom. *Charlotte and Emily Brontë: Literary Lives*. London: Macmillan, 1989.

Wion, Philip K. "The Absent Mother in *Wuthering Heights*." Peterson 315–29.

Woolf, Virginia. "The Brontës." *The Common Reader*. 1925. New York: Harcourt, Brace and Company, 1953. 159–65.

Wright, Andrew H. *"Persuasion." Jane Austen: A Collection of Critical Essays*. Ed. Ian Watt. Englewood Cliffs, N.J.: Prentice-Hall, 1963. 144–53.

Wright, Edgar. *Mrs. Gaskell: A Reassessment*. London: Oxford UP, 1965.

Yeazell, Ruth Bernard. "Why Political Novels Have Heroines: *Sybil*, *Mary Barton*, and *Felix Holt*." *Novel* 18 (1985): 126–44.

# Index

abolitionism 139
*Absalom, Absalom!* 128n., 139, 142
*Adam Bede* 116, 157, 178, 191
Adams, John R. 133n., 136n.
adultery 79–80, 92
*Age of Innocence, The* 178
Allen, Walter 80n., 96n.
Allott, Miriam 118
alter ego 155, 156
Anderson, Amanda 162n.
androgyny 156, 159, 161n.
anger 56, 59, 73, 138, 190–91
animal imagery 179
*Anna Karenin* 83n., 84–5, 90, 92
anonymity 2–3, 115
anti-hero 24, 61, 118, 185n.
anti-heroine 9, 13–15, 17, 186, 189
anti-semitism 154, 167
archery 169–70
architecture 101–102
Armstrong, Nancy 98n.
art 10–11, 13, 18, 27, 37, 54, 56, 59, 70,
    116, 118, 155, 190
    and life 134
    and patriarchy 127–9
    *see also* female artist
Auden, W.H. 7
Austen, Jane 1–3, 50–52, 55, 56, 124, 131
    character 5–6
    and Charlotte Ramsey Lennox 7–13, 15
    and community 189
    craft of 2, 7, 14, 18, 27, 30, 54
    critics of 5–7
    and detective novel 40
    and female initiation 62
    influences on 7–9
    'Plan of a Novel' 9, 13
    style 53
    and world 6–7, 18, 28
authority 80, 127, 139, 169
authorship 2, 10, 37
    *see also* women writers

autobiography 65, 38, 72n., 80n., 87

Babb, Howard S. 53n.
Bachelard, Gaston 27n., 114
Bailey, John 34
Baker, William 161n.
Baldwin, James 67n., 132n., 137, 140, 142,
    146
Balzac 91
Banfield, Ann 14n.
Barker, Juliet 79n.
Barnard, Robert 95n.
Bataille, Georges 99
Bath 16, 19–20, 32, 44, 51
Bayley, John 83n.
beauty 11, 13, 55, 56, 67, 142, 166
Beer, Gillian 161n., 164n., 168n., 171n., 176n.
Belsey, Catherine 167n.
Bennett, Joan 165n.
Benvenuto, Richard 98n.
Bible 79, 144, 153, 185, 186
*Bildungsroman* 25, 34, 56–7, 86
*Billy Budd* 81–2, 93
biography 38
bird imagery 59, 62, 75, 101n., 111
black people 79n., 102, 139–40, 146
    families 145
    males 143
    women 141–3
*Bleak House* 63–4, 102, 147, 179
blonde-brunette antithesis 66–7
Bodenheimer, R. 72n., 148n.
Bodichon, Barbara 139
body 58–9
Book of Daniel 153, 159
books 16–17, 43, 62–3, 80–81, 89, 99, 106,
    108, 115–18, 121, 128
Booth, Wayne C. 7
boredom 91–2, 166
Boren, Lynda 54n.
Boudjedra, Rachid 144
Bouraoui, Hédi 191

Brontë, Branwell 71, 78, 99, 116
Brontë, Charlotte 1–3, 96, 105, 116, 127,
    131, 145, 186, 189, 191
    anger of 56, 59, 73
    critical reactions to 5, 56–7
    craft of 59ff.
    and female sexuality 73
    heroines 56, 58
    influence on male writers 81–2ff.
    and Jane Austen 6, 62
    and Mrs Stowe 135, 137
    and *Wuthering Heights* 99–100, 109
Brontë, Emily 1–3, 96, 98, 113, 116, 131, 189
Brontë, Rev. Patrick 78–9
Brophy, Brigid 3
Browne, Sir Thomas 95–6
Brownstein, Rachel 17
Burgan, Mary 127n.
Burlin, Katrin 27, 29
Burney, Fanny 2–3, 7–8, 19, 30
Burton, Antoinette 28n.
Bush, Douglas 47, 53n.
Butler, Marilyn 14n., 47n.
Byron, Lord 41

Canada 145–6, 153
capitalism 140
Caribbean 74
Carpenter, Mary Wilson 159n.
castration 79
Cecil, Lord David 57–8, 96n., 97n., 100,
    110n., 127, 132n., 145
characters 14, 20, 31, 57, 66, 98, 113, 115,
    138, 151
charades 71, 72n., 172–3
Chase, Cynthia 163n.
Chase, Richard 78, 98
chastity 12–13, 76, 165
child abuse 117, 124–5
childbirth 60, 151–2
childhood 62–3, 103–104, 109, 118, 128
Chraïbi, Driss 191
Christian, R.F. 83n.
Christianity 64, 67–8, 76, 78–9, 84–5, 98n.,
    144, 153, 157
Church, Richard 10
civilization 118, 121
Cleopatra 10–12
closet image 114, 117–18

clothing 164–6
coincidence 57–8, 145
Collick, John 95n.
Collins, Wilkie 105
colonization 164, 169
communication 190–91
communion 190
community 148n., 153–4, 164n., 189
conscience 165
consciousness 48–9, 84n., 155, 184
constancy 33, 37, 40–41, 46, 48–9, 53–4,
    56, 100
Court of Love 9, 40n., 67, 90
Craft, Catherine 8n., 10, 12
Craig, G. Armour 79
Craig, Sheryl 101n.
Craik, W.A. 28, 34, 58, 70n., 74, 77n., 97n.,
    117, 123
*Cranford* 166n.
creativity 63, 114–15, 127, 132, 146
Cross, J.W. 155n.
Crozier, Alice 132n., 148n.
'crystallization' 90

Daiches, David 7, 97n.
Daleski, H.M. 159n., 176n.
dancing 21–2, 28, 49
Daniel see Book of Daniel
*Daniel Deronda*
    colonization theme 164, 169
    double plot 151, 156ff.
    and female failure 190–91
    'female' hero of 154–5
    Jewish theme 153–63, 186
    quest for origins in 157, 168, 176
    violence in 169–71
Dante 180, 182, 185
Darwinism 84–5
dates 100, 112, 116
David, Deirdre 164n., 185n., 190n.
Davies, Stevie 101n., 114n.
death 75, 90, 92, 96, 117, 119, 122, 124,
    126–7, 178, 184, 186
deception 40
decoding 116
deformities 144
desire 110n.
devil 118, 124

Dickens, Charles 60, 63–4, 78n., 102, 105, 135n., 136–7, 147
Dickinson, Emily 1–2, 96, 119, 126
Dingly, R.J. 74n.
disintegration 83
Disraeli 148
dissociation 184
dogs 112, 124, 178
domesticity 28n., 37, 114, 134, 155, 169, 190–91
*Don Quixote* 160
Dostoyevsky, F. 85n., 110
Dowling, Andrew 183n.
drama 72, 166, 179, 182
dreams 75, 99–100, 104–105, 110, 114, 118–21, 123, 125, 127, 178
*Dred* 140
Dreiser, T. 173
drowning 160, 174, 184
dualism 147–8
Dunn, Richard J. 72
duty 12–13, 35, 91, 155

Eagleton, Terry 68n., 71, 128n.
Edgeworth, Maria 2–3
education 30, 32, 57, 65, 89, 90, 116, 139, 158
Edwards, Anne-Marie 19n., 28n.
Eliot, George 1, 4, 6, 23n., 80, 110n.,131, 137
    ambivalence of 153, 155–6, 160
    anger of 190–91
    and community 189
    and *Jane Eyre* 67–8
    and public sphere 190
    quest for origins 168
    and self-destructive heroine 191
    and Zionism 153, 159n., 187
Ellison, Ralph 79n.
Emerson, Ralph Waldo 115, 153n.
emigration 145, 153, 177
*Emma*, 6, 8–9, 11ff., 14, 16, 20, 29, 32, 34, 51, 55, 58, 62, 69n., 71
emotions 2, 52, 77, 155, 156, 161, 175
England 32, 78, 85, 139, 147, 153, 158, 160, 171, 173, 189
epistolary novel 2–3, 17, 38, 43, 116
    *see also* letters
equality 68–70, 75, 139
Eros *see* romantic love

escape 116, 118, 145–6, 189
Esther 186–7
evil 47, 98, 109, 140, 174, 183–4
Ewbank, Inga-Stina 119n., 126n.
'eye' 33, 43, 57

'factory novels ' 139
facts 24
fairy tale 58n., 69, 84, 105–106, 108
family 53, 84, 98, 141, 144–5, 148, 157, 178
father 97n. 15, 17–18, 78, 103, 127, 143, 157, 167
Faulkner, William 101–103, 112n.,123n., 128n., 139, 141–2
feeling 48–9, 59–60, 160
female artist 8, 10–11, 13, 31, 37, 54, 56–7, 62, 70, 100, 116, 128–9, 155, 161–3, 172–3, 190n.
female initiation 57, 62
female narrator 93
*Female Quixote, The* 8–13, 15, 62
female voice, 2–3, 31, 50, 56, 84, 99, 113, 117, 161, 172, 191
    *see also* narrative voice; women writers
femininity 28n., 134, 154–5, 159, 169, 177
feminism 6, 8, 25, 59, 97n., 98, 110n.,132–3, 147–8, 151
    and Judaeo-Christan tradition 153–4
Fergus, Jan 33n.
Feuillide, Eliza de 23n.
fiction 7, 24, 27–8
    *see also* novel
Fielding, Henry 9, 21
films 3, 37n., 43, 48n., 50n., 73, 86n., 95, 99, 101, 104, 107n., 111n., 118, 125n., 151–2
Flaubert 92, 110, 133
flowers 90
*Flying Dutchman* 183–4, 185n.
food 87
Forster, E.M. 7, 87, 96n.
Foster, Charles H. 136n., 139
France 2–3, 8–9, 10, 15, 18, 58, 63, 70, 74, 92, 97, 146, 151, 191
Frazier, Franklin 139
freedom 65–6, 117–18
friendship 25, 45, 96
French romances 8, 9ff.

Freudianism 7, 79n., 97n., 143, 164n.
Friedan, Betty 151
frigidity 171
Frost, Robert 78
future 7, 110

Galef, David 104n.
gambling 165–6, 171, 176
Gard, Roger 47n.
Gaskell, Elizabeth 1, 4, 166n., 173, 186
   anger of 191
   critical responses to 131–2, 133n., 134
   earnings of 135
   feminism of 148
   and Mrs Stowe 134–6ff.
   productivity of 134
   and public world 190
   social awareness of 147
   subversive aspects 137–8
   and working-class 136–7, 144–5
Gates, Barbara 72n.
gaze 166, 175
   Lacanian 26n., 113, 169
gender 42, 66, 72, 84, 98, 159, 169
Genlis, Madame de 14, 62n.
Gérin, Winifred 113, 117, 133n., 135–6
ghost 60, 75–6, 88n., 93, 101, 104, 121–2,
   127, 179
'ghost-text' 99, 105, 112ff.
Gilbert, Sandra M. 70n., 92
Gilbert, Sandra M. and Gubar, Susan 37,
   59n., 71, 73, 97n., 113n., 115n.116n.
God 60, 63, 76–7, 84, 98, 138
goddess 76, 87
Goetz, William 107n.
*Golden Bowl, The* 17, 40n., 178
Golding, William 118
Goldsmith, Oliver 28n., 62
goodness 63, 174
Goodridge, J. Frank 98n., 117
Gothic novel 12, 14–15, 19, 29, 82, 114
   delusion in 24–6
   male and female 21, 82
   'new Gothic' 66, 69, 82
governess theme 30, 55, 83, 88, 165, 176–7
Great Britain 139–40
Greene, Sheila 138
Gubar, Susan see Gilbert, Sandra M. and
   Gubar, Susan

Guerard, Albert 101
guilt 145, 164n., 166, 169, 185
*Gulliver's Travels* 62–3, 116
Gutman, Herbert G. 145

Hagar 186–7
Haight, Gordon 83n., 159n.
hair 66–7
Halperin, John 185n.
*Happy Ever After* 83–93
*Hard Times* 136
Harding, D.W. 7, 28, 44n.
Hardy, Barbara 36n., 50n., 147, 157n., 179n.
Harris, Jocelyn 20n., 31n., 54n.
Hawthorne, Nathaniel 6–7, 82n., 95, 115,
   119, 129, 133
Heilbrun, Carolyn 98
Heilman, Robert B. 66, 69, 87n.
Heine 133
heiress-plot 15, 17
hero 4, 16, 23, 42, 47, 61, 86, 88–9, 96, 102,
   105, 118, 124, 154–5, 160, 185
heroine 9, 14, 16–17, 56, 58, 93, 105, 143,
   149, 154, 156, 171, 186, 189
   blonde-brunette antithesis 66–7
   Gothic 26–7
   as mentor 33ff.
   self-destructive 190–91
   working-class 137
heroism 147, 171
history 10, 18, 23, 28, 38, 110n., 147,
   158–60, 171–2
Hobbs, E.A. 165n.
Hochman, B. 166n.
Hoeveler, Dianne 24n., 27n., 28n., 29, 31n.
Homans, Margaret 97n.
Honan, Park 19n., 23n., 28n., 31n., 33n.,
   40n., 47n.
honor 12–13
Hopkins, Robert 39n.
Horowitz, Barbara 23n., 30n., 36n., 44n.
horse symbol 69, 77, 80, 91, 171, 174, 185
*House of Mirth, The* 164–5, 175n., 176n.
Hughes, Kathryn 166n.
human nature 31, 47, 70
humanity 148
Hutchinson, Stuart 164n.
Huxley, T.H. 156

Ignatieff, Michael 87n.
imagery 58–9
imagination 5, 9, 12, 15, 18, 24, 27, 45, 80,
    114, 118, 154
individual action 148
individualism 39n.
Industrial Revolution 143–4
integration 83
intelligence 24, 41, 155, 157, 164, 191
Internet 191
intertextuality 8, 20n., 113, 115, 153n.
intuition 48, 91, 109
irony 23n., 25, 28, 155
irrationality 109
Isles, Duncan 8
Israel 151
*Ivanhoe* 66, 159n.

Jacobs, Carol 104n., 114n.
James, Henry 3, 5, 7, 17, 30, 90n., 117–18,
    129, 133, 151, 155, 171n., 173,
    178–9
*Jane Eyre* 30, 93, 95, 98, 101–102, 113,
    128, 145, 177, 179, 186
    books in 62–3, 80
    castration theory 79
    as confessional 57–9
    craft and structure of 59–61
    'doubles' in 71–6
    ending 78–80
    and female initiation 57, 62
    Gothic elements 66–7, 82
    heroine 56
    independence theme 63, 65, 67–8, 80
    male contrasts 66–8
    melodrama of 57–8
    Melville and 81–2
    name of 58–9
    as quest novel 57–8, 65
    starvation motif 61
    subversive elements 69, 72, 80
    Tolstoy and 82–93
jealousy 35, 52–3, 72, 92, 119, 142, 160,
    183
Jerinic, Maria 15n., 29n.
Jews 66, 151–2, 157, 159–60, 162–4, 166–7,
    169, 178, 186
Johnson, Claudia 33n., 39n., 44n., 48n.
Johnson, Samuel 8–9

Joyce, James 122
Jung, Carl 97n.

*Kadosh* 151–2, 186
Keats, John 39, 166
Keeldar, Shirley 82
Kelly, Gary 28n.
Kettle, Arnold 98, 133n.
kidnappings 15, 22
*King Lear* 72–3
knowledge 75, 124, 157–8, 170

'La Pia de'Tolomei' 180–82
Lacan 26n., 97n., 113, 169
Laclos 175
Lafayette, Madame de 2, 9, 11n., 12, 50
landscape 38–9, 110n., 119, 122, 126
Lane, Maggie 19n., 22n., 32
language 10, 12, 23n., 29, 31, 40, 58, 72n.
Lawrence, D.H. 87, 96n., 100
Leavis, F.R. 151, 153–6, 167
Leavis, Q.D. 96n., 98, 106
Lennox, Charlotte Ramsay 2–4, 7–13, 15, 17
Lerner, Laurence 180n.
letters 26, 37–8
Levine, George 180n.
Levy, Anita 110n.
Lewes, George Henry 6–7, 57–8, 161n.
Lewis, Matthew 12, 21
library 115–16
life 27, 33, 56, 58, 93, 134, 147
*Life of Charlotte Brontë, The* 134
Lincoln, Abraham 131
Linder, Cynthia Ann 71
literature 38, 41, 62–3, 128
    *see also* books; poetry
Litz, W. 28, 39n.
locality 96, 103, 145
Longfellow 146
love 20, 39n., 40n., 56, 63, 66, 71, 83,
    90–91, 99, 125, 155, 174
    diachronic and synchronic 127
    transcendent 126
    types of 67, 76, 84
    *see also* romantic love
Lovesey, Oliver 162n.
lyric 38

Macbeth 170

McCarthy, T. 104n.
McKillop, Alan D. 24n.
McKinstry, Susan 110n.
McMaster, Juliet 127n.
*Madame Bovary* 10–11, 58n., 84, 86, 89, 92, 171
madwoman 30, 71, 73
Mailer, Norman 18n.
male authors 2, 10n., 33, 40, 60, 84n.
male characters 57, 66
    as 'female' heroes 155–6
male-female relationship 7, 56, 79, 80, 155, 159, 170
male gaze 113, 175
male readers 3, 40
male tyrant 63–4
Manchester 136–7, 139, 147
*Mansfield Park* 6, 13–15, 26n., 33, 62, 71, 84, 169, 171n.
Marenco, Charles 182
marriage 13, 17, 20, 22, 24, 28, 58, 77, 80, 88, 117, 152, 157, 162, 171, 175ff.
    Christian 67–8, 83, 90
    dissatisfaction with 91, 180, 182
    equality in 139
    independence of 55
marriage market 2, 25, 55, 167, 170, 183, 189
Marshall, Gail 162n.
Martin, Robert B. 67, 79n.
Martineau, Harriet 139
Marxist critics 7, 98, 132, 136n., 147
*Mary Barton* 136–8, 139ff., 147–8
    compared to *Uncle Tom's Cabin* 136
    sexual abuse in 140–41
masculinity 40, 42, 56, 71–2, 84, 92, 128, 152, 156, 158–9, 169, 171, 174, 177
master-servant relationship 63
Mead, Margaret 142
melodrama 57–8, 123–4
Melville, Herman 81–2, 96n., 133, 159
mentor 9, 88
    false 19
    female 10, 19, 33–4, 42
    male 8, 10–11, 18, 22, 25, 27ff., 70, 86
*Merchant of Venice, The* 153–4, 166–7, 178n.
metaphor 22, 23n., 28–9, 53, 63, 77, 123, 168, 190–91
middle-class 135, 137–9, 143, 148

*Middlemarch* 6, 60, 62, 83n., 153, 155–7, 168, 171n., 175–6, 178–9, 183, 186
*Mill on the Floss, The* 75n., 168, 177
Miller, J. Hillis 96, 98
'mirror' image 63, 91, 163n., 178, 183
mistaken identities 15
Moers, Ellen 60, 75n., 134–5, 140, 161n.
Moglen, Helene 64n., 68n.
*Monk, The* 12, 21
moon 66–7, 76, 87, 90–91
morality 63–4, 82, 174
Morris, Jane 180, 182
Morrison, Paul 29n., 30n.
Morrison, Toni 1, 42n., 84n., 191
Moser, Thomas 111n.
mother 15, 97n., 134, 144, 157, 159, 162, 167
Mudrick, Marvin 7, 14–15, 52
mulattoes 139–40
Munro, Alice 1, 133, 191
music 49, 172–3
*Mysteries of Udolpho, The* 21–2, 29n., 82
    mythic dimension 58, 67, 76, 82, 147, 178–9

names 107, 115, 127–8
narrative voice 2, 28, 31, 50, 93, 99ff., 113, 137–8
    *see also* female voice
narrators 97, 103–112, 137–8
    multiple 112–13
    unreliable 106
nature 41, 70, 75, 86, 97n., 109, 118
navy 6, 40n., 42n., 44, 49, 53
Nereid 165, 174, 179
Newman, Beth 113
*North and South* 136, 138, 142, 148, 186
*Northanger Abbey* 3, 8–33, 46, 62, 124, 177n.
    and female novel 14–15
    Gothic delusion in 24–6
    Gothic heroine 26–7
    as satire on travel literature 19
    text 13–14
novel 2–3, 7, 11, 31, 58
    experimental 131, 133
    place-name titles 14, 17, 100

observer 104

onomastics 58
opera singers 161
oppression 116, 139, 144, 161, 191
Orwell, George 137, 147
palimpsest 116
*Pamela* 2, 9, 58, 60, 62, 81, 84, 114, 124
passion 59, 73, 86, 174, 177–8
past 12
Patmore, Coventry 106n.
patriarchy 2–3, 6, 12, 14, 17, 40, 43–4, 53,
    64, 70, 107, 115, 128, 142, 164–5,
    169, 191
    *see also* father
Payn, James 163n.
performance 161–2, 169, 172–3, 191
*Persuasion* 3, 6, 8, 13–14, 19–20, 22, 32–54
    'artist-critic' in 36ff., 43, 54
    ending of 36
    female mentor in 33–4
    and female passion 59
'persuasions' 13, 34–7, 49
Peterson, Linda 98n., 101n.
Pierre 82
*Pilgrim's Progress* 62
place 14, 17, 100–103
plot 15, 24, 111, 136–8, 141, 143, 145–6,
    151, 156
poetry 38–9, 67, 115, 126, 145, 160, 172
Poggioli, R. 87n., 88n., 90n.
politics 18, 28, 133n., 137–8, 144, 147, 190
Poole, Adrian 153n.
Poovey, Mary 39n.
Pope, Alexander 16
*Portrait of a Lady, The* 17, 167n., 175–6,
    178–9, 180n., 183
postmodernist critics 58, 133
poverty 63–4, 78
power 64, 79–80, 140, 154–5, 169–70, 183,
    185
Price, Reynolds 84n.
*Pride and Prejudice* 14, 20, 34, 56, 70, 77
Pritchett, V.S. 108
private sphere 2–3, 37, 48, 56, 72n., 81, 99,
    148n., 155, 190–91
*Professor, The* 58
prose 38–39, 41
prostitutes 12, 141
Proust, M. 86–7
psychoanalytic critics 97n., 114, 185n.

psychology 14, 18, 168, 174, 177–8
psychosomatic illness 109–10
public sphere 2, 37, 48, 51–2, 56, 72n., 97n.,
    99, 148n., 155, 190–91
publication 2
punishment 60–61, 79–80, 121, 185
puns 58
Putzell, Sara 151n., 163n.
Pygmalion 173–4

quest 57–8, 65, 147, 157, 168, 176, 184, 186

racialism 74, 131, 142, 144–6, 154, 167, 169
Radcliffe, Mrs 21, 31, 82
readers 3, 10, 40, 104–105, 116, 133
realism 20, 29, 38, 69, 98, 145, 155
reality 7, 13, 82, 119
reason 60
rebellion 57, 63, 98, 117, 161, 189
'Red Room' 60, 75, 114
religion 64, 67, 76, 79–80, 84, 92, 117–19,
    144, 152–3, 186
revenge 69, 119, 122, 124, 128, 142, 191
revolution 6, 18
Rhys, Jean 73–4, 189n.
Rich, Adrienne 80n.
Richardson, Samuel 2–4, 8–9, 17, 20, 44,
    58n., 60, 84, 86, 105
Richmond, Henry 135
risk 35, 37, 53–4, 67, 141
Robinson, Carole 156n.
Roe, Sue 131n.
romances 3, 8, 9ff., 18, 20, 23, 69, 80, 86,
    105, 108, 146, 177
    Gothic 14
    lyric 38
romantic love 40n., 83–4, 86, 90, 96, 98, 117
Romanticism 18, 39, 40n., 44, 98n.
Rossetti, Dante Gabriel 180–82
Rougemont, Denis de 67, 90, 96
Rubenius, Aina 133n., 140
Ruth 186–7

Said, Edward 6, 54n., 147
salvation 75, 79
Sanger, C.P. 98, 100, 112
sarcasm 23, 158, 164, 178
Sartre 90–91
satire 9, 12, 17, 19, 52

Sayers, Dorothy 96
*Scarlet Letter, The* 95, 118, 127, 141, 185n.
Scheherazade 37, 40, 54, 62
Schlesinger, Arthur, Jr. 147
Schopenhauer 165n.
Schorer, Mark 7
Scott, Sir Walter 6, 8, 31, 66–7, 72n., 104n., 118, 154, 159n., 163n.
Scudéry, Madame de 8–10
seduction 3, 15, 141
self-reflexiveness 3, 8–9, 33
Semmel, B. 159n., 165n.
Senf, Carol A. 110n.
*Sense and Sensibility* 8, 12–13, 33–4, 40, 56, 88n.
sensuality 73
serpent image 166
sexual abuse 140–42
sexuality 12, 20–21, 42, 71, 73, 77, 79, 84, 87, 90–91, 97n., 107, 127
Shaffer, Julie 15n.
Shakespeare 4, 7, 16, 72, 111, 153–4, 167, 176, 180
Shelley, Mary 32n.
*Shirley* 59, 73, 82, 174
Showalter, Elaine 190
Siegel, Carol 100n.
sin 119
Sisken, C. 31n.
slavery 74, 84, 135, 139, 142, 144, 169
    and factory workers 139–40, 147
    and families 141, 145
Smith, Sheila 97n.
Smollett, T. 16, 19
snobbery 11, 44–6
social class 43–5, 47, 158, 171, 173
social reform 139–40, 148, 160
socialization 115, 117–18, 123
society 7, 43, 92, 98, 139, 147, 190
Solomon, Eric 97n.
songs 144–5
spirit 48, 69, 101, 114–15, 119, 128, 167, 184
Stanhope, Lady Hester 170
statues 173–4, 177, 183
Stendhal 86, 90
Stone, Wilfred 163n., 166n.
Stoneman, Patsy 132, 133n., 138, 148n.
Stowe, Harriet Beecher 1, 2, 4, 5n., 159n.

anger of 191
complexity of 147
critical responses to 131–4
domestic life of 134–5
as family earner 135
feminism of 147–8
and Mrs Gaskell 134–6ff.
and racism 132, 144, 146–7
and slavery 136, 141–2
social awareness of 147
subjectivity 57, 63
subplot 144, 146
suffering 53, 61, 64, 65–6, 76, 90, 102, 118, 147–8, 191
supernatural 27, 69, 74
symbolism 70–71, 74–5, 79, 87, 91, 97n., 102, 114–15, 144
Sypher, Eileen 154n.
systems 6, 12, 137–8, 140

Tandrup, B. 29n.
Tanner, Tony 7, 14n., 23n., 27n., 29n., 30n., 32, 35n., 44n., 46n., 47n., 51n.
Tate, Allen 190
Teale, Polly 189n.
Tennyson 7
text 3, 58–9, 99, 104–105, 112–13, 115–16, 123, 127, 147
Thackeray, William 60, 64–5, 70–73, 166, 173
theatricals 59, 71
    *see also* drama
Thompson, Andrew 185n.
Thompson, James 23n.
Tillotson, Kathleen 60, 64, 136–7, 139
Titans 82
Tolstoy, Leo 82–93, 133
    and *Jane Eyre* 82–3ff.
*Tom Jones* 9, 12, 21
Tompkins, Jane P. 133n.
Tonna, Mrs 140
trade unions 137
tragedy 173, 185
*Tragic Muse, The* 173
transcendence 111, 126
Traversi, Derek 121n.
Trilling, Lionel 5, 7
Trollope, Mrs Frances 139–40
Turgenev 90

*Turn of the Screw, The* 30, 90n., 117
Turnell, Martin 86
Twain, Mark 6, 61, 146
tyranny, familial 15, 18, 29, 32, 63–4, 114, 116, 191

*Uncle Tom's Cabin* 135, 140
    compared to *Mary Barton* 136
    critical reactions to 131–3
    double plot 138–9
    North-South contrast 147
    plot coincidences 145
    popularity of 133
    sexual abuse in 141
Unitarianism 138–9
United States 139, 146, 151n., 173
universality 96, 103, 159–60
university education 158
utopianism 153–4, 187

Van Ghent, Dorothy 103, 114
*Vanity Fair* 60, 64–5, 70–72, 166
Vashti 186–7
verbal art 116, 124–6, 175
*Villette* 58, 73, 100, 143, 186
Vine, Steven 100n.
violence 169–71
virginity 27, 76, 90, 127n., 141
virtue 12
Visick, Mary 100n.
visual artists 3, 58, 70, 116, 164
Vogler, Thomas A. 97n., 98, 108

*War and Peace* 85
Warhol, Robyn 137n.
*Washington Square* 17
Watt, Ian 113n.
wealth 17, 166, 169
Weissman, Cheryl 34n., 48n.
Weissman, J. 112n.
Wharton, Edith 164–5, 178
Whicher, G.F. 96, 135
Wiesenfarth, J. 27
white men 142
Wilson, A.N. 83n., 87n.
Wilt, Judith 163n., 164n., 173n.
*Wings of the Dove, The* 17
Winnifrith, Tom 80n., 98
Wion, P. 97n.

wit 31, 43, 45, 50, 172
Wollstonecraft, Mary 6, 25, 29n., 55–6, 60, 80
women 40–42, 151, 164, 174
    and blacks 142
    and community 153–4, 189
    disenfranchisement of 137
    in domestic sphere 2
    economic position 17, 26, 55, 166, 173
    Jewish 152, 153ff., 161, 162
    oppression of 162, 170, 191
    public role of 190
    and social change 43
    silencing of 56, 88
    slave, and sexual abuse 141
women writers 7, 10, 13, 31, 38, 59, 123, 128–9, 140, 191
    craft of 14, 30, 54, 116, 118
    intertextuality 8–9
    problems of 132, 134, 191
Woolf, Virginia 1–2, 7, 38, 77, 87, 98, 133–4, 158
    and Charlotte Brontë 56–7, 59
    and Mrs Gaskell 132
working-class 136–8, 142
    culture 144–5
    and slaves 139–40, 147
    women 143
world 147, 190
Wright, Andrew 34
Wright, Edgar. 132, 145
writing 42–3, 118, 123, 128, 175
*Wrongs of Women, The* 140
*Wuthering Heights* 26, 61, 72, 75, 189
    authorship of 99
    bleeding hand image 122
    blonde-brunette contrast 67
    blood imagery 125, 127n.
    Charlotte Brontë and 9–100
    critical views 95–8
    female voice 99
    'ghost-text' 99, 105, 112ff.
    hiding images 114, 117
    house images 101–102, 104, 114
    ledge/table images 114–15ff., 123
    'multiple choice technique' 115
    narrative techniques 97, 103–12
    place in 100–103
    rooms in 114

symbolism 102
textuality 99, 104–105, 112–13, 115–16,
     123, 127
tree image 122–3
verbal skills 124–6
world 6–7, 18, 114

Wyler, William 3, 99, 101, 104, 107n., 125n.
Yaeger, Patricia 127n.
Yeazell, R.B. 133n.
Yorkshire 103, 108, 111, 117, 122

Zionism 151n., 153, 159n., 163, 187